AN EXEMPLARY
HISTORY OF THE
NOVEL

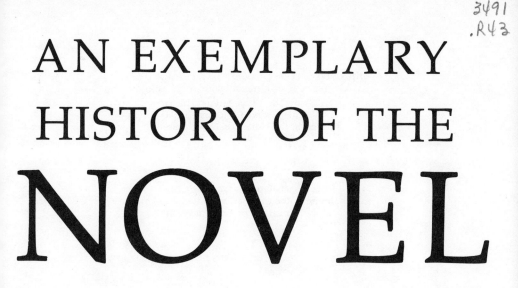

AN EXEMPLARY
HISTORY OF THE
NOVEL

The Quixotic versus the Picaresque

WALTER L. REED

THE UNIVERSITY OF CHICAGO PRESS • CHICAGO & LONDON

THE UNIVERSITY OF CHICAGO PRESS, CHICAGO 60637
THE UNIVERSITY OF CHICAGO PRESS, LTD., LONDON

WALTER L. REED
is associate professor of English
and chairman of the Comparative Literature Program
at the University of Texas at Austin.

Library of Congress Cataloging in Publication Data

Reed, Walter L
  An exemplary history of the novel.

  Includes index.
    1. Fiction—History and criticism. 2. English
fiction—18th century—History and criticism.
3. English fiction—19th century—History and
criticism. 4. American fiction—19th century—History
and criticism. I. Title.
PN3491.R43   809.3'1   80–17908
ISBN 0–226–70683–4

Contents

Acknowledgments

This book has been a number of years in the making and it has been helped along its way by many generous people and institutions. Its beginnings go back to several fine teachers, become friends, who introduced me to the novel in general and *Don Quixote* in particular: Martin Price, Harry Berger, Jr., and George Fayen. Their exemplary meditations have had a deep effect on my thinking about prose fiction. The book was also tempered and tested by my own students at Yale in a course called "Problems in Fiction." They made my problems their own and gave them back to me in a much clarified form.

A Morse Fellowship from Yale University enabled me to begin serious research in England. A summer stipend from the National Endowment for the Humanities allowed me to pursue the byway of late classical romance. A John Simon Guggenheim Memorial Fellowship gave me the time to do most of the actual writing of the book, and two grants from the University Research Institute at the University of Texas allowed me to revise and prepare the manuscript. To all of these foundations I am grateful indeed for confidence and support.

A shorter version of the first chapter appeared in *Novel* 9 (1976), 101–13 and in *Towards a Poetics of Fiction*, edited by Mark Spilka (Bloomington, 1977); I am grateful to the editors of *Novel* and to Indiana University Press for permission to reprint this copyrighted material. I also acknowledge permission to quote from Kafka's *The Great Wall of China*, translated by Willa and Edwin Muir, copyright ©1946 and copyright renewed ©1974 by Schocken Books, Inc.; published in Great Britain by Secker and Warburg, Ltd.

In my attempt to deal with the novel over several centuries, I have benefited from the expertise of friends and colleagues at Yale and Texas. I can only mention some of these here: for the introductory and Renaissance chapters, Janice Haney-Peritz, Alfred MacAdam, Wayne Rebhorn, and Ramón Saldívar; for the eighteenth-century chapters, Michael Seidel, Dustin Griffin, and Larry Carver; for the nineteenth-century material, R. J. Kaufmann, John Farrell, Warwick Wadlington, Wayne Lesser, and James Duban. Though they are not responsible for my persistent errantry, their good advice has saved me from many errors of judgment. The inspiration and encouragement of Michael Holquist preside over the book as a whole, even in the few sections that he has not read, argued over, expanded, and improved. The probes and queries of Alexander Welsh, whose book on the Quixotic novel is appearing at the same time as this one, have been most useful to me in my final revisions. The manuscript was flawlessly typed by Ona Kay Stephenson.

My last acknowledgment is my most heartfelt. My wife, Loree, has lived this book in a more existential fashion than Don Quixote lived *Amadis of Gaul:* endured it, encouraged it, sought funding for it, corrected it, kept it from going completely astray over the many stages of its progress. Her love and sustenance of its author ought to be acknowledged in a dedication, but she introduced him to a love and sustenance greater still. As Sancho says to Don Quixote, "That's the kind of love I've heard them preach about," and all our dedications fall short of His example.

1

The Problem with a Poetics of the Novel

The night before, two doubtful words had halted him at the beginning of the *Poetics*. These words were *tragedy* and *comedy*. He had encountered them years before in the third book of the *Rhetoric;* no one in the whole world of Islam could conjecture what they meant.

Borges, "Averroës' Search"

The notion of a poetics for the novel is being advanced today on many different fronts. French, Anglo-American, and German critics are leading a new assault on an old literary problem. Can the "loose baggy monster," as Henry James called the nineteenth-century novel before him, be classified and comprehended within a new and better taxonomy? Can the "outlaw on Parnassus," as a recent critic has dubbed the novelist in European tradition, be legally accommodated in a broader and less classically biased literary system? There is a growing body of criticism at present pointing the way "towards a poetics of fiction."[1]

This study, while concerned with the nature and form of the novel in general, pursues a history of the novel rather than a poetics. The history aims at being exemplary, in two senses of the word. It is defined by the relations between particular examples of the novel, beginning with the Spanish picaresque novels of the sixteenth and seventeenth centuries and Cervantes's *Don Quixote* and continuing with other examples of this double series in the three centuries following. The discussion of the way these novels relate to one another also tries to serve as a model of what the novel is and does, of the ways in which the novel is and is not historical. A theory of the novel, which has been advanced more economically and more polemically in another context, will emerge in the course of the study as well.[2] But the history and the theory will take as their point of departure this question of a poetics. In a roundabout fashion, a better understanding of the problems inherent in a poetics of the novel will lead to a better understanding of this problematical literary form. Thus our discussion will proceed not towards a poetics of the novel but away from it.

Many recent poetics, of course, claim not to deal merely with the novel but with "fiction," "narrative," or even "prose."[3] But since all

1

these schemes give novels a place of prominence in the conceptual spectrum, it seems fair to address oneself initially to this historically significant type of prose fiction and ignore for the time being the wider reaches. It is also true that "poetics" may be loosely used, applied simply to a group of essays on different aspects of the novel by different hands. Even in this case, a clarification is worthwhile.

The term "poetics," as is well known, comes from Aristotle's *peri poetikes*—"on the poetic [art]"—and has become the generic name for a certain kind of literary study. Like Aristotle's treatise, later poetics have involved two distinctive elements: "a tendency toward system or structuration," as Claudio Guillén puts it,[4] and a tendency to establish literary norms and a literary canon. The full Aristotelian system was lost when the second book of the *Poetics*, on comedy, disappeared; but, as Guillén has shown, European poetics have continually conceived of themselves in terms of totalities and hierarchies of genres, not simply as series or enumerations. Thus there is a difference between a poetics, such as Frye's *Anatomy of Criticism*, and a work of criticism, such as Brooks's *The Well Wrought Urn*.

The Aristotelian practice of aesthetic judgment, based on a work's approximation to an ideal form, and the practice of indicating canonical examples (the *Iliad*, *Oedipus Tyrannos*) have also been part of the tradition. Since the later eighteenth century, as the Princeton *Encyclopedia of Poetry and Poetics* points out, there has been an emphasis on the descriptive, classifying element, after an overemphasis on the prescriptive and the canonical in neoclassical poetics. But there is a difference between a theory of literature (or some branch of literature) and a poetics, just as there is a difference between a poetics and a piece of literary criticism. If a theory of literature is primarily descriptive and largely assumes the questions of norms—what is literature and what isn't—it is not a poetics in the true sense of the word. Staiger's *Grundbegriffe der Poetik* is a poetics; Wellek and Warren's *Theory of Literature*, as the authors point out, is something different. The distinction revolves around the question of literary value. Explicitly or implicitly, a poetics is concerned with judging literature according to some standard of aesthetic good and bad—whether the judgment is elitist and restrictive, as in the case of Staiger, or democratic and expansionist, as in the case of Frye. The recent structuralist *poétiques* of literary discourse, with their claim to a more value-free systematics, may challenge this traditional conception. In effect, they would deny the distinction between poetics and theory. But I should like to defer the question of this usage until later in the chapter.[5]

A final distinction must be made on the historical side. Since the later eighteenth century many poetics have assumed a genetic or historical orientation, static taxonomies giving way to dynamic models of evolution, as in Hegel's *Aesthetik*. But though poetics have been influenced by literary history, they have not been subsumed by it. Renato Poggioli used the phrase "unwritten poetics" to refer to the fact that literary genres and forms inevitably exist in the minds of authors and audience before being codified by critics and theorists.[6] Greek tragedy existed, after all, before Aristotle anatomized it. But once written down, the "unwritten poetics" loses its collective, historical character; an actual set of general habits is transformed into an ideal set of specific rules. It is with the fully articulated systems that we are concerned here. Furthermore, and this brings us to the question of the novel, while there have been many implicit or partial sets of rules available to people writing novels, the novel has generally tried to keep its methods from explicit recognition, or has delighted in flouting its own conventions. As Guillén puts it elsewhere, "the modern novel, . . . from Cervantes to our time, could be described as an 'outsider' model that writers insist on regarding as essentially incompatible with the passage from an unwritten poetics to an 'official' system of genres."[7]

It is this sense of itself as "outsider," in fact, that I would single out as the most basic feature of the novel as a literary kind. The novel is a deliberate stranger to literary decorum; it insists on placing itself beyond the pale of literary tradition. Its ethos of opposition is fundamental and should not be ignored. It is one reason that the term "novel" (from the Latin *novellus*, "news") has proved so difficult to define, a term not even available in most modern European languages, which unlike English do not distinguish between "novel" and "romance."[8] Most definitions strike one as overly vague (Forster's "any fictitious prose work over 50,000 words") or overly specific (Frye would limit the term to fiction whose narrative and dialogue are "closely linked to the conventions of the comedy of manners" and whose characterization attempts to approximate "real people"), or else avoid the issue by a historical pluralism, as with Ralph Freedman's suggestion that "it is simpler to view all of prose fiction as a unity and to trace particular strands to different origins, strands which would include not only the English novel of manners, or the post-medieval romance, or the Gothic novel, but also the medieval allegory, the German *Bildungsroman* or the picaresque."[9] Nevertheless, the term does continue to mean something to educated readers, as repeated critical usage attests. It is the idea of a novelty confronting literary tradition that is of the essence.

The novel, I would argue, is a long prose fiction which opposes the forms of everyday life, social and psychological, to the conventional forms of literature, classical or popular, inherited from the past. The novel is a type of literature suspicious of its own literariness; it is inherently antitraditional in its literary code. The dialectic of "literature" and "life" is of course relative—"life" may not always have the last word—and it is historically conditioned. As Borges notes of *Don Quixote*, the antithesis that Cervantes posits between the idealism of the chivalric romances and the reality of contemporary Spain has been confused by our historical distance from the text. But Borges also acknowledges that a novelist of our own time would use details equivalently mundane, like filling stations, to oppose the literary.[10] The term *nouveau roman* is a redundancy (now redoubled in *nouveau nouveau roman*), necessary in mid-twentieth century French culture and language, perhaps, but stating nothing really new in the strategies of the novel as it has existed over the last four centuries. At least from *Don Quixote* onward the novel has adopted an antagonistic stance both toward the literary canon and toward its own precursors—even in novels like *Joseph Andrews*, written in mock-neoclassical "imitation" of *Don Quixote*.

The problem of accommodating the experience of the present to the authority of the literary past is of course not unique to the novel. All kinds of literature, since the later Middle Ages at least, have felt and responded to the demands of representation, the need to modify or transform the inherited types and formulas the better to approximate the contemporary experience of author and audience. But the novel is distinctive in the prominence and autonomy it gives to forms which are unliterary or uncanonical. I say "forms" because I do not consider that anything in a novel is truly formless. I agree with critics like Martin Price who argue that there is little "unshaped" material in the most realistic novel, that we find "relevance itself expanding to acquire new detail, and the irrelevant detail becomes the boundary at the limit of expansion."[11] However, it seems to me crucial to distinguish between forms which acknowledge their literary standing and forms which claim to lie beyond the conventional literary repertoire: forms of speech (the peasant proverbs in *Don Quixote*), forms of commerce (the inventories and contracts in Defoe), forms of architecture and landscape gardening (the country estates of Jane Austen), forms of the landscape itself (the archaeology of Wessex in Hardy)—not to mention the subliterary forms of journalism, the detective story, comic books, and dirty jokes which find their way into novels of today in Mailer, Robbe-Grillet, Pynchon, and Barth.

4

The novel creates the illusion of a dichotomy by establishing different fictional levels, "so separated," as Richard Predmore says of *Don Quixote*, "that the difference which separates them seems to the reader to be the difference between literature and life."[12] It is in these terms that I would rephrase the critical commonplace that the novel deals with the difference between appearance and reality. The novel explores the difference between the fictions which are enshrined in the institution of literature and the fictions, more truthful historically or merely more familiar, by which we lead our daily lives. If we adopt the term "fiction" in its older, less pejorative sense of "that which is fashioned or framed" and use it to include not only stories or texts which have been designated, honorifically, as literary, but also the numerous structures of culture and behavior which are demonstrably fictive or mind-made,[13] we can say that the novel is the literary genre which gives the greatest weight to those human fictions—economic, political, psychological, social, scientific, historical, even mythical—which lie beyond the boundaries of the prevailing literary canon. Literary paradigms are not simply modified in the novel, they are confronted by paradigms from other areas of culture.

A more extended example of this confrontation might be useful at this point. There is the famous passage in *Middlemarch* in which George Eliot focuses her authorial attention on the match-making activities of Mrs. Cadwallader; she raises the question of motivation and of plot. "Now, why on earth should Mrs Cadwallader have been at all busy about Miss Brooke's marriage; and why, when one match that she liked to think she had a hand in was frustrated, should she have straightway contrived the preliminaries of another? Was there any ingenious plot, and hide-and-seek course of action, which might be detected by a careful telescopic watch?" Not at all, the author answers, and uses the image of the telescope, figurative of the conventionally panoramic perspective of the Victorian novelist, as a means of introducing an explicitly unliterary image of point of view:

> Even with a microscope directed on a water-drop we find ourselves making interpretations which turn out to be rather coarse; for whereas under a weak lens you may seem to see a creature exhibiting an active voracity into which other smaller creatures actively play as if they were so many animated tax-pennies, a stronger lens reveals to you certain tiniest hairlets which make vortices for these victims while the swallower waits passively at his receipt of custom. In this way, metaphorically speaking, a strong lens

> applied to Mrs Cadwallader's match-making will show a
> play of minute causes producing what may be called
> thought and speech vortices to bring her the sort of food
> she needed.[14]

The "scientific" analogy here appeals to a model of vision outside the literary even as it acknowledges its own metaphorical quality. The sweeping overview of Eliot's predecessors—Dickens or Thackeray, for example—is opposed and criticized by the more limited but more discerning point of view of the biological researcher; a literary convention is criticized by a scientific one. There are many other examples in *Middlemarch* of this formal dialectic: the medical procedures and habits of mind in Lydgate conflict with his melodramatic perception of the French actress Laure and his sentimental vision of Rosamond; the threads of Reform politics picked up by Mr. Brooke confound the grand generality of his Johnsonian view of human nature ("Let observation with extensive view..."); these same politics and his journalistic rendering of them transform Will Ladislaw from a "Shelleyan" aestheticism to a position as an acknowledged legislator of the world; Dorothea's hero-worshipping view of Casaubon as a Milton or a Pascal is shattered by the legal expression of his jealousy in the codicil to his will.

This unliterary material which Eliot brings into the novel (on the basis of careful research, one might add) is not simply raw content or subject matter; it is a fund of structures or codes quite apart from the structures and codes of literature as Eliot knew them. When Milton describes the "Optic Glass" of Galileo in Book I of *Paradise Lost*, the formal possibilities of the telescope are subordinated to the forms of poetry, to the epic simile, in this case. When Newton demands the Muse somewhat later, his theories must submit to the formal requirements of poetic tradition. Poetry or drama may include a good deal of extraliterary material, but these genres retain a much greater commitment to their own aesthetic ceremony or etiquette. There are also modernizing attitudes in poems and plays of any literary period, attitudes that call older codes or conventions into question. The *Odyssey* offers an implict critique of the more fatalistic physical heroism of the *Iliad*; *The Tempest* reveals the "baseless fabric" of some of the major conventions of Elizabethan drama; the Preface to *Lyrical Ballads* rejects the ennobling formulas of "poetic diction." But in all these examples the revisionary thrust of the critique is contained by the traditional sanctions of poetic voice and dramatic *agon*. In the novel, such deep performative sanctions, radical formalizations of ordinary speech and action, no longer bind the prose of a more various world, and no equivalent sanctions arise to take their place. As a novel, *Middlemarch* is not concerned with purifying prose fiction from outmoded conventions so much as it is concerned with "reforming" the novel reader's cultural perceptions, with expanding literature's repertoire of forms to achieve a broader representation of human life in society. At the same historical moment that Matthew Arnold was reemphasizing the literary canon in *Culture and Anarchy*, Eliot was trying to move her readers toward a less exclusive conception of civilizing form. This is not to say that *Middlemarch* is a formal anarchy. As a number of critics have shown in the last dozen years, there is consierable coherence and unity in the design of the novel as a whole. But this is a "higher formalism," an organizing pattern which functions on a different level. It may synthesize the literary and nonliterary paradigms in a more appropriate form, but the significance of the synthesis cannot be appreciated without a recognition of how this novel, in its own cultural moment, moves dialectically back and forth between literature and other human institutions.

It should be obvious by now that a poetics proper of the novel proper is a highly problematic undertaking, attempting, as it must, to systematize the antisystematic and to canonize the anticanonical. The opposition is often implicit (there are of course exceptions to the rule), and it is an opposition which might be related to more fundamental antinomies of the human mind, but I would offer the following generalization: the novel characteristically opposes itself to the view of literature that a poetics implies. Not only does it oppose itself to types of literature more traditional than the novel. As I have already mentioned, a novel characteristically opposes itself to other novels. This is not to say that novelists are not formally indebted to other novelists, but that the rules of the game forbid overt acknowledgment of this debt, except in the form of parody; such is not the case with poetry or drama. "There is need of a book showing in detail that every novel bears *Quixote* within it like an inner filigree, in the same way as every epic poem contains the *Iliad* within it like the fruit its core," Ortega y Gasset wrote.[15] There is a good deal of truth to this assertion, but the difference between the way the epic relates to its ancestor and the way the novel does to its great original is extreme.

This basic incompatibility between the novel and a poetics has been obscured and complicated by certain developments in the literary history of the last two hundred years, particularly by two developments that were both specialized and influential. The first was the reaction against the neoclassical canon by certain German romantics, who used the novel as one of the banners of their revolt. For a number of reasons, a significant one being the popularity of Fielding, Richardson, Sterne, and Diderot, German romantics like Goethe and the Schlegels elevated the novel to a new prominence in their countercanon. Goethe compared the novel to the drama in *Wilhelm Meister* in a way that placed the two genres on a par. Friedrich Schlegel spoke of the novel as "a Romantic book," the epitome of romantic literature as distinguished from the classical, and his brother August saw it as the genre which included all other genres.[16] The other development was the creation of a modernist aesthetic which elevated the novel not so much by comparison to other types of literature as by comparison to the other arts, particularly music, painting, and architecture. In a sense, the novel is here projected beyond the older humanistic arena of literature into a higher, more sacred precinct of art, just as in German romanticism there is a tendency to ground the novel not simply in literature but in a more basic conception of myth. The most influential figure in this latter development is of course Henry James, although one might mention Proust and Mann as well. Although he is wary of prescribing it, James insists on the high seriousness of the art of the novel. His famous image of "the house of fiction" reveals his desire to represent the novel as a solid and enduring institution, at least as important to the present age as poetry and the drama. James is responding implicitly to Victorian critics like Arnold, who were not disposed to include the novel in the best that had been thought and said. In response to those who would keep the novel beyond the pale, James demands that it be admitted to the privileged circle of culture.

As far as the definition of the novel itself is concerned—the novel as outsider model which opposes other forms of life to the forms of literary tradition—one would have to make some adjustments for the novels of German romanticism and the novels of European modernism. In both these movements, the novel claims more centrality for itself within the sphere of literature and culture, and the opposition becomes one between the forms of a semisacred myth and/or art and the forms of a meretricious life. However, the forms or fictions of everyday life are still represented in breadth and detail, even as they are being criticized or subsumed by the forms or fictions of art. Goethe shows the petty financial and erotic troubles behind the company of actors in *Wilhelm Meister* as well as their production of *Hamlet;* James insists on the particulars of Strether's Woollett character as well as on the synthesizing power of his imagination of

Paris; Proust presents the redemptive world of art deeply imbedded in the snobberies of contemporary French society. Only in what Ralph Freedman has called the "lyrical novel," in Hesse, Gide, and Virginia Woolf and certain German precursors, has there been a significant weakening of the novel's commitment to the extraaesthetic world.[17]

Furthermore, even in many earlier novels, the opposition between inherited and experienced fictions is not as one-sided as in works of realism like *Moll Flanders, L'Assommoir,* or *One Day in the Life of Ivan Denisovitch.* In *Don Quixote* the literary fictions often come out ahead of the overconfident assumptions about "truth." The barber and the curate, those figures of normative sobriety, turn out to be avid consumers of romances themselves, and Sancho's proverbs are applied with the same imaginative irrelevance as Quixote's chivalric scenarios. A similar ambivalence toward the structures of "reality" (a word that should always be used in quotation marks, as Nabokov says) can be found in *Tristram Shandy, The Confidence-Man,* or *Lolita.* What is different for Goethe, Flaubert, James, and their heirs is that "culture," to follow Raymond Williams's argument, had begun to be seen itself as a form of opposition, opposition to the increasingly dominant forces of democratic and industrial society.[18] Some novelists preferred to join forces with a canon increasingly on the defensive rather than continue to oppose a less influential establishment—some of the greatest, but by no means all.

As far as a poetics of the novel is concerned, there were no real attempts at official classification until the twentieth century. James was adamant in refusing to lay down rules for the art of the novel. Schlegel's *Brief Über Den Roman* was cast not as a systematic treatise but as a dialogue, a romantic form which, as one critic puts it, "rebels against systematic order" and which cultivates the "chaotic."[19] Schlegel also ignores the formal distinction between the novel (*Roman*) and romantic literature in general, in which he includes Dante and Shakespeare. In Percy Lubbock's *The Craft of Fiction,* however, we have a genuine poetics of the novel based on James's practice, and in Lukács's *Theory of the Novel* we have a historical poetics of the novel based on German romantic methods, particularly those of Hegel. The inadequacy of Lubbock's system and canon, with *The Ambassadors* and *The Wings of the Dove* as his *Oedipus Tyrannos,* has generally been realized by now; it was most fully exposed by Wayne Booth's *The Rhetoric of Fiction,* which unfortunately tended to set up a counterpoetics of its own, based not on Lubbock's dramatic model of representation but on a rhetorical model of narration, and which proscribed, in turn, James and other modern novelists for their "confusion of distance." The limitations of Lukács's theory are less obvious; it has been less influential than that of Lubbock, it is more catholic in its tastes, and it recognizes more fully the novel's negative ethos. But while Lukács begins with a direct contrast between the novel and the epic, he ends by envisioning a synthesis of the two genres in novelists like Goethe and Tolstoy. Lukács expresses his own dissatisfaction with this Hegelian poetics in the preface he wrote for a reissue of the book in 1962. "Suffice it to point out that novelists such as Defoe, Fielding and Stendhal found no place in this schematic pattern, that the arbitrary 'synthetic' method of the author of *The Theory of the Novel* leads him to a completely upside-down view of Balzac and Flaubert or of Tolstoy and Dostoevsky. . . ."[20] Both Lukács and Lubbock have particular difficulty in assimilating Tolstoy's work to their systems.

It may be true, as one critic has recently claimed, that the epic-oriented theory of Lukács is a healthy corrective to the drama-centered theory of Lubbock and others, but as both try to reunite the novel with the more regular, more tradition-minded forms of epic and drama, they falsify the nature of the genre. In his later writing Lukács continues to collapse the distinction between ancient and modern narrative modes. "The really great novelists are in this respect always true-born sons of Homer," he says in *Studies in European Realism*.[21] "The want of a received nomenclature is a real hindrance," Lubbock complained, "and I have often wished that the modern novel had been invented a hundred years sooner, so that it might have fallen into the hands of the critical schoolmen of the seventeenth century."[22] The teaching of literature in schools in fact has been an important stimulus to the creation of poetics throughout the ages, as E. R. Curtius has observed.[23] As schoolmen of the twentieth century, dealing with a type of literature increasingly studied within the academy, we must resist the temptation of order and norm which can easily distort the nature of the material we are trying to understand.

The existence of this ancient quarrel between the novel and literature does not mean that the idea of a poetics is simply irrelevant to the novel and should be discarded by all critics concerned, however. It is an idea against which the novel, since it is after all literary in the wider sense of the word, must struggle. If we think not of a poetics *of* the novel but of poetics *and* the novel we may understand better both these antithetical categories. "The theoretical orders of poetics should be viewed, at any moment in their history, as essentially mental codes—with which the practicing writer... comes to terms through his writing," Guillén has suggested.[24] If we adopt this more phenomenological view, we can see this coming to terms as an important aspect of a novel, and a significant constituent of its meaning.

Without pretending to be exhaustive or systematic myself, I would say that there are three fundamental ways in which the novel comes to terms with the alien order of a poetics. The first is the realist strategy of rejection: the novel asserts its place not within the literary universe but within the "real" world of nonliterary discourse. *Moll Flanders* is "a private history" in which the author has merely edited the style and diction of the woman who lived the life. *Pamela* is a series of letters "which have their foundation in Truth and Nature" and are assembled by an editor. Twain posts the "Notice" as the beginning of the colloquial narrative of *Huckleberry Finn:* "Persons attempting to find a motive in the narrative will be prosecuted; persons attempting to find a moral in it will be banished; persons attempting to find a plot in it will be shot." Form and function are not ostensibly conditioned by literary priorities, as they are in *Paradise Lost,* Pope's *Pastorals,* or, in a subtler way, Wordsworth's lyrics; they are dictated by the types of persons and places involved. In Robbe-Grillet's *Jealousy* the rejection of literary convention is dramatized by the discussions of the African adventure novel which take place in this strangely neutralized and noneventful narrative.

The realist strategy in *Jealousy* shades off into the second way in which the novel declares its independence of poetics, the fictionalist strategy of incorporation and transcendence. Here the novel becomes its own poetics, in a parodic and subversive way, including encyclopedically within itself examples of other genres along with critical discussion of them. The best example of this tactic is *Don Quixote,* which mocks in its preface the absurdities of Aristotelian classification, but which incorporates a great variety of genres—epic, pastoral, ballad, Greek romance, picaresque novel, Moorish history, and others—alongside Quixote's chivalric romances and which includes a number of learned debates on literary subjects. Fielding follows Cervantes's lead. Where Richardson declined to write a preface for *Pamela,* letting nature speak for itself, Fielding writes a mock *Poetics* for *Joseph Andrews,* taking up where Aristotle left off and defining the novel, with tongue-in-cheek neoclassicism, as a "comic epic in prose." Throughout the novel Parson Adams is made to find that

11

nature and Homer are not, in fact, the same. *Tristram Shandy* devours, digests, and regurgitates the whole eighteenth-century system of the arts in its eccentric and unbalanced *paideia*. In *Ulysses* this need to free oneself from another's system by creating one's own becomes an obsession; Homer himself is subsumed and redistributed in Joyce's fictive universe. Barth's *Giles Goat-Boy* attempts a similar incòrporation of the ancients in the modern, although, one may feel, with less success.

The third way the novel has resisted the embrace of a poetics—used by Barth and Joyce as well—might be called the populist strategy of vulgarization. Popular literature, beneath the contempt of a poetics if not beyond its pale, is made to challenge the canonical, as in *Great Expectations*, where Mr. Wopsle's recitation of Collins's "Ode on the Passions" and his ill-fated performance in *Hamlet* compare unfavorably with Pip's obsessional acting out of the patterns of the fairy tale, or with Miss Havisham's reenactment of the creature-creator dialectic of Mary Shelley's *Frankenstein*. Or popular literature may stand in for the canonical and reveal the emptiness of the literary universe itself, which is how I read Emma's immersion in the popular romances and keepsakes in *Madame Bovary*—not as a criticism of this trivial literature alone but as an exposure of the literary imagination in general. More explicitly, Pynchon reduces classical and Renaissance tragedy to the communications of the postal service in *The Crying of Lot 49*.

I would not go so far as to say that all novels resist the claims of a poetics in one or more of these ways. The pressure of systems that classify and canonize has not always been felt by novelists as needing such specific resistance.[25] I would also grant that, for any writer in any genre, coming to terms with the theoretical order of poetics requires a certain amount of struggle and assertion of independence. But the novel arose, first in Spain and then in England, out of the attempt to create a vernacular literature addressed to the middle classes that neither submitted to the classical ordering of genres nor acknowledged the superiority of that ordering by a traditional cultivation of native and popular modes. The rise of the novel in eighteenth-century England is generally acknowledged and has been much discussed. The rise of the novel in late sixteenth-and early seventeenth-century Spain is less widely admitted.

In *Don Quixote* and the numerous picaresque novels of this earlier period we have the first fully developed examples of an extended prose writing which opposes the fictions of everyday life to the fictions of a literary tradition. In *Lazarillo de Tormes, Guzmán de*

Alfarache, El Buscón and other Spanish picaresques, the injunctions
of the Counter Reformation against the idealizing and entertaining
literature of the Renaissance bore fruit. The prose of the world is
played off against the prose of belles-lettres, out of a basically religious reaction against the Renaissance celebration of the nature and
dignity of man.[26] In a rather different spirit, Cervantes's ironic
genius reacted to the strictures of the neo-Aristotelians against the
popular romances of chivalry, strictures that would limit the freedom
of the artist to imagine, observe, and above all involve the reader in
an imaginative world.[27] At a time when many theorists were subjecting the romances to a new poetics—a project Cervantes himself
was to underwrite in *Persiles y Sigismunda*—*Don Quixote* gave the
uncanonical and the unliterary fictions of the day a major voice in
literary politics.

Thus at the same historical moment Cervantes and the authors of
the Spanish picaresque novels subjected the literary humanism of
the Renaissance to its first major critique from within the province of
literature more broadly conceived. At the same time that poetry was
winning its battle against philosophy and religion, as in Sidney's
Apology, with its Aristotelian basis, the novel was launching the
literary tradition of the new which was to make serious inroads on
literature, in the classical, canonical sense of the word, in the
nineteenth and twentieth centuries. The novel, of course, has undergone a great many changes since Cervantes's time, most notably in
the way it has risen in literary prestige. And poetics have changed a
good deal since Sidney, becoming less dogmatic, and less influential
as well, in their prescription of literary laws. Nevertheless, the basic
antagonism has persisted. Now, it would seem, the novel itself is
being challenged by a new imaginative medium, the film—though it
would be unwise to proclaim the death of our distinctively modern
genre. As Wellek and Warren remind us, the evolution of aesthetic
forms is not like the evolution of biological species. Old genres never
die, they just reach a relatively smaller audience, which may expand
at a later time. New genres never take over the earth, they just create
new and larger audiences for their art—which may not prove as
lasting over the years.

An adequate *theory* of the novel, therefore, would have to be
something more than a poetics. It would have to combine a poetics
with a prosaics, so to speak, in order to describe the interaction
between existing conceptions of literature and conceptions of nonlit-
erature that are brought critically to bear upon the literary. It is in
this context that I would like to raise the question of the adequacy of

the recent poetics of structuralist persuasion emanating from France. The work of such critics as Roland Barthes, Tzvetan Todorov, Gerard Genette, and Julia Kristeva has been renewing the possibility of a poetics of fiction and attracting considerable attention in Anglo-American criticism.[28]

In the first place, one might well question the applicability of the term "poetics" to the structuralist analysis, a term used freely by Todorov, and more restrainedly by Genette. At issue is not merely the apparent lack of concern with a canon or with aesthetic value-judgments, but the lack of focus on the *literary* specificity of the texts that are being analyzed. Todorov cites Jakobson as a precedent for his use of the term "poetics," but where Jakobson insists that "the main subject of poetics is the *differentiae specifica* of verbal art in relation to other arts and in relation to other kinds of verbal behavior,"[29] both Todorov and Barthes are more concerned with illuminating literary structure by analogy with linguistic structure. Instead of taking up Jakobson's question, "What makes a verbal message a work of art?" Todorov tends to ask, "How is a work of art like a verbal message?" The terms of his "Poétique" are a curious mixture of categories taken from linguistics and logic and categories taken from traditional theorists like Aristotle and Henry James. In spite of his claims to the contrary, he offers no satisfactory definition of the literary *specificum*, something that Jakobson has been able to provide, at least for poetry. "Introduction à l'analyse structurale des récits" elaborates the different levels on which a text and the exposition of it may operate, but the term *récit* effectively levels the distinction between the special and the general use of language that poetics is usually concerned with making.[30]

Nevertheless, one may use the term "poetics" to describe the systematics of structuralists like Todorov and Barthes if one realizes that there has been a transvaluation of critical values. The literary humanism of traditional poeticians like Aristotle, Sidney, Staiger, or Frye, is replaced by a scientific holism which explicitly rejects the humanist assumptions. Rather than a defense, the structuralists offer an attack on poesy, a counterpoetics which takes as its field not "poetry" or "literature" but a much broader range of narrative discourse—popular, classical, informal, formal, oral, and written. This is a valuable contribution in its own right and a serious challenge to traditional methods of literary study, but as it deliberately ignores the inherited notions of literary form against which the novel has struggled, it would not seem to be able to grasp the novel's dialectical nature. In fact, in its opposition to the idea of a literary canon and to the idea of literary value-judgment, the structuralist *poétique* can be seen as a novelization of traditional poetics—a poetics by the novel, or at least by the *nouveau roman*.

These objections may be formulated more specifically in reference to three of the most illuminating studies of this French school which share several essential features: Barthes' *S/Z*, Genette's "Discours du récit," and Kristeva's *Le texte du roman*. All three of these conceive of themselves as antitraditional systematics, as *poétiques ouvertes*, in Genette's phrase, rather than the *poétiques fermées* of literary tradition.[31] All three are focused predominantly on the "modern" or "new" mode of structuration, conceived in opposition to the ancient or old. And all three derive a set of virtually universal narrative features from the analysis of a single text: Balzac's *Sarrasine* in the case of Barthes, Proust's *À la recherche du temps perdu* in the case of Genette, and a little-known late medieval narrative, Antoine de La Sale's *Jehan de Saintré*, in the case of Kristeva. "The single text is valid for all the texts of literature," Barthes writes, "not in that it represents them (abstracts and equalizes them), but in that literature itself is never anything but a single text."[32]

Without claiming to do justice to the subtle and often brilliant insights generated in each of these studies, I would nevertheless like to call attention to the following theoretical limitations of them all, as far as a possible poetics of the novel is concerned. First of all, a historical distinction—between the old and the new, the classic and the modern, or in Barthes' terms, the "readerly" (*lisible*) and the "writerly" (*scriptible*) text—is introduced with an extremely uncritical historical attitude. Historical change is represented in a crude binary opposition, whose terms are essentially political, logical, or semiotic: the difference between bourgeois and antibourgeois in Barthes, between open and closed in Genette, between symbol and sign in Kristeva. The fact that the supposedly pivotal text can be located anywhere from the fifteenth to the twentieth century only underlines the historical uncertainty.

Secondly, in championing the openness of the narrative text without adequate attention to the possibilities of closure, these *poétiques ouvertes* exaggerate the indeterminacy that particular novels are capable of achieving. Instead of specific analysis of the ways in which narrative limits and controls are transgressed and removed, we are given a generalized ideology of liberation. Barthes' writerly texts (between which and the readerly text, *Sarrasine* is only a halfway house) seem to have little or no concrete embodiment:

> the writerly text is not a thing, we would have a hard time finding it in a bookstore. Further, its model being a productive (and no longer a representative) one, it demolishes

15

any criticism which, once produced, would mix with
it: . . . the writerly text is *ourselves writing*, before the infinite play of the world (the world as function) is traversed,
intersected, stopped, plasticized by some singular system
(Ideology, Genus, Criticism) which reduces the plurality of
entrances, the opening of networks, the infinity of languages.[33]

In such vertiginous openness the question of the novel itself becomes
irrelevant. "The writerly is the novelistic without the novel, poetry
without the poem."[34]

The final objection I would raise is that paradoxically, in spite of
their theoretical commitment to dynamic multiplicity, these modernizing poetics in practice effect a curious kind of hypostasis of their
categories, in which they turn out to resemble more classical poetics
after all. The generic level of generality on which a traditional poetics
would operate is subverted, but it is then reconstituted on both a
lower and a higher level of abstraction. On the lower level are the
textual particulars of the single narrative chosen for discussion,
which however they are dissected constitute a highly determinate
order of their own. On the higher level are the (primarily) linguistic
universals—the codes (Barthes), figures (Genette), or grammatical
transformations (Kristeva) which constitute a putative totality of
available structuration.

In this double reconstruction of formal order, structuralist poetics
look suspiciously like Aristotelian poetics writ large. The historically dynamic and historically divergent modalities of the novel
either tear or slip through these extremely fine and extremely coarse
meshes. On the one hand, we are invited to consider, with Genette, a
narrative's deviation not from shared generic constraints but from its
own implicit norms. On the other hand, we are invited, as with
Barthes, to entertain such macro-concepts as the subject and predi-
cate, "the mother cell of the entire Occident."[35] In Kristeva's argument in particular, the analysis of a particular narrative is conducted
at a level of generality that ends up including virtually all of Western
culture since the fifteenth century under the rubric of *le roman*.

An important precedent for these structuralist poetics of prose, as
Todorov and other critics freely acknowledge, has been the writings
of the Russian Formalists of the 1920s. Indeed, it is in their writings,
carried on in the West, and up to the present most authoritatively, by
Roman Jakobson, that the term "poetics," reconceived by analogy
with the scientific study of language termed "linguistics," under-
went the sea change from humanistic to scientific usage that has

created a certain critical confusion about the enterprise at present. There was also, however, a profound critique of Russian Formalism undertaken in the 1930s by the Soviet critic Mikhail Bakhtin and his circle. This historical semiotics, still being discovered and assimilated in the West, does in fact point the way to a potential closing of the gap between "novel" and "poetics" that has been the burden of this chapter. Since the most relevant of this material, some of it still in the process of being translated, became available to me after my own argument here was essentially complete, I can only conclude this chapter by pointing out its existence. I admit its challenge to my thesis about the incompatibility of *any* poetics with the heterodox nature of the novel, but I also claim its support for my contention that the phenomenon of the novel can only be understood in a thoroughgoing historical investigation.[36]

In his critique of formalism, Bakhtin speaks of a "sociological poetics" in which literature would be studied not in isolation but in the larger system of cultural "ideologies." Thus the nonliterary is as important as the literary material itself, and the distinction between the different subsystems must be acknowledged and respected. Even more important, this broader poetics must be oriented toward historical change: "sociological poetics itself, lest it become dogmatic, must be oriented toward literary history. There should be constant interaction between these two fields. Poetics provides literary history with direction in the specification of the research material and the basic definitions of its forms and types. Literary history amends the definitions of poetics, making them more flexible, dynamic, and adequate to the diversity of the historical material."[37]

When he comes to write about the novel specifically, on the other hand, Bakhtin talks less in terms of this "historical" or "sociological poetics" of the future and more in terms of the older poetics of literary tradition, against which the novel must always stand in opposition. The coincidence of Bakhtin's argument with my own is striking here, and it would be something of a scholarly embarrassment if the scope and originality of his thinking were less apparent. "Faced with the novel," Bakhtin writes, "literary theory exposes its utter helplessness."

> With other genres, literary theory works confidently and precisely—there is a completed and already-composed object, definite and clear. In all the classical epochs of their development these genres retain their rigidity and their canonic quality; their variations from epoch to epoch, from trend to trend and from school to school are peripheral, and

do not affect their ossified genre-skeleton. Up to the present day, in fact, theory dealing with these completed
genres can add almost nothing essential to that which was
already established by Aristotle. His poetics remains the
stable foundation for the theory of genres (although this
foundation is sometimes so deeply embedded it is almost
invisible). Everything works as long as no one mentions
the novel. But as other genres have become novelized, they
have led theory into a dead end. Dealing with the problem
of the novel, the theory of genres finds itself face-to-face
with the necessity of radical reconstruction.[38]

A recent reviewer of these essays speaks of "the [Russian] formalists, whose early work in semiotics and literary theory . . . seems
capable of turning our best contemporary thinkers into re-inventors
of the wheel," and he goes on: "We may take comfort in the fact that
after re-inventing early and middle formalism, we have finally begun
to be 'anticipated' by its last and greatest genius, Mixhail Baxtin."[39] I
can only point the reader interested in pursuing the problem of a
poetics for the novel to the recent and forthcoming translations of his
work.[40] But my own study must turn here from the problem of a
poetics to the question of a history for the novel, the question of the
ways in which particular novels might be said to constitute a historical series of examples. In this perspective, my divergence from
Bakhtin's type of historicism will become clearer.

2

On the Origins of the Novel

For it is no such easy task to distinguish between what is natural and what is artificial in the present constitution of man, and to make oneself well acquainted with a state which, if it ever did, does not now, and in all probability never will exist, and of which, notwithstanding, it is absolutely necessary to have just notions to judge properly our present state.

Rousseau, *Discourse on the Origin and Foundation of Inequality among Mankind*

One of the obvious appeals of a poetics for the novel is the prospect of rising above the familiar yet confused terrain of the more traditional historical understanding of prose fiction. A poetics of the novel conjures up a brave new world for criticism; a history of the novel peers into a dark backward and abysm of time. The historical study of the novel in this century has produced a vast array of sequences, selections, and juxtapositions of texts, arrangements which neither harmonize nor conflict with one another and which leave the nature of the object under investigation unclear. Some historians of the novel have aimed at all-inclusiveness, along the lines of evolutionary biology, and trace the family tree of the modern realistic novel from the Greek romances through the Middle Ages and the Renaissance. Ernest Baker devotes some three of his ten volumes of *The History of the English Novel* to fiction before Defoe.[1] Others, like F. R. Leavis, would limit the significant history of the English novel to the work of a few great writers. *The Great Tradition* is more an act of canon-formation than a historical analysis, but it does articulate a developing sequence of the best that has been thought and said in prose fiction, taking note of the second best and acknowledging some nonevolutionary "sports" like *Wuthering Heights*. But in most of these histories the crucial question of the origins of the novel as a literary form is generally dissolved in relativities or ignored. Arnold Kettle is perhaps the most honest when he says, "We might as well start—when we have finished our preliminaries—with Bunyan and Defoe. The starting point is neither original nor inevitable, but it is convenient."[2]

There are, however, two influential accounts of the history of the novel that deal seriously with the question of origins, accounts that many readers find persuasive today. One is set forth by Ian Watt in

The Rise of the Novel: that the novel began in England in the early eighteenth century, as the product of epistemological and sociological changes, that its essential feature is the circumstantial narrative that Watt calls "formal realism." The other account is more philosophical, deriving ultimately from Hegel. It defines the novel in opposition to the epic, and locates its exemplary instance in *Don Quixote.* Lukács's *Theory of the Novel* is one example of this historical argument. But it informs Ortega y Gasset's *Meditations on Quixote* as well, and it has been expanded brilliantly by the Soviet critic Mikhail Bakhtin.[3] The one account is nationalistic, the other cosmopolitan or "world-historical," in the Hegelian phrase.

The main limitation of Watt's account of the novel's origins is that it fails to weigh adequately the claims of earlier prose fiction to the status of "novel." He assumes "as is commonly done . . . that [the novel] was begun by Defoe, Richardson and Fielding,"[4] and then defines "formal realism" in such a way as to account for the distinction between English novels of the eighteenth century and the "prose fiction" of earlier periods and other countries.

> Formal realism, in fact, is the narrative embodiment of a premise that Defoe and Richardson accepted very literally, but which is implicit in the novel form in general: the premise, or primary convention, that the novel is a full and authentic report of human experience, and is therefore under an obligation to satisfy its reader with such details of the story as the individuality of the actors concerned, the particulars of the times and places of their actions, details which are presented through a more largely referential use of language than is common in other literary forms.[5]

Thus formal realism is the narrative "embodiment" of a prior "premise"; behind the form is an intention, but one that can only be deduced from the form itself. The logic of Watt's argument is circular. Alternatively, Watt provides an explanation by referring to the author's "obligation" to "satisfy" the reader's need. Too much depends on these elusive commitments and desires. There are also significant problems of discrimination, particularly if Fielding's new species of writing is kept in mind. Watt admits that some earlier writers "professed a wholly realistic aim," but claims that "they did not follow it whole-heartedly."[6] The criterion here is again one of intention or commitment, but now it is one that may not be sincere, or efficient. Watt concludes with an appeal not to intention itself but to the consciousness of intention: "The aim of verisimilitude [in earlier writers of prose fiction] had not been deeply enough assimilated . . . to bring about the full rejection of all the non-realistic conventions that governed the genre."[7] The equivocation between a distinction of kind and a distinction of degree shows that "formal realism" is simply too loose a theoretical construct to allow for a discussion of origins.

Indeed, the following criteria that Watt uses to describe the novels of Defoe and Richardson can with almost equal justice be applied to the anonymous *Lazarillo de Tormes,* Aléman's *Guzmán de Alfarache,* and Quevedo's *El Buscón:* "Defoe and Richardson are the first great writers of our literature who did not take their plots from mythology, history, legend or previous literature" (p. 14); "Defoe initiated an important new tendency in fiction: his total subordination of the plot to the pattern of the autobiographical memoir" (p. 15); "[Defoe's] fiction is the first which presents us with a picture both of the individual life in its larger perspective as a historical process, and in its closer view which shows the process being acted out against the background of the most ephemeral thoughts and actions" (p. 24); and finally, Defoe and Richardson are original in "the adaptation of prose style to give an air of complete authenticity" (p. 27). With some allowance for differences in emphasis, these are all apt descriptions of the three earlier Spanish picaresque novels. Watt's criteria have been convincingly applied to *Don Quixote* as well, and in a more deliberate tour de force to Longus's *Daphnis and Chloe* and other late classical Greek romances.[8] The circularity of Watt's argument is perhaps inevitable, a version of the hermeneutic circle of all interpretation. Nevertheless, it is a circle too closely drawn.

If Watt bases his history on an entity which turns out to be more diverse and widespread than he allows, Lukács and Bakhtin define the novel in terms of a difference that is not as exclusive as it pretends to be. *The Theory of the Novel* is a historical poetics, as we noted in the first chapter, and is more concerned with broad dichotomies than with concrete sequences. It characterizes the novel as antithetical to the epic, but then asserts a continuity of spirit or mind between the two forms that undermines the sense of a difference. "The genre-creating principle which is meant here does not imply any change in mentality," Lukács writes; "rather it forces the same mentality to turn towards a new aim which is essentially different from the old one."[9] The derivation of novel from epic turns out to contain a nostalgia for return:

> The epic and the novel, the two major forms of great epic
> literature, differ from one another not by their authors'

fundamental intentions but by the given historico-
philosophical realities with which the authors were confronted. The novel is the epic of an age in which the extensive totality of life is no longer directly given, in which the
immanence of meaning in life has become a problem, *yet
which still thinks in terms of totality.*[10]

The question of specific origins is thus avoided in the essential continuity of history. The novel becomes a later manifestation of the epic
spirit, and although Lukács identifies *Don Quixote* as "the first great
novel of world literature," he also insists on the overlapping of categories. The "chivalrous epic of the Middle Ages" is seen as "the
curious case of a novel form existing in a period whose absolute
belief in God really encouraged the epic,"[11] while *Don Quixote*
"overlaps still more obviously into the epic in its formal and
historico-philosophical foundations."[12]

Bakhtin draws on Lukács in his essay "Epos and Novel," and,
although he maintains the distinction between the two categories
with greater clarity, he dramatizes the historical weakness of this
negative definition as the novel becomes the focus of a more general
cultural change. Bakhtin defines the epic as the genre of "absolute
past," "irrefutable tradition," and "absolute distance," but then goes
on to assert that these characteristics are "to a greater or lesser extent
also essential to the other major genres of classical antiquity and the
Middle Ages."[13] Conversely, the so-called low genres of all earlier
periods become assimilated to the novel, and we find that such diverse things as the Socratic dialogue, Menippean satire, and "popular laughter" are "the first authentic and essential step in the development of the novel as a 'becoming' genre."[14] Even more than Lukács,
Bakhtin illuminates the nature of the novel with brilliant theoretical
formulations, but as history his account is too all-embracing and too
partisan in its championship of historical "becoming." "With [the
novel] and in it is born the future of all literature," Bakhtin writes,
and in this absolute ascendency the particulars of the literary past are
left behind.[15]

It seems clear now that any history of the novel and any argument
for its origins must mediate between the nationalistic and world-
historical extremes. I would argue, in fact, that the novel can only be
understood as a multinational phenomenon, rooted in European national cultures although eventually spreading to almost every modern nation-state, continent, or local region. The novel does not simply arise at one point in history and geography and go on developing
steadily thereafter. Rather it arises and rearises in different regional

cultures at different times. The Russian novel of the nineteenth century is a revolutionary "renovelization" of the contemporary European novel, a renovation that was widely regarded in twentieth-century Europe as peculiarly modern, ahead of its time. The novel also renews itself within national literatures in different historical periods. The Victorian novel in England shows an awareness of the eighteenth-century English novel (Dickens looks back to Smollett, Thackeray to Fielding), but it also conceives of itself as raising the novel to a new level of moral seriousness and social responsibility—a level which it was not considered capable of in the romantic era, in spite of Sir Walter Scott.[16] The novel can even define itself as the vehicle of a particular region or ethnic group, recently fallen or risen, as has been the case in the United States with the novel of the Southern renaissance or with the contemporary Jewish novel.

This is not to say that the concept of the novel originates separately or spontaneously in each literary tradition. The Japanese novel is to a large extent a late nineteenth-century importation from the West, as is, according to Edward Said, the twentieth-century novel in modern Arabic.[17] As I shall show in a later chapter, even Defoe, the trueborn Englishman, was quite aware of his Continental predecessors. But the precedent that earlier novels offer is less a definitive or imitable form than an invitation to explore the *mismatching* of forms immediately experienced with forms more remote and traditional. "New novels" may declare themselves in opposition to novels of the past—such is clearly the case in the *nouveau roman* of the past few decades in France—but the reaction is more against the institutionalization of certain novels—those of Balzac, for example, by academic and bourgeois culture—than against the project of the novel in general.[18] In the case of Tolstoy, the rejection of "literature" reaches truly epic proportions, but it can be argued that in this Tolstoy is the most deeply typical of novelists.

Nevertheless it would be false to conclude from this centrifugal plurality of the novel that it has no construable history at all and no discernible point of origin. If we accept the insight of recent theorists that a truly literary history is a history of readings of the past, it should be possible to locate the historical moment when the past began to be read novelistically. "In contrast to a political event, a literary event has no lasting results which succeeding generations cannot avoid," writes Hans Robert Jauss. "It can continue to have an effect only if future generations still respond to it or rediscover it—if there are readers who take up the work of the past again or authors who want to imitate, outdo, or refute it." Such a history would be based on a history of reception, and it would mediate between the tracing of an entity (the novel) that has no natural or positive existence, and the setting up of a canon (the great tradition or the great antitradition) which has no suprahistorical validity. Such a history "demands on the one hand—in opposition to the objectivism of positivist literary history—a conscious attempt to establish canons, which, on the other hand—in opposition to the classicism of the study of traditions—presupposes a critical review if not destruction of traditional literary canon."[19] In the chapters that follow, I will go on to offer such a history, which I call an "exemplary" history of the novel in the several senses of that word. But here I will try to describe the point of origin, the moment, in fact, that the canon becomes identifiably canonical and the novel a critical departure from it. Such an origin is thus not a unitary source but a disruptive event, a differentiation within a cultural system that had previously been perceived as homogeneous.

It will hardly be surprising if I locate this moment and event in Spain during the late sixteenth and early seventeenth centuries. In spite of the influence of Watt, a large number of readers continue to feel that *Don Quixote* is "the exemplary novel of all time," in Harry Levin's phrase.[20] And a growing critical bibliography in the last decade on the picaresque novel testifies to the validity of the parallel claim that the picaresque "may well serve as a *paradigm* for the novel as a whole."[21] Some of these readers are themselves novelists—Mann and Bellow, Borges and Barth—and have deliberately eschewed the requirements for the novel of sociological verisimilitude and/or architectonic form that had helped to obscure the standing of the Spanish Golden Age novels. "Every writer *creates* his own precursors," in Borges's paradoxical formulation. "His work modifies our conception of the past." The experimental fiction of the last decades has played a significant role in helping us see that Cervantes and some of his contemporaries are not simply aberrations in the line of the novel's development.[22]

What, then, was the literary event that inaugurated this novelistic project? We are not concerned with a particular efficient cause so much as with what might be called the enabling conditions. We need not posit an extrinsic cause, philosophical or sociological, of which the novel is an effect, if we can find something, both inside and outside the literary field, that will account for the new sense of half-outsiderhood that we have defined as the novel's essential feature. The novels themselves provide an important clue.

"I think it's a good thing that important events which quite acci-

24

dentally have never seen the light of day, should be made public and not buried in the grave of oblivion," begins *Lazarillo de Tormes*. "It's possible that somebody may read them and find something he likes and others may find pleasure in just a casual glance."[23] The narrator of this *vida* or "life" directs his story to a priest or nobleman, whom he periodically addresses as "Your Honour," but he also has a keen sense, conceited or ironic, of a broad and casual reading public. The author invokes the reader more specifically and pointedly at the beginning of *El Buscón*:

> Dear Reader or Listener (for the blind cannot read) I can just imagine how much you want to read about my delightful Don Pablos, Prince of the Roving Life. Here you will find all the tricks of the low life or those which I think most people enjoy reading about: craftiness, deceit, subterfuge, and swindles, born of laziness to enable you to live on lies; and if you attend to the lesson you will get quite a lot of benefit from it. . . . You are well aware of the price of the book, as you already have it, unless you are looking through it in the bookshop, a practice which is very tiresome for the bookseller and ought to be suppressed with the utmost rigour of the law.[24]

As in the opening joke about blindness, the reader is first flattered and then humiliated. He is a consumer whose motives and morals are suspect. A more gentle but more succinct irony is presented by Cervantes at the beginning of the Prologue to *Don Quixote*: "Idle reader. . . ."[25]

The audience for these literary fictions is both specific and uncertain. It is not a community of listeners attending to an epic "song," or a member of an aristocratic coterie glancing over poems circulated in manuscript ("illustrious, or maybe plebian reader," Cervantes says in the Prologue to The Second Part of *Don Quixote* [467]); nor is it the patrons of the drama in a listening and viewing audience. Rather it is a solitary, anonymous figure, scanning a bulk of printed pages, out of a sense of nothing better to do. In these three textual moments (which are cumulative and interrelated) the ethos of the novel is realized. The raison d'être of the novel is the ambiguity introduced into literature by the technology of the printed book. This is the thesis that the rest of this chapter will attempt to establish.

The effects of the development of the printing press on the culture of fifteenth- and sixteenth-century Europe are only beginning to be explored. They have been overdramatized, and unfortunately somewhat discredited, through the work of Marshall McLuhan; they have been more soberly assessed, although with a clear partiality for the pre–printed word, by Father Walter Ong; and they are being most challengingly discussed by the historian Elizabeth Eisenstein. Eisenstein is especially persuasive in her argument for the diversity of effects of the revolution of the book: religious, political, and literary. "One of the advantages of considering the effects produced by printing is that we can come to terms with the coexistence of incompatible views and the persistence of contradictory movements without treating any as anomalous and without forcing them into oversimple grand designs. The many changes introduced by the new technology, . . . far from synchronizing smoothly or pointing in one direction, contributed to disjunctions, worked at cross purposes, and operated out of phase with each other."[26] The Protestant Reformation, the classicizing Renaissance, and the consolidation of the modern nation-state are all demonstrably bound up with this new technology, though all exploit and react to it in different ways. To call attention to such a crucial medium is not to argue for a simple technological determinism in which culture is a subfunction of machinery. Indeed, one can and should argue from the other side as well—that, for example, it was the demand by an increasing number of readers for texts that led to the invention of the printing press, or that the wide and immediate popularity of both *Don Quixote* and *Guzmán de Alfarache* contributed significantly to the expansion of the publishing trade in Europe and helped undermine the still powerful ethos of the manuscript as the norm of literary production. It is important to distinguish between the acquisition of the technology of print alone and the transformation of the culture by this new means of communication. Thus Eric Havelock argues that the culture of Athens only becomes literate in a modern sense in the late fifth century B.C., some two centuries after the Greeks had acquired the knowledge of writing.[27]

It would also be misleading to minimize the importance of the individual intelligence that realizes and interprets the implications of the new technological mode—Plato and Aristotle in Greece, for example, or Luther and Erasmus in Europe. If Luther had merely nailed his ninety-five theses to the door instead of publishing them in Latin and allowing them to be translated and printed in the vernacular, the Protestant revolt might have been contained much longer. If Erasmus and other humanists had not insisted on printing the Greek and Latin classics, many of the newly found manuscripts might subsequently have been lost again. And if Cervantes and a handful of other Spanish authors had not reflected on the revolu-

26

tionary implications of the printed book for the literary tradition, the novel might indeed have arisen later in England or in France. But Cervantes and others did realize some of the paradoxes of the new author-reader relationship, the potential mass popularity of a book, the new privacy of literary consumption, and the potential freedom from the authority of tradition. They realized these paradoxes in such a way that a new kind of imaginative writing, outside the prevailing literary canon but self-consciously aware of it, seemed both possible and inevitable.

One must emphasize that the relationship between the novel and the printing press is a complex of factors rather than a simple cause and effect. The new form of the novel was a response to as well as the creation of a particular cultural moment, and it created new needs and habits of its own. The analysis of the cultural place of art by Clifford Geertz is particularly relevant here. The subjectivity that the spectator or viewer or participant experiences in art "does not properly exist until it is thus organized," Geertz argues. "Art forms generate and regenerate the very subjectivity they only pretend to display. Quartets, still lifes, and cockfights are not merely reflections of a pre-existing sensibility analogically represented; they are positive agents in the creation and maintenance of such a sensibility."[28] The novel is one such agent, in which the sensibility so created, augmented, and maintained is precisely that of the "idle reader," drawn into the new cultural arena of the printed text. It is a sensibility to which literate people have become thoroughly accustomed, although critics remind us still of its peculiar illogic and uncertainty.[29]

For both the humanist and the Christian institutions of the sixteenth century, the role of the idle reader is a subversive one, at least if it is extended beyond a well-educated and responsible class. For the humanists, the prime function of reading is moral edification, the building up—and testing through the play of mind—of ethical responsibility and awareness. *Prodesse* takes precedence over *delectare* in the Horatian formula, and the authoritative texts for this exercise of virtue are those of classical Greece and Rome. For the Reformers, the main function of reading is individual salvation, and the personal study of the Bible in the vernacular takes precedence over all other reading—except of course in the countries of the Counter Reformation, like Spain, where the vernacular reading of the Bible is itself declared subversive and, in a certain sense, "the Priest reads for all."[30] A third important role in the Renaissance might be called that of the courtly or civic reader—the political advisor whose breadth of knowledge was important in the practical affairs of state. It is this last role, in fact, that launches Don Quixote on his third expedition in Part Two; he would advise the king on a way of defending the country against the invasion of the Turk. Such an amateur role may well be outmoded in the growing bureaucracy of the Counter Reformation state, but the more obvious irony is that Quixote's plan is based on the chivalric romances.[31]

For Cervantes, the reader is in practice less morally, religiously, or politically motivated. Like Don Quixote before his madness, the reader is unoccupied, out of work; "in the times when he had nothing to do—as was the case for most of the year—[he] gave himself up to the reading of books of knight errantry" (31). In fact it was these reprinted and rewritten medieval romances, having only tenuous connections with either the classical or the scriptural traditions, that became the first best-sellers of the new literary age.[32] As Eisenstein points out, the revolution into print often "was accomplished in a most deceptive way—not by discarding the products of scribal culture but by reproducing them in greater quantities than ever before. . . . Augmented book production altered patterns of consumption; increased output changed the nature of individual intake."[33] On the one hand, the reader read more freely and widely than in an earlier age when the manuscript copy was often the occasion for a communal reading aloud.[34] On the other hand, he was more able to reflect on the absurdities and inconsistencies of the characters and events displayed before him.

The role of the author also changed with the spread of the printed book, and again Cervantes reflects on this change with a self-consciousness that is constitutive for the novel. In claiming that he is not Don Quixote's father but his "step-father," and in introducing the intermittent fiction of the Arab historian Cide Hamete Benengeli, along with the Moorish translator of the Arabic manuscript, Cervantes continually demotes himself from author to publisher.[35] He is an author who continually denies hs own authority. This denial or subversion extends to the classical and biblical traditions as well, however, for when "Cervantes" laments the lack of scholarly apparatus in his book in the Prologue to Part One, his "intelligent friend" gives him the mechanical formula for producing such authority:

> 'As to quoting in the margins the books and authors from whom you gathered the sentences and sayings you have put in your history, all you have to do is work in some pat phrases or bits of Latin that you know by heart, or at least

that cost you small pains to look out. For example, on the
subject of liberty and captivity you might bring in:
'"Non bene pro toto libertas venditur auro."
'And in the margin cite Horace, or whoever said it. . . . If
you are dealing with friendship and the love God bids you
bear to your enemy, come to the point at once with Holy
Scripture, which you can do with a little bit of research by
quoting the words of no less an authority than God himself: "Ego autem dico vobis: diligite inimicos ves-
tros." '(28)

The friend then goes on to pry the novel free from such religious and
literary rules entirely, first by observing that no one will take the
trouble to see whether Cervantes follows his authorities or not and
second by noting that these authorities are irrelevant to the kind of
book he has written, "an invective against books of chivalry, which
Aristotle never dreamed of, Saint Basil never mentioned, and Cicero
never ran across" (29). The fictitious dialogue here is the novel's
declaration of independence.

And yet this declaration on the part of the novel keeps undermining its own counterauthority. It is not a new rule so much as a
critique of regulation itself. At the very end of the Second Part of *Don
Quixote* Cervantes apparently reaffirms the idea of his book as an
invective against the chivalric romances: "For my sole object has
been to arouse men's contempt for all fabulous and absurd stories of
knight errantry, whose credit this tale of my genuine Don Quixote
has already shaken, and which will, without a doubt, soon tumble to
the ground. Farewell" (940). But as Ramón Saldívar points out, this
conclusion is not spoken by Cervantes in propria persona to the
reader; it is spoken by Cide Hamete, the fictive and suspect historian, to his pen.[36] The author himself disappears, in a literary equivalent of the Indian rope trick.

This dubious authority of the author is dramatized differently in
the contemporary picaresque novels, but it is equally evident. The
putative author of *Lazarillo de Tormes* is a self-advertised rogue, who
confesses his sins and achievements to his interlocutor while vainly
posturing as a Renaissance self-made man, spicing his life story with
classical commonplaces and twisted religious pieties. Is the narrator a
satirist himself or the butt of the author's satire? Is he first one and
then the other, or both at once? Critics argue both sides of the case,
but it is the very ambiguity of Lázaro's stance that is significant.[37]
Quevedo's picaro, Pablos, is forced into a less equivocal posture; he

is repeatedly deceived, mocked, beaten, and humiliated. Yet he continues to speak for himself and to appeal to the reader with a disturbing empathy. We are given little or no sense of an author behind the narrator with whom we can more comfortably identify. We are disingenuously invited to share in Pablos's debasement: "who can realize how I felt, what with shame, a disjointed finger and the fear that they would cramp my legs? They had the ropes round me already so I pretended to come round. But they were trying to hurt me and before I could open my eyes they had already twisted the cords deep into me" (111). Pablos's authority is his experience, but his experience is one of a frightening lack of self-determination.

Thus these original Spanish examples of the novel respond in different ways to the new literary economy of the printed book. The responses are similar in the way they challenge, both seriously and playfully, some of the traditional values and functions of literature. Yet we must be more specific about what it is that is being challenged, and from what vantage point. Much valuable work has been done in this regard by Hispanists, in particular by Alban Forcione for Cervantes and by Alexander Parker for the picaresque. Both Forcione and Parker show how these earliest forms of the novel are part of a reaction against Renaissance humanism, in its more classicizing and idealizing modes. *Don Quixote* shows a complex ironical reaction by Cervantes to the neo-Aristotelian criticisms of the vernacular romances. These fictions, including Ariosto's *Orlando Furioso* as well as the more pedestrian chivalric romances in prose, were measured against the standards of Aristotle's recently discovered *Poetics* and found wanting.[38] *Don Quixote* is a "double-edged parody," rendering the popular romances absurd but also confounding the rational principles of this particular neoclassicism:

> Cervantes is highly conscious of both the general and specific aspects of the tradition of literary theorizing in the Renaissance and generally sympathetic with its aims. . . . On the other hand he is suspicious about the burdens with which the critical movement saddled the creative artist and perhaps sceptical about its assumption that truth is within easy reach of reason's grasp. Consequently he does not hesitate to subject its major ideas to a careful examination and to assert openly his independence of many of them.[39]

The picaresque novel grows out of an ethical and religious critique of literature rather than a logical and aesthetic one. As Parker shows, attacks on the irresponsibility of the chivalric romances by such Spanish humanists as Vives and Valdés were extended during the Counter Reformation to the idealizing tendencies of literary humanism itself. Thus Pedro Malon de Chaide writes, "We are naturally prone to evil, and require no incitements to sin, such as these lascivious and profane books . . ., these love stories, and the *Dianas*, the *Boscans*, the *Garcilasos*, the monstrous books and collections of fabulous tales and lies, as the *Amadises, Florisels, Don Belianis*, and a fleet of similar prodigies—what else are they but a knife in a madman's hand?" The picaresque is a more implicit critique of such literature, an alternative, as Parker puts it, to such humanistic distortions of the true human condition.[40] The picaresque emphasis on the lowliness of men is a response to the literary assertion of man's dignity. "The most pressing of all these problems in the world of the Counter-Reformation was the relationship of religion to the humanist culture of the Renaissance," J. H. Elliott writes. "This fundamental incompatibility meant that sooner or later there was likely to be a reaction both against the idealism of Renaissance culture and against its anthropocentric emphasis."[41]

The complex of forces, parties, and interpretations in the consciousness of literature in this period of European history attest to the truth of Walter Benjamin's observation in "The Work of Art in the Age of Mechanical Reproduction": "the technique of reproduction detaches the reproduced object from the domain of tradition. By making many reproductions it substitutes a plurality of copies for a unique existence. And in permitting the reproduction to meet the beholder or listener in his own particular situation, it reactivates the object produced. These two processes lead to a tremendous shattering of tradition."[42] What was shattered, partly by the dynamic force of the printing press, was the delicate balance of Christian religion, classical literature, and the popular, vernacular imagination that is usually designated as Christian humanism.[43] The shattering took many forms. One was the direct proscription of certain kinds of aesthetic experience, as in the *Index of Prohibited Books* or the English Puritan closing of the theaters. Another was the growth of restrictive types of neoclassicism, such as the neo-Aristotelian movement in Italy or the Pléiade in France, which self-consciously attempted to purify the new by a closer imitation of the old. A third form of response, much less influential until the Renaissance was well over, was the form that we now call the novel. Thus one might say on a more general level that the novel and neoclassicism are dialectical opposites in literary culture, and that the idea of the "novel" is hardly conceivable until the idea of the "classic" has newly limited literature's supposed range—until the tradition has been declared less able or less willing to accommodate the new.[44] As we shall see, the twin forms of the novel and neoclassicism gained headway in France in the seventeenth century and in England in the eighteenth century. But by then both these countries had the precedent of the Spanish novel before them.

Why should the novel have been developed first in Spain, rather than in the other European countries? Or why might conditions there have been more conducive to the establishment of this countercanonical critique of literary tradition? Three distinctive features of Spanish Golden Age culture seem important. The first is the relative thinness of the Renaissance humanist movement in Spain. The second is the special restriction put by the Spanish Inquisition and Index on the production and distribution of books. The third, paradoxically, seems to be the relative weakness, or lack of cultural identity, of the Spanish middle class. These three conditions are facets of literary history in the way they define the possibilities of readership in Spanish society, in the way they help to create the role of the idle and ambiguous reader.

It is widely observed by historians of Spanish literature that the literary classicism of the Italian Renaissance was more "belated" and less deeply rooted in Spain than in any of the other countries of Western Europe. As Otis Green puts it, "The medieval background is, in many respects, the background also of the Golden Age, to its very end."[45] This does not mean that there is no Renaissance in Spain, but that the Spanish reception of Renaissance themes and forms was less than wholehearted. Of the Golden Age period E. R. Curtius writes,

> The Spanish literary system preserves the crossing of styles, genres, and traditions which we have found to be a distinguishing characteristic of the Latin Middle Ages. Italy had no Middle Ages in the sense in which the northern nations had, France broke with her Middle Ages about 1550. Spain preserved hers and incorporated it into the national tradition. The waves of Italianism which swept over to Spain in the fifteenth and sixteenth centuries exerted a formal influence but they never touched the core of Spain. The literary theorists of the Italian cinquecento were scandalized by the lack of a "classical" Spanish literature, but fortunately they were unable to change the course of things.[46]

One notable symptom of this persisting medievalism in Spain was the broad popularity, among all the social classes, of the chivalric romances, a popularity which lasted until the very end of the sixteenth century. Thus an aclassical or anticlassical literature was quite conceivable, especially as the unclassical nature of the Spanish tradition became more evident.

The Council of Trent further aided the Spanish sense of alienation from Renaissance traditions with its creation, in 1558, of a new Spanish Inquisition and Index. This "drastic shock to Spanish intellectual life," as J. H. Elliott calls it,[47] took the form of an unusual scrutiny of the reading matter available to the public. The Spanish Index was more liberal and more discriminating than its Roman counterpart, but its policy involved a closer monitoring and investigation of individual texts and passages.[48] It may be, of course, that such scrutiny was an effect, as well as a cause, of a peculiar Spanish attitude toward the dangers of literacy. For example, Luis Vives was outspoken in his condemnation of the chivalric romances in his *De institutione foemenae* as early as 1524. The crown officially banned "idle and profane books such as *Amadis*" from the American colonies in 1531.[49] And in the view of Americo Castro, the influence of Moorish culture in Spain, with its oriental notion of sacred books, had quite early given Spanish culture a distinctive attitude toward books, "not as coldly objectified realities, with certain ideas or tales to present, but as being read, as a personal experiencing of values, in which a person reveals his individuality while incarnating the living substance of the book into his own life."[50]

Nevertheless, it seems to have been the Council of Trent that institutionalized and enforced this peculiar self-consciousness about reading, creating a generation of readers who were quite literally *desocupados*. Cervantes dramatizes such inquisitorial proceedings, albeit in a comic vein, in Chapter 6 of Part One, "Of the great and pleasant Inquisition held by the Priest and the Barber over our ingenious gentleman's Library" (56)—except that Cervantes discreetly avoids the Spanish word for Inquisition.[51] Not only were many of the works of humanists like Erasmus banned or selectively excised, but there was also a strict prohibition on the translation of the Bible into the vernacular. On the other hand, the vast array of the chivalric romances was virtually untouched. Where in Reformation countries the free pursuit of learning and the imperative reading of Scripture allowed a wide exercise of literacy in the burgeoning field of the printed book, Spanish readers were systematically curbed in these pursuits. Such measures had the double effect of depriving the reader of his "library that has no other limits than the world itself" and of dramatizing the subversive power of a desire for it.[52]

A third factor in the distinctive literary milieu of Golden Age Spain is sociological: there was a notable absence of a strong middle class. It is difficult to see at first what this might have to do with the rise of the novel, especially in view of the customary association of the novel with the growth of the middle class. The idea that the picaresque novel developed in Spain because there were more beggars there than elsewhere in Europe has been properly discredited,[53] but the structural parallels between the form of the novel and the form of society in Spain at this time have not been sufficiently explored. Speaking of the contrast between the wealth of the nobility and the poverty of the peasants, Elliott notes,

> The uniqueness of Spain lay not so much in this contrast, as in the absence of a middling group of solid, respectable, hardworking bourgeois to bridge the gulf between the two extremes.... The contempt for commerce and manual labour, the lure of easy money from the investment in censos and juros, the universal hunger for titles of nobility and social prestige—all these, when combined with the innumerable practical obstacles in the way of profitable economic enterprise, had persuaded the bourgeoisie to abandon its unequal struggle, and throw in its lot with the unproductive upper classes of society.[54]

Many from the would-be mercantile class simply left Spain, and others, especially in the economic collapse of the 1590s, found their lot cast willy-nilly with the lower classes.

Correspondingly, much of the social and psychological interest of Alemán's *Guzmán de Alfarache* comes from the picaro's precarious social standing—exacerbated by the fact that his father is a Jew as well as a merchant. Guzmán periodically manages to find a place on the fringes of respectability, and at one point late in the second part he actually becomes a good bourgeois. He marries, buys a house, and as a merchant pursues "an honest and honourable calling."[55] Nevertheless, he is soon plunged back into poverty, begging and thieving, and he ends up in the galleys, ripe for conversion. Quevedo's Pablos finds it still more impossible to occupy a middle ground between the aristocrat's honor and the beggar's disgrace. The point is less that these novels are an accurate reflection of social conditions in Spain than that they dramatize a problem faced by the readers of the novels themselves. As Claudio Guillén points out, such readers could not have come primarily from the lower classes, given the wide popularity of the novels, but must have been largely the declassé members of the Spanish middle class. Thus, Guillén suggests, "the rise of the novel in sixteenth-century Spain seems to have been rooted not in the triumph but in the frustration of the bourgeoisie."[56] The novel seems to derive an impetus to its break from literary tradition from the social displacement of a large group of readers, from their growing awareness of their lack of identity as readers with the literature of the ruling class, or of the people. *Guzmán de Alfarache* has two prefaces, one "To the Vulgar" and one "To the Discreet Reader," but the "Curious Reader" addressed at the beginnng of Chapter 1 belongs to neither category.

Thus in the literary history, the literary politics, and the literary sociology of sixteenth-century Spain one can see similar structures, structures of polarization with a relatively weak middle between the two extremes. I would argue not that these structures are a direct cause of the early Spanish novel but that they are homologous with the form of the novel in a culturally significant way. They both reflect and produce the structure of the Spanish picaresque, where divine transcendence and human degradation conspire against the middle estate of man. They also mirror and project the structure of *Don Quixote,* where an incorrigible idealistic imagination keeps colliding with an incontrovertibly material world. In these novels and in this society, it is a game of both ends against the middle. And it is in the book itself, that mechanically reproduced and privately consumed text of uncertain authority and value, that these extremes are brought most intriguingly together.

What we see in this reflection of literary and social organization is a homology of structures like that envisioned by Lucien Goldmann. In *Towards a Sociology of the Novel*, Goldmann speaks of the need for considering the relations between "the *novelistic form* itself and the *structure* of the social milieu within which it developed"; he goes on to say that "the two structures, that of an important novelistic genre and that of [economic] exchange, should appear rigorously homologous, to the extent that one might speak of a single and identical structure which would manifest itself on two different planes."[57] The idea of a single informing structure is in my view too extreme, and a rigorous homology would seem to be inevitably reductive, either of the literary or of the socioeconomic form. But the validity of the argument here may at least be tested by considering a contrary case. Would such a theory of the origin of the novel in the Spanish Golden

Age suggest why, for example, the novel did not arise in Elizabethan England? It would seem to if the following generalizations about Elizabethan literary culture are allowed.

First of all, there is a notable lack of self-consciousness in the Elizabethan prose fiction of the sixteenth century about the ethos of the printed book. Walter Ong has called attention to the "residual oralism" of Tudor prose, "in part endemic to the native tongue because of the still largely non-literary oral grounding of this tongue, and in part due to the positive encouragement from the oral residue and emphases in Latin."[58] This lack of awareness of, or lack of interest in the reader as silent consumer of the printed text is confirmed by Walter Davis in his analysis of the "histrionic sense of writing" in Elizabethan fiction: "For whatever the causes—'oral residue' or a sense of the spoken word behind the written word, or traditions of oratory like the 'ethical' appeal—we find common to much Elizabethan poetry and prose the sense that to write is essentially to speak, to speak essentially to act out a part."[59] Thus the concept of the idle reader is essentially foreign, and the implications of the revolution of the book in Elizabethan literature are unrecognized—or repressed.

Second, the enabling conditions of Spanish literary culture are notably lacking. It is true that the Italian Renaissance came to England relatively late, but it is also true that it was eagerly received and deeply absorbed. Where Cervantes took the precedent of Ariosto in the direction of the modern novel, for example, Spenser in *The Faerie Queene* took it back in the direction of medieval allegory and romance, with a play-medievalism that affirmed the power of the humanistic imagination to synthesize, idealize, and edify. Instead of the conflict of native genres and the classical canon, Spenser offers a harmony—"hobgoblin run away with the crown from Apollo," as Gabriel Harvey said of *The Faerie Queene*. Sidney also emphasizes the harmony of Aristotelian theory and popular practice in "An Apologie for Poetry." And it is precisely the mediating power of literature, between the moral idealism of philosophy and the empirical truth of history, that Sidney, following Aristotle, insists on. The poet can improve on the laws of nature: "onely the Poet, disdayning to be tied to any such subjection, lifted up with the vigor of his owne invention, dooth growe in effect another nature, in making things either better than Nature bringeth forth, or, quite a newe, formes such as never were in Nature, such as the *Heroes*, the *Demigods*, *Cyclops*, *Chimeras*, *Furies*, and such like."[60] In *Don Quixote*, such a vision of literature qualifies as madness.

The strength of the literary middle is further paralleled in the middle way of the reformed Anglican church, which rejected both Catholic and Protestant extremes and effected a "compromise between contending forces." The English Reformation was informed by humanist ideals of literacy and education, and saw "a dramatic broadening and diversification" of printed materials after the Elizabethan settlement of 1559, according to A. G. Dickens—even as the Council of Trent was engaged in its very different deliberations.[61] There was also in England a socially powerful and culturally secure middle class; the contrast with Spain is particularly striking in Louis B. Wright's description:

> Political changes favored the growth of the middle classes in England. The rise of the Tudors saw the ascent of a bourgeois dynasty. Henry VII may have had the habits of a usurious merchant, but his son enjoyed wealth with the abandon of any *nouveau riche* and stood not upon high birth for advisers, companions, or mistresses. Though the mythical ancestry of the Tudors went back to King Arthur, Queen Elizabeth had a near progenitor, a great-grandfather, who was a London merchant. . . . Many of the great names of Elizabethan England had lowly origins. The Cecils and the Walsinghams were upstart gentry; perhaps Burleigh's bourgeois heritage was responsible for his canny financial and economic policies, which lay behind much of Elizabethan strength. From Elizabeth, rich merchants and daring seamen in the service of trade won knighthoods, for her government honored business and awarded it the trappings of greatness.[62]

The contrast between the Spanish Golden Age novel and the more rhetorical, less novelistic mode of Elizabethan English fiction can be best appreciated in the closest thing to a picaresque novel that Elizabethan literature produced, Thomas Nashe's *The Unfortunate Traveller*. Nashe may well have known *Lazarillo de Tormes*, which was available in Rowland's translation of 1576, but he shows little inclination to imitate or borrow from it.[63] As Davis and other critics emphasize, the narrative is a deliberately rhetorical performance, addressed initially to a patron, Lord Henry Wriothesley, then to the "dapper Mounsier Pages of the Court," who comprise an imagined listening audience—"Oh my Auditors," as Nashe addresses them.[64] He refers to his book alternately as natural "leaves on trees," which he is seeking to engraft on a branch of nobility, and as "wast paper," for wrapping packages or wiping one's mouth. Like its own heavily metaphorical language, the book strains to name itself as something else.

Nashe's rhetoric is hyperbolic and satirical and mocks the orations of others in the course of the narrative—of Reformers, humanists, poets, and villains. Nevertheless, Nashe's excesses are a critique of excess, and constitute in the end a defense of the literary, the religious, and the social middle way. The hero, Jack Wilton, becomes the servant of the well-known poet Surrey, and while Surrey's Petrarchan love for Geraldine is shown as artificial, the poet, in his humanistic pursuit of fame, remains a strong idealizing presence: "Destinie never defames hir selfe but when shee lets an excellent Poet die, if there bee anie sparke of Adams Paradized perfection yet emberd up in the breastes of mortall men, certainelie God hath bestowed that his perfectest image on Poets," Jack Wilton claims.[65] Such praise is a far cry from Quevedo's proclamation in *El Buscón* "Against All Idiot, Useless and Rubbishy Poets" (133). Nashe also has his hero listen to Protestant religious debates at Wittenberg and observe a battle in the wars of the Reformation, upon which Jack delivers a sermon in defense of religious moderation. Such a stance is very different from the anticlerical satire of *Lazarillo de Tormes* or the Counter Reformation moralizing on the nothingness of man in *Guzmán de Alfarache*. And as a bourgeois servant of an aristocratic master, one who even changes places with the aristocrat during a period of disguise, Jack enjoys the protection and benefits of upper-class life while looking down on the lower orders of society. "Verie devout Asses they were," he says of the Lutherans, "for all they were so dunstically set forth, and such as thought they knew as much of Gods minde as richer men."[66] In the Spanish picaresque novel poverty is given a voice of its own, and it frequently denounces the pretensions of "richer men."

These elements are thematic as well as formal, but they all point to the greater emphasis on unity and harmony in the literary culture of England and the lack of that sense of a shattering of tradition that prepared the way for the emergence of the novel in Spain. Other factors may of course be relevant—the centrality of Elizabethan drama, for example, in which many of the potentially countervailing elements of the picaresque novels and *Don Quixote* find a more traditional literary framework. The comic delinquency of Falstaff in Shakespeare's Henriad, the lyrical roguery of Autolycus in *The Winter's Tale*, the satirical overreaching of Volpone or the Alchemist in Ben Jonson's plays, or the direct adaptation of *Don Quixote* in Beaumont and Fletcher's *Knight of the Burning Pestle*, with its mockery of middle-class enthusiasm for chivalric romance, all show the power of Elizabethan drama to assimilate elements eccentric or subversive to literary tradition. There is also the more popular Elizabethan pamphlet tradition, in which picaresque themes get treated in a more straightforward journalistic fashion, as in the criminal biographies, the beggar books, the cony-catching pamphlets, and the prison tracts, or, as in the jest-books and fabliaux, in a purely comic and farcical manner.[67] But in these unambitiously popular genres, in spite of their increasing tendency to adopt Spanish surnames and picaresque episodes, there is no attempt to engage canonical literature in a novelistic dialectic. There are significant imitations of the Spanish novel in France as early as the 1620s, with Sorel's *Francion* and *Le Berger extravagant,* but it was only in the eighteenth century, with Defoe and Fielding, that the stature and nature of the earlier Spanish novels were understood and the novels themselves creatively adapted in England.

It is in this historical perspective that one final question about the origins of the novel needs to be addressed; that is, the relevance and possibly novelistic nature of the late classical romances of Greece and Rome. Are these surviving prose fictions really misnamed? Did they simply fail to emerge as full-fledged novels because of the breakup of the Roman Empire? Are they paradoxical cases of "the novel before the novel," which expose the inadequacy of our theoretical understanding of the term?[68] Chariton's *Chaereas and Callirhoe,* Longus's *Daphnis and Chloe,* Achilles Tatius's *Leucippe and Clitophon,* Heliodorus's *Aethiopica,* and in Latin, Petronius's *Satyricon* and Apuleius's *Metamorphoses* all form a body of prose fiction with undeniable novelistic elements. They concern contemporary characters, show detailed psychological analyses, reflect on social conditions, and reveal a sophisticated awareness of the conventionality of literary tradition. Above all, they are something decidedly new and beyond the bounds of the classical canon. As one scholar describes it, "It is difficult to learn whether narrative prose fiction grew up outside the circle of fashionable literature and never sought entrance within the magic circle, or, seeking admission to the inner orbit of established classical works, it was shut out. Regardless of the methods or reasons for exclusion, ancient novels make up a kind of underground literature."[69]

A full investigation of the claims of these complex and interesting narratives is beyond the scope of this study, but the following generalizations may be offered. The Greek and Latin romances resemble later European novels in many ways, but they are finally a different

39

type of literature because of the different relationship they bear to the classical literary canon. On the one hand, they conceive of themselves as extending the canon and/or reclaiming popular narrative forms for high, aristocratic art. On the other hand, they transcend the literary canon altogether, in their invocation of a higher religious power, an authority which eclipses the more conventional rule of genre. With the expansion of Christianity, this transcendence becomes a thoroughgoing conversion of Western literary culture away from the older Greek and Roman standards. The extension and transcendence of the canon can often be seen operating within the same work. But in no case do these works establish the kind of dialectical half-outsiderhood that the European novel is founded upon.

In Chariton's *Chaereas and Callirhoe*, probably the earliest of the surviving Greek romances, one can see an unselfconscious extension of canonical forms in the frequent allusions to the Homeric epics as precedents and parallels, and in the rather competitive allusions to the drama. "What dramatist ever produced so incredible a situation on the stage?" Chariton asks his readers. "Indeed, you might have thought you were in a theater, filled with a multitude of conflicting passions."[70] Heliodorus makes such connections with the drama in a more psychological vein, as when he says of one of his characters, "He wondered what this could be which had the air of a recognition on the stage."[71] It is important to realize that these are not ironic subversions of an existing epic or dramatic tradition so much as transferals of such conventions to a new medium. The romances were published on papyrus scrolls, scholars argue, for a new audience, the widely scattered citizenry of the Alexandrian and Greco-Roman empires, which had succeeded the more local and homogeneous units of the Greek city-state.[72] But the shift to papyrus was more gradual than the later shift to the printed book and resulted in a more evolutionary diffusion of the tradition.

Most of the surviving classical fictions are more sophisticated than popular, however. In the elegant pastoralism of *Daphnis and Chloe* or the exaggerated rhetorical self-consciousness of *Leucippe and Clitophon* one sees a reabsorption of the more popular romance motifs by canonical literature, especially through the conventions of sophistic rhetoric.[73] Amid Petronius's parodies of a great many Roman literary forms in the *Satyricon* there is a generous burlesque of Greek romance, but the aristocratic bias of all the parody hardly challenges the authority of the Roman canon. Apuleius is less overt in his allusions to high literary materials, but, as P. G. Walsh shows, there is still a pervasive evocation in the *Metamorphoses* of Greek and

Roman literary models, as in the "mosaic of Virgilian phrases" in the story of Psyche's journey to Hades, which recall the descent to the underworld in Book VI of the *Aeneid*.[74] The very choice of Latin as the language of the narrative, which Apuleius alludes to disingenuously in his preface, is an act of literary sophistication. As Perry puts it "The literary language of the poor-in-spirit was not Latin but Greek"—that is, the *Koiné* of the empire.[75] It may be true that the *Metamorphoses* is part of "a general trend, partly based on the development of regional cultures now asserting themselves against the breaking-up 'classical' systems,"[76] but it is also true that an independent critique of the classical system as such is never formulated.

What happens instead in almost all these romances, and Apuleius provides the most spectacular instance of the process, is that an appeal is made to a higher reality, beyond the plane of the literarily human. The surprising conversion of Lucius to the worship of Isis and Osiris at the end of the book is not simply a pious coda but the logical culmination of his quest for transformation. It is a quest that begins in foolish curiosity but becomes increasingly urgent as the hero suffers the degradations of his asshood. And it is a quest that is mirrored in the lyrical, mythological metamorphosis of Psyche in the famous interpolated tale. Apuleius's *Metamorphoses*, despite its comic tone, is ultimately a ritual process of atonement, curiously opposite to the Christian pattern, where multiple sufferings on the part of others point the way to salvation for the one initiate, out of his lowly incarnation.

The religiosity of the other romances (the *Satyricon* is an exception in this) is based on a cult conception of deity. The conventional chastity of the lovers who undergo the trials of separation is supported in varying degrees by the local powers of particular gods and goddesses: Aphrodite of Aphrodisia in Chariton, Pan of Lesbos in Longus, the Ethiopian sun-god in Heliodorus. The priestly interpretations of Heliodorus provide a transition to the Christian appropriation of romance. As one of his priest characters says, "Men skilled in divine and human knowledge have not chosen to disclose to the vulgar the hidden significations contained under these natural appearances, but veil them under fables; being however ready to reveal them in a proper place, and with due ceremonies, to those who are desirous and worthy of being initiated." Only Achilles Tatius, in his highly mannered display of human passion, avoids explicit reference to some form of religious cult. Yet even here, the spectacular mock-deaths of Leucippe, which Clitophon is forced to

41

observe, point in a mock-religious direction. "Consider how often she has died and come to life again," Clinias reminds Clitophon at the end of the narrative.[77]

The theological profundity of classical romance is of course open to question. Yet the ethos of this type of fiction, in which the ordinary limits and vicissitudes of human experience are triumphantly overcome in the service of some higher power, is clearly different from the ethos of the novel, as succeeding romances, from the third- and fourth-century saints' lives to the sixteenth-century chivalric romances, demonstrate. The influence of the classical romances on the European novel are also negligible—or rather instructive—in the way it dramatizes the differences between the two types of fiction. When Cervantes responded directly to Heliodorus's *Aethiopica* he wrote not another novel but a Renaissance romance, *Persiles y Sigismunda.* When the author of the spurious sequel to *Lazarillo de Tormes* tried to use Apuleius's *Metamorphoses* as a guide, he had the picaro changed into a tuna fish, clearly missing the point of the emerging novelistic form.[78] And this is not to mention the numerous more straightforward imitations of classical romance in the sixteenth and seventeenth centuries.

There is an incident from Apuleius that Cervantes incorporates into *Don Quixote* with an instructive shift in causality. During the reading of "The Tale of Foolish Curiosity" in Chapters 33 and 34, Quixote has been asleep upstairs at the inn. He dreams he is fighting a giant and slashes some full wineskins hanging from the rafters. When awakened to the reality of his conquest, he falls back on his chivalric defense mechanism, the explanation that such reality is the work of an evil enchanter. In the episode from the *Metamorphoses* on which this incident is based, Lucius thinks he is attacking three thieves at the gate of his host in Thessaly. It is revealed after a mock trial the next day that these are only three wineskins. But behind this empirical truth lies a further revelation: these skins had been accidentally brought to life by the magic of the witch Pamphile. Romance can and does deal with such supernatural transformations. The novel must deal with a more partial magic, in Borges's phrase: the transformation of literary tradition in a field of nonconforming human codes. In romance, the reader's allegiance is finally to some deeper power, higher ideal, or stronger fulfillment of desire. In the novel, his allegiance is divided, and his perception is directed along a horizontal rather than a vertical axis. The enchantment of the novel is a personal and psychological phenomenon, derived from the experience of idle reading, on the part of a readership untrained in or uncommitted to aristocratic definitions of the arts of leisure.

3

The Advent of the Spanish Picaresque

He has chosen things low and contemptible, mere nothings, to overthrow the existing order.

1 Corinthians 1:28

Lazarillo de Tormes, published in three separate editions in 1554, appeared just before the onset of the Counter Reformation in Spain, and it shows some distinctive features as a picaresque novel. Most notably, it is closer to the spirit of humanistic satire, with its critique of ecclesiastical abuse, than the later Spanish novels were to be. Scholars have frequently suggested that the author of the anonymous *Lazarillo* was a Spanish follower of Erasmus. Although this hypothesis has been discredited,[1] one can see a number of structural and imaginative affinities between this first instance of the novel and a satirical encomium like Erasmus's *Praise of Folly*. Both works present an ambiguously colloquial address by a speaker of doubtful integrity, a situation that Barbara Babcock calls the framing paradox of the Cretan liar.[2] Like Lazarillo's obviously self-serving apology, the praising of folly is done by "Folly" herself. Both works also pay special attention to the sins of the church, a critique which goes beyond medieval clerical satire by invoking the reforming authority of the New Testament. The attack on religious orders is oblique in *Lazarillo* and direct in *The Praise of Folly*, but it is an attack on the corruption of the office more than simply on the corruption of the officeholder. The protagonist's name in *Lazarillo* alludes to the biblical Lazaruses in the Gospels of Luke and John, both of whom are resurrected after death; Folly's claim that "all Christian religion seems to have a kind of alliance with folly and in no respect to have any accord with wisdom" more forcefully recalls Paul's first letter to the Corinthians.[3] In both these texts we see the alliance of a low secular spokesman with a high religious authority, an alliance that conspires against the authority, dignity, and self-sufficiency of the existing order, of church as well as of state. The spokesman is not himself (herself) religious; he or she alludes to the generic humility of the Christian vision without embodying it.

This autonomy of the speaker in Erasmus, grounded in the classical techniques of satire, helps prepare the way for the sudden and virtually accidental appearance of the kind of writing we now call the novel. Yet *Lazarillo de Tormes* moves in a different direction from *The Praise of Folly*. It gives the autonomous voice a more radical freedom. Erasmus insists on the traditional oratorical medium of his discourse, and dramatizes a particularly responsible audience by addressing an introductory letter to Sir Thomas More. He cites numerous classical precedents for his playful exercise—Homer, Democritus, Virgil, Ovid, Lucian, and others—at the beginning and alludes directly to numerous precedents in Scripture for valuing "folly" as the discourse proceeds. Indeed, the fiction that a pagan goddess named "Folly" is speaking becomes quite thin by the middle of the text. The author of *Lazarillo*, on the other hand, has his character address an anonymous "Vuestra Merced," an ambiguous character who seems himself implicated in Lazarillo's morally dubious situation. The arch-priest, to whose mistress Lazarillo is married, is the interlocutor's friend, and on one level Lazarillo is trying to defend himself against the rumors circulating against this ménage à trois. But Lazarillo also has his eye on a broader kind of audience when he cites Pliny's maxim that "there is no book, however bad it may be, that doesn't have something good about it" (23). He makes a gesture in the direction of classical literature by citing Pliny and Cicero, but these authorities are merely pretexts for his advertisements for himself. If anything, the allusions only serve to undermine the notion of the classics as morally improving literature; a little of such learning is a dangerous thing.[4] And where Folly increasingly reveals the biblical subtext behind her rhetorical pretext, Lazarillo shows his spiritual potential only fleetingly in his narrative, when he shares his food with his indigent *hidalgo* master. Thereafter he becomes more worldly, as he serves more venial and more reliable employers, which leads one critic to speak of his social success as his spiritual "death."[5] Such religious judgments are rendered secondary by the text, as I will show later on, but the narrative voice in *Lazarillo de Tormes* does detach itself from the scriptural chorus and speak of the low and humble world, the material and social realities, as things in and of themselves.

It is useful to compare *Lazarillo* in this regard with another prose fiction that comes out of the Erasmian matrix, the books of Rabelais's *Gargantua and Pantagruel*. In Rabelais's five books one can see a structure broadly similar to that of *Lazarillo* and *The Praise of Folly*: an alliance of high moral ideals and low secular clowning, of the spiritually elevated and the physically debased. High and low together attack a pretentious and inadequate middle, an established order that no longer mediates but rather, with its prohibitions and its nonsense, oppresses both mind and body. One can also see how Rabelais, like the author of *Lazarillo*, tips the Erasmian balance toward the realities of the lower world, where flesh is flesh and not merely a vehicle for the Incarnation, where folly is foolish and not merely a trope for God's truth. Food and drink have some sacramental associations in Rabelais but are more significant as a means of celebrating or sustaining the life of the physical man. And the spokesmen for these realities achieve a subversive freedom from all apparent rules, defeating the official hierarchy by appeal to popular culture.[6]

It is sometimes proposed, and has been increasingly of late, that *Gargantua and Pantagruel* be considered as an early example of the novel.[7] The terms of the previous chapter suggest why I do not agree with this view. While reacting in unprecedented ways to the revolution of the book, Rabelais's narratives are deeply committed to the humanist ideals of the Renaissance and are also deeply involved in the oral media of literary presentation. The critique in Rabelais is not so much of the institution of literature per se as of the official norms of academic scholastic culture in general. I will have more to say on the question of Rabelais and the novel in the following chapter on *Don Quixote*. But I would like here to insist on the important differences between the two types of innovation represented by Rabelais's *Oeuvres* and the anonymous *Lazarillo*.

The most obvious difference involves the physical and imaginative scale on which the two narratives operate. Gargantua and Pantagruel are giants, human in form but grossly larger than life, and although Rabelais is not consistent in his use of his fiction, even exploiting the incongruity of normal and gigantic proportions, the gigantic is the norm against which most of the actions and achievements are to be judged. Lazarillo is of ordinary stature; the attention to his childhood and the diminutive of his titulary name render his presence particularly unimposing. He is notable for his lacks rather than for his fulfillments, and his bouts with hunger and thirst contrast markedly with the surfeit of food and drink in Rabelais.

The contrast between excess and minimality functions on an intellectual level as well. The figure in Rabelais most like the picaro is Panurge, the trickster whom Pantagruel encounters begging and in rags, whom he takes on as his servant. But Panurge's quest for food is imaginatively redundant. He begs in twelve different languages, several of them literally unheard of, in a staggering display of erudition rather than a practical sharpening of the wits. Panurge becomes Pantagruel's comrade more than his menial; his tricks are exuberant and gratuitous, motivated by a sense of comic play, where Lazarillo's are calculating and constrained, motivated by physical and psychological needs. As Thomas Greene observes, the pranks of Panurge belong to a widespread Renaissance "art form," a traditional trickster behavior common in poetry and drama.[8]

The differences between these two fictions, then, are a function of the difference in ethos: of all-inclusiveness in *Gargantua and Pantagruel*, of deprivation in *Lazarillo de Tormes*. As Erich Auerbach puts it, "everything goes with everything" in Rabelais—high culture with low culture, the body with the spirit, modernity with antiquity. Auerbach's comments on Rabelais's humanism are particularly relevant to my argument on the origins of the novel:

> His humanistic relation to antique literature is shown in his remarkable knowledge of the authors who furnish him with themes, quotations, anecdotes, examples and comparisons; in his thought upon political, philosophical, and educational questions, which, like that of the other humanists, is under the influence of antique ideas; and particularly in his view of man, freed as it is from the Christian and stratified-social frame of reference which characterized the Middle Ages. Yet his indebtedness to antiquity does not imprison him within the confines of antique concepts; to him, antiquity means liberation and a broadening of horizons, not in any sense a new limitation or servitude; nothing is more foreign to him than the antique separation of styles, which in Italy even in his own time, and soon after in France, led to purism and "Classicism."[9]

Rabelais's fiction is thus prior to neoclassicism rather than being anti-neoclassical. It attacks the established order not from the excluded and humble viewpoint of the half-outsider, to use Guillén's phrase, but from the all-inclusive vision of the polymath and the polyglot, a vision that overwhelms structure, inverts hierarchy, and subverts significance in its sheer plenitude. It is the world in Pantagruel's mouth, not the world from Lazarillo's jaundiced eye. As we have been discovering, the novel is a critique of the neoclassical purification of literature; such a separation of the old and the new had not become a significant enough adversary for Rabelais.

As I shall argue in the next chapter, with *Don Quixote* the novel later developed its own strategies of inclusiveness, by channeling the multiplicity of literary forms through the consciousness of a character who is himself a reader of texts. But at this earlier point of departure it is fair to describe the difference between *Lazarillo de Tormes* and *Gargantua and Pantagruel* as a difference between novel and satire. Rabelais anticipates the novel in interesting ways, and he is reinterpreted novelistically by later writers like Sterne and Melville. But the ethos of his prose fiction is finally the ethos of satire, before his time and after. I would describe this as an ethos of exaggeration, as distinct from the ethos of displacement peculiar to the novel. The label of "satire" is certainly not definitive of Rabelais's work, but at the level of definition on which I have been discussing the novel so far, it is clearly the more appropriate term.[10]

The type of satire known as Menippean or Varronian includes many examples of narratives in prose, in which characters and incidents predominate and in which contemporary manners and morals are directly represented. *Gargantua and Pantagruel* shares many features with Lucian's dialogues and stories, with Petronius's *Satyricon*, with Erasmus's colloquies and with Swift's later *Gulliver's Travels* and *A Tale of a Tub*. Such satires resemble novels in many ways, not the least of which is their generally subversive and antinomian quality. As Alvin Kernan notes, satire seems to disregard the formal order and decorum of good literature so-called.[11] But it is in the question of literary rules that the difference between satire and the novel is most important. Satire deliberately violates the rules of literary decorum and of representational form; physical and moral faults are grossly exaggerated, while conventional aesthetic distinctions between one kind of form and another are deliberately confused. "The scene of satire is always disorderly and crowded, packed to the very point of bursting," writes Kernan.

> The deformed faces of depravity, stupidity, greed, venality, ignorance, and maliciousness group closely together for a moment, stare boldly out at us, break up, and another tight knot of figures collects, stroking full stomachs, looking vacantly into space, nervously smiling at the great, proudly displaying jewels and figures, clinking moneybags, slyly fingering new-bought fashions. The scene is equally choked with things: ostentatious buildings and statuary, chariots, sedan-chairs, clothes, books, food, houses, dildoes, luxurious furnishings, gin bottles, wigs.[12]

The effect of such formal confusion and proportional excess, paradoxically, is to affirm the validity of the formalities in question, to reaffirm the rules by dramatizing their necessity. Norms and ideals themselves are represented only fleetingly in the satiric fiction, and when they do appear at any length they often seem thin and inadequate. The real force of rules in satire, which belong more to the domain of custom than to the domain of ethics,[13] is only revealed in the flagrant violation of them that the satirist depicts. A kind of negative jurisprudence is thus entailed. A satire is an adversary system, a case for the prosecution, and the particular rule that is violated is given all the force of law—of the spirit of the law rather than its letter. Satire presents offenses against customs and mores as if they were violations of a legal covenant.

The legal sanction that satire lends to literary rules is by no means a simple one. There are innumerable reversals, dialectics, and shiftings of logical ground in the case presented. In *Gargantua and Pantagruel,* for example, the exaggerated human scale of the giants is frequently itself the law by which the physical pettiness and false modesty of ordinary human beings are implicitly condemned—a complex equation of physical excess and moral largesse that Swift reproduces in the Brobdingnagians in *Gulliver's Travels.* Or there is the self-defense of Folly in Erasmus's *Encomium,* which impreceptibly turns into a defense of Christian humility and an attack on Stoic philosophical pride. In these early humanistic satires, the overestablished order of the medieval church is the chief offender, and the simpler virtues of Scripture, the classical authors, and folk tradition are the main sources of a countervailing principle or spirit of the law. Nevertheless, the relation of exceptional instance to normative standard is essentially judicial. A particular character, action, or expression is considered as if it were trying to live up to a particular standard of wisdom or virtue—which in point of fact it often is not—and failing miserably in the attempt.

Thus where the institution of literature is concerned, satire pretends to regard the rules of "good literature" as more legally binding than mere generic convention. To write bad epic verse is not simply to be an indifferent poet but to commit a crime against the literary community. Furthermore, satire pretends to regard other forms of human culture and behavior as if they were aspiring to the status of "good literature." The strategy of the mock-heroic is to look at a particular modern sub- or extraliterary phenomenon as if it were trying consciously to emulate canonical forms like the epic—as if it were trying to crash the cultural gate. The strategy of the carnivalesque in Rabelais is to regard medieval theology as if it were trying to take part in a classical symposium, as if scholastic logic, with its intricate formalities and terminologies, were trying to join the convivial colloquium, with its free speculation, drunken rapture, and popular laughter.

In the novel, on the other hand, exception and norm are placed in a different kind of relationship. The exception, like the excluded servant Lazarillo, is given a new autonomy and becomes *another* norm, a new law unto itself which to a significant extent eludes the embrace of the canonical law that would judge it and find it wanting. The relation between competing or conflicting forms is thus not judicial, rather it is diplomatic. The novel takes a stand outside a particular system of values, or between competing systems, and while its apparent norms are more visible than the norms of satire, they are also more problematic. The dialectical relationship of the novel to literary tradition entails a conflict of rules, a competition among values, and a general lack of codified precedent for the formal result. It seems to me that the term which best describes the relation of divergent forms in the novel is a diplomatic rather than a legal one; forms are arranged according to a *protocol*.

The word "protocol," in English, is used outside the general legal vocabulary. Coming from a Greek word meaning "a flyleaf glued to a manuscript describing its contents," it refers to an original record of a particular negotiation carried on outside the authority of a given system of law. It is a record that serves as the basis for further negotiations that may become more binding, as in a treaty. The term has been used in analytic philosophy to describe the syntax of basic statements of truth. Protocol sentences are models of verifiable scientific observation of the world. But I would like to use it in this study to define the kind of rules by which the novel, as distinct from other types of literature, tends to operate. A protocol is an agreement sui generis, but its terms are rendered formal and public. A novelistic protocol informs the text on a number of different levels, but it does not establish order or unity in any widely shared literary sense. A protocol is formal, but its form is not necessarily organic, harmonious, or logically coherent. The protocol of a particular novel is often adopted and adapted in subsequent novels, but it is also considerably less normative, as I will argue shortly, than what is generally understood by the term "genre" in literature more oriented toward tradition. If a genre is "a challenge to match an imaginative structure to reality," as Rosalie Colie suggests, a protocol may be said to reverse the definition: it is a warning against the attempt to match reality with a preexistent literary form.[14]

Finally, a secondary meaning of "protocol" helps to explain the way in which the original diplomacies of the novel may easily become highly conventionalized themselves. The term also refers to the rigid rules of ambassadorial precedence, behavior, and dress, which are necessary where no deeper, more organic system of rights and privileges obtains. As in the mass of "popular" novels which remain comfortably and predictably within the formulas of the detective story, science fiction, or the historical romance, a protocol, when it *is* followed, often produces a proliferation of examples in which even the dialectical tension of traditional literary genres is never achieved. The so-called "realism" of the novel is best seen as a series of protocols in which novels reach out to engage new areas of sign and structure beyond the domain of literary convention, beyond even the cumulative conventions of the novel itself. But the realism of one novel or group of novels may easily become a matter of convention or cliché in novels that exploit the original terms—plot formulas, settings, character types, manners of speech—on a superficial level. The concept of the protocol thus captures one of the paradoxes of the novel that this study had not yet dwelt on sufficiently, the paradox of a kind of writing inherently committed to innovation which at the same time seems so prone, in the mass of its examples, to the stereotypical and the formulaic.

One might say, then, that the novel and satire are opposing revaluations of the nature of literary rules. Satire is conservative and reactionary in the way it appeals to an earlier standard, to literary rule as a spirit of the law. The novel is liberal and progressive in the way it dramatizes a negotiation between new and old species of writing, juxtaposing rather than subordinating one kind to another. Such political labels, of course, can be misleading. One might put the contrast in terms of economics and say that satire affirms standards of value by radically bankrupting the currency of the modern, where the novel describes with more relativity the mechanics of devaluation and exchange. Or one might use categories of logic, as Julia Kristeva does, and say that the novel deals with the "nondisjunction" of logically opposite terms.[15] Whatever terminology is preferred, it should convey the idea that the novel is countersystematic: beyond a system, between systems, or against system altogether. Thus it is finally to the protocol of particular novels that one must turn, and to the way in which these protocols are renegotiated by subsequent novelistic texts.

Lazarillo de Tormes is a text that emerges from the matrix of satire, as I have already noted. It is in this sense not fully novelistic, and some critics have insisted that it is more a precursor than a true example of the picaresque.[16] There is no point in exaggerating its resemblances to later instances of the novel. As a narrative it is quite short; its precision and economy are effective but rarely expand either character or setting with the plenitude of *Guzmán de Alfarache* or even the relatively economical *El Buscón*. None of the other characters besides Lazarillo is given a proper name, and Lazarillo's masters are a gallery of social types familiar from the medieval satire of "estates": the conniving blind man, the miserly priest, the false pardoner.[17] Similarly, the language is not particularly committed to objective description; it is rather made up of conventional phrases and proverbs. As Lazarillo says of his first master, "He relied on the proverb which says that a hard man will give more than a man who hasn't anything at all" (32).

Nevertheless, there are subtle but important dislocations of this apparently traditional material. We have a character who is both knave and gull, who is exploited by others and who deceives them in turn, with no clear standard of virtuous conduct or superior wit. As Francisco Rico has argued, we have in *Lazarillo* a primary instance of novelistic "point of view," in which the individual perspective is a primary constituent of value and significance, placing rather than placed within the world.[18] The proverbial and conventional language is ironically twisted, recombined, and misapplied. "I think it's a good thing that important events which quite accidentally have never seen the light of day, should be made public and not buried in the grave of oblivion," the narrator says, slyly and pompously, of his own paltry *vida* (23). The wise words of the community are revealed as detachable clichés and can be manipulated to the speaker's advantage. "God (to grant me revenge) had blinded his good sense for that instant" (36), Lazarillo says of his success in luring his blind master to smash his head into the stone pillar. A major theme of *Lazarillo* is "the opposition of authentic and uniquely personal experience (resulting in this case from the hero's exposure to hunger, cold, blows and justice) and the commonplace terms which the community applies to experience and with which it hopes to dismiss experience," writes Stephen Gilman.[19]

Yet to call Lazarillo's experience "authentic" and "uniquely personal" is to miss the protocol of the novelistic text. In fact, *Lazarillo de Tormes* is a systematic exploration of the inauthentic; it is informed throughout by a protocol of the ersatz, in which a substituted object or experience is made to serve, provisionally, as a replacement for something else. The substitute is offered deliberately, with an awareness of its lesser value and reduced efficacy. But it serves as a challenge to the intrinsic worth of that which it replaces, a challenge to the status of the status quo.

The operation of the protocol can be seen most easily in the peculiar treatment of objects in the narrative. In a well-known incident, in which the hero is initiated into the picaro's way of life, Lazarillo is asked by his blind master to put his ear close to a stone animal that resembles a bull: "put your ear close to the bull, and you'll hear a loud noise inside it" (27). Lazarillo obeys and has his head smashed against it. In place of the promised sound, which suggests a special message or revelation, he discovers the brute materiality of the object, an object which is itself a replica of something else. The experience acts as an ersatz revelation, nevertheless: "at that moment I felt as if I had woken up and my eyes were opened. I said to myself: 'What he says is true; I must keep awake because I'm on my own and I've got to look after myself'" (27–28). His curiosity is satisfied in a way that he did not expect.

Lazarillo learns this lesson of substitution very well. He gives his blind master smaller coins than the ones actually donated by passersby, putting a *blanca* into his mouth and passing a half-*blanca* on to the beggar who has been saying the prayers. In a more complicated series of substitutions, he steals the blind man's sausage, takes the sausage from its pan and puts a thin rotten turnip in its place. When the blind man discovers the switch and suspects his servant, he pokes his long sausage- (and turnip-) like nose down Lazarillo's throat, which prompts Lazarillo to vomit "his property" back up: "his nose and the half-digested sausage came out at the same time" (34). Lazarillo has the last word in these exchanges when he lures the blind man to jump head-on into the pillar, as an appropriate reprisal for the stone bull. He jeers at the beggar as he runs away, "What! You smelled the sausage and you couldn't smell the post? Olé! Olé!" (37). Just as the physical objects can replace one another, they can also turn out to serve radically different functions. The blind man's wine jug brings Lazarillo pleasure when he sips through a straw from a hole he has made in the bottom of it, but it brings him pain when the blind man discovers the trick and smashes the jug down on his face: "the jug, which had been the source of pleasure and was now to be the instrument of pain" (30).

On the level of character as well, this protocol of the ersatz informs Lazarillo's relationships with his different masters. With the miserly priest he is forced to act like vermin by breaking into the chest that contains the priest's supply of bread. The priest finally catches him, beats him, and tells him, when he regains consciousness, "By God, I've hunted down the mice and snakes that persecuted me" (48). With the impoverished *hidalgo*, his third master, the master changes places with his servant. The *hidalgo* ends up depending on Lazarillo for his food and it is finally he who runs away from Lazarillo. In Lazarillo's marriage to the archpriest's mistress in the last chapter, the husband becomes a knowing replacement for the lover, part-time.

Thus on the level of plot, in the interaction of characters and objects, we see a series of bad bargains being made, exchanges which are instrumental rather than ends in themselves and whose success is either temporary or highly ambiguous. Nevertheless, these exchanges are not purely ironic or absolutely devaluing. They involve dubious likenesses that dramatize the instability of life in the social and psychological world, but they do not reveal, even negatively, a clear otherworldly standard of truth. To speak of Lazarillo's success and dishonor simply as his spiritual "death," as Gilman and others do, is to overemphasize the vertical reference of the text and to overestimate the force of Christian precept in the horizontal relationships of society. The sympathy Lazarillo shows for the impoverished *hidalgo* is like Christian charity but it is finally not the same. As with the other forms of ersatz, a potential metaphoric identity keeps collapsing into metonymic proximity or juxtaposition. In fact, there is even a scriptural precedent for this frustration of religious message in the Lucan parable of Lazarus to which the novel alludes. In Luke the beggar Lazarus dies after being ignored by the rich man (*dives* in the Vulgate); the rich man also dies and finds himself in hell. When he sees Lazarus far off in the bosom of Abraham and is denied any relief for himself, the rich man asks Abraham to send Lazarus back to earth to warn his five brothers. "But Abraham said, 'They have Moses and the prophets; let them listen to them.' 'No, father Abraham,' he replied, 'but if someone from the dead visits them they will repent.' Abraham answered, 'If they do not listen to Moses and the prophets they will pay no heed even if someone should arise from the dead.'"[20] The idea of the resurrected beggar as a stand-in for the prophets is explicitly rejected here; Lazarus is a type for the rejection of new typologies.

Nor is it clear on a more practical level that, as some critics have tried to argue, Lazarillo's wits become less sharp as he becomes less hungry. Gilman describes the Prologue, delivered by the older man, as a dull performance, an "epilogue post-mortem,"[21] but it is equally possible to argue that Lazarillo is here, as elsewhere, the creator rather than the butt of the irony. Thus R. W. Truman considers that Lazarillo "comes before us as one who feels he had made substantial material progress in life and yet is so far conscious of the limited nature of what he has achieved that he enjoys the comedy of pretending to have achieved more than he has in fact done."[22] Even at the end of his narrative, when he accepts his wife's adultery with apparent unconcern, he shows that his wits are still alive and his tongue still sharp. When the archpriest has told him to ignore the gossip about his wife, he reports his reply: " 'Sir,' I said to him, 'I made up my mind a long time ago to keep in with respectable people. It's quite true that my friends have said something to me about my wife. In fact they've proved to me that she had three children before she married me, speaking with reverence because she's here.' Then my wife began to swear such fearful oaths that I was sure the house was about to fall down about our ears" (78). What we see here is not so much an irony directed at Lazarillo, who remains too evasive to be anyone's dupe, but an irony directed at the social concept of honor itself. Lazarillo wears the manners of the socially respectable as a disguise, in a way that exposes the fictionality of these manners. Thus he says to anyone who would hint at his wife's infidelity, "I swear on the Sacred Host itself that she is as good a woman as any in Toledo. If anyone says the opposite I'll kill him" (79). The boundary between 'worse than' and 'as good as' is challenged, and the ersatz man of honor installs himself in the midst of respectability. "That was the same year as our victorious Emperor entered this famous city of Toledo and held his Parliament here. There were great festivities, as Your Honour doubtless has heard. At that time I was at the height of my good fortune" (79).

The reader, of course, is made a party to the protocol of the text. The book that he holds in his hands is a substitute for the letter to "Vuestra Merced"—a replacement underlined in Spanish by the general use of *Vd.* as the polite form of the second-person address. It is not a case of someone's private letters being presented to the world by an editor, as in the later fiction of the epistolary novel, but of a self-confessed public performance presenting itself as a private communication—and vice versa. Similarly, Lazarillo's life story or *vida* is a surrogate for the explanation of his dubious circumstances or *caso* that his fictional correspondent has supposedly requested: "And since Your Excellency has written to ask a full account of this subject I thought best not to begin in the middle but at the beginning, so as to present a complete narrative of myself." The idea of beginning at the beginning rather than in the middle implicitly disclaims any epic ambitions on Lazarillo's part, yet the final phrase of his prologue ironically presents him as an ersatz Aeneas: "how much more they have accomplished who have had Fortune against them from the start, and who have nothing to thank but their own labor and skill at the oars for bringing them into a safe harbor."[23]

The protocol of substitution in *Lazarillo de Tormes* thus suggests from the start a view of the novel as surrogate literature, as a humble yet arrogant pretender to cultural respectability. Its pretense, at the same time, lays the respectability of literature open to question. If there is no book however bad that does not have some good in it, as Lazarillo reminds us Pliny has said, it may be that the greatest of books have some bad in them as well, or—more to the point—can be used for morally dubious ends like self-advancement in the hands of a vulgar class of readers.

This is not to say that all its readers, especially the initial ones, responded to Lazarillo according to the terms of the protocol I have sketched out here. On the contrary, there is evidence that the book was read along quite different lines—for example, by the author of an anonymous and spurious "sequel," who went on to describe Lazarillo's transformation into a tuna fish in the manner of Apuleius and to report his scholarly disputations with the doctors of the University of Salamanca in the manner of Rabelais.[24] Though less popular than the original, which appeared in four separate editions within two years, parts of this spurious sequel found their way into translations from the Spanish for some time. Other evidence of the fact that Lazarillo was misunderstood—or rather read unsympathetically—is its appearance on the Index Expurgatorius in 1559 and the appearance of a censored edition in 1573, which cut out the chapters with the worldly friar and the false pardoner but left the chapter with the miserly priest. The Council of Trent itself abolished the granting of indulgences for offerings of money and thus got rid of pardoners, but the Inquisition was apparently most sensitive to criticism of the itinerant functionaries and mendicant orders. In spite of its initial popularity, Lazarillo had to wait until the end of the century until it was widely recognized as a new species of writing; until, that is, it became more than one of a kind.

The argument over the novelistic status of Lazarillo de Tormes—whether it belongs to the class of subsequent picaresque novels or whether it is merely a "prototype" of the genre—has been resolved, for all intents and purposes, by Claudio Guillén, who shows that historically considered, it is both.[25] Guillén traces the publication history of Lazarillo and observes that its popularity dwindled in the half-century after its publication, until the appearance of Guzmán de Alfarache in 1599. Then it went through nine editions in four years, and in most cases it was the editors of Guzmán who produced the new Lazarillos. The final seal was put on the process of recognition, Guillén argues, when Cervantes's character, Ginés de Pasamonte, speaks in the First Part of Don Quixote of his own life story, "so good . . . that Lazarillo de Tormes will have to look out, and so will everything in that style that has ever been written or ever will be" (176).[26] The form of the novel as a particular literary kind is constituted not by one example or even by two, but by a reader who singles out the kind (*género*, says Cervantes) and commits his recognition to the medium of print.

The term "genre," as applied to the picaresque in particular and the novel is general, is misleading, however. It implies a more stable set of rules than in fact ever pertained, and a greater commitment to the idea of such rules than can be discerned from the texts. As the spurious sequels to *Lazarillo, Guzmán*, and *Don Quixote* attest, the novel was from its inception a particularly open invitation to other authors; it encouraged expropriation more than imitation, a cashing in on the marketable material rather than an observation of literary decorum. Both *Guzmán* and *Don Quixote* were immediate and unprecedented best-sellers, and respect for tradition or rules seems to have played a small part in the proliferation of narratives "in that style." The novelistic protocol, as I have suggested, allows considerably more latitude in the observance of literary formalities than do poetic or dramatic genres. Similarly, the novelistic *series*, as I would prefer to call the succession of novels bearing family resemblances to one another, is a more open-ended affair than a generic tradition, however much genres might themselves have been combined or transformed. As Rosalie Colie argues, it was "the *concept* of generic form" that was important for the Renaissance humanists, much more than the definition of specific generic norms. And that concept had a "*social* force and function," setting forth "definitions of manageable boundaries, some large, some small, in which material can be treated and considered."[27]

It is precisely the lack of such a shared belief in separable (and combinable) literary kinds that gives the novel its impetus in literary history. Instead of conforming to a generic type, a novel follows another novel in a historical series. The novelistic series may be a matter of explicit sequels: *The Second Part of the Life of the Picaro, Guzmán de Alfarache; Lazarillo de Manzanares; James Hind, the English Guzmán; The Spiritual Quixote; Sir Launcelot Greaves.* The changes are rung on a local habitation or a name.[28] Or the series may be made up of less explicit successor novels that exploit a plot and setting formula (the Gothic novel, the sea story, the Western), a character-type and professional role (the detective story, the *Bildungsroman*, the portrait of the artist). As I noted earlier, many of these series resemble genres in their tendency to the stereotypical and the formulaic, but the conventions have much more to do with their subject matter than with any formal characteristics—plot structure, mode of characterization, diction, or "point of view"—and have much less normative power than the rules of genre. Novelistic series are by nature more loosely defined, in part because of their focus on the "history" or "adventures" of a particular character or group. Such a focus promotes the idea of additive sequence. How can my book be finished, asks Ginés de Pasamonte, when my life isn't over yet? No matter what sense of an ending is given by a particular novel, there is an implicit "to be continued"—a promise that is explicit from *Lazarillo* onwards: "I will inform Your Honour of my future in due course"; "Something further may follow of this Masquerade." [29]

Recent scholarship on the picaresque novel has unfortunately blurred this distinction between novelistic series and poetic or dramatic genre. The most lucid and informed discussion of the subject is again that of Claudio Guillén, in "Toward a Definition of the Picaresque," where distinctions are drawn between (1) picaresque novels "in the strict sense," (2) "another group of novels [that] may be considered picaresque in a broader sense of the term only," and (3) "a picaresque myth: an essential situation or significant structure derived from the novels themselves." For the strict sense of the term, Guillén offers a list of seven shrewdly chosen characteristics. These however exclude a number of early Spanish successors to *Lazarillo* and *Guzmán* (such as Salas Barbadillo's *La hija de Celestina* and Espinel's *Marcos de Obregón*, both influential abroad). Furthermore, these defining characteristics are somehow independent of "the picaresque genre," which Guillén identifies only as "an ideal type, blending, in varying degrees or fashions, *Lazarillo de Tormes* with *Guzmán de Alfarache* . . . with the addition of other novels according to the case." In other words, the normative genre, with its supposedly "stable features" is kept in isolation from specific criteria in Guillén's analysis, and has only a putative existence in the possible community of texts. In spite of his keen insight into the dynamics of literary history, Guillén here finally refuses the novel its full literary difference. [30]

At the other extreme of Guillén's historical flexibility lies the procrustean attempt of Stuart Miller in *The Picaresque Novel*, which frankly avows its model in Aristotle's *Poetics*: "a forthrightly systematic attempt to construct an 'ideal genre type' for the picaresque novel, showing how a number of coherent formal devices unite to produce a specific picaresque content and emotional response."[31] There is something deeply contradictory about Miller's desire to formalize the rules of a genre that he finds reflecting "a total lack of structure in the world, not merely a lack of ethical or social structure" (p. 131). He abstracts, or chooses examples, from eight different picaresque novels, from *Lazarillo* to *Roderick Random;* he sees 1550–1750 as the "classic period" of the picaresque (p. 4), and thus surreptitiously canonizes the anticanonical form.

Like attempts at a poetics of the novel discussed in Chapter 1, most definitions of the picaresque as a genre go astray in considering it on the model of poetry, of drama, or even of myth, rather than as an early instance of the novel. Ulrich Wicks is in fact specific on this point: "I suggest that . . . we leave out of consideration for the time being one half of our term, namely *novel,* a formidable job of definition itself."[32] Like so many of the nets cast by literary criticism, genre theory allows the novel, in its genuine yet not unlimited novelty, to escape.

It is more accurate, therefore, to think of *Lazarillo de Tormes* as a pretext for *Guzmán de Alfarache* and certain other novels than to think of it as a prototype for a genre. There is, in fact, little direct evidence that Alemán had *Lazarillo* foremost in his mind, or that he considered resemblances worth advertising. There are reminiscences in the form of the title and in the occasional references to "Guzmanillo"; there is an allusion to the trials of being a blind man's servant, although Guzmán never has a blind master. And there is a picaresque conversion that recalls Lazarillo's, though it lacks the specificity of the stone bull. "I plainely began to perceive," Guzmán says, "how Adversitie makes men wise: in that very instant, me thought, I discovered a new light; which as in a cleare Glasse, did represent unto mee things past, things present, and things to come" (Mabbe, I, 236). But as one critic puts it, Alemán's novel is most notable for the way it enlarges the scope of *Lazarillo*—its geography, its social spectrum, and its range of cultural reference.[33] Thus Ben Jonson wrote in a dedicatory poem to Mabbe's translation:

> Who tracks this Authors, or Translators Pen
> Shall finde, that either hath read Bookes, and Men;
> To say but one, were single. Then it chimes,
> When the old words doe strike on the new times,
> As in this Spanish Proteus; who, though writ
> But in one tongue, was form'd with the worlds wit.
>
> (I,31)

The neoclassicizing rhetoric of Jonson's verse, the assumption that books and "old words" are a primary source for describing the "new times" and that Guzmán is a Proteus redivivus, misrepresents *Guzmán* as a novel, perhaps, but it does describe the greater bookishness and broader worldliness of Alemán's text.

The major problem for a modern reader, in fact, is in coming to terms with the overabundance of commentary on the simple story line of Guzmán's adventures. Instead of the spare understatement of *Lazarillo*, we have a voluminous moralizing on the part of the older narrator, a moralizing that takes off from the behavior of the picaro or of the characters he encounters, but extends itself into general expositions of doctrine, proverbs, *sententiae*, exemplary anecdotes, and other narrative digressions. The digressions are not made without a certain self-consciousness on the narrator's part; some of the asides anticipate *Tristram Shandy*. "O what a gentle disparate, what a pretty absurdity is this of mine, yet well grounded in Divinity? how am I leapt from the Oare to the Helme? What a Saint John the Evangelist am I become on the sudden that I reade you such a lecture?" (I, 83), Guzmán remarks ironically at one point. And at another: "I treat in this of mine owne life, and therefore will not meddle with other mens; but I doe not know, whether I shall be able, when a ball offers it selfe so fairly, to pull backe my hand or no? For there is no man that is Master of himselfe, when he is on horsebacke" (I, 103). English and French translations, particularly in the eighteenth century, frequently omit this homiletic material, but a historical reading of the novel must take it into account.[34]

If we cease to look for traditional literary form and search instead for the peculiar protocol of Alemán's narrative, however, we need not apologize for the lack of unity or symmetry. There is clearly a double structure or duality at least in the narrative, but it is not simply a "precarious equilibrium" in which both sides "lessen" or "weaken" one another.[35] There is a function and purpose in the pervasive dichotomy, a symbolic action that may best be identified as that of punishment, chastisement, or castigation. The edition of *Lazarillo* that was approved by the Inquisition was the *edición castigado*. Alemán, in effect, makes such "chastisement" an integral part of his text, the dominant protocol of his own version of the picaresque. As Guzmán says himself at one point, "It stood with me as with prohibited bookes" (II, 60). A new novelistic protocol is simply written over the older protocol of *Lazarillo de Tormes*.

The protocol of castigation is most obvious in the moralizing commentary, which functions almost as a gloss or marginalia on the primary narrative line of autobiography. Indeed, the "discreet reader" is invited to collaborate: "In this Discourse, thou maist moralize things, as they shall be offered unto thee, Thou hast a large margent left thee to doe it" (I, 18). The *prodesse* is intrinsically separated from the *delectare* in the Horatian formula; moral "profit" is to be brought in from beyond any unified literary text.[36] A characteristic moralizing sequence in *Guzmán* is the report on an immoral act by the protagonist, followed by a criticism of that act, followed by a general condemnation of the offense as common to all mankind, followed by proverbs and a brief exemplum. It is this moral policing of literature that Cervantes mocks so brilliantly in his picaresque fantasia "The Dog's Colloquy": "All this is preaching, Scipio my friend," Berganza interrupts his canine companion. "I agree with you, and so I'll be quiet," Scipio replies—whereupon Berganza launches into a long moralizing digression of his own.[37]

Yet the chastisement is not merely extrinsic to *Guzmán de Alfarache*. It is also represented, vividly and realistically, in the psychology of the picaro himself. Realism in the novel, I have suggested, is simply a certain type of protocol, one that engages certain formalities of an extraliterary world. In *Lazarillo* it is most fully rendered in the attention to physical objects, to their manipulation and substitutability for one another. The thoughts and feelings of the character are more hidden, more ambiguous. In *Guzmán*, the world of objects is of less concern; the focus of novelistic realism is the emotional and cognitive experience of the corrected offender. We see clearly Guzmán's ambivalence toward morality, and his psychological dependence on the approval of others. He becomes addicted to certain gratifications beyond all physical need, as when he compulsively steals sweetmeats at the house of the Cardinal. He experiences humiliation and then struggles to assuage it. His response to correction is a mixed one, involving rationalization, self-condemnation, and criticism of the offense in other people. The older narrator, supposedly converted and redeemed at the end of his story, looks back on his earlier self and belabors it with moral truths, but the earlier self has internalized the psychic drama of crime and punishment as well.

It is important to see that the scene of this crime and punishment is the self rather than society; Guzmán is considerably less than a hardened criminal. Alexander Parker rightly insists that a picaro is a "delinquent" rather than a felon, a character whose social acts are more in the nature of misdemeanors than gross violations of the law.

The law Guzmán is most concerned with is moral and religious, and when he is finally sent to the galleys it is for misappropriation of funds rather than robbery or murder. While he is in the galleys he is most severely punished for a theft he did not commit. There is considerable attention to Guzmán's family as causal factors in his delinquency—to his father, a converted Jew and a merchant of varying fortunes and shady practices; to his mother, who is a fortune hunter and a whore; and to his one-time wife, whose death causes him multiple hardships. He is often punished for and by the failings of those he depends on, yet Alemán conveys little sense of protest at the injustice.

Guzmán's own attitude might be called both pessimistic and masochistic. He even has some insight into the way his attitude limits his prospects. "I have learned long agoe couragiously to suffer and abide the changes of Fortune with an undaunted minde, for I always suspect the worst, looking for the hardest measure she can give me, and prevent her better usage, by expecting no good at her hands" (III, 131–32). But in Alemán's imagination the precise justice of a particular punishment is less important than the rough justice of human suffering for human sinfulness. As one critic has suggested, the religious stress of the novel is less on the New Testament law of love and redemption than on the Old Testament law of persistent original sin.[38]

The castigation or chastisement that is so pervasive in Guzmán's experience is a means of preserving the intrinsically wayward self. As Guzmán says at one point, "All which I did, that by correcting my selfe, I might conserve my selfe" (II, 35). Dissipation is more than a metaphor; it becomes a threat to one's very identity. Or as Guzmán says to the reader, "My only purpose was (as I told thee before) to benefit thee, and to teach thee the way, how thou mightest with a good deale of content and safetie, passe thorow the gulph of that dangerous sea wherein thou saylest. The blowes I shall receive, thou the good counsels" (III, 28). Guzmán is a scapegoat for the self in Counter Reformation society, one, in whose sacrifice every reader may vicariously participate, just as he, in his moral castigation of the sins widespread in that society, participates vicariously in the survival of the reader.

Thus we see in the structure of *Guzmán de Alfarache* the picaresque's characteristic alliance of the high and the low against the middle, but the alliance works in a different way than in *Lazarillo de Tormes*. Here high religious doctrine continually chastizes low secular practice, subjecting it to corrective punishment. Low practice does not insinuate itself into the honorable middle estate, as in the ironic upward mobility of Lazarillo; rather it drags this middle estate down with it, into its own abasement. Thus in *Guzmán* the picaro and the novel are allowed many of the trappings of humanistic dignity and culture. There are dedicatory poems and prefaces advertising the artistry of Mateo Alemán, and we are told in one of them that Guzmán has "(by his study) come to be a good Latinist, Rhetorician, and Grecian" (I, 19). Guzmán spends a good deal of time in cultivated Italy, and pursues a degree in the liberal arts at the University of Alcalá de Henares. Yet all this residual humanism is of little consolation as Guzmán continually experiences the collapse of his higher aspirations. He visits Florence at one point in his travels and marvels for a time at the beauty and fine artistic form of the city. But his aesthetic valuation is soon subjected to an economic one as he runs out of money; Florence "began now (me thought) to stinke, I could not endure the sent of it; every thing seemed so foule and filthy to my sight, that I did now long to be gone. . . . You may see (my masters) what wonders want of money can worke" (III, 213).

It is a similar case with the three interpolated romances that Alemán introduces into Guzmán's narrative, a device uncharacteristic of other picaresque novels. They are, in their mode, more idealizing and "entertaining" than Guzmán's picaresque adventures, but they also deal, thematically, with more cruel and unusual punishments. The first, a Moorish romance, allows the hero to convert to Christianity and escape his execution. The third, taken from Masuccio, involves a rape which revenges itself and leaves the husband in blissful ignorance of his wife's violation. The middle tale, "Dorido and Clorinia," is a macabre story in which a man cuts off the hand of a woman and has both his hands cut off in return. The hands are nailed to the dying woman's door with some verses in which the first offender proclaims the "sentence / . . . too small a punishment for my Offence" (II, 291). In effect, Alemán creates a fictional arm of the Inquisition itself through his protocol of corrective punishment. But like the irony of the impetus given to modern capitalism by the theology of Luther and Calvin, the irony of Alemán's project is that his didactic religious purpose considerably extended the developing secularity of the novel as a literary form.

The publication of a spurious Second Part of *Guzmán de Alfarache* by a certain Juan Martí apparently led Alemán to intensify and complicate, though not essentially to change, the protocol of the First Part. There is not the major transformation of the rules of the First Part that we see in the Second Part of *Don Quixote*, but like Cervantes, Alemán manages to incorporate the counterfeit sequel into his continuation of the novel while taking an imaginative revenge on its author. Alemán's revenge is indirect. He has Guzmán meet a character named Sayavedra (Martí's pseudonym) who identifies himself as Juan Martí's brother. Sayavedra first robs Guzmán, but then becomes his servant; he recounts his life to his master, which is a pure, unmoralized version of the picaresque. Finally, during a storm at sea, Sayavedra goes mad, claims that he is Guzmán de Alfarache, jumps overboard, and drowns. Guzmán laments his death with apparent sincerity, making Alemán's punishment of his rival seem an impersonal fate:

> It would have griev'd a mans heart and moved much compassion, to see the things that he did, and the fooleries which he uttered; . . . he would crye out in a loud voyce, I am Guzman de Alfarache's ghost, I am that ghost of his, which goes thus wandring up and downe the world; whereat he made me often both laugh and feare. . . . he would not leave his talking, but by flashes would fall a ripping up of my life, and bolt out by fits, all that which I had formerly recounted unto him concerning the courses I had taken, composing a thousand extravagancies. (IV, 38–39)

Whether Martí's sequel is the main cause of the change or not, we can see how Alemán's Second Part of *Guzmán* further criticizes and corrects the narrative energy of the simple picaresque *vida*. Guzmán is himself the master in this relationship, not the servant. The picaresque account of trickery and deceit is attributed to another character, and this understudy is then killed off. The picaresque scapegoat is given a picaresque scapegoat of his own. Alemán complains in the Second Part that he does not want his book to be known as the book of the picaro, but as "The Watch-Tower of mans life" (III, 127). The subtitle *Atalaya de la vida humana* (the "watchman" is borrowed from Ezekiel), appears on the title page, and though one may well question Guzmán's status as a latter-day prophet, there is a substantial increase in moralizing in this sequel. Whole chapters go by with only the briefest allusion to specific events from Guzmán's life story, and the narrator loses all self-consciousness about his digressions. As a character, Guzmán is also a more public and official figure than in the First Part—he is a courtier, a master of servants, a husband, a merchant, and a scholar. His final position is that of a convict in the galleys, but this dramatic degradation can also be seen as part of the heavier castigation of the picaresque in the Second Part. He does undergo a conversion in the galleys but, as Norval notes, "Guzmán's most spectacular conversion has been followed by his most hideous act of revenge," the entrapment and betrayal of Soto, a convict who had earlier borne false witness against him.[39] "Soto, and one of his Companions, who were the Ring-leaders of this rebellion, were condemned to be drawne in pieces with foure Gallies; and five others to bee hang'd: Which sentence was executed. And as many as were found to have a finger in this businesse, were confined to the Gallies for terme of life, being first publikely whipt, passing from Gally to Gally, till they had rounded the whole Fleete" (IV, 352–53). After this orgy of correction, Guzmán himself is pardoned and set free, and his narrative comes to an end. The clearest thing about his conversion is that it finally enables the old offender to join forces with the police. Alemán promises a third part of *Guzmán de Alfarache* but it seems never to have appeared. His only subsequent works were a book on spelling, a life of the archbishop of Mexico, and *San Antonio de Padua,* a saint's life.

There were many successors to *Guzmán,* however, in the series of picaresque novels that developed in Spain. The series became not a single line of development but a branching in several directions. Ignoring for the moment the picaresque novellas of Cervantes, which will be taken up in the following chapter, one can describe three different lines of succession. The first was inaugurated by *La Pícara Justina* (1605), more properly a parody of the picaresque. It is "an implicit satire on the aims and structure of *Guzmán de Alfarache,*" Parker notes, "whose appearance was, as the Prologue states, the spur of its own publication." "Its style . . . is a treasure-house of the language of burlesque, a riot of verbosity in which popular speech is given an exuberant ornamentation by being overladen with the language of polite literature."[40] But this parody was reclaimed by more straightforward picaresque novels, as Parker shows, like Salas Barbadillo's *Hija de Celestina* (1612) and Castillo Solorzano's *La Garduna de Sevilla* (1642), in which the protagonist is female, the narrative is in the third person, and there is little or no moral emphasis. As one critic points out, Salas Barbadillo tries to give his version of the picaresque a unity of form and a coherence of effect that would bring it in line with neo-Aristotelian principles.[41]

A second line of succession tended to bypass *Guzmán de Alfarache* and hearken back to *Lazarillo de Tormes*. The ironic tone of *Lazarillo* becomes more playful and comic, and there is a notable lack of moral commentary. The lower-class rogue continues to survive on the fringes of society by his wits alone. Examples of this line include Jean de Luna's "corrected and emended" second part of *Lazarillo de Tormes* (1620), Tolosa's *Lazarillo de Manzanares* (1620), and the apparently eponymous *Estevanillo Gonzalez* (1646). In *Estevanillo* in particular, the hero becomes a more traditional jester, and the spirit of the Counter Reformation is conspicuously absent.

Finally, there are a number of Spanish texts that adopt certain forms or themes of the picaresque novel for essentially other kinds of writing: Espinel's *Marcos de Obregón* (1618), a largely autobiographical series of adventures with a minimal emphasis on deceptive transactions; Carlos García's *Desordenada Codicia* (1619), combining one rogue's confession with a general anatomy of thieves and thieving, extending to classical and biblical precedents; and Enríque Gómez's *El siglo pitagorico* (1644), probably based on a satire of Lucian, which deals with the transmigration of a picaro's soul. Though these last works clearly derive from the picaresque, they move well beyond the novel into the miscellaneous "literature of roguery," as Chandler calls it. The novel arose in Golden Age Spain, but it was perfectly capable of declining then as well, or of passing into other kinds of literature. *Estevanillo Gonzalez* was the last picaresque novel of any significance written in Spain until the nineteenth century. It is probably this curious loss of the novelistic initiative in Spanish literature itself that has led literary historians to underestimate its importance in the reorganization of the novel in France and in England, when the challenge of the novel to canonical literature was to become more permanently established.

The most brilliant of all the successors of the original *Lazarillo de Tormes* and *Guzmán de Alfarache* was Quevedo's *El Buscón—La vida del Buscón llamado don Pablos,* which may have been begun as early as 1604 but which was not published until 1626. What is most interesting about this version of the picaresque is that Quevedo appears quite hostile to the values and techniques of *Lazarillo* and *Guzmán,* indeed to the idea of the novel itself. He was one of the most learned classical scholars of his time and a virulent defender of aristocratic privilege. As far as editors can tell, he never authorized the publication of *El Buscón* as a book, but instead had it circulated in manuscript, in the older courtly manner of transmission.[42] The narrative is literarily self-conscious; its stylistic brilliance is heavily indebted to the baroque conceit rather than to literal description. The story is "The Life of the Swindler, Called Don Pablos," a generic rather than a specific title and one that calls attention to the hero's unreliability and social pretensions rather than to his proper name and birthplace. Quevedo's reception of the picaresque resembles that of Cervantes, who saw the emergent novel as a literary kind rather than as something unique.

Nevertheless, Quevedo's literary mimicry is such that he produces a novel of his own—not a parody like the *Pícara Justina*, nor a satire like his own *Sueños*, which freely mingle the natural and the supernatural in their visionary denunciation of human vice and folly. Unlike Cervantes, Quevedo did not create the broadly different counterfiction to the picaresque that *Don Quixote* represents, but, like Ginés de Pasamonte in Cervantes's novel, he turns out one of the best of the kind ever written.[43] To use a current theoretical term, Quevedo deconstructs the picaresque novel as he knew it, dismantles its formality and its ideology from within. Yet in the ongoing history of the novel as a form, this deconstruction is virtually indistinguishable from a new novel in the series, another novel informed by a different protocol. As we have seen, in the emergence of the novel such opposition became the rule rather than the exception.

The stance of *El Buscón* toward its predecessors can be seen most clearly in a preface "To the Reader," which is apparently not Quevedo's own but was added by the bookseller, Roberto Duport, who arranged for the first printed text.[44] If such is the case, Duport is an attentive reader of Quevedo, making explicit what the author leaves his audience to discover on its own: that the reader of this text will pick it up expecting entertainment but will find his pleasure quickly turning to embarrassment and pain. "Here you will find all the tricks of the low life or those which I think most people enjoy reading about," the preface advises. The admission of our pleasure becomes somewhat unsettling as we follow the list: "craftiness, deceit, subterfuge and swindles, born of laziness to enable you to live on lies." The pleasure principle becomes a still more disturbing kind of profit: "and if you attend to the lesson you will get quite a lot of benefit from it." Such benefits one would hardly want to acknowledge. The final humiliation comes as we are advised to reform ourselves, on the basis of something not even in the text: "Study the sermons, for I doubt if anyone buys a book as coarse as this in order to avoid the inclinations of his own depraved nature." The nonexistent "sermons" are a jibe at *Guzmán de Alfarache*, but the more serious accusation is leveled at the *hypocrite lecteur*.[45] It is not only the picaresque novel that Quevedo calls into question but the picaresque reader who would consume them, the "idle reader" treated so much more liberally by Cervantes.

Thus while there are many signs of Quevedo trying in *El Buscón* to outdo *Lazarillo* by presenting exaggerated versions of episodes in the earlier text,[46] and while there is much evidence that *El Buscón* is a thoroughgoing thematic rejection of the social and moral values of *Guzmán* (in the version of Juan Martí as well as of Alemán),[47] the most powerful assault is made on the expectations and the sensibilities of the reader. The protocol of this novel is a protocol of mortification, like the chastisement of *Guzmán* in some respects, but different in the means and the purpose of the punishment meted out. Where Alemán intends the punishment as corrective and finally beneficial to the self, Quevedo holds out little hope for anyone's reform. And where Alemán effects his chastisement by a heavy application of moral wisdom from outside and beyond, Quevedo mortifies the pleasure of the text by subversion from within. The focus of this protocol is not on objects in the world, nor is it on psychology of the main character as an actor in the world. It is rather on the vicarious experience of reading a first-person novel, where we experience objects and psychology through the medium of another self, or, more strictly speaking, through the medium of another's printed discourse. Pablos's first initiative in the novel is to reject the careers his parents envision for him—his father wants him to be a thief, his mother a male witch—and to pursue an education: "I told them I wanted to learn to be an honest man and that they ought to send me to school, because you couldn't do anything without knowing how to read and write" (87). Literacy is easily acquired, but honesty (virtue, *virtud* in the Spanish) is not. As readers we are quickly led to sympathize with Pablos's desire to escape his demoralizing origins, but we are repeatedly shown the impossibility of his doing so.

As recent critics of the novel point out, there is a persistent pattern in Pablos's adventures of the past returning to haunt him, humiliate him, and finally destroy him. "The structure of the *Buscón*, based on a repetition of motifs, is designed to block Pablos' exit from the family of which he is so ashamed," writes C. B. Morris.[48] Thus Pablos's moment of picaresque awakening comes from the realization that the insults other children have heaped on his mother—that she is a witch and a whore—are true. "When I realized the truth it was like a kick in the stomach" (89). Thus he is "paralyzed with shame" in the middle of his career by the fact that his uncle is a hangman (142) and he is forced to leave Madrid. And thus toward the end of the novel, when he is trying to pass himself off as a nobleman, his childhood friend Don Diego reappears and inadvertently reveals his antecedents. Speaking of the remarkably similar person he used to know, Don Diego exclaims, "You won't believe this, sir, but your mother was a witch, your father a thief and your uncle a public executioner, and he was the worst and most unpleasant man you ever saw" (189). Of course Don Diego soon discovers the truth of Pablos's identity.

Nevertheless, as Leo Spitzer observed long ago, it is difficult to maintain that a coherent moral judgment on Pablos is being elicited from us as readers.[49] In the first place, such a judgment is so easily passed as to be uninteresting. Pablos's wrongdoing and dullness are obvious and self-confessed, and his singular lack of success as a trickster can hardly evoke the indignation of satire. Secondly, the main impetus of his adventures is the emulation of someone else's example. Much more than Guzmán, Pablos is overanxious to please; he is less a servant of many masters than a student of many teachers. "I went to school," he says, "and the master greeted me very cheerfully, saying that I looked a quick bright lad. As I didn't want to disabuse him I did my lessons very well that day" (88). He adopts the role of picaro later on out of a similar desire to conform: " 'when in Rome do as the Romans do,' says the proverb, and how right it is. After thinking about it I decided to be as much a tearaway as the others and worse than them if I could. I don't know if I succeeded but I certainly tried hard enough" (112). And even at the lowest moral point in his career, when he kills two policemen in Seville, he has been inspired by the example of others, in particular by a former classmate, Mattoral, whom he calls "the master of novices" (212). Pablos is an incurable reader of other persons' *vidas.* Conversely, the reader of his *vida* is continually and disarmingly solicited to identify with Pablos's emotions, rather than to pass judgment on his acts. "How can I explain my feelings?" he asks rhetorically (96). "You can imagine what sort of life we led under these conditions" (97). "You can't imagine how disgusted I was," he says of a meal with his uncle where the meat pies are made of human flesh—an understatement more effective than any exaggeration (143).

The ruling passion of Pablos as a character, and the dominant affect with which the reader finds himself involved, is the feeling of shame. With Guzmán, it is more proper to speak of a sense of guilt, of the internalization and partial grasp of the sense of wrongdoing and suffering for wrong. But in Pablos's case the sense of self is bound up with externals and surfaces, with the image reflected to the self by others. This personal shame-culture of the main character is reflected in the hyperbolic conceits and understated euphemisms that pervade the narrative style. As Parker puts it, "The exposure of human self-conceit is apparent . . . in a particular type of verbal witticism that is a constant thread running through the style. In describing people or objects connected with them, Quevedo uses an epithet or a phrase that ennobles them, and then, by word-play, shatters the illusion by turning it into its opposite."[50] For example, Pablos mentions his younger brother, who picks pockets in their father's barbershop. "He was caught in the act," Pablos says, "and the little angel died from a few lashes they gave him in prison. My father was very upset, because the child stole the heart of everybody who saw him" (85). We are mortified by our initial assent to the sentimental metaphors.

The focus on surfaces can also be seen in the emphasis on clothing in the novel, on disguises which dignify temporarily but which only heighten the sense of shame when they ultimately fail. Pablos dresses up as the "boy-king" in carnival time and ends up smeared with excrement. Don Torribio and his beggars' fraternity dress in bits and pieces of respectable attire, and their "honor" depends on only being seen from the right angle. Don Diego insists on trading cloaks with Pablos at the end, only to set him up for a beating and slashing by Don Diego's men. As a picaro, Pablos is for the most part a bad imitation, a parody of the more honest and honorable substance of the aristocrat. But as readers we are forced to identify with the parodic figure; we are given no access to the character of authentic social value.[51]

This mortification of character and reader is intensified by Quevedo's specific denial of religious transcendence to this lowest of the low. The alliance of the high and the low found in *Lazarillo* and in *Guzmán* is explicitly rejected in *El Buscón*, as when Pablos is spat upon and beaten. "Please don't," Pablos protests; "I'm not Christ on the Cross, you know" (108). In a theological as well as an emotional sense, Quevedo's narrative is merciless. One might argue that the ultimate purpose of Quevedo's mortification of Pablos's flesh and of the reader's spirit is religious salvation, as in the *autos da fé* which allowed the heretic to recant. But such a prospect would be radically extrinsic to the text, which ends instead in a confirmation of mortal hopelessness. Like Lazarillo, Pablos ends his story joined up with a proven whore, but, unlike Lazarillo, Pablos is radically displaced from European society.

> When I saw that this situation was going to be more or less permanent and that bad luck was dogging my heels, I made up my mind, not because I was intelligent enough to see what was going to happen but because I was tired and obstinate in my wickedness, to go to America with

Grajales. . . . I thought things would go better in the New World and another country. But they went worse, as they always will for anybody who thinks he has only to move his dwelling without changing his life or ways. (213–14)

The manuscript versions of the text promise that we will see this worsening in a "second part," but Quevedo apparently thought better of a sequel. It is perhaps proper to speak of *El Buscón* as a dead end of the Spanish picaresque, as it is hard to envision any sequel following its particular lead into any further negation.

4

The Counterfiction of DON QUIXOTE

> Menard (perhaps without wanting to) has enriched, by means of a new
> technique, the halting and rudimentary art of reading.
>
> Borges, "Pierre Menard, Author of the *Quixote*"

The historical relationship between *Don Quixote* and the picaresque
novel that both preceded and followed it is a complex one. As we
shall see in later chapters, these two earliest manifestations of the
European novel have sometimes been conflated with one another by
later novelists and have even been confused with one another by
modern critics. An increasing distance from the original moment of
the texts, geographical as well as historical, has tended to smooth
away the distinctive features of the two counterfictions. There are
undeniable structural resemblances, as a recent study of the problem
notes, between them.[1] Both types of novel deal with the episodic
adventures of contemporary characters, masters and servants, significantly dislocated from their society. The adventures take place
along roads and in inns, engaging a wide variety of other social types
and insisting on the humble physical necessities of existence. Don
Quixote is a reader of *Amadis of Gaul* and *Palmerin of England,* but the
world he inhabits is the world of *Lazarillo de Tormes* and *Guzmán de
Alfarache.* And as a reader of fiction, Don Quixote becomes involved,
however unwittingly, in the basic situation of the picaresque hero—
the marginal man's career of deception.

Nevertheless, Cervantes does not simply work within the terms of
the picaresque novel as he knew it. He did write several novellas of a
picaresque sort—"Rinconete and Cortadillo," "The Illustrious
Kitchen-Maid," and "The Dog's Colloquy"—which function, like
Quevedo's *El Buscón,* as sophisticated deconstructions of the ongoing novelistic series.[2] But in *Don Quixote* he stood apart from this
series and created a radically different version of the novel form. One
of the ways in which he achieves this imaginative distance is by
including a picaresque character within *Don Quixote* and the sketch
of a picaresque narrative within his own text. In Chapter 22 of the
First Part, Quixote and Sancho encounter a group of prisoners in
chains on their way to become slaves in the galleys. Among these

71

prisoners is Ginés de Pasamonte, alias Ginesillo de Parapilla, according to one of the guards, who has written *The Life of Ginés de Pasamonte* and anticipates writing a sequel to it when he reaches the galleys for a second time. There are some ironic allusions to *Guzmán de Alfarache* here, for example, a suggestion that Guzmán's conversion when he was in the galleys may not have been a long lasting one. But Cervantes significantly makes no direct mention of what was to be his main competitor in the literary marketplace.[3] Instead he has Ginés compare his *vida* to the earlier, less popular example. "It's so good . . . that Lazarillo de Tormes will have to look out, and so will everything in that style that has ever been written or ever will be. One thing I can promise you, is that it is all the truth, and such well-written, entertaining truth that there is no fiction that can compare with it" (176).

There are two elements of this self-advertisement of the picaresque that signal the different nature of *Don Quixote* as a novel. The first is the consciousness of literary genre and style. As I argued in the last chapter, the idea of a genre is a subtle undermining of the novel's claim to authenticity and uniqueness. In mentioning *Lazarillo* and others of the *género* (when in fact only two or three others were then in existence), Ginés enthusiastically resituates the picaresque novel back within the literary system that it had purported to stand beyond. The second subversive element of the passage reinforces this ironic reconventionalizing of the unconventional. Ginés claims to tell the truth, but it is "such well-written, entertaining truth" that it outdoes fiction. As I pointed out in my discussion of *Guzmán* and *El Buscón*, the picaresque was conceived in opposition to the literature of idealizing and entertainment. The author of the picaresque life story deals with two levels of experience on which aesthetic pleasure is a liability—the level of harsh empirical realities and survival in a hostile world, and the level of spiritual salvation in a world hereafter. For Cervantes, in contrast, aesthetic recreation is the central truth of whatever experience is represented in art. As he writes in the Preface to his *Exemplary Stories*, "My intention has been to set up in the square of our republic a billiard table where each one can come to amuse himself without fear of injury; I mean, without hurt to soul or body, for honest and pleasant exercises bring profit rather than harm. For one is not always in church, places of prayer are not always filled, one is not always at one's business, however important it may be."[4]

Guzmán de Alfarache is always in church or about his business—often both at once. Don Quixote, on the other hand, is continually playing the game of literature, according to his own adaptation of the rules. In his meeting with the galley slaves he decides, according to the rules of chivalric romance, that the issue in question is not crime and punishment but pleasure and liberty; thus he sets the captives free. At the same time, Quixote clearly adapts the rules of chivalry here to incorporate something of the alien genre he has encountered. This is the only explanation for his unprecedented speech to another of the prisoners in praise of the sexual procurer in the well-ordered state. The lover of Dulcinea is clearly speaking out of character, but he is doing so in the spirit of the new generic context he has entered. The essence of literary rules for Cervantes turns out to be their inter-changeability.

The ethos of the picaresque novel, as we have seen, is one of exclusion: the exclusion of literature as a cultural institution, the ex-clusion of social codes as definitions of the individual *vida*, the exclu-sion of other points of view in the first-person presentation of experience. Even in *Guzmán de Alfarache*, which does include several stories and discourses other than the picaro's own, the thrust of the narrative is to cut out and cast away a whole realm of illusory values. The ethos of *Don Quixote*, on the other hand, is ironically inclusive. Alternative versions of experience are conjured up and entertained, even as their claims to truth and substance are put into question. The picaresque touchstones of the belly and the purse, the forms of alimentary and economic reduction so prevalent in *Lazarillo, Guz-mán*, and *El Buscón*, are transposed in *Don Quixote* from a metonymic to a metaphoric field.

> That day happened to be a Friday, and there was no food in the inn except some portions of a fish that is called pollack in Castile and cod in Andalusia, in some parts ling and in others troutlet. They asked whether his worship would like some troutlet, as there was no other fish to eat.
> "So long as there are plenty of troutlet they may serve me for one trout," replied Don Quixote, "for I had just as soon be paid eight separate *reals* as one eight *real* piece. What is more, these troutlet may be like veal, which is better than beef, or kid, which is better than goats' meat. But, however that may be, let me have it now, for the toil and weight of arms cannot be borne without due care for the belly." (40)

In the picaresque novel such analogical equivalences of sustenance are continually denied. When Guzmán is served ass's meat disguised as veal, his stomach tells him the truth and he vomits it up. When Lazarillo is given one coin by a passerby, he substitutes another of lesser value in giving it to his blind master. In modern rhetorical terms, one might say that the picaresque novel deals with false metaphors which turn out in experience to be metonymic. *Don Quixote* deals in apparent metonymies—accidental and contingent juxtapositions—which paradoxically reveal an underlying metaphoric relatedness.

This metaphorical or analogical inclusiveness in *Don Quixote* is most noticeable on the level of narrative type and literary genre. Other literary modes are simply imbedded in the story of Quixote's adventures. He meets spokesmen for the pastoral romance, for the ballad, for the Italian novella, for the Renaissance epic, and for the Moorish novel—representatives of "virtually the whole range of fiction available in his time," as one critic puts it,[5] and representatives of the discourse of literary criticism as well. Not all these figures embody their literary modes in the same way that Don Quixote embodies the chivalric romances. Some stories are interpolated, some are reported indirectly, and some are merely alluded to. But they do dramatize a pluralistic literary field, albeit ironically displaced from its normal position in human experience. In a history of the novel per se, the picaresque is the primary counterfiction to *Don Quixote*, but in the contemporary system of Renaissance literature it is only one of a wide variety of alternatives that *Don Quixote* manages to entertain.

There are two possible precedents for this inclusive or collective quality of *Don Quixote*, and they both raise questions about the originality of Cervantes's novel as a novel. One possible precedent is the satura or carnival form so brilliantly deployed by Rabelais. We have already considered *Gargantua and Pantagruel* in connection with the picaresque novel, but we must consider it in relation to *Don Quixote* as well. The other possible precedent for Cervantes's innovation is the collection of novellas within a frame-story, such as Boccaccio assembled in *The Decameron*. Cervantes's own *Exemplary Stories*, though less elaborate than *The Decameron*, show his interest in this form of prose fiction. It has been claimed for both these earlier texts that they anticipate *Don Quixote* in essential ways—that they are, in effect, significant earlier examples of the novel.

In his influential study of Rabelais and the carnival tradition, Mikhail Bakhtin argues that this eclectic and populist form of festival is merely continued in Cervantes. "The carnivalesque basic element in Cervantes' *Don Quixote* . . . is quite obvious," he writes; "his novel is directly organized as a grotesque play with all its attributes. The depth and consequent nature of his realism are also typical of this pathos of change and renewal."[6] This is a view which has been furthered recently by Julia Kristeva and Barbara Babcock, as in the latter's claim that "the insertion of the semiotic of carnival into that of the epic and the romance [is] the necessary prerequisite to the development of complex prose fiction in the form of the novel."[7] Cervantes follows Rabelais, we are told, in the way that he gathers together a wide variety of imaginative forms—classical and popular, spiritual and corporeal, noble and base—and in the way the hierarchies of official culture are stood on their heads.

Apart from the lack of immediate historical influence between Rabelais and Cervantes, a condition attributable to the Counter Reformation,[8] there is an important difference in the terms on which the diverse literary elements are brought together in their two books. In *Gargantua and Pantagruel* the terms are resolutely oral and incorporative. In spite of their awareness of themselves as printed texts, Rabelais's *livres* are a recreation of the oral symposium, where truth is ingested and expressed through the mouth. In *Don Quixote*, as we have already seen, the terms are those of the printed book. The dialogue of characters is always mediated through the literature they have read, and the generic alternatives are juxtaposed with, rather than assimilated to, one another. Instead of Cervantes's "idle reader," paradoxically divided in the privacy and the publicity of the lore he has mentally consumed, Rabelais's audience is designated as "most noble boozers" and is invited to participate in an urgently physical and communal cameraderie: "Now be cheerful, my dear boys, and read joyfully on for your bodily comfort and the profit of your digestions. But listen to me, you dunderheads—God rot you!—do not forget to drink my health for the favour, and I'll return you the toast, post-haste."[9]

Anything that can be drunk or spoken or spoken under the influence of drink may be brought into Rabelais's narrative. The swallowing up and spewing forth of oral formulas is the etiquette by which different elements of the narrative associate. At later points in the history of the novel, beginning perhaps with Sorel and Scarron, as Bakhtin suggests, but certainly with Sterne and Melville and Joyce, the Rabelaisian etiquette becomes assimilated to the etiquette of Cervantes and the novel. But *Gargantua and Pantagruel* is only a novel after the fact, after the fundamental bookishness of this new literary form was firmly established and the more philosophical, festive, and oral qualities of Rabelais's antibook were dominated by the typographical situation.[10]

In the case of *The Decameron* a similar argument has been advanced for the essentially derivative nature of *Don Quixote*'s strategy of inclusion. Viktor Shklovsky, a precursor of Bakhtin in the theory of prose fiction, makes the most emphatic claims. In considering the strategies of combination typical in story cycles like *The Decameron*, Shklovsky argues that these methods are simply extended in the case of what we regard as the novel. "One can say generally that both devices, the composition by framing and the composition by stringing together, have the effect of integrating more and more external material in the body of the novel. This phenomenon can be seen especially well in the famous example of *Don Quixote*." Shklovsky goes on to argue that Don Quixote himself was originally conceived as a simple character, but that he grew in complexity because of the demands upon him as a connecting thread between the different stories and different types of discourse contained in the novel.[11]

There is something to be said for this argument, particularly in view of Cervantes's own experiments with the novella collection in his *Exemplary Stories*, which he advertised as the first novellas written originally in Spanish and written with a collective as well as individual significance. Nevertheless, as far as *Don Quixote* is concerned, the imaginative totality of the text cannot be so easily divided into its component parts as can *The Decameron*, and the strategy of inclusion is strikingly different. The consistently developed frame of *The Decameron*, where the fugitives from the plague tell traditional tales to one another for amusement, and the rationally organized sequence, where stories told on different days address different topics, are much more architectonic and ontologically stable structures than anything in *Don Quixote*. No single character or narrator is preeminent in *The Decameron*, and the epistemological boundary between the tellers and the tales is firmly established. In *Don Quixote*, a single character dictates essentially unpredictable terms of the literary engagement, and the narrative boundary between teller and tale is continually being broken and/or redrawn. Characters step in and out of the stories they present—as protagonists, as narrators, and as critics. Authors and historians and translators emerge unaccountably in the text. What Cervantes introduces is a radical dislocation of the storyteller and the story as they were conceived by oral tradition. The fictional "frame" of his narrative is the consciousness of the hero who inhabits it. Both author and audience are drawn into a confusing intermediate realm, the realm of the printed text. *Don Quixote* is unprecedented primarily in its existential realization of a new cultural being—the reader.

It is quite probable that Cervantes did not fully understand—or even highly value—the innovation of his exemplary novel. He could certainly not envision the extent to which *Don Quixote* would become, along with the picaresque novel, the charter for a new type of

European literature. After the publication of the First Part of *Don Quixote* he continued to work in more conventional literary forms like the Italian novella, the poetic dream vision, and the classical-Christian romance. But there are distinctly Quixotic or novelistic features in some of these alternative productions—for example, the strange intercalation of "The Dog's Colloquy" with "The Deceitful Marriage" at the end of the *Exemplary Stories*, where one character reads another character's manuscript report of a dialogue he has supposedly overheard between two dogs about their picaresque service of many masters. There is also the redoubling of novelistic innovation in the Second Part of *Don Quixote*, where Cervantes writes a sequel literally to end all sequels and completely reconstructs the original situation of the idle reader and the illusive text. Whatever Cervantes's artistic understanding of his own discoveries, the protocol of realizing the reader is fundamental to *Don Quixote* in both its parts, and it is according to this protocol that I would like to pursue a discussion of this originary novelistic text.

The distinguishing characteristic of Don Quixote, his *daemon* as a hero, is the fact that he has read chivalric novels until, as the author puts it, "his brain dried up and he lost his wits" (32). He briefly considers taking up the pen himself, but instead begins on a much different literary project involving the sword. His mimesis is an existential one, an imitation not of nature but of literature, and not even of particular texts so much as of a certain class of texts. Furthermore, as E. C. Riley notes, his behavior is directed *toward* as well as *by* a textual ideal, for as readers we are made aware of "the account of his adventures that Don Quixote believes his personal enchanter will one day be writing, as distinct from the one that is in fact written about him."[12] Quixote's behavior has no ulterior motivation in Cervantes's account of it. It is not the result of a previous trauma—like, for example, the madness of Cardenio whom he encounters in the Sierra Morena—and it is not directed at any goal or acquisition of power, other than the diffuse literary aspiration "to increase his renown and to serve the state" (33). His career is rather the transformation of the passive activity of reading into an active mode. Don Quixote internalizes his experience of books and performs them.

The role of Cervantes himself, the author as announced on the title page and in the Prologue, involves a similar reorientation toward the role of the reader. From the first hint of other sources of information in Chapter 1 ("They say his surname was Quixada or Quesada"; "that is no doubt why the authors of this true history, as we have said, assumed") to the abrupt interjection of the Arab historian Cide

77

Hamete Benengeli in Chapter 9, the author repeatedly transforms himself into a reader of an already existing text. As he explains on discovering the rest of Don Quixote's story in manuscript, "I have a taste for reading even torn papers lying in the streets" (76). There have been careful attempts on the part of critics to establish the imaginary provenance of the text we are given in *Don Quixote,* but such systematizing of the putative layers of fictionality misses the point.[13] The rules of a particular fictional contract are not to be understood and followed from beginning to end, but the actual reader is to be forced to adjust again and again to the shifting boundaries of his ongoing aesthetic experience.

This realization of the figure of the reader for the actual reader's consideration is rather specifically defined in *Don Quixote.* It is not the general metaphysical project that Borges attributes to the novel in his essay "Partial Magic in the *Quixote,*" where he concludes from the mention of "Cervantes" in Chapter 6 that the reader is made aware of his own existence as fictional.[14] On the contrary, the reader of *Don Quixote* is generously validated in his own time and space. The author mentions "the amusement and pleasure which an attentive reader may now enjoy for as much as two hours on end" (76), and the actuality of contemporary Spain where both the fictional adventures and the actual reception of them are represented as taking place is never called into question. What the reader of *Don Quixote* is confronted with instead is the novelty and the potential power of his intermediary role *as* reader in rearranging unwritten experience.

The First Part of *Don Quixote* structures this potential power as a dialectic of interpolation and interruption. On the one hand, texts both actual and ideal are inserted into the fabric of other texts—texts that had seemed to be directly referential and hence transparent. There are full-fledged interpolated tales, such as "The Tale of Foolish Curiosity," which the innkeeper reads aloud from a manuscript to an audience of the characters of *Don Quixote,* and there are stories of those characters themselves: Chrysostom, Dorothea, Cardenio, the captive, the goatherd, and others. There are also more subtle and minute interpolations in the ubiquitous phrases "it must have been" and "it seemed to be," which insinuate other possible ways of seeing a particular situation.[15] Between these two extremes Cervantes creates a vast array of fictive spaces within his fictive space, local arenas of narrative where the reader is released from one set of generic constraints, only to be captivated by others.

On the other hand, there are numerous interruptions, the breakings-off of these tales within the tale before they are properly concluded. Often these interruptions are caused by members of the audience or readership in the novel, the result of responses or interrogations that the stories themselves cannot contain. Sancho interrupts his story of the goatherd carrying his three hundred goats across the river because Don Quixote cannot keep count of how many goats have been transported. Cardenio interrupts the story of his misfortunes when Don Quixote cannot resist reacting to his mention of *Amadis of Gaul*. Cervantes interrupts his own narrative at the end of Chapter 8 with the sudden discovery that the first author's manuscript was incomplete. And Quixote himself continually finds his chivalric exploits interrupted by an evil enchanter. "What a way that scoundrel of an enchanter, my enemy, has of transforming things and making them invisible! You must know, Sancho, that it is a very easy thing for enchanters to give things whatever appearance they please. For this wicked sorcerer, my persecutor, being envious of the glory he saw I was sure to gain from this battle, has turned the hostile squadrons into flocks of sheep" (139). The successive realizations of the reader are as precarious as they are persistent.

The subtleties and complications of this process of interpolation and interruption can be seen in "The Tale of Foolish Curiosity," the most palpable interpolation in the First Part of the novel. We have first of all a "second Don Quixote" (280), as Dorothea calls him, in the innkeeper who provides the manuscript of the story. He is a champion of the old chivalric romances, and his arguments with the priest in their defense recall the "inquisition" of Chapter 6 when Quixote's books are removed and destroyed. The innkeeper stops short of going out as a knight-errant, yet he seems to restrain himself largely on stylistic grounds. "I see quite well that it's not the fashion now to do as they did in the olden days when they say those famous knights roamed the world," he says (281). The priest criticizes the shortcomings of the romances, but he succumbs to the temptation of another literary genre. When he agrees to read "The Tale of Foolish Curiosity" "if only out of curiosity" (282) (*Curioso/curiosidad* in the Spanish), we find him ironically exemplifying his reading matter in a way that suggests a third Don Quixote.

In the tale itself, the parallels and alternatives continue to proliferate. Anselmo's lack of confidence in his wife Camilla contrasts with Quixote's faith in Dulcinea. Yet Anselmo's insane empiricism ironically leads him to place complete trust in Camilla's eventual deception, acted out on the stage with Lothario, in her closet. Quixote's idealizing madness suddenly appears less credulous. There is also a lesson for Cardenio, the disillusioned suitor of Lucinda, in this episode. Like Anselmo, he has overseen and misread the staged behavior of his beloved, who apparently went along with the marriage forced on her by Don Ferdinand. As Cardenio will shortly learn, Lucinda has in fact been true to him, and his earlier wish that she "draw her dagger in defence of her honour" (233) is ironically realized in Camilla's theatrical gesture of stabbing herself, the seal on her deception of Anselmo. In the most curious parallel of all, the story itself is interrupted at this point by Don Quixote, who has been asleep upstairs and has begun attacking the wineskins. His stabbing of the skins and the gush of red wine from them appear as an unconscious imitation of Camilla spilling her own blood. This interruption from without is finally replicated by an interruption from within the tale as Anselmo tries to write down his confession and forgiveness. The text of the story is broken off: "it was clear that his life had ended before he could finish his sentence" (323).

The reader reads characters reading one another's stories, or acting as if they had read them. Even when he is asleep, Don Quixote is drawn into the gestures and motifs of other narratives, and the coincidental analogues between one level of fictionality and another complicate our sense of linear causality. The priest complains at the end of Chapter 33 that there "is something impossible" about the story of Anselmo that he has just finished reading. Yet in the very next chapter we find an even more impossible meeting and reconciliation of Dorothea and Cardenio with their lost lovers, on a supposedly more "realistic" level of the text. All the readers are unexpectedly drawn into fictional replications of their experiential worlds, discovering their experience in simplified, clarified, inverted, or caricatured form.

It is true that individual characters rarely seem to learn from such revisions of their own adventures in any direct or sustained fashion. Cardenio never seems to perceive the analogy between his premature judgment of Lucinda and Anselmo's false perception of Camilla. Don Quixote ends the First Part of his adventures in as deluded a condition as he began them. But on a more figurative level, these realizations of the reader produce realizations in the reader. It is not that characters are educated, as in the later romantic mode of the *Bildungsroman* and model of progressive education, but that the reader is *recreated* in the older Renaissance sense of this term. Recreation is both edification and escape. The mind is led away from the external contraints of its habitual surroundings into a reduced world of play. But within this second world a mastery of issues deriving from the first world may be built up and achieved. In this respect, *Don Quixote* may be seen as a novelistic version of the more widespread recreative culture of the Renaissance, where the ideal pattern of experience is one of withdrawal and return.[16] *El Buscón,* as we have seen, is a deconstruction of the literary sensibility; *Don Quixote* is a reconstruction of its possibilities. The reader is not so much mortified as put through a series of imaginative exercises.

On a more literal level of the narrative, this recreative function is presented in terms of illness and cure. The priest and the barber discover that removal of the source of Quixote's curious disease is not enough, and they are forced to adopt more homeopathic methods in attempting to restore him to his sanity. As Quixote's madness runs its course we encounter a series of analogical illnesses and treatments: Chrysostom's suicidal complex of pastoral motifs, which is already beyond cure; Cardenio's compulsive and unpredictable catatonic states, which are dispelled by the reappearance of Lucinda. There are also the physical injuries sustained by Quixote and Sancho in their encounters, which are variously alleviated: by the herb lore of the goatherds in Chapter 11, by the fickle "balsam of Fierobras" in Chapters 17 and 18. But on a more figurative level, the figure-*making* level of the reader's experience, it is the fact that Don Quixote's madness cannot be cured that provides the occasion for recuperative play.

The First Part of *Don Quixote* has generally been considered random and shapeless in its plot, but it is in fact clearly structured according to the recreative pattern of withdrawal and return.[17] After an appropriate interruption of his adventures on the occasion of his first sally, which sends him back home, Quixote moves further and further from the domestic setting of his unnamed village in La Mancha. He leaves its confining relationships, social and familial, and enters a simplified country landscape where he can project his imaginings more freely and where he can meet various counterparts in the flesh, analogously entangled in literary fictions. The ultimate point of retreat in his progress, coming halfway through the First Part, is the barren Sierra Morena. From here he sends Sancho with a message back to Dulcinea, with the result that the priest and the barber come out after him. In the second half of the First Part Quixote returns to his village. The larger company moves in successive stages, meeting up again with several of the same characters Quixote encountered on his way out: the barber who provided the helmet of Mambrino, Andreas, the servant ineffectually rescued from a beating, the innkeeper, and Maritornes. But Don Quixote's position has changed on the journey back. He is less the projector of his own fictions than the audience for the supposedly restorative fictions of the others. When the plot of the "Princess Micomicona" is introduced, with Dorothea in the lead role, Quixote is put on the defensive and remains more or less in this posture until the end of Part One.

Don Quixote thus shifts from an active to a passive mode in his chivalric mimesis as he enters the second half of the First Part of his adventures. Yet this loss of mobility and initiative is accompanied by a gain in critical sophistication. He moves from the position of the maker to the position of the interpreter in the world of fictions, and it is in the realm of discourse *about* fictions that Cervantes achieves the positive purpose of his recreation. It is not that Quixote learns the "truth" in the First Part; such radical disillusionment belongs to the different protocol of the Second Part. It is rather that he teaches a deeper appreciation of literary feigning. The bulk of his adventures in the First Part are framed by two critical debates about the worth of the chivalric romances, and a comparison of these debates provides a measure for the reader's own ideal education.

In Chapter 6 the barber and the priest hold an "inquisition" over Don Quixote's library. (Cervantes's *escrutinio* avoids a dangerous mention of the Holy Office, but the allusion is evident.) Preceded by the housekeeper who, with her peasant superstitions, wants to sprinkle the library with holy water to keep off evil enchanters, the representatives of spiritual and physical well-being (barbers being the provincial surgeons) proceed to destroy some of the most popular reading material of the day. As the judgment goes on, the priest and the barber reveal some complicity with their victims. They gradually shift their criteria for judgment from ethical to aesthetic grounds and begin to spare some books on account of their style. Their own literary enthusiasms undercut their authority, but the fact remains that all the reading matter is banned, including some books that would have been spared had it not been for "fate and the laziness of the inquisitor" (64). Through all this attack on fiction Don Quixote has been asleep.

In Chapter 47, Quixote encounters another clerical critic of chivalric romances, the canon from Toledo, and this time he is wide awake. There is no burning of books here. Instead, as Alban Forcione has shown, Quixote engages the canon in critical debate and emerges the victor on the canon's own terms. Using the resources of classical rhetoric and arguing on neo-Aristotelian principles, Quixote confounds the canon's attempts to distinguish literary truth and falsehood. Quixote "accepts the canon's doctrine of verisimilitude and through ironic distortion illuminates the problematic foundations on which it rests; i.e., that in the last analysis belief depends on what the reader will accept as true."[18] The aim of Cervantes's defense has thus shifted from religious critics, like the priest, with literary tastes, to literary critics, like the canon, who are invested with religious authority. The priest and the barber confiscate the printed volumes but Don Quixote escapes with the essence of the chivalric romances in his head. After proving the symbolic vitality of these fictions in the course of his adventures, Quixote meets the canon and from within the province of the literary imagination evades his more educated strictures. The critic here is left in a state of neo-Aristotelian *admiratio:* "The canon was astonished at this well-reasoned nonsense of Don Quixote's, at his description of the adventure of the Knight of the Lake, and at the impression made on him by the deliberate lies in the books he had read. And he marvelled, too, at Sancho's foolishness in so ardently desiring the countship his master had promised him" (443). Although literally he has been brought back home in a cage, on the field of the literary text Don Quixote emerges as the successful champion of "idle reading."

In the Second Part of *Don Quixote,* published ten years after the First Part, new kinds of problems present themselves, and a new protocol of literary experience is created to deal with them. Most simply, the problem that the Second Part must confront is the existence of the First Part. Don Quixote must succeed himself as a character. For a less ironic and reflective author like Alemán, such succession is not so fraught with novelty. Guzmán de Alfarache is simply a more public and a more officious figure in the Second Part of his adventures, and the presence of a spurious sequel is dealt with summarily. But for Cervantes, the existence of Quixote's previous adventures in print and the possibility as well as the eventual fact of a rival sequel led to a thoroughgoing reconstruction of the original fictional contract. *Don Quixote* still pursues its realization of the reader, but in the Second Part this realization is more melancholy and less triumphant. Instead of interpolating his adventures into the prose of the world, Quixote now finds his imaginings appropriated and usurped.

Don Quixote first learns of the publication of the First Part of his adventures from Sancho, who has heard about it from the bachelor of arts Sampson Carrasco. Both Quixote and Sancho are anxious about the way they have been presented; they are proud and amazed, but also irritated and jealous. Quixote particularly objects to the interpolated stories. " 'Now I believe that the author of my story is no sage

83

but an ignorant chatterer,' said Don Quixote, 'and that he set himself to write it down blindly and without method. . . . I do not know
what induced the author to make use of novels and irrelevant stories,
when he had so much of mine to write about' " (489–90). There are in
fact no interpolated tales in the Second Part, and the principle of
interpolation is succeeded by a principle of rivalry. In the First Part
Don Quixote's precedents were secure in his own literary memory
and could be generously extended to the actions of others. In the
Second Part, he must live up to his published reputation and he is
never certain of what that reputation consists. His imaginative mastery, so comically resilient in the First Part, becomes more tragically
insecure. He ceases to be man reading and becomes man read.

Many of the people Quixote and Sancho meet in the Second Part
have read the First Part. They have preconceptions about the knight
and squire and, like the Duke and the Duchess, they manipulate the
knight and squire in ways that will realize their particular interpretations of what they have read. These staged encounters, in which
Quixote is constantly on the defensive, are different from the staged
encounters in the latter half of the First Part of the novel, for they aim
at the manipulator's amusement rather than Quixote's cure. People
know Don Quixote like a book, and that knowledge is shown to be a
dangerous thing. The barber and the priest are replaced by Sampson
Carrasco as the local force of opposition to Quixote's project, and
Carrasco's motives are clearly suspect. In his first challenge as the
"Knight of the Mirrors" Carrasco claims to have already beaten Don
Quixote in battle and to have usurped his renown. "Since I have
conquered him, his glory, his fame, and his honour are transferred
and have passed to my person," he boasts, prematurely (551). Carrasco's eventual triumph over Quixote in Barcelona as the Knight of
the White Moon (another image of reflected glory) is a matter of
personal vindication rather than an altruistic regard for Quixote's
own well-being.

Thus Don Quixote is defeated not by the forces of reality in the
Second Part but by the power of rival fictions. His return to sanity
coincides with his death, and it is hard to follow those critics who see
his simultaneous disillusionment and demise as the ultimate lesson
about literature that Cervantes was trying to inculcate.[19] Whatever
conclusions one does draw from the Second Part of *Don Quixote* must
necessarily be more melancholy and more complex. They should
center on the loss of control that the literary author experiences when
his printed book enters the public domain, and on the way in which
reading can become a means of asserting control over others instead

of a means of recreating oneself. One might say that in the Second Part of *Don Quixote* Cervantes is most deeply concerned with the political dimensions of the reading of the printed book.

One can see such issues in the new relationship of Don Quixote and Sancho Panza, who now begin to compete with one another in their chivalric roles. The "Sanchification" of Don Quixote and the "Quixotization" of Sancho in the Second Part, observed by Salvador de Madariaga long ago, are simply one form of the pervasive rivalry of literary reputations.[20] The Duke and the Duchess consider Sancho "madder and more entertaining than his master" (677), and by providing him with his long-awaited governorship they insure that he upstages his master through a number of chapters. While Sancho is dispensing the wisdom of Solomon on the "Isle of Barataria," Quixote is left at the castle giving advice and being scratched in the face by cats. More subtly and more importantly, Sancho's own fiction of the enchantment of Dulcinea early in the Second Part robs Quixote of his most vital imaginative resource from the First Part. Sancho pretends to see the peasant girl as a princess in Chapter 10, and Quixote, "very much downcast" (532), must struggle with this disillusioning scenario for the rest of the book.

One can also see Quixote's loss of imaginative authority in the device of Cide Hamete Benengeli and the Moorish translator of the "history." These formerly supporting figures of fictionality now play a subtly derogatory role in the narrative, casting doubt on its authenticity rather than (comically) validating it as they did in the First Part. The translator announces that he thinks the fifth chapter apocryphal because of Sancho's high style and superior wisdom. Cide Hamete openly doubts the reliability of Quixote's adventures in the Cave of Montesinos. "I cannot persuade myself that all that is written in the previous chapter literally happened to the valorous Don Quixote," Cervantes has him write in the margin of the "original" manuscript. "The reason is that all the adventures till how have been feasible and probable, but this one of the cave I can find no way of accepting as true, for it exceeds all reasonable bounds" (624).

In this new imaginative context, the appearance of an actual spurious Second Part, Fernandez de Avellaneda's *Segundo Tomo del Ingenioso Hidalgo Don Quixote de la Mancha*, is a less crucial factor than is sometimes assumed. As E. C. Riley puts it, "one could almost believe that if the spurious sequel had not existed [Cervantes] would have had to invent it."[21] He may have learned of Avellaneda's rival text before he mentioned it in Chapter 59, but in the new vision of literary politics that informs his own Second Part, the appearance of a

competitor is less a threat than a fortuitous validation of his argument. As we have seen in the case of *Guzmán* and *Lazarillo*, Cervantes
seems to mention only the literary rivals who are not the most serious
competitors.[22]

It is the literary imagination in general that is on the defensive in
the Second Part of *Don Quixote*. The most notable qualities of the
fictions that Don Quixote encounters are their thinness and their
fragility. The principle of interpolation in the First Part creates a
textuality that is both elastic and internally spacious; the principle of
usurpation in the Second Part shows the text as brittle and of the
surface. Here the readerly imagination is put in the position of defending old worlds rather than of creating new ones. The loss of the
idealizing power of love, the greater attention to "hunger and continued poverty" (608), to the animal side of human existence, and to
the presence and pressure of death are all distinctive features of the
Second Part of the novel as compared to the First. After the adventure
of the "enchanted bark" in Part Two, where Quixote shows an un-
customary lack of courage, the author concludes: "Don Quixote and
Sancho went back to their beasts, and to their beast-like existence"
(661).

This is not to say that the Second Part of *Don Quixote* is inferior to
the First, rather that it deals more directly with the inferiority of the
literary imagination. As far as Quixote's own character is concerned,
we find a greater depth of awareness in him, an introspective quality
in the midst of his disillusionments. His inner moods and motives
become more important than his external actions. In a number of his
adventures now, as with the enchanted bark but also with the theatrical Parliament of Death or the belligerent braying aldermen, Quixote wisely backs away from physical confrontation, revealing new
qualities of discretion in his valor. In the adventure of the lion he
shows a more desperate kind of bravery, proving himself in existential rather than conventional chivalric fashion. The greater reflective-
ness of the Second Part also appears in the long passages of homiletic
discourse that both Sancho and Quixote fall into, in which they vie
with one another in expressions of wisdom. "When I speak of matters of pith and substance, this master of mine's in the habit of telling
me that I ought to take a pulpit in hand and go about the world
preaching pretty sermons," Sancho complains. "But, as for him, it's
my opinion that once he begins to string sentences and give advice,
it's not only one pulpit he should take in hand, but two on every
finger. . . . The devil take him for a knight errant, so many things he
knows" (609). It is as if the self-consciousness of the author in the

First Part has been internalized by the hero in the Second Part. The extensive play of recreation becomes an intensive struggle of personal doubt.

The new phenomenology of vision and the new skepticism are revealed most starkly in Quixote's descent into the Cave of Montesinos in Chapters 22 and 23. For the first time the reader discovers that he has no check on the truth or falsity of what Quixote has seen, and for the first time Quixote's chivalric scenario is itself infiltrated with melancholy and physical disgust. The vision of Durandarte's heart cut out and preserved in salt and of Belerma's face with "great rings around her eyes" and a "sickly complexion" (619) is a nightmare image of the knight-errant's immortality. There is an uncharacteristic allusion to classical epic in the motif of an underworld descent and a more specific reference to the *Aeneid* in the image of Dulcinea fleeing Quixote like Dido from Aeneas. And there is an unusual scriptural allusion in Quixote's conviction that he has been underground for three days. It is as if Quixote falls back on these more venerable classical and Christian precedents to shore up the sagging authority of his own chivalric romances. It is also as if he retreats to a dream world of his own unconscious in an effort to revive his melancholy fortunes in the world of waking awareness.

In some respects, the Second Part of *Don Quixote* is closer to the ethos of the contemporary picaresque novels than to the ethos of the First Part of the novel. There is more emphasis on emotional deprivation and physical need, on deception for economic gain, on the nastiness and brutishness of the world, and on the brevity of life. Yet in its conservation of the literary facts of life, in its inclusion of alternate examples of the literary text, however ominously or disappointingly these are presented, it remains a distinctly Quixotic counterfiction to the picaresque. Its continued counterpointing of the picaresque mode is nowhere clearer than in the renewed confrontation of Don Quixote with Ginés de Pasamonte, the arch-picaro of Part One who reappears as Master Peter the puppet player.[23]

In his reappearance in the Second Part of the novel, the picaro is significantly disguised as such. In the First Part Ginés was contemptuous of aliases, rejecting "Ginesillo de Parapilla." Here he is so thoroughly disguised as Master Peter that we only learn his identity after the adventure is over, and even then we must credit this revelation on the dubious strength of Cide Hamete's oath "as a Catholic Christian" (646). The old Ginés advertised himself; the new Ginés is a purveyor of fictions about others and dubious ones at that. The puppet show is a device he uses to gather a crowd for his talking ape, who then tells people, for money, the supposed truth about themselves.

In his encounter here with Don Quixote, however, Ginés seems oddly legitimate. He takes no money for the ape's supposed revelations, and he is forced to haggle for the price of his puppets after Quixote has destroyed them. The roles that they played when they met in the First Part, when Ginés was one of the galley slaves, are significantly reversed. Now it is Ginés rather than Don Quixote who is the purveyor of chivalric fiction, both in his puppet presentation of the rescue of Melisendra and in the praise which he has the talking ape lavish on Don Quixote and Sancho Panza. And it is Quixote who is the disrupter of the chivalric scenario. He suspects the ape of being in league with the devil and wonders why he has not been denounced to the Inquisition. He smashes the puppets and the theater to pieces. In the latter instance, Quixote's iconoclasm is supposedly due to a recurrence of his old chivalric madness, yet his attack on Master Peter's fiction is curious for its ferocity, for the blatant inequality of the combat, and for the calm, rational way that Quixote subsequently explains his madness. "I assure you gentlemen that all that has passed here seemed to me a real occurrence. Melisendra was Melisendra; Sir Gaiferos, Sir Gaiferos; and Charlemagne, Charlemagne. Therefore I was stirred to anger" (643). In fact, Quixote had complained earlier of the lack of verisimilitude in Master Peter's performance. His reaction is such that it suggests he is acting out his resentment at the chivalric romances for his recurrent humiliations in their service.

What has happened in this episode, as in many other episodes involving rival fictions in the Second Part of *Don Quixote,* is that the competing mode of the picaresque has been completely drawn into the Quixotic at the same time that Quixote himself has been disenfranchised in his literary project. The rogue is the apologist for imaginative literature; the knight is the delinquent antagonist. Fiction is either deceptive and brutish, as in the talking ape (or in the story of the braying aldermen which frames this episode), or it is fragile and trivial, like the puppet show, which relies heavily on the verbal commentary of Master Peter's young assistant to communicate its message. Quixote's readiness to pay for what he has destroyed only underlines the debasement of the illusion.

Nevertheless, in making the defeat of a fiction divided against itself the theme of the Second Part, Cervantes still manages to keep the memory of literature alive. The reading of books no longer affords a positive means of recreating the world, but literature still asserts an elegiac presence; it is a trace that refuses to disappear. The chapter describing the puppet show begins with a composite quotation from the *Aeneid*—"Here Tyrians and Trojans, all were silent" (638)—an allusion to the beginning of Book Two of the *Aeneid*, which is in turn Virgil's most direct recapitulation of the *Iliad*, when Aeneas tells Dido and the Carthaginians of the fall of Troy. There is of course considerable irony in this novelistic echo of the epic past, but as with the ostensible "parody" of the chivalric romances throughout, *Don Quixote* conserves the experience of literature even as it shows that experience's fundamental incongruity. Literature is not only incongruous with the reader's experience of the contemporary world but is also incongruous with itself. The rudimentary art of the novel here reveals that the permanence of the classic is in the end a readerly illusion.

It is not in its literary self-consciousness per se that *Don Quixote* establishes the novel's claim to literary uniqueness, to be sure. Even in the literary culture of sixteenth- and seventeenth-century England, where the innovation of the novel was furthest from the horizon of literary possibilities, the reflexivity of literature was a widespread phenomenon. Spenser's *Faerie Queene* is a self-consciously archaic and poetic rendition of many of the same chivalric materials that *Don Quixote* treats in self-consciously contemporary and prosaic fashion. Donne's *Songs and Sonets* are elaborately contrived lyric exercises that play with the received conventions and conceits of Petrarchan love poetry. Shakespeare's plays are deeply informed with a theatricality constantly reflecting back upon itself: plays within plays, the world as stage and the stage as world, actors stepping in and out of roles. Milton's *Paradise Lost* incorporates and criticizes the literary succession of epic poetry from Homer onward. Such poetic and dramatic works share with *Don Quixote* its ironic awareness of a disjunction between the literary materials of the past and the performative moment of the present.

What is distinctive about Cervantes's novel, however, and what continued to stimulate later recreators of this new species of writing, is the definition of the performative moment itself. The paradigmatic literary situation in *Don Quixote* is the encounter between an idle reader and a printed book. The self-consciousness of the narrative keeps returning to this radical of presentation and reception, reimaging it and redefining it but never letting its "audience" forget for long the displacement of more immediate kinds of *literary* experience that it entails. The self-consciousness of *Hamlet*, in comparison, is a critical awareness of the theater rather than of the printed text.

Hamlet himself is actor, stage manager, and spectator in his performance, alternately and simultaneously. A fruitful way of understanding his development in the play is to chart the progress of his growing understanding of what it means to "act." From his initial perception of acting as obedience or correct behavior (in response to his
father's memory and ghost), through his notion of acting as deception (with Ophelia), as experiment or test (with "The Mousetrap"),
as passionate reaction (with the stabbing of Polonius and the
graveyard struggle with Laertes), to his final definition of acting as
improvisation in "The readiness is all," the expressive function of
the hero's theatrical performance is the focal point of the play. Hamlet is a character who must defend himself against the external roles
that others would cast him in. He must delay his own definitive
action until he can define his own role—neither in complete subjection to the designs of others nor in complete control himself—in the
play to which he gives his name. He cannot finally read his fate, but
neither will he allow it to be read. His model of performance remains
the *agon* of drama. In this respect his project is the opposite of Don
Quixote's. Hamlet sheds one provisional role after another as he
purifies his acting from fiction. Quixote embraces a ready-made role
at the start and frames all his actions in a recognizable, though unpredictable, fictional form. The difference between these heroes is
symptomatic of the difference between the novel and the drama.

Paradise Lost may serve to distinguish the example of the novel
from the example of poetry. Less obviously reflexive than *Hamlet*,
Paradise Lost nevertheless dramatizes the disjunction between its
numerous literary precedents and its own reenactment of them. The
poet performs the repertoire of classical epic and biblical narrative,
but the performance continually revises and reformulates the inherited motifs. As he invokes the Muse at the beginning of Book I,
Milton repeatedly relocates the dwelling place of his inspiration:

> Or if *Sion* Hill
> Delight thee more, and *Siloa's* Brook that flow'd
> Fast by the Oracle of God; I thence
> Invoke thy aid to my advent'rous Song
> That with no middle flight intends to soar
> Above th' *Aonian* Mount....[24]

This rearrangement of topoi or places is characteristic of the poem.
The Greco-Roman forms are conjured up only to be subordinated to
the Judeo-Christian, and the epic imagination moves from outer,

cosmic spectacle to inner, spiritual audience as the providential plot of things unfolds. Books V and VI, where Raphael relates verbally to Adam the earlier war in heaven, is an important turning point in the evolution of the poem. Here we have an epic narration within the epic narration, the structural equivalent of Cervantes's interpolated tales and of Shakespeare's plays within the play. The angel recounts the supernatural events at one remove, with an important reminder of the insufficiency of human language to express them.

The model of imaginative performance that informs these books and *Paradise Lost* as a whole is a model of the voice. From the opening imperative "Sing Heav'nly Muse" to the final relation of the future course of biblical history by the angel Michael—"Henceforth what is to come I will relate, / Thou therefore give due audience, and attend" (XII, 11–12), the text of *Paradise Lost* imitates the oral presentation and auditory reception of the literary message. It is not a simple recreation of the oral medium of Homer, which Milton of course would not have known in its original oral dimensions in any case. Rather the poem is a literate rendition of an oratorical situation, an oratorical situation deriving both from classical rhetoric and the Puritan sermon, itself the vocal expounding of a biblical text. "Whereas the bardic performance is mythical and traditional, the oratorical performance is ethical and individual. The character of the speaker is carefully manipulated in order to achieve his goal of persuading an audience."[25] Milton addresses not the idle reader but the energetic auditor of his narrative.

Milton was to provide an important example for later poets—at least for English poets of the eighteenth and nineteenth centuries. But the force of the example of *Paradise Lost* was essentially archaizing as far as the growth and expansion of European literary culture was concerned; it provided a source of literary authority that intimidated even as it inspired.[26] One might argue that the fascination of the English romantic poets with *Paradise Lost*, like their fascination with the folk ballad as a lyrical form, was in part a desire to recover for poetry an oratorical authority that it had lost in an increasingly typographic literary culture. The example of *Hamlet* was possibly even more influential, affecting the novel itself as well as poetry and drama. But here as well, the authority of Shakespeare and the more generic and conservative form of the drama often functioned—as, for example, in Goethe's *Wilhelm Meister*—as a reassertion of literary order and stability in an increasingly unstable "novelistic" field of literary possibilities.[27]

In the case of *Don Quixote*, on the other hand, later writers were to find a precedent for the unprecedented, a locus classicus of the typographic dislocation of the literary work and a charter for the innovations of a type of literature that repeatedly declared its independence from literary tradition. Although in the singularity of its example and the breadth of its scope *Don Quixote* was more susceptible to being regarded as an authoritative classic than any of the various picaresque novels was, its example was generally a liberating rather than an imperious one. The Quixotic offered a pretext for exploring the insufficiencies of literature rather than a subtext for asserting literature's power. Along with its still less commanding counterfiction, the picaresque, *Don Quixote* initiated a new kind of literary history—ambiguously historical, suspicious of genealogies and filiations, often even challenging history itself as a basis of knowledge. It is this diachronic afterlife of the Quixotic and the picaresque, the earliest forms of what has come to be known, in English, as "the novel," that the rest of this study will explore.

5

MOLL FLANDERS *and the* Picaresque
The Transvaluation of Virtue

HECTOR. Brother, she is not worth what
she doth cost
The keeping.
TROILUS. What's aught but as 'tis valued?
Shakespeare, *Troilus and Cressida*

The novel first emerged as a significant literary phenomenon in Spain. *Don Quixote* and the Golden Age picaresque novels constituted a popular and self-conscious innovation within Spanish literary culture that rapidly passed beyond that national literature to the rest of Western Europe. As the vitality of the Spanish experiment exhausted itself, it is to countries like France and England that a history of the novel must turn. Through international publication, followed by translation and imitation, the Spanish examples quickly penetrated the literatures of these two emerging nation-states. What is interesting is the different ways in which the Spanish novels were assimilated to the two literary traditions. In France, with the growing authority of its neoclassical literary culture, the Spanish innovations were for the most part absorbed into a canonical system of genres. In England, with the diversity of Elizabethan modes, the antiliterary polemics of Puritanism, and the more belated and tenuous classicizing movement of the Restoration, the Spanish novels were generally relegated to the status of popular, subliterary narrative. The peculiar place of Defoe in the history of the novel needs to be considered in this wider context.[1]

The debates over the status of the *roman* in France were plentiful and complex, and the examples of prose fiction were numerous. There were first of all the *romans héroiques*, by such authors as Mlle de Scudéry and La Calprenède, which closely adhered in theory if not in practice to the rules of the classical genres. Although often taken as representing the "moderns" in the ongoing *Querelle des anciens et des modernes*, these narratives were well within the orbit of neoclassicism, enough for a critic to say of them in 1664, "It will not be thought strange if in this discourse I submit novels to the same rules as epic poems, for they are only distinct by their versification, and have the rest in common."[2] Opposed to these voluminous tales with their historically and geographically exotic settings were the shorter and more realistic *nouvelles* which continued the older Italian and Spanish form of short fiction and prepared the ground for the psychological masterpiece of Madame de Lafayette, *La Princesse de Clèves*. Yet the realism of these more immediate and contemporary narratives was still conceived as fulfilling the neoclassical requirement of *vraisemblance*. "The theorist, whether of the *roman* or the *nouvelle*, bound the novel to the severe limitations of classical aesthetics, which are in precise opposition to the particularizing realism associated with the novel," English Showalter writes.[3]

A third type of novel common in seventeenth-century France, represented by Sorel's *Le Berger extravagant*, Scarron's *Roman comique*, and Furetière's *Roman bourgeois*, is the comic novel. In spite of its frequent parody of the more heroic and sentimental romances, this kind of fiction was also easily contained within the neoclassical theory of genres. The French reception of the Spanish picaresque novel brought the ironic half-outsider back within the literary canon of tradition by treating it as a self-contained comic or low literary form. "A resolutely Aristotelian criticism could not help identifying the prose manner of the picaresque tales as *le style bas*—the language of low comedy in which interesting heroes did not speak. . . . Furetière and Scarron assume a reader of *Le Roman bourgeois* and *Le Roman comique* who joins them in looking down on the fictional characters from a superior height."[4] This reclaiming of the novel by the neoclassical system occurred in the case of *Don Quixote* as well, which was either regarded as a comic and satiric work or was treated as a model for the collection of *nouvelles*.[5] Sorel imitated both the Spanish picaresque and *Don Quixote* in his *Histoire comique de Francion* (1622) and *Le Berger extravagant* (1627) respectively. In his *Bibliothèque françoise* he categorizes the genre—"We speak of comic novels in general, but we also divide them into satiric and burlesque, and some of them are both together"—and mentions the Spanish novels, Apuleius's *The Golden Ass*, and Rabelais's *Gargantua and Pantagruel* as examples along with his own and his contemporaries' works.[6] As we shall see in the next chapter, a growing body of seventeenth-century French criticism began to value *Don Quixote* as a classic text of the *modernes*, but it was only in the eighteenth century, with Lesage, Marivaux, and the less well-known Robert Challe that the Spanish exemplars of the novel were really freed from the matrix of neoclassicism, a conception of literature they had originally stood over against.[7]

In seventeenth-century England, on the other hand, both *Don Quixote* and the Spanish picaresque were received into a popular literary substratum, a literary culture that was scattered and fragmentary and had no particular designs upon higher or more classical literary tradition. The corpus of prose romances, more amenable to neoclassical regulation, was itself small in England as compared with the chivalric romances in the previous century in Spain or the heroic romances in the same period in France.[8] And while there were a number of English translations of the Spanish novels, the imitations and the critical comments show that the literary innovation and critique of canonical forms were not at all recognized. The picaresque novels were generally treated as more comic versions of the popular criminal biographies or as more circumstantial versions of the Elizabethan jest-books and cony-catching pamphlets. The few overt imitations of the picaresque, such as Head and Kirkman's *The English Rogue* (1665–71), were moralized beyond recognition. *Don Quixote* was imitated only in poetic or dramatic form in England in the course of the century, never in prose, and, as Edwin Knowles has shown, the overwhelming English impression of Cervantes's novel until well into the eighteenth century was of a work of crude burlesque.[9] The only surviving piece of seventeenth-century English criticism devoted to Cervantes's masterpiece, Edmund Gayton's *Pleasant Notes Upon Don Quixot* (1654), treats the text largely as an occasion for the critic's own facetious banter and regards the hero, in a manner that anticipates Butler's *Hudibras,* as a knave and a fanatic.

By the time Defoe began to reinvent the novel in the eighteenth century, the disposition of English literary culture toward prose fiction had begun to change. There was a growing awareness of the French *romans* and *nouvelles* and there was a neoclassical movement of growing prestige in the writing of authors like Dryden, Swift, and Pope. Defoe's relationship to both these developments is still a matter of speculation, but there is enough evidence to suggest that a novel like *Moll Flanders* should not be considered in isolation from the cultural debate, finally making its appearance in England, over the value of new types of imaginative writing as opposed to the classically sanctioned literary forms. Defoe's education at Charles Morton's academy for Dissenters at Newington Green may have given him a less solid grounding in the classics than his contemporaries had who attended university, but the evidence of his allusions to literature and the sale catalogue of his library show that he was widely read in literary as well as historical and economic works.[10] He probably knew several modern languages, possibly Spanish among them,[11] and during his early success as a London merchant he had, as Sutherland puts it, "ambitions to be classed among the 'polite' writers in the neo-classical mode."[12] With the publication of his long-winded, unreadable, and relatively unpopular satire *Jure Divino* in 1706, Defoe's Augustan aspirations came to an end, and he devoted himself to journalistic and polemical kinds of writing. Yet in his poem "To the Athenian Society" and his satire *The Pacificator*, his literary aspirations in the 1690s show surprising parallels with those of Swift, which may account for the indignation of Defoe's reply to Swift's condescending dismissal of him a decade later, when their careers had notably diverged. As a satirist Swift became a strong defender of the ancients against the moderns. As a novelist, Defoe became an exemplar of the modernity which turned away from classically sanctioned forms. But the fact that they were both at one time contributors to the same literary subculture, and that Defoe continued to respect Swift's learning ("an orator in Latin; a walking index of books; he has all the libraries of Europe in his head")[13] suggests that the Augustan Age and the rebirth of the novel in eighteenth-century England have more in common than is usually recognized.[14]

Both the Augustan restriction of the literary canon and the novelistic departures from it, I would argue, were responses to the continuing questions of Renaissance Europe over the value and the validity of imaginative writing in general. I would go further and claim that it was only with the development of a significant neoclassicism in England that the novel became conceivable as such—as a sophisticated prose narrative defining itself in opposition to authoritative literary norms. As in Spain more than a century earlier and as in France at roughly the same time, though proceeding from the opposite direction, the novel developed most rapidly and creatively in England when the forces of classical tradition and the forces of popular innovation were brought into competition with one another in the same literary field. This is not to say that *Moll Flanders* is an explicit critique of classical literary form—any more than *Gulliver's Travels* is an explicit vindication of it. But it is to say that Defoe's recreation of the novel is not as innocent of literary precedent, positive and negative, as it is often taken to be. The assumption has often been made from the subject matter and the lack of overt literary allusion in Defoe's fiction that his readership, both ideal and actual, would be limited to the lower middle and upper servant classes, relatively restricted in their awareness of the larger literary field. But recent scholarship has challenged this assumption. Where printed materials are concerned, the boundaries of class are most easily crossed. As Maximillian Novak puts it, "Some attempt has been made to describe certain works as 'popular fiction' as opposed to fiction for an elite audience, but such a distinction, unless carefully defined, does not hold up under close analysis. *A Tale of a Tub* and *Robinson Crusoe* are cases in point."[15]

The horizon of expectations around a novel like *Moll Flanders*, to use H. R. Jauss's phrase, must therefore be widened, at least provisionally, to consider more of the available literary culture of Defoe's time. As far as our history of the novel is concerned, this broader view would include two kinds of novelistic models that *Moll Flanders* engages, obliquely but significantly, in its self-definition as a narrative. One of these models is the idealizing romance of the higher levels of culture that had been developed in France and was now being produced in England on a somewhat more popular level. The other model was the Spanish picaresque novel that had been received in England as a popular comic tale and combined with the more serious criminal confessions and biographies. It is between these two polarities of prose fiction as Defoe and his readers knew it that *Moll Flanders* situates itself.

Defoe's allusions to these other novelistic models are elusive, to be sure, which is why critics continue to speak of his "nearly pure and certainly naive mimesis."[16] But there is a growing recognition among critics of the way in which the circumstantial realism of a novel like *Moll Flanders* is filtered through the typical patterns of romance: the childhood abandonment, the quest, the ordeal, the perilous—or scandalous—erotic encounter, the surprising revelation of identity.[17] No specific genre of romance is entailed—the situations recall everything from the Greek romances to the recently popular *chroniques scandaleuses*—but these subliminally idealizing formulas hover in the background of Moll's adventures and achievements.

Yet while she draws power from these precoded heroic situations, Moll also resists and frustrates their conventional resolution. Martin Price notes particularly Defoe's "parodies of tragic situations" in *Moll Flanders*, as in the pragmatic response she makes to the discovery that one of her marriages is incestuous.[18] Defoe invokes romantic formulas only to evade them, as when Moll mentions her early orphanhood among the gypsies but is "not able to be particular in that Account" when questioned about it (9).[19] The episode of

Moll's seduction and marriage in the Colchester household holds up two romantic stereotypes for critical scrutiny. The older brother who seduces her is a typical Restoration rake, but Moll undercuts his erotic mastery by noting the superfluous ingenuity of it all. The younger brother who marries her is the more sentimental type of the "conscious lover," and Moll finds his romantic attitude even more inappropriate to the realities of their relationship. As Price observes, Defoe characteristically "robs life of its climactic structure,"[20] and this may be seen as a deliberate strategy for breaking down the forms of closure most typical of romance narrative. After her seduction Moll bewails her loss of innocence: "and thus I finish'd my own Destruction at once, for from this Day, being forsaken of my Vertue, and my Modesty, I had nothing of Value left to recommend me, either to God's Blessing, or Man's Assistance" (29). Yet her fortunes revive in the very next sentence: "But things did not End here."

The relationship of *Moll Flanders* to the picaresque novel involves a similar transvaluation of literary values, though Defoe's use of the narrative formulas in this case is still more oblique and complex. The critical consensus has been that *Moll Flanders* cannot legitimately be considered as a picaresque novel on the Spanish model. "It would seem, then, more misleading than instructive to call *Moll Flanders* a picaresque novel" Robert Alter writes; "It derives from the English criminal biography, not from the line of *Lazarillo*."[21] There are two misunderstandings in this view, however. The first is to assume that a novel must follow the rules of a prior example without significantly transforming them. The second is to assume that the line of the criminal biography in England was separate and distinct from the line of the picaresque—of which, as Alexander Parker is quick to point out, *Lazarillo* itself is hardly the definitive example.[22] The evidence points rather to the wide popularity of a composite "literature of roguery," to use Chandler's phrase, which freely mixed a comically debased form of the Spanish picaresque with a melodramatic elaboration of the early seventeenth-century criminal biography. The extended title of *Moll Flanders* would certainly arouse the expectations of contemporary readers that the book was written according to the formulas of this popular and generally loosely organized mode. The fact that Defoe gives this mode a surprisingly different character, both more serious and more ironic, is only an indication of his powers as a novelist. At the same time that *Moll Flanders* devalues the literary conventions of romance, then—explicitly, implicitly, and by conspicuously ignoring them—it revalues a contrasting form, the picaresque, which in translation had

fallen into disrepute. As the relationship of *Moll Flanders* to the picaresque novel is an important aspect of our exemplary history, I shall
describe this latter revaluation in greater detail.

As the Spanish picaresque novel was received in England—
indeed, even as it was continued in Spain in the seventeenth
century—the paradoxical alliance of secular lowliness and high religious ideals effectively broke down. The lowliness of experience was
presented in a more traditionally comic or satiric mode, while the
religious spirit displayed itself in the moralistic condemnation of the
rogue as a criminal. This breakdown of the novelistic synthesis in the
best of the Spanish picaresque was facilitated in England by the presence of other literary genres for dealing with the life of the half-
outsider, genres more purely popular in their isolation from the
forms and themes of the classical tradition. Although the earlier
jest-books, cony-catching pamphlets, and satirical "characters" may
have contributed to the sense of the Spanish picaresque as essentially
comic (many English commentators refer to it, not inappropriately,
as the picaresque *tale*), it was the criminal biographies which helped
divide the genre into its entertaining and its edifying sides. Unlike
the picaro (who as Ginés de Pasamonte observed, can never finish his
story because he goes on living), the criminal tells his tale, or has it
told of him, from the perspective of his punishment, usually of his
imminent death. This confrontation with death leads necessarily to
an increase in seriousness and the passing of moral and religious
judgment on the central character. The stratagems of the criminal are
more vicious than those of the picaresque rogue; there is less clever-
ness, more violence, and more vice. Also, because of the ostensibly
historical nature of the criminal biography (although many were in
fact apocryphal, in whole or in part) there is less concern with the
development of coherent episodes, and a tendency, as Novak notes
of *The English Rogue,* to rush rapidly from one adventure to another
with little development of character or scene.[23]

The comic picaresque is exemplified by John Stevens's translation
of Ubeda's *Picara Justina,* published in 1707 in a drastically reduced
and streamlined version in *The Spanish Libertines.* The original was,
as I noted in an earlier chapter, a baroque and burlesque parody of
the picaresque novel, full of sophisticated literary and linguistic
games. Stevens notes that his version is "an Extract of all that is
Diverting and Good in the Original, which is swell'd up with so
much Cant and Reflection, as really renders it tedious and unpleasant," a procedure of simplification that Lesage also followed in
his translations from the Spanish.[24] The result is a tightly knit series

of episodes, narrated in the first person by the heroine in an ironically polite style: "he show'd him his Fist in such an undecent manner, as made the Fore-Teeth he had left drop out with Fright, and so his Gums were left quite destitute of Company."[25] This is a tone which Defoe was capable of assuming, as in his *Street-Robberies Consider'd* (1728),[26] but which he carefully avoids in *Moll Flanders*. Indeed, the avoidance of irony, the avoidance of such a condescendingly figurative language that was quite common in these latter-day picaresques, is a key to Defoe's transformation of the genre. Moll often falls into a polite style, but periodically punctures it with a cruder, more literal definition: "for 'tis scarce credible what Practice she had, as well Abroad as at Home, and yet all upon the private Account, or in plain *English*, the whoring Account" (169). She refuses to assume a conventional picaresque voice for her narrative.

Justina is much less single-minded than Moll in her tricks and deceptions. Some of them are motivated by self-defense, as when she avoids being raped by a band of traveling scholars, but others are motivated by revenge. Thus she tricks a man into exchanging his gold watch for a piece of cheap jewelry not so much for the value of the object as to gain revenge for an earlier insult. Seen against this background, Moll's concern with replenishing her stock emerges as a more sensible goal. Some of Justina's deceptions are purely antic, as in her smearing of a fat hostess of an inn with bacon grease and honey. "As soon as I spy'd this Figure," she says, "I began to contrive what Trick I might put upon her."[27] It is not that Moll Flanders lacks a sense of humor but that she disciplines her energies in the interests of survival. Justina lives in the security and freedom of the comic, where danger never threatens. Only at the end of her career does she consider marriage and when she does marry she enters a relationship where her picaresque talents will presumably lie fallow. We are left to assume that in true comic fashion she will live happily ever after.

It is not necessary to claim that Defoe read this particular picaresque novel. (Though he may well have; a copy of the original Spanish text is listed in the sale catalogue of his and Phillips Farewell's library.) Rather one may use the novel to point out some of the codes or sets of literary expectations that Defoe might expect contemporary readers to bring to *Moll Flanders*, codes and expectations that modern readers need to recover to appreciate the thrust of Defoe's reformulations. In a similar way, one can use a criminal biography like Francis Kirkman's *The Counterfeit Lady Unveiled* to show how Defoe reworks some of the formulas of this related genre.

The Counterfeit Lady Unveiled shows an interesting use of the comic picaresque in its latter half, where the narrative becomes noticeably livelier, the character more consistent, and the scenes more dramatically structured. The narrative formulas of the criminal biography proper are used with less confidence. Thus after describing the heroine's rather successful gulling of an old man who keeps her as his mistress, the narrator inserts the obligatory moralizing in an awkward, ex post facto fashion: "And now I have related this story of her, is she not a base, ungrateful woman thus to leave a man who so handsomely provided for her?"[28] What Defoe does is put this kind of moralizing in the mouth of Moll herself, which has led many critics to accuse either the author or the heroine of hypocrisy. But, in the context of the criminal literature of the period, Moll's self-critical remarks are better seen as an internalization of an often artificially external point of view. Moll's penitential reflections offend against a twentieth-century ethic that values consistency to a personal standard more highly than submission to an external norm, but they show a dramatic change in the way the criminal was conventionally presented in literature in Defoe's own time.

The first-person narrative of *Moll Flanders* does not go so far as to become a spiritual autobiography. This related Puritan genre has been shown to be a significant determinant of Defoe's writing,[29] but, like the patterns of romance, the idealizing paradigm of God's providence in an individual life is something that Moll's life story flirts with but easily evades. In spite of Moll's conversion in Newgate, the Preface acknowledges what most readers have felt about the older narrator, that she "was not so extraordinary a Penitent, as she was at first" (5). Again, it is against the formulas of the criminal biography that Defoe's novelistic achievement is most clearly revealed. Where Defoe deftly incorporates the moralizing commentator into Moll's own complex personality and suppresses the comic overtones of her deceptions of other people, Kirkman works more awkwardly as he brings Mary Carleton to her final repentance. He recounts a story of a merry prank she is supposed to have carried out while actually in prison, but then rejects it as inconsistent with her penitential role. "This is a story that I have heard of her . . . but I cannot believe it and am confident no such thing was done at Newgate; she was not in so merry a mood; for after her trial, to her sentence, she was another creature."[30]

Defoe was capable of making other variations on this moralistic theme. In his pseudo-autobiographical narrative "John Sheppard's Own Story," for example, he has Sheppard judge himself with a most unusual dignity and detachment. "A clear and ample account have I now given of the most material transactions of my life," Sheppard writes, "and do hope the same will prove a warning to all young men." He goes on to thank various reverends for their ministrations to him, to ask mercy for his "Poor distressed mother," and to ask God to pardon his soul. The sensationalism of the genre, its excesses of violence, condemnation, and repentance, are severely, almost comically chastened.[31] It is worth noting that all of Defoe's ventures into the genre of criminal biography proper—his longer accounts of Sheppard and Jonathan Wild, his various letters purporting to be from criminals or their admirers—were composed after he wrote *Moll Flanders*. His fictitious letter to *Applebee's Weekly Journal* from "Betty Blewskin" cites Moll Flanders as a precedent and makes several self-conscious jibes at more canonical, moral literature: "I rarely came emptyhanded from the *Theatre*, especially if the play was anything Popular: I assure you, *Cato* was worth 100 Guineas to me...."[32]

The other feature of seventeenth-century criminal biography that Defoe uses creatively in *Moll Flanders* is the fiction of historical accuracy. This is not the *vraisemblance* of neoclassical literary theory, but a more naive journalistic appeal to the actual event and a more pragmatic concern with putting down one's competitors. In fact, many criminal biographies are full of unsubstantiated rumor and outright plagiarism from other sources, but the rules of the form demand a serious claim of factuality, often supported by an appeal to legal documents and the machinery of the courts. This feature of criminal biographies is certainly one literary precedent for Defoe's insistence on authenticity in *Moll Flanders*—an insistence which is not nearly so marked, for example, in his subsequent novel *Colonel Jack*. Moll, of course, manages to use the authenticating apparatus of the law to her own advantage, as a means of preserving her anonymity even as it supposedly validates her existence. "My True Name is so well known in the Records, or Registers at *Newgate*, and in the *Old-Baily*, and there are some things of such Consequence still depending there, relating to my particular Conduct, that it is not to be expected I should set my Name, or the account of my Family to this Work" (7). As the modern version of this formula goes, the names are changed to protect the innocent—although questions of guilt and innocence are more complicated in Defoe.

Again, *The Counterfeit Lady Unveiled* provides an interesting illustration of this rule, interesting in its awkward inconsistency. Kirkman is at great pains to reproduce Mary Carleton's own published narrative but makes very little of the fact that her legal self-vindication and written *Case* are completely false. The will to convince others of the truth of one's own lies is at the heart of Defoe's imagination, but in Kirkman the narrative contretemps is never developed. When he comes to deal with Mary's behavior after her capture and sentencing, the author introduces himself into the story as witness: "And I, being near her, told her it was a great work she had to do and that yet she had time to repent of all her ill deeds to a merciful God, who refused none that came with a true repenting heart. She replied 'The Lord grant me true repentance'... and truly I believe she was truly sorrowful."[33] Here the legal witness becomes a religious witness, and the reiteration of "true" and "truly" seeks to validate this all-important character change. As we shall see in more detail, Defoe has Moll take the law into her own hands. She uses the authority of both civil law and religious doctrine to reinforce and authenticate her "life."

The Spanish picaresque novel had been reabsorbed into a complex of formulas for representing the experience of the delinquent, a complex which combined low comic modes with high religious ones. It is to this literature of roguery that *Moll Flanders* most directly alludes, at the same time that it effects a thoroughgoing transformation in the value of the subliterary material. In Defoe's hands it is no longer a socially inferior form of polite literature, nor is it a sensational subject matter in the service of a pious moral. It is true that the insubordinate nature of *Moll Flanders*, its opposition to the forms and themes of Augustan neoclassical literature, is more implicit than in the case of the Spanish picaresque novels I have earlier considered. It is also true that some of the staunchest defenders of the neoclassical mode, like Swift, wrote in forms that Aristotle and Horace never imagined. But as in *Lazarillo* and *Guzmán*, the preoccupation in *Moll Flanders* with the value of a self excluded from the validating forms of cultural discourse leads beyond the received traditions of literature, both in ideology and technique.

Defoe does occasionally echo Puritan attacks on classical literature, as when he speaks contemptuously of the *Iliad* as the story of the rescue of a whore.[34] But his achievement as a novelist is less to criticize than to ignore the strictures and sanctions of neoclassical poetics and insist on alternative values best represented in the popular literature of criminals and rogues. The ignoring is not a function of ignorance on Defoe's part; his novels emerge as something new only in the broader context of early eighteenth-century English letters. As a novelist, Defoe takes for granted the loss of influence of classical literary learning that Swift as a satirist deplores. Like earlier satire, the satirical writing of the Augustans depends on a strong presumption of normative cultural value, against which the aberrations of "modern authors" can be measured and condemned. Swift identifies value with a civilization that exists preeminently in the past, that has been sublimated, in its historical decline and fall, into literary artifact and precept. Defoe, on the other hand, is concerned not with the structures and fixities of civilization but with what Henry James was to call "the terrible fluidity of self-revelation," the moral and aesthetic dilemma of the self whose civilization of supporting values has collapsed. Defoe's novels are notorious for their failure to realize the classical trope of irony. They locate value instead in a metonymy of alternative structures that characters build up as a means of survival. In Swift, value is *sub*stantial; it exists as an ethical ground for aesthetic structure. In Defoe value is inevitably transactional; a loss in one system of values seeks out compensation in another system. Value must be recreated by aesthetic structures against a background of ethical ruin.

There are clear sources in Defoe's own experience for his lack of confidence in the literary humanist imagination as a conservator of value. One source is the intellectual heritage of English Puritanism, in which he was formally educated, with its emphasis on the insecurity of all human achievement and endeavor. "Indeed what is our whole life, but a continued deliverance?" one Puritan journalist wrote. "We are daily delivered, either from the violence of the creature, or the rage of men, or the treachery of our own hearts; either our houses are freed from firing, or goods from plundering, or our bodies from danger, or our names from reproaches or our souls from snares."[35] Literature is not simply evil, but in its celebration of various forms of human self-sufficiency it can be a temptation to false security. Defoe was not consistently critical of any type of secular literature,[36] but the deeper sense of threat to human values which informs his writings certainly derives in part from the Puritan literary temper. On the other hand, in the more widespread area of his thinking about economics and mercantile value, his two experiences of bankruptcy clearly underlie his concern with economic security. The collapse of his financial credit not only led to severe legal sanctions, from which he was never entirely to escape, but also had the effect of cutting him off from the society of polite men of letters, for whom the pursuit of literary excellence was supposed to be independent of economic considerations, although as W. B. Coley has argued, this pursuit actually involved a series of "serious games . . . with the system, with its aristocratic representatives, and with its Rules."[37] Defoe continued to play the game of Augustan politics, but as far as Augustan literature was concerned, he abandoned the field.

From the perspective of the humanistic neoclassical culture, Defoe's literary alliance of religiosity and trade is inconsistent and hypocritical, but in terms of an evolving Puritan structure of thought about religion and trade—and in terms of a reemerging dialectic of the novel—the neoclassical view is itself partial and presumptive.[38] As I am finally concerned in this study with the novel in its particularity, I must turn to the text of *Moll Flanders* to see how this general literary problem of value is articulated.

One of the strongest objections to Defoe's art from the first has been not that moral notions are lacking in it but that these notions are not made an integral part of his narratives, that they are somehow added on from the outside. Thus Charles Gildon complained in 1719 in the postscript to his attack on *Robinson Crusoe*, "You seem not to understand the very Nature of a Fable, which is a sort of Writing which has always been esteem'd by the wisest and best of Men to be of great use to the Instruction of Mankind; but then this use and Instruction should naturally and plainly arise from the Fable itself, in an evident and useful Moral, either exprest or understood."[39] Mark Schorer voices much the same objection in "Technique as Discovery": "Because he had no adequate resources of technique to separate himself from his material, thereby to discover and to define the meanings of his material, his contribution is not to fiction but to the history of fiction, and to social history."[40] Ralph Rader suggests, in a more shrewdly Aristotelian vein, that Defoe, in his lack of concern with a morally structured plot, should not be considered as a novelist at all.[41]

There is ample evidence for these charges in the Preface of *Moll Flanders* alone. But even in the Preface, one can see the locus of the value attributed to the novel undergoing a significant shift. At first value is assigned to the story itself, in that it is historical truth rather than literary fiction, a "private History" as distinct from "Novels and Romances." But the ground shifts as Defoe allows that he has put the heroine's original narrative "into new Words," that he has gone to considerable trouble as an author himself to "wrap it up so clean, as not to give room, especially for vitious Readers, to turn it to his Disadvantage." An important distinction is implied here between historical content and literary form. The original narrative is in effect denied its intrinsic value ("the whole relation is carefully garbl'd of all the Levity, and Looseness that was in it," Defoe goes on to say) and the locus of its merit shifts to the decorum of the retelling.

Moral value does not remain secure in this notion of formal style, however, for as the defense progresses the emphasis shifts to the role of the reader, no longer seen as an antagonist ("vitious Readers") but as an ally. "But as this Work is chiefly recommended to those who know how to Read it, and how to make the good Uses of it, which the Story all along recommends to them; so it is hop'd that such Readers will be much more pleas'd with the Moral than with the Fable; with the Application, than with the Relation. . . ." Moral and fable are now quite separate, and in the term "application," a crucial term in Defoe's protean aesthetic, the concept of literary value is presented in increasingly extrinsic and pragmatic terms. The reader can draw religious inferences from the narrative "if he pleases to make use of it"; the choice is now up to him. Finally, the argument shifts to a more practical and more extrinsic kind of lesson: "All the Exploits of this Lady of Fame, in her Depredations upon Mankind stand as so many warnings to honest People to beware of them." The value of the story now seems to be in the reader's learning how not to be robbed.

Most of these defenses of the tale are quite conventional and each one tends to contradict the others as a critical principle. Defoe offers neither originality nor consistency in this Preface; rather he offers an etiology of the idea of literary value, where value changes from intrinsic to extrinsic. The discussion moves the idea of worth from content through form to audience response and on to the audience's own possessions. Defoe's final position—that people can learn practical safety measures from literary narratives—is no more illogical than the earlier position—that excellence of literary style can redeem an obnoxious subject. Nor is the overall structure of the argument itself illogical, as no single system of value is given preeminence. There is a priority given instead to the idea of a life behind the narrative, an original of the book that can be referred to a number of different standards of value for judgment. What is especially interesting is the way the Preface ends with this original itself being subject to division. We learn of two other "Parts still behind" Moll's own life, "whole Volumes of themselves"—the life of her governess and the life of her transported husband, the highwayman. What is still more interesting is that Defoe refers to these stories as "two of the most beautiful Parts" of Moll's life. In this fragmentation we seem to leave the preoccupation with moral and practical value behind altogether and move into a realm of aesthetic delight. This new criterion of judgment seems to be reflected back on Moll's narrative when we find the author/editor now referring to the "elegancy" of Moll's original narrative, a quality it had hardly been allowed at the start. In effect, Defoe's Preface moves the concept of value through a number of different axiological frames, from the ethical to the aesthetic. Instead of being structurally identical, as in neo-Aristotelian theory, the profit and the pleasure of the tale are arranged in a series of stages which devolve from intrinsic to extrinsic. Pleasure only emerges as the last of the frames of reference for the notion of worth.

It is this procession through different systems of value, I will argue, that informs *Moll Flanders* as a whole, a procession which rearranges a hierarchical structure of values into a narrative sequence. This is the protocol of Defoe's novel, the specific code that governs its inner structure as well as its stance toward the literary tradition. Moll's career is neither a harlot's nor a pilgrim's progress, although it does use structural elements of both biographical models. Rather it is a search for ethical place in a world where ethics have become multiple and pragmatic, a search in which the origins of the heroine are too obscure for her to occupy any ethical place with security. Defoe is by no means contemptuous or even subversive of moral values, but he conceives of character at a pre-ethical level. In a sense, Moll's career is a devolution of value, but it so successfully problematizes the universalist assumptions of ethics that it emerges as a critique of the very notion of moral absolutes.

The stages along Moll's way can be seen at different levels of narrative organization, on the level of sentence in some instances, on the level of episode, and on the level of plot. Most locally, for example, there is Moll's description of her seduction by the elder brother of the Colchester household:

> My Colour came, and went, at the Sight of the Purse, and with the fire of his Proposal together; so that I could not say a Word, and he easily preceiv'd it; so putting the Purse into my Bosom I made no more Resistance to him, but let him do just what he pleas'd; and as often as he pleased; and thus I finish'd my own Destruction at once, for from this Day, being forsaken of my Vertue, and my Modesty, I had nothing of Value left to recommend me, either to God's Blessing, or Man's Assistance (29).

The essence of Defoe's syntax is its parataxis; the basic unit is the clause, and there is relatively little suspension or subordination in the sentence structure. The first clause is quite self-incriminating in that Moll responds initially to the purse (whether to the contents or the exterior is not clear), but the succeeding clause—"and with the fire of his Proposal together"—introduces a somewhat different frame of reference. The qualification "together" has the effect of cancelling some of the superficiality or venality of the purse being put in the initial position. The following clause further deepens our sense of Moll's reaction; she is robbed of her power of speech, and the fact that the elder brother "easily" perceives it casts her as the victim of his designs. The causal "so" and the reference of the participial phrase "putting the Purse into my Bosom" to Moll rather than the brother come as something of a surprise; we suddenly see Moll as a more active agent, accepting payment and delivering services. The diction suggests no longer the shy maiden but the brisk tradesman; "just what he pleas'd; and as often as he pleas'd" is not a coy euphemism but what Defoe calls elsewhere "the language of trade."[42] But this is quickly succeeded by another frame of reference that both Moll and her creator recognize, the language of morality: "and thus I finish'd my own Destruction at once." She begins with a standard of judgment by which she is rendered valueless—not only is the occasion her "Destruction" but she is an active agent in bringing it to completion—but the ethical frame shifts thereafter as the sentence moves into the next clause and the abruptness of the judgment begins to be extenuated. "At once" yields to "from this Day" and the active "I finished" becomes a passive "forsaken of"; her "Vertue" becomes substantive and independent, and is partially transformed by the introduction of another, less intrinsic quality, "my Modesty." Both these qualities are translated into a third term, still more extrinsic—"Value"—which is then presented in terms of its visible appeal to an audience: "nothing of Value left to recommend me." The undermining of the purely moral judgment is completed by the dual reference to a transcendent "God's Blessing" on the one hand and a highly practical "Man's Assistance" on the other. As she implicitly refers her case to this double audience, she effectively moves it beyond the jurisdiction of the general ethical judgment of mankind. This prepares the way for her to continue— "But things did not End here."

Each clause in the sentence provides a kind of closure and imparts a definite judgment of value. But no closure of judgment is final; value can only be fixed temporarily. One can see this instability of value on a semantic level as well, in the problems Moll encounters with the referential ambiguities of language. She seizes on the term "gentlewoman" offered ironically by her first protector, her old nurse, as a means of fixing her identity. She uses it to refer to a life of industry and independence, but we see that it can mean both more and less. On the one hand, it can describe a member of the middle class, as in the Colchester family, whose members are attracted by Moll's innocent assumption of the title; on the other hand, in the particular example Moll selects, it can refer to a woman of ill-fame with two bastards.

If we move from the structure of style to the structure of episode in Defoe's narrative, we can see the same general pattern of value exchanged. Moll's involvement with the Colchester family, for example, is organized around the question of her worth within the family, in terms of the complex of rules that make up its middle-class code. Moll's place in the family is ambiguous from the start, institutionalizing the ambiguity of the term "gentlewoman" she seized on as a younger child. As Defoe knew from his own experience, middle-class gentility was an unstable commodity in eighteenth-century England.[43] Moll is not an adopted member of the family either formally or practically, but she is not a member of the servant class either. She acquires the accomplishments of the well-to-do middle-class woman—music, dancing, and French—picking up the education given to the daughters, and even claims the "advantage" of them in her physical attributes. But her description of herself at this early stage shows a good deal of uncertainty about her intrinsic worth. She defines her character as reputation: "I not only had the Reputation of living in a very good Family, and a Family Noted and Respected every where, for Vertue and Sobriety, and for every valluable Thing; but I had the Character too of a very sober, modest and vertuous young Woman." "And," Moll adds, showing how externalized her notion of character is, "such I had always been" (19).

When the elder brother begins to show interest in Moll, the lack of definition of her "value" becomes a problem—not the ambiguity itself so much as the fact that Moll is unable to reflect upon it. As an older woman, she judges herself harshly, but she criticizes the elder brother as well for failing to realize how easily he might have had her. She is concerned less with her own integrity, according to a single norm, than with the possibilities and problems of exchange. Her fascination with the gold he gives her, like her fascination with the purse in the passage quoted above, is not crass commercialism but a fetishism of capital, of which the older Moll is quite scornful: "as for the Gold, I spent whole Hours in looking upon it; I told the Guineas over and over a thousand times a Day. Never poor vain

Creature was so wrapt up with every part of the Story, as I was, not Considering what was before me, and how near my Ruin was at the Door" (25).

Luckily for Moll, the older brother's overelaboration of the seduction leads him into a verbal contract with her; he promises he will marry her after he comes into his estate. This is one of many contractual agreements in Moll's life, all of which have a curiously binding force in a world of such apparent immorality. A contract is a crucial instrument in the transformation of intrinsic into extrinsic value, and Moll will subsequently learn to use such instruments to her advantage. But in the case of this contract, as one critic has put it, Moll has neglected to read the fine print.[44] When she tries to hold the older brother to his promise, he insists on a strict interpretation of the clause, "when he was come to his Estate." "I could not deny a Word of this," Moll confesses (38). After much forensic argument on both sides, and after an illness which is both symptomatic and symbolic of her change of social identity, she enters into marriage with the younger brother, Robin.

This new role gives Moll a different conception of value. On the one hand she has lost both substance and potential as a member of the middle-class household. Her romantic attachment to the older brother was profound enough to allow no transfer of her affections, and even obliges her to judge herself by strict New Testament standards: "In short, I committed Adultery and Incest with him every Day in my Desires, which without doubt, was as effectually Criminal" (59). On the other hand, she has gained a more legally defined worth as wife, and a more measurable economic value, which can be expressed in pounds sterling. Defoe neither sentimentalizes what has been sacrificed nor satirizes what has been gained. We are given little latitude in our own assessment of Moll's fortunes and misfortunes simply because Moll is so persistent and so various an evaluator of them herself. Her value within the context of the Colchester family finally collapses, but her value as a wife and a widow launches her into a new sphere.

In each of the major episodes of *Moll Flanders* there is a similar progression from the ambiguously intrinsic to the specifically extrinsic. Thus her second marriage to the gentleman-tradesman involves her with an "amphibious creature" and her money is squandered in a conspicuous consumption out of scale with the trade upon which it uttimately depends. She is left "upon casting things up" with a mixture of capital and commodities, and must change her name—give herself a surname, as far as her narrative is concerned—in order to free herself from the bonds of marriage. With each succeeding episode, Moll's "character" and the value she assigns it become more and more dependent upon externals for definition, and the contracts she draws up to define the limits of her obligations become more and more concrete. Her marriage to the Virginia planter is preceded by a contest in verse which is in effect a written contract absolving her from accountability for a nonexistent fortune. When she breaks the news of her limited resources to her new husband, she produces what she does have piecemeal as a means of increasing his estimate of its worth. "I had brought him so near to expecting nothing, by what I had said before, that the Money, tho' the sum was small in its self, was doubly welcome" (83). They then move to Virginia, where the extrinsic value of their income, that is, its purchasing power, will be increased. When the totally unforeseen disaster of her husband being her brother comes to light, Moll faces the problem not in tragic recognition of a catastrophe but with a written contract. "So I ran in and fetch'd Pen, Ink, and Paper, and he wrote the Condition down in the very words I had proposed it, and sign'd it with his Name" (102). Later on, with her fourth and fifth husbands, we find Moll having two contracts at once; when the marriage to her Lancashire husband goes bust she can fall back on the written agreement with her financial advisor, the bank clerk—though not before the arrangements with her "Mother Midnight," where Moll presents three itemized bills, detailing services provided and the cost in pounds, shillings, and pence. This famous list, which through Franklin becomes an important form in American literature, is only the most explicit of the many contractual agreements that Moll is involved in in the book.

I do not mean to imply that the plot of *Moll Flanders* is an orderly or coherent unfolding of events. Since the canons of valuation are constantly devolving, there is no plot at all in the Aristotelian sense, and, as noted before, there is a deliberate avoidance of rhetorical or dramatic closure in Defoe's narrative method. There is recurrent suspense, but nothing of the quality of the well-made play that Congreve, for example, felt it necessary to import from the drama[45] and that Fielding was later to bring, in his more self-conscious way, to the novel. What I am describing is rather a deep plot, a structure of argument in Defoe's novel, with a logic and a formalism of its own. The code of the contract, with its related rules of inventory, specification ("VIZ"), and exclusion of the metaphorical dimension of language, provides the main formal antithesis to the various literary codes—comic, tragic, satiric, romantic, picaresque—which this novel gestures toward but rejects. The contract is a mechanism for

111

the determination of value between two parties, and as such is a neutral instrument. Nevertheless, in the devolution of value that *Moll Flanders* chronicles, the instruments which Moll uses to define and protect her personal worth lead to an increasing alienation and an increasing fragmentation of her character. As Maximillian Novak has demonstrated, Defoe is not a spokesman for laissez-faire economics; he cannot accept the complete relativity of value and has no conception of a regulatory fiction like the benevolent "unseen hand" of Adam Smith.[46] Like Marx after him, although from an opposite point of view, Defoe insists on deriving the fluctuating value of capital from more concretely human activities. Marx describes a positive creation of value by human labor; Defoe describes the way value devolves out of the private attempt to secure an accumulated wealth.

Thus while Moll sees herself as being taken out of the marriage market because of her age, her turning to thievery is also a logical development of her quest for value as it leads her into a more various pursuit of property, a property now fragmented, material, and dangerously remote from her being. Moll's last marriage is buttressed by "a great Bundle of Papers" (180), but the best of contracts provides no permanent defense against the larger vicissitudes of existence. As in earlier cases, Moll must face a terrifyingly formless futurity, in which all value is swallowed up in the prospect of "poverty." There is no substance to fall back on: "We liv'd in an uninterrupted course of Ease and Content for Five Years, when a sudden Blow from an almost invisible Hand, blasted all my Happiness, and turn'd me out into the World in a Condition the reverse of all that had been before it" (189). The hand here is closer to the Puritan hand of an angry God than the hand of laissez-faire economics.

In one of the best recent readings of Defoe, Homer O. Brown notes the importance of defensive structures in his writings. "Hiding behind the disguise of Robinson and his factual-seeming narrative, Defoe is doing what Robinson does—constructing and hiding inside a 'natural' fortification which cannot be perceived as a 'habitation' from the outside."[47] This is an apt description of Moll Flanders's use of contractual forms, although in Moll's case it is as if the rigidity of her various legalistic self-enclosures leads on the one hand to a collapse of interest in the things within them (thus the characteristic dismissal of the long period of ease and content) and on the other to an exaggerated sense of the hostile chaos of the world beyond her defenses. The more fixed her defenses, the more terrifying her ap-

112

prehensions of futurity and the further afield she must range in an effort to replenish her "stock."

When she begins her career as thief, the rhythm and pace of Moll's narrative accelerates. Her adventures in the Colchester household receive the most lengthy and elaborate development, and the procession of subsequent husbands and lovers receives a variable narrative treatment. But as she becomes increasingly caught up in particular acts of appropriation, Moll's descriptions of her exploits succeed one another more rapidly. More specific objects and places are entailed by the narrative, concrete commodities replace money, and Moll has trouble getting the full monetary value of the goods she has stolen. Moll still clings to her legalism, as when she supports her governess's oath that no man had been in her house all day (Moll having been disguised as a man) with the triumphant "and that was very true indeed" (217) or when she produces material evidence in the form of a silver spoon and a purse of nearly 20 guineas to support her claim to be a legitimate customer of the goldsmith she has tried to rob. But the legality is increasingly a fiction, an outright deception rather than a strict construction of phrases. She adopts the name of Moll Flanders—as with so many of her identities it is given to her by someone else—and she even goes as far as to disguise her sex and her class. As her acquisitions become more various, she becomes more protean. Indeed, at this stage of her life Moll's narrative most closely resembles the earlier Spanish picaresque novel: "generally I took up new Figures, and contriv'd to appear in new Shapes every time I went abroad" (262).

What happens at this stage of her career is that value gradually loses its economic character and becomes increasingly aesthetic. As she admits at several points, it is no longer economic necessity that impels her, but a compulsion to try her luck. She goes as far as to gamble literally at one point, and though she realizes the dangers of the "itch of play" in this particular form, she compromises her quest for value by treating her thievery as a game.[48] This phase of Moll's pursuit of value does not represent a sudden change of heart on her part. It is more the outcome of her methods than a specific defect of her character. Indeed, this posteconomic stage of Moll's development is quite similar to the final stage of literary evaluation in Defoe's Preface—from virtue to value to "elegancy" and "incredible variety."

It is in this context that Moll's conversion experience in Newgate must be understood. The conversion is not the thematic climax of a spiritual autobiography, as Starr tries unconvincingly to suggest,[49] but the invocation of a religious paradigm in a novel to redeem the collapsing pursuit of secular value. The experience of conversion was not entirely alien to the Spanish picaresque—occurring for example at the end of the Second Part of *Guzmán de Alfarache*—and it was a virtually obligatory feature of the criminal biography. In a sense, Defoe counters the picaresque gamesmanship of Moll as thief with the otherworldly sobriety of the criminal life-story when she becomes a condemned prisoner. Moll is as close to a character like Mary Carleton as she is to the repentant Puritans who published their spiritual histories.

Moll manages to give her conversion her own peculiar stamp, however. This is not to say that it is not genuine but to note that it is consistent with her character, or rather continuous with her quest. She first experiences Newgate as the negation of all human value, as "an Emblem of Hell itself, and a kind of an Entrance into it" (274). This is her final ruin, and as Moll endures it she loses her very ability to weigh and judge and compare. "I degenerated into Stone; I turn'd first Stupid and Senseless, then Brutish and thoughtless, and at last raving Mad as any of them were; and in short, I became as naturally pleas'd and easie with the Place, as if indeed I had been Born there" (278). In a terrible way, Moll has at last found a place, at the bottom of the scale of social and cultural value.

In fact, as we have learned at the beginning of the novel, Moll *was* born in Newgate. That Moll does not remember this fact does not seem to me forgetfulness on Defoe's part nor does it seem to be an irony at Moll's expense. It is instead symptomatic of the collapse of the evaluative faculty in Moll, an indication of her inability to find even negative values in this return to origins. If she were to remember that Newgate was where she began her life, the inevitable irony of the perception would provide some independent perspective on her present situation. As it is, her recovery from this nadir proceeds not simply from her adherence to Christian doctrine but from the appearance first of her Lancashire husband, then her "governess" as emblems of distress. Earlier Moll had defined herself in isolation from her criminal accomplices; her failure to be impressed by the example of their arrests was symptomatic of the growing alienation of her character from any emotional base. Now the presence of those she had been closest to allows her to evaluate her own position. The minister who brings her to repentance is sent by her governess, and his "friendly" concern has the effect of breaking down Moll's by now purely habitual structures of defense: "This honest friendly way of treating me, unlock'd all the Sluces of my

Passions: He broke into my Soul by it; and I unravell'd all the Wick-
edness of my Life to him" (288). What we witness here, in effect, is
the birth of the "original" of *Moll Flanders*. The heroine commits her
character to the order of narrative. But it is only by appeal to a
transcendental scheme of value that this secular, extraliterary literature can assume its place in the world. "I now began to look back
upon my past Life with abhorrence, and having a kind of view into
the other Side of time, the things of Life, as I believe they do with
every Body at such a time, began to look with a different Aspect. . . . I
had nothing in my Thoughts, but what was so infinitely Superior to
what I had known in Life, that it appear'd to me to be the greatest
stupidity in Nature to lay any weight upon any thing tho' the most
valuable in the world" (287). On one level a rejection of the moral
content of her life, this conversion allows it to assume its literary
form. Quevedo's Pablos is cruelly bound to the shame of his worthless origins; Moll Flanders, with the sanction of eternity, can translate her life into the mode of narrative. Things do not end here.

   This rather obscure moment in *Moll Flanders* should not be seen as
any kind of formal climax, to be sure. Nor is Moll's ability to tell her
life story of any permanent value. Instead of turning Moll inward,
her conversion turns her out again, into a "New World" that gives
her final new frame of reference a concrete geography. But when the
otherworldly values are relocated in the economics of Virginia there
is something like an inflation of the value problem which has informed the novel up to this point. The excess of commodities and
capital on the one hand, and the offhand resolution of the old problem of incest on the other ("Thus all these little Difficulties were
made easy" [342], Moll says when she confesses the incest to her
current husband) make this part of the novel a coda rather than a
continuation of Moll's quest. The New World is the best of both
worlds, ethically secure as the terms of Moll's punishment but economically profitable as an opportunity for legitimate trade. If Newgate represents the ultimate emptiness of Moll's structures for the
defense of value, Virginia represents an ultimate embarrassment of
riches. Quevedo's Pablos is held to a single standard of judgment,
and finds that things go worse for him in America. For Moll Flanders,
allowed to experience a procession of standards in her pursuit of
place, America—on her second visit—is a place where things do go
better. Nevertheless, she fulfills the "limited terms" of her transpor-
tation and returns to England, where old age and extreme wealth
allow her to pass into an obscurity similar to that from which—under
the opposite extremes—she emerged in the arena of evaluation. "The

nature of the character in a novel," Walter Benjamin writes, "cannot be presented any better than is done in the statement, which says that the 'meaning' of his life is revealed only in his death."[50] Like the characters of earlier picaresque novels, Moll avoids this final stamp of significance, just as she has avoided the marital closure of comedy or romance and the punitive closure of satire. With the final note "Written in the Year 1683," Defoe submerges the resolutions of literary plot in the more abstract resolutions of historical chronology. The date comes as a surprise—it is the only such historical marker in the novel—but it marks the story with the authority of chronicle. The documentary past is the court of final appeal for this ambiguously literary text—though of course this historicity is itself a fiction.

6

JOSEPH ANDREWS *and the Quixotic*
The Politics of the Classic

> When first young Maro in his boundless Mind
> A Work t'outlast Immortal Rome design'd,
> Perhaps he seem'd above the Critick's Law,
> And but from Nature's Fountains scorn'd to draw:
> But when t'examine ev'ry part he came,
> Nature and Homer were, he found, the same.
>
> Pope, *An Essay on Criticism*

Fielding's public career as a novelist began with his *Quixote*-like critique of Richardsonian fiction, although it is possible that he had already experimented with the picaresque form by 1742. *Jonathan Wild* and *A Journey from This World to the Next* appeared in Fielding's *Miscellanies* in 1743, but they may well have been conceived, if not completed, before Fielding decided to imitate the manner of Cervantes in prose fiction. In any case, the immorality of the literature of roguery called forth an essentially satiric response from Fielding, and both these narratives have the traditional mock-heroic structure of Augustan satire rather than the experimental form of the "new species of writing" that Fielding was later to be credited with founding. *Jonathan Wild* recasts the criminal biography as a mock-heroic commentary on the "great man" of politics. *A Journey from This World to the Next* transforms the realistic rogue into a Pythagorean travesty.[1] In neither case was Fielding drawn significantly beyond the satiric codes of Augustan neoclassical culture.

Richardson's *Pamela* initially provoked a more traditional response as well, in the burlesque *Shamela*, but the challenge of Richardson's novel soon led Fielding to the more innovative and autonomous fiction of *Joseph Andrews*. As his title page advertised, this innovation was also a reworking of an earlier precedent—an "Imitation of the Manner of Cervantes, Author of *Don Quixote*." The balance of novelty and conventionality in Fielding's experiment, which of course was a major event in the emergence of the European novel in England, has never been fully or fairly assessed. Most criticism of Fielding's art, from Dr. Johnson onward, has used the opposition

117

between Fielding and Richardson for the terms of its discourse.[2] The relationship of his novels to the broader field of earlier European prose fiction and the theory thereof has received much less attention. As with Defoe, the most important elements of this relationship have to do with the way earlier European fiction and theory of fiction were being absorbed by English literary culture. There is first of all the question of the English reading public's reception of the more idealistic and/or erotic romances, then the question of the standing these romances were felt to have in the literary canon, and finally the question of the English understanding of *Don Quixote* itself—Cervantes's creative response to this long-fought battle of the books.

As I noted in the last chapter, the vogue of prose romances was relatively slow in coming to England, and it was only in the eighteenth century that a version of this type of fiction was as widely read as it had been in France or Spain. If anything, there was a recrudescence of the more sophisticated Continental narratives, as Dieter Schultz has observed. "The development of fiction in England in the late seventeenth and early eighteenth centuries reversed the realistic trend so prominent in French writers of the second half of the seventeenth century. Perhaps as a consequence of the 'romancy' cultural climate after the Restoration, the popular 'novel' in England resurrected the high mode of the courtly novella, although . . . its exalted rhetoric usually degenerated into a veneer for sensationalism and pseudo-romantic eroticism."[3] There was also a tendency in England to associate this type of reading with a particularly female audience. Thus the library of "Leonora" imagined by Addison in 1711 contained five heroic romances from the French, a copy of Sidney's *Arcadia*, the more scandalous *New Atlantis*, and "A Book of Novels" (i.e., novellas) among some thirty miscellaneous volumes and sets.[4] It seems to have taken several decades of this fashion in reading before the "female Quixote"—a young woman whose judgment had been distorted by her reading of such romances—was widely comprehensible in the form of the novel.[5] Before the middle of the century the challenge that the romances might pose to literary tradition was simply not evident.

Only with the growing experience of the romances, in other words, was the relevance of the Continental debates about the relationship of romance to the classical canon widely appreciable in England—the debate that began in Italy over Ariosto, spread to Spain in the strictures of the neo-Aristotelians, and achieved its fullest elaboration in France in the seventeenth-century "quarrel of the ancients and the moderns." Some Englishmen had joined the debate peripherally in the seventeenth century, as with Davenant's Preface to *Gondibert* (heavily indebted to the French theory and practice that Davenant had observed in exile) and with Hobbes's "Reply." But neither Davenant nor Hobbes had much to say about the romances themselves, concentrating on the classical genre of epic or, in the case of Hobbes, on a "Heroique" poetry that included both epic and tragedy. It was only in France that champions of the modern prose romances as distinct from the classical epic emerged, and it was only much later in England that the significance of this complex polemic began to permeate English literary culture.

What the English began to perceive, belatedly and at a distance, were some of the paradoxes and inconsistencies of the ongoing Continental debate. In some cases, the French *modernes,* like Chapelain and Fenelon, were extremely rule-conscious themselves. "The curious thing . . . about this quarrel of the Ancients and the Moderns is that the real moderns were the champions of the ancients. That is, the champions of the moderns, while protesting that their own times were superior to the ancients in various ways, nevertheless based their arguments for superiority largely upon the superiority of the moderns in *following the rules.*"[6] Such defenses of modernity were hardly liberating. In other cases the defenders of romance showed a schizophrenic attitude toward this popular and amorphous genre. One of the most influential of the French treatises, Pierre-Daniel Huet's *Letter on the Origin of the Romances* (first translated into English in 1672) provides the best example of the tensions between classical order and vernacular energy that Fielding was eventually to exploit—with of course the example of *Don Quixote* before him as well.

Huet begins his argument with a distinction between romance and epic. The distinction involves both style and subject matter but does not make verse a necessary condition for epic. He makes a further distinction between romance and fable that hinges on the neoclassical criterion of *vraisemblance:* romance is "the Fiction of things that might have happened but never did," fable "the Fiction of things that never were and never can be."[7] Here romance is rationalized and comprehensible according to an extension of Aristotelian rules. But when Huet begins to talk about the "origin" of romances— largely oriental in his view—the neoclassical criteria begin to disappear. He mentions the "lies" of the Arabians and the Persians, the truth of "Holy Scripture," and a great variety of fabulous and legendary material. His eclectic pluralism at this point contrasts strongly with his earlier categorical exclusivity. Only when Huet reaches the

Greek romances does his neoclassicism reassert itself. "Rough and unshapen as it [i.e., romance] was among the Orientals, [the Greeks] have worked it into a better Form by confining it to the rules of *Epopea*, and uniting in a complete Body, the several Parts that lay without Order or Relation to each other."[8] He considers Apuleius's *Golden Ass* as a "Milesian fable," one of those stories which as Cervantes's canon had noted "are extravagant tales whose purpose is to amaze, and not to instruct" (*Don Quixote*, p. 424), and speculates that Petronius's *Satyricon*, which he claims was intended as a satire but is in fact a romance, was originally a well-ordered narrative before being reduced to its fragmentary state.

Huet's neoclassicism disappears completely before the vernacular European romances, and instead of a defense of ancient rules he gives a defense of the patriotic notion that all the European romances originated in France. Although admitting the crudity of these medieval narratives, Huet nevertheless manages to see in them redeeming signs of reason—that is, of the mind's curiosity and desire for knowledge. Thus a double theory of romance emerges. On the one hand it is the expression of an emerging natural vitality; on the other, it is the product of an established cultural order. Huet never resolves the ambiguity of the genre; he merely shifts his emphasis, as when he comes to contemporary neoclassical France:

> It will be sufficient to tell you, that all these writings being
> the fruits of ignorance, carried in them the marks of their
> original and were no other than a heap of Fictions bun-
> glingly stitched one to another, and infinitely beneath that
> Sovereign degree of Art and Elegance to which our nation
> has since raised the Romance.... Monsieur d'Urfey was
> the first who retrieved them from Barbarity, and brought
> them under a Regulation in his incomparable Astrea, a
> Piece the most ingenious and Polite... which eclipsed the
> Glory Greece, Italy, and Spain had acquired before.[9]

I have dwelt on Huet in order to suggest the kind of tensions that existed in the critical discussions of romance with which Fielding could hardly have avoided being familiar when he came to write his Preface to *Joseph Andrews*.[10] It is true that there was much less of this discussion going on in England than there had been on the Continent, but it is interesting that William Warburton wrote a "Dissertation on the origins of the Books of Chivalry." This essay was prefixed to Jarvis's translation of *Don Quixote* published in 1742, the same year that *Joseph Andrews* was published. Warburton, in fact, criticizes Huet for slighting the vernacular romances in his discussion, and with less neoclassical prejudice of his own he sees the romances as having a serious religious purpose in their association with the Crusades. Thus Warburton is able to value the popular romances by giving them the sanction of Christianity as a counterbalance to classical precepts. It is also interesting, and symptomatic of the relative proverty of the romance tradition in England, that when Warburton tries to explain the nature of the chivalric romances to his readers he falls back on an analogy with the mystery and morality plays in the history of English drama. Both Fielding and Warburton have read Cervantes and apparently Huet with enough understanding to perceive the problem these earlier naive narratives pose for a neoclassical theory of literature, even though their own English literary tradition was less abundant in such narratives. It is this persistent critical problem that seems to me to be behind the artful theorizing of Fielding's famous Preface to *Joseph Andrews*.

The lack of specific reference to romance in the Preface has led some critics to claim that Fielding was strangely negligent in acknowledging his debt to his Continental predecessors in discussing the comic epic in prose—that he was either "guilty of unacknowledged literary theft" or that he "independently deduced many of the principles they had enunciated a century before."[11] It seems rather the case that Fielding is ironically exploiting this venerable critical tradition and exposing the inconsistencies of the neoclassical efforts to subdue or banish the recalcitrant popular genre. When Fielding supposes that "the mere *English* Reader may have a different Idea of Romance with the Author of these little Volumes" (3), he signals that his own construct will contain some surprises.[12] Since most discussions of Fielding's Preface take it as a relatively straightforward piece of theorizing,[13] I shall develop this point at greater length.

The idea of a preface seems first of all a reaction to Richardson's disavowal of the need for a preface to *Pamela*. Relying on the "Foundation [of the letters] in Truth and Nature," Richardson as editor vouches for his book on the grounds of his own affective response ("he can Appeal from his own Passions [which have been uncommonly moved in perusing these engaging Scenes]"), and on the grounds, somewhat contradictory, of his impartiality.[14] Fielding's lofty beginning—"this kind of Writing which I do not remember to have seen hitherto attempted in our Language"—takes Richardson at his word and excludes his "new species of writing" (as Richardson himself called it) from the literary field. At the same time, as he launches into his rehearsal of Aristotle's *Poetics*, Fielding makes an exaggerated claim for his own literary production. The exaggeration is not immediately evident, and a recognition of it depends on some familiarity with the terms of neoclassical literary debate, but the first few paragraphs are clearly a form of affectation, subspecies vanity, that Fielding goes on to anatomize as the source of the comic. There is an interesting precedent for this play with Aristotelian sanctions in the Prologue of *Don Quixote*, where Cervantes speaks ironically of books "never mind how fabulous and profane, so full of sentences from Aristotle, Plato and the whole herd of philosophers, as to impress their readers and get their authors a reputation for wide reading, erudition and eloquence" (*Don Quixote*, p. 26). But where Cervantes's irony is broad and obvious, Fielding lays a more subtle trap for the "Classical reader," as he calls him. There is first of all the irony that the supposed Homeric model, the *Margites*, is missing, as is the part of Aristotle's *Poetics* that dealt with the nature of comedy. The so-called rules of the comic epic are conveniently lost, although the author confidently assures us that "this great Pattern . . . had it survived, would have found its Imitators equally with the other Poems of this great Original" (3).

The second problem, also obvious to the genuine classical reader, is the easy way Fielding glides over the two centuries of controversy about the relation of romance to epic. Fielding uses the term "romance" in his first sentence, allowing that the English reader may have a different idea of it than the one he is proposing, then launches into a discussion of the rules of epic, agreeing with the common opinion that the epic can be written in prose, and following what seems to have been a common conservative view in England, that Fenelon's *Telémaque* should be included in the genre.[15] He rejects out of hand the claim of the heroic romances to canonical status, but in the phrase "those voluminous Works commonly called *Romances*" (4) he deftly avoids the problem of distinguishing his own work from these deficient ones—a distinction he will in fact claim to have made at the end of the Preface. In his famous definition, "Now a comic Romance is a comic Epic-Poem in Prose," the problematic gap between genres is closed by the shift from the serious genres to a comic one. The shift is perfectly logical but also a sleight of hand, and it allows for a more explicit criticism of the Aristotelian apparatus as the argument proceeds. Comedy is not merely different from tragedy, it begins to assert its superiority: "Nay, I will appeal to common Observation, whether the same Companies are not found more full of Good-Humour and Benevolence, after they have been sweeten'd for two or three hours with Entertainmer.ts of this kind, than when soured by a Tragedy or a grave Lecture" (5). Further on, the author speaks of *"Aristotle*, who is so fond and free of Definitions" (7). By now the reader realizes that the application of these prefatory observations to the narrative that follows is hardly a perfect fit.

This is not to say that Fielding rejects high literature or that the theorizing in the Preface is irrelevant to the moral structure of Fielding's comic exposures. But the evasions and ironies of the Preface do suggest that it partakes itself of the comic action of the novel, and that it dramatizes the ambivalent relationship of *Joseph Andrews* to the neoclassical canon. There are numerous parallels to this comic undercutting of neoclassical expectations in Fielding's writings. The first chapter of Book V of *Tom Jones* provides one example. In defense of the prefaces to each separate book "which we have determined to be essentially necessary to this kind of writing, of which we have set ourselves at the head," Fielding declines to justify this rule of "prosai-comi-epic Writing." "Who ever demanded the Reasons of that nice Unity of Time or Place which is now established to be so essential to dramatic Poetry? What Critic hath been ever asked, Why a Play may not contain two Days as well as one?"[16] There is a subtle but important difference here from the Augustan mock-epic, as in *The Dunciad*, or the Augustan mock-poetics, as in *Peri Bathos*. In Pope and the Scriblerus Club writings, classical forms and themes constitute a standard, a set of rules which may be misapplied to contemporary material with satiric intent, but whose authority is itself unquestioned. In Fielding these rules are treated as more relative. They constitute one of many language games or literary codes, but not the dominant one. Not identified, as in Pope, with "Nature" in its rationally ideal sense, neoclassical rules cease to have such extensive jurisdiction over the realm of literary discourse. Fielding liberalizes the rules of literature to allow a greater pluralism of standards. The traditional hierarchy of genres is not overthrown, but a new respect is accorded to the "low" as distinct from the "high."

In so freeing the classical imagination from its own imperial tendencies and in putting forward the insubordinate claims of more popular forms—including Richardson's *Pamela*, Cibber's *Apology*, and the fairy tales mentioned in the first chapter of *Joseph Andrews*—Fielding had before him the example of *Don Quixote*. We come here to the question of Fielding's "imitation" of Cervantes and the degree to which *Joseph Andrews* subordinates itself to an authoritative model from the literary past. In some respects it would seem that Fielding's innovations are nothing new at all in the history of the novel. The answer to this question depends on the status of *Don Quixote* in English letters at that time.

It has been shown by a number of critics how the English attitude toward Don Quixote himself changed in the course of the seventeenth and eighteenth centuries. Cervantes's hero was initially regarded as a rogue and a burlesque figure, then as a vehicle for satire, later as amiable humorist, and finally as pathetic idealist.[17] But what is of more interest in a history of the novel is the way the book as a whole was regarded. The initial view of it as a jest-book or burlesque, evident in Gayton's commentary, John Phillips's translation and Phillips's plays (which were attacked by Thomas Rymer) began by the turn of the century to give way to a more serious and positive evaluation. The dominant interpretation for many years thereafter was that *Don Quixote* was a satire, not of literary fashions (although Pope recognized its affinities with "Mock-Epick"),[18] but of the social institutions of Spain. Defoe voices this opinion, probably derived originally from Rapin, in his *Memoirs of Captain Carleton* (1728), where the hero is told by a Spanish gentleman that before Cervantes wrote,

> it was next to an impossibility for a man to walk the streets with any delight, or without danger. There were so many cavalieros prancing and curvetting before the windows of their mistresses, that a stranger would have imagined the whole nation to have been nothing less than a race of knight errants. But after the world became a little acquainted with that notable history [i.e., *Don Quixote*], the man that was seen in that once celebrated drapery, was pointed at as a Don Quixotte, and found himself the jest of high and low.

Carleton's informant goes on to claim that "to this, and this only, we owe that dampness and poverty of spirit, which has run through all our councils for a century past."[19] This view of Cervantes as a satirist and a social reformer reappears in Charles Jarvis's Preface to his translation of *Don Quixote*, and it is only in Warburton's "Supplement" of 1742 that the essentially literary object of Cervantes's critique is identified: "For the ridicule of Cervantes does not so much turn upon *that*, "he corrects Jarvis, "as upon the *ideal* of chivalry, as it is to be found only in the old romances."[20] Even Warburton calls *Don Quixote* "this incomparable satire," however, and it is out of this traditional generic view that Fielding's more novelistic interpretation emerges.

In French critical writing the uniqueness and modernity of Cervantes was more appreciated. In Perrault, De Callières, and Saint-Evremond in particular, *Don Quixote* was singled out and praised as worthy of comparison with the classics in the Quarrel of the Ancients and the Moderns.[21] Fielding refers to Saint-Evremond in other contexts, and may well have derived the sense of Cervantes as more than a traditional satirist from him. In this context the idea of an "imitation" of *Don Quixote* becomes especially paradoxical: the authority of Cervantes is an authority which challenges the traditionalism of neoclassical poetics itself, a poetics in which imitation is such a central concept. Nature and Cervantes are not the same, but neither are they entirely opposed. As with the evasive identification of romance and epic in the Preface, the "imitation of the manner of Cervantes" in *Joseph Andrews* places the novel in a doubly ambiguous relationship to the literary canon. Somewhat more openly, the author of "An Essay on the New Species of Writing" follows Fielding's ironic lead a decade later: "The first Critics drew their Rules from the first Professors of the Art they made their Observations on; which were afterward the settled Standards by which the Worth of their Successors was to be determined. In Imitation of so great an Example are the Rules for future Historians of this kind drawn from the works of their Original Mr. Fielding."[22] Fielding is called "our English Cervantes" here but the precedent and authority of Cervantes receive no other notice. And in his review of Charlotte Lennox's *The Female Quixote* in 1752, in an ostentatiously "judicious" proceeding, Fielding gives Mrs. Lennox the edge over Cervantes in several departments, including the regularity of her story. Fielding says significantly that, in *Don Quixote*, Cervantes, "in many Instances, approaches very near to the Romances which he ridicules."[23]

In his play *Don Quixote in England* published in 1734, Fielding shows himself the victim rather than the master of the ambiguous nature of Cervantes's masterpiece; that is, his imitation of *Don Quixote* is divided against itself. On the one hand, Quixote and Sancho continue to be deluded by the chivalric romances; on the other hand, Quixote's madness is declared exemplary—"All mankind are mad, 'tis plain"[24]—and is thus symbolic of a universal human weakness. There is a conflict between the aesthetic specificity of the Quixote who has been deluded by chivalric romances, and the ethical universality of a Quixote who moralizes for all mankind on their own delusions. Cervantes's hero, it is true, is unpredictable in his madness, and periodically amazes his critics by his rationality. But Don Quixote never steps out of character in Cervantes's novel; rather he shows his character to be more flexible and more comprehensive than others imagine it to be. What Cervantes dramatizes is the idealizing power of the literary imagination. Fielding, on the other hand, finds the literary imagination a restriction and an embarrassment; his Quixote does not expand his literary delusions to include ethical ideals but rises above them to pronounce the moral of the play. Thus when Dr. Drench refers to him as a madman in the last scene, Fielding's Quixote admits his own limitations and speaks in the name of a higher and more general human nature:

> I have heard thee, thou ignorant wretch, throw that word in my face, with patience. For alas! could it be proved, what were it more than almost all mankind in some degree deserve? Who would doubt the noisy boistrous squire, who was here just now, to be mad? Must not this noble knight here have been mad to think of marrying his daughter to such a wretch? You, doctor, are mad, too, though not so mad as your patients. The lawyer here is mad, or he would not have gone into a scuffle, when it is the business of men of his profession to set other men by the ears, and keep clear themselves.[25]

The romances themselves never become a vehicle for this tenor, as they do in Cervantes, and the play in general suffers from the division.

In *Joseph Andrews* Fielding overcomes the limitations of his earlier treatment of Cervantes by a subtle but significant revision. Instead of a Quixote deluded by the absurdities of romance, we have in Parson Adams a Quixote who is deluded by classical literature, and a Quixote of the ethical rather than of the aesthetic precept. The initial Quixote figure is of course Joseph Andrews, who supposedly follows the moral doctrine of his sister Pamela's published letters. But when Parson Adams is introduced and assumes the burden of the Quixotic role Fielding reverses Cervantes's dialectic and gives us a hero deluded not by the native romances but by neoclassical culture itself. This is how I interpret the movement away from *Pamela* as direct adversary in Fielding's novel. The specious moralism of Richardson's anticanonical writing is seen as a danger inherent in Augustan neoclassicism as well: the "profit" of the aesthetic pleasure may be in the end too self-centered or self-serving to live up to an ethical ideal. Parson Adams is a demonstration by example that Nature and Homer are not in fact the same—not at least in the way that neoclassical theory was tempted to assume. Fielding locates his own Quixotic novel in the gap between precept and example. Where Cervantes shows how the most critical epistemological stance is inevitably bound up with the literary imagination, Fielding shows how the noblest forms of the moral sensibility are always extrinsic to the ethical act. The best that has been thought and said is not exempt from this discrimination.

This ethical revision of Cervantes entails a number of formal differences between *Joseph Andrews* and *Don Quixote*. There is first of all the diferent role played by the author. Fielding, it has been observed, owes as much here to the English tradition of the rehearsal play as he does to *Don Quixote* for the reflexive commentary of his novels,[26] but the difference can be seen as a corrective revision of Cervantes as well. Where Cervantes uses the fiction of the Arab historian Cide Hamete Benengeli and thus puts a problematic distance between the story and the storyteller, Fielding assumes the role of historian himself and allows for no recessive depths in his imaginative construct. He praises *Don Quixote*, in fact, for its lack of geographical and chronological specificity; it is "the History of the World in general" (188), and in describing "not Men, but Manners; not an Individual, but a Species" (189) in *Joseph Andrews*, Fielding deliberately collapses the distance between himself as author and other selves, other nations, or other times. Cervantes uses the fiction of the Arab historian to distance his reader from the text and to undermine the reader's confidence in its authority. It is true that at several points Fielding descends from his genial omniscience and professes to have learned a fact from conversation with one of his characters, but even this potentially Cervantean touch insists on an immediate access to the world of the story rather than an undermining of its claims to truth. The largest consciousness in the novel is that of the author, who may feign ignorance for the purpose of irony, but whose ultimate aim is the transparency of his medium, the transparency of the particular before the general. This is certainly not the case with the authorial persona Cervantes assumes in *Don Quixote*.

A similar reversal occurs in the use of the interpolated tale, a device which Fielding dutifully takes over from *Don Quixote* but uses for an opposite effect. The interpolated tales of the First Part of *Don Quixote*, as we have seen, are stories within the story, recreative spaces within the larger play world of the narrative, into which various levels of reader are drawn and from which they return. They dramatize or give play to the potential for freedom in the readerly imagination; they are microcosms of literary form which reflect back on the macrocosm of a more realistic form of life. In *Joseph Andrews* the tales are windows on a larger world rather than mirrors held up to nature. They look beyond the comic confines of the novel proper to other modes of experience and expression. This is not to say that the "History of Leonora," Mr. Wilson's tale, or the history of the two friends Leonard and Paul are notably more realistic than the history of *Joseph Andrews,* but they all deal with more problematic visions of life. None of the interpolated tales is presided over by a benevolent "Author"; none of them is capable of any graceful romantic resolution. Leonora and Horatio live unhappily ever after, apart; Mr. Wilson is rescued from his urban degradation by the love of his wife but is forced to retreat to the country and even there is subject to the incursions of a savage world. The friendship of Paul and Leonard is on the point of being sacrificed to domestic politics when the story itself is interrupted. It may be too extreme to say, as Howard Weinbrot does, that "there are several moments at which *Joseph Andrews* is grim, savage, and terrifying, and these are largely in the interpolations," but Weinbrot is surely correct in observing that in these tales "the author has relinquished the reins of the narrative" that he elsewhere holds onto tightly.[27] At these points the comic epic in prose looks out on a larger uncomic world through alternate genres. In *Don Quixote,* on the other hand, Quixote's chivalric romance incorporates and subsumes such alternate literary perspectives within itself.

Fielding's conception of literary character is also fundamentally different from that of Cervantes. Don Quixote's is a character in which self and role are obviously incongruous and whose relation to other characters is distorted by its preconceptions. But the progress of his adventures is a paradoxical overcoming of these manifest gaps. We find it increasingly difficult to distinguish the reality principle from the fiction-making potential in Quixote, and we find that characters who set themselves in opposition to his madness are generally involved in a collaboration with it. Melville's romantic observation is to the point: "The character sheds not its characteristic on its surroundings, whereas, the original character, essentially such, is like a revolving Drummond light, raying away from itself all round it."[28] Fielding's characters are characters in the former, unoriginating sense: the roles they project upon their surroundings, less palpably fantastic than those of Don Quixote himself, can be distinguished from the more genuine selves that they are in their more unguarded moments. This is as true of the amiable Parson Adams, whose practice is often better than his preaching, as it is of the more hypocritical facades of the other characters he meets.

For Fielding character is revealed preeminently in interaction, and his Quixote figure is really double: Parson Adams *and* Joseph Andrews. We can focus exclusively on neither. Their relationship is different from the relationship of knight and squire in *Don Quixote*. Sancho Panza is an understudy to Quixote, an apparent contrast who comically converges with his master at numerous points along the way. Joseph Andrews and Abraham Adams are superficially similar in their innocence, but they continually contrast with one another in a kind of Quixotic counterpoint: youth and age, ignorance and learnedness, romantic passion and philosophical disinterest. They divide the attributes of Quixote among them. There is also the deployment of the two main characters in what Ronald Paulson has called the "touchstone structure" and Martin Price the "dance of attitudes"; that is, Fielding's tendency to dwell less on the actions of Joseph and Adams themselves than on the reactions of other characters to them.[29] It is by their reactions alone that many characters—Miss Gravairs, Mrs. Tow-wowse, the falsely generous gentleman—exist in the novel and are known. A developed character is responded to, inadequately, by a more limited one. The thrust of Fielding's imagination of character is from the round to the flat. Often this thrust extends, through satiric similes, beyond the world of the novel to contemporary society:

> Suppose a Stranger, who entered the Chambers of a Lawyer, being imagined a Client, when the Lawyer was preparing his Palm for the Fee, should pull out a Writ against him. Suppose an Apothecary, at the Door of a Chariot containing some great Doctor of eminent Skill, should, instead of Directions to a Patient, present him with a Potion for himself. Suppose a Minister should, instead of a good round Sum, treat my Lord—— or Sir—— or Esq.——, with a good Broomstick. Suppose a civil Companion, or a led Captain, should instead of Virtue, and Honour, and Beauty, and Parts, and Admiration, thunder Vice, and Infamy, and Ugliness, and Folly, and Contempt, in his Patron's Ears. Suppose when a Tradesman first carries in his Bill the Man of Fashion should pay it; or suppose, if he did so, the Tradesman should abate what he had overcharged on the Supposition of waiting. In short—suppose what you will, you never can nor will suppose any thing equal to the Astonishment which seiz'd on *Trulliber*, as soon as *Adams* had ended his speech (165–66).

From Adams to Trulliber's reaction to Adams to a catalogue of comparable comedies of manners: Fielding moves our attention from the center to the periphery, from the fully developed narrative of adventures to the single-sentence vignette. Rather than shedding their characteristics on the world, the characters of *Joseph Andrews* serve as a pretext for the self-revelations of others.

A final contrast between *Don Quixote* and *Joseph Andrews*, deliberately effected by Fielding's imitation, lies in the concept of plot. Fielding later criticized the randomness of Cervantes, complaining that the order of incidents in *Don Quixote* could be changed at will with no effect on the whole.[30] *Joseph Andrews* is less elaborately plotted than *Tom Jones*, which is so astonishing in its formal symmetries as to call into question the substantiality of orderly Aristotelian action, but it does show, as in Fielding's description of the *Odyssey*, "a series of separate adventures detached from and independent of each other, yet all tending to one great end."[31] The "end" is both thematic and literal: the exposure of affectation as a barrier to charity and the removal of the obstacles to the love between Joseph and Fanny as a specific instance of this charity. In *Don Quixote* the plot is based on a conflict of ends, a conflict between the ends of the hero and the ends of the society around him. Quixote pursues an imaginative quest on its journey outward, the other characters attempt to contain him and return him to his rational place in the world. When Quixote is returned from enchantment it is either in a cage or on his deathbed. In *Joseph Andrews*, on the other hand, the quest of the hero and the reintegration of society are finally brought together. There is a linear progression from city to country, from the public disorder of London to the private reordering of Pamela's family romance. It is not that many of the adventures on the road in *Joseph Andrews* could not also be rearranged, but that these more random episodes are parts of a passage from one society to another. The movement of *Don Quixote* is withdrawal and return (in Part One) and continuous disillusionment (in Part Two). The movement of *Joseph Andrews* is one of retirement from the great world to the country.[32]

Thus Fielding's imitation of the "manner" of Cervantes assumes a freedom to revise and improve upon his original. *Don Quixote* is no more sacrosanct than any other cultural form. Fielding also imitates the matter of Cervantes in places; certain episodes from *Don Quixote* are recognizable in the action of *Joseph Andrews*. The most extensive of such borrowings is the "scene of roasting" in Book III, where Adams, Joseph, and Fanny are mockingly entertained by the unprincipled squire. This episode is clearly modeled on Don Quixote's reception by the Duke and the Duchess in Part Two. It is interesting that this most explicit imitation of the earlier novel involves a character who is least susceptible to Fielding's methods of comic exposure, a character who is more "vicious" and less "affected" than the claims of the Preface of *Joseph Andrews* would seem to allow.[33] Like many readers, Fielding has recognized the darker aspects of the practical jokes that Cervantes's Duke and Duchess perpetrate on Don Quixote and Sancho, but he responds in his imitation by exaggerating both the offense of the jokers and the moral idealism of the hero. In *Don Quixote* we see that the Duke and Duchess are bored, that their pranks are attempts to continue the adventures of their favorite literary character, that their deficiencies are failures of imagination. The humiliation of Quixote and of Sancho is not their main intent, but a side effect of their cruder sense of play. In *Joseph Andrews* we see the squire not as a defective artist but as an anti-artist, a willful and deliberate perverter of the goodness of human nature. We see this viciousness because the author, uncharacteristically, makes an explicit statement; there is very little irony or indirection: "What distinguished him chiefly, was a strange Delight which he took in every thing which is ridiculous, odious, and absurd in his own species" (245). We also see it because Parson Adams for once applies his moral idealism appropriately and denounces the perversions of charity at the squire's table, and we are reminded of it yet again in the attempted rape of Fanny which follows. In the course of this latter episode, however, Fielding recovers much of his comic balance. He interpolates a more digressive and oblique imitation of *Don Quixote* in the discourse between the poet and the player over the relative importance of the text and the performance. This recalls the discussion of the theater between the canon and the curate at the end of Cervantes's First Part. Once the Squire himself is left behind, the novel returns to its more characteristic interplay of romantic adventure and farce, its comedy of narrative manners.

In his reenvisioning of *Don Quixote*, Fielding transforms a plurality of imaginative perspectives into a plurality of moral actings out. The construct of literature, the verbal text of the story, is constantly criticized and constantly exposed in its artificiality. A text in Fielding is an occasion for performance; it is not a thing of permanent value or beauty in and of itself. The discourse between the poet and the player during Fanny's abduction makes the conflict between text and performance explicit. The poet considers his writing as the true event, the player's acting as merely an inferior transcription of his words. The player argues that the playing is the thing, and that his performance on the stage redeems an otherwise indifferent text. Fielding as author, of course, is both poet and player; through his periodic reflexive commentary and through his constantly shifting levels of style, he continually acts out the telling of the story. Where *Don Quixote* insinuates the idea of a readable text into the actions of all the characters (as in the fiction of Cide Hamete Benengeli's ur-history), *Joseph Andrews* construes the text as an occasion for performance. The value of a speech or literary formula is measured against the actions which proceed from them. In some cases, the actions fail to live up to the profession, as, for example, in the case of the liberal gentleman who promises Parson Adams a living and fails to deliver; in other cases, as in Adams's inconsistent, unstoic grief at the supposed drowning of his son, the actions are greatly to be preferred. But in either case, the physical, material transactions between people—the giving of food, lending of money, offering of love or of combat—provide a contrasting standard by which the value of language as a speech act may be judged. Language is significant as verbal behavior in Fielding, not as mental vision.

Martin Battestin has shown how biblical texts like the parable of the Good Samaritan lie behind many of the episodes in Fielding.[34] As we shall see with *The Confidence-Man*, the authority of Scripture may itself be undermined by novelistic irony. But in Fielding's case these biblical passages remain an ultimate authority, and they do so in large part because they never assume explicit verbal form. It is Adams's classical literature which is expounded and exposed in the novel, not his Christianity. The Old and New Testaments belong to a realm of the spirit for Fielding; it is Greek and Roman literature that are caught up in the dangerous realm of the letter. As the action of the novel unfolds, there is a shift in the balance of spiritual authority between Parson Adams and Joseph Andrews. Adams's classical texts, the tragic and stoic sweep of his reading of human nature, become increasingly irrelevant in the contracting rural and domestic world of the latter half of the novel. On the other hand, the texts of popular romance which, consciously and unconsciously, guide Joseph Andrews, along with *Pamela*, various pastoral interludes, and Shakespeare's *Macbeth*, prove more appropriate to the problems of the reintegration of society. Indeed, when Pamela herself enters the novel at the end, Richardson's heroine is no longer a simple object of parody and burlesque. Rather she is incorporated into Fielding's fictional universe. Her calculating virtue is not so much exposed as fulfilled by Joseph's genuine romantic chastity. Here the Richardsonian text is finally transformed into Fieldingesque performance.

In the course of the novel as a whole, I would argue, the relationship of *Joseph Andrews* to *Pamela* is a shifting one, just as the relationship between *Don Quixote* and the chivalric romances is more complex and equivocal than the terms "parody," "burlesque," or "satire" allow. Initially, Richardson's fictional creation is held up to ridicule, along with Colley Cibber's *Apology* and other abuses of Augustan neoclassical norms. But by the end of the novel, Richardson's new species of writing is reintegrated into the society of literary forms. Its place is subordinate and peripheral, to be sure. The strategy by which Fielding is able to effect this accommodation is the same strategy by which he transforms the restrictive neoclassical canon into a broader definition of the literary field: literature is treated as a form of political activity. Fielding's actual political career involved him for a long time in "serious games ... with the system, with its aristocratic representatives, and with its Rules," as W. B. Coley puts it.[35] Interestingly enough, the game of Augustan politics, with its precarious balance of principles and patronage, seems to have failed for Fielding at about the time he was writing *Joseph Andrews*. This disaffection expresses itself in some curiously complimentary remarks about Walpole, although Fielding had long supported the Opposition.[36] In the novel that he was writing at the time of this disillusionment, one might say, Fielding translates the game of Augustan politics into a game of literary texts, the protocol of his new species of writing.

In *Tom Jones* the politics of the Ancients and the Moderns becomes quite explicit.

> The Antients may be considered as a rich Common, where every Person who hath the smallest Tenement in *Parnassus*, hath a free Right to fatten his Muse. Or, to place it in a clearer Light, we Moderns are to the Antients what the Poor are to the Rich. By the Poor here I mean, that large and venerable Body which, in *English*, we call The Mob. Now, whoever hath had the Honour to be admitted to any Degree of Intimacy with this Mob, must well know that it is one of their established Maxims, to plunder and pillage their rich Neighbors without any Reluctance; and that this is held to be neither Sin nor Shame among them.[37]

The overt defense of the modern authors is of course ironic, and the irony cuts both ways. The vehicle of the metaphor, the unruly poor, is as much the object of censure as the tenor, the modern writers who borrow freely from the ancients. But the terms of the analogy are significant nevertheless in the way they extend the terms of the literary debate beyond their proper literary contexts. As in many of Fielding's analogies, the content of the figurative language is social and

Chapter Six

political. But as in even more cases, the form is political as well. The analogy violates the neoclassical decorum that seeks to separate high and low styles, presents this decorum as the code of the subgroup rather than the code of the whole, and deliberately overextends the rules by applying them to a subject matter over which they have no authority. Thus the phrase "their established maxims to plunder and pillage" applies the notion of neoclassical rules to the behavior of those who have nothing to do with literature. It does not condone "pillage and plunder" in the least, but in the comic exuberance of its *translatio* it puts the "established maxims" in question.

A good example of this politicizing of the republic of letters is provided by the discussion "Of Divisions in Authors" in *Joseph Andrews* which plays on the idea of the divisions between authors as well as the divisions within their works. "Authoring" is presented as a "trade," and although the dignity of the political is ironically questioned in the passing analogy to "Prime Ministering," the chapter ends with a figurative displacement of literary authority into the realm of commercial enterprise. Homer hawked the books of his epics separately, anticipating the modern practice of publishing by number. Virgil's twelve books show his modesty, while Milton's twelve show his belated pride. The rug is pulled out from under the literary profession in the final analogy: "it becomes an Author generally to divide a Book, as it doth a Butcher to joint his Meat" (72).

Thus literary form in Fielding is culturally relative. No particular code is absolute. Fielding follows Cervantes in this respect, although what is a plurality of genres in Cervantes becomes a plurality of styles in Fielding. The scope and inclusiveness of the various literary forms have been restricted and reduced; they are part of an aesthetics of action rather than an aesthetics of reception. Fielding's novelistic stance in this respect resembles that of Defoe, in that both authors dramatize the independence of prose fiction from its subordination to the neoclassical genres. There is, of course, a crucial difference in the modes of their dramatizations. Defoe's mode is metonymic, as we have seen. It sets itself apart from the hierarchy of neoclassical poetics, alluding to traditional forms and values only obliquely. It offers a series of alternative structures, derived from institutions other than literature, as more adequate for the defense of human nature. Fielding's mode is essentially metaphoric. It challenges the hierarchy of neoclassical poetics from within, showing how even the most established literary terms have a limited range of reference, how the canon can be comically expanded rather than satirically

134

purified, and, most important, how style is a form of interaction among people rather than an institution unto itself. Fielding's metaphoric alternatives redeem the institution of literature by incorporating in the republic of letters the broader literacy of the commonwealth.

In a history of the novel then, the more obvious comparison of Fielding and Richardson needs to be supplemented by a comparison of Fielding and Defoe. Fielding takes little note of Defoe directly, although in the London disasters of Mr. Wilson's tale it is hard not to feel an allusion to the picaresque realities of *Moll Flanders* as well as to the moral strictures of "The Rake's Progress." As in his other experiments with picaresque matter, Fielding presents the adventures of the rogue in a clear moral frame quite alien to the picaresque novel, but he also mocks his own moral framing in the overanxious, overpious interruptions of Parson Adams as he listens to Mr. Wilson's tale. Like the countergenres of *Don Quixote* and the picaresque in Spain a century and a half earlier, the contrasting but complementary forms of the novel in Fielding and Defoe define the extremes of novelistic opposition to neoclassical tradition.

The novels of Richardson fall in between these two extremes, and are not so clearly a critique of neoclassicism itself. *Pamela* and *Clarissa* represent a different version of the "new species of writing," and they are best seen as radical transformations of romance. Pamela's letters do not play off polite literature in the way that Moll Flanders's redressed narrative does, nor do they exploit the ambiguous relations between popular and canonical literature in the manner of the history of *Joseph Andrews*. Rather they appropriate and reassert the values of the older heroic romance tradition in the colloquial expressions of a young servant girl. The aristocratic ethos of heroic romance—moral purity supported by an incredible strength of will in the relationship of men and women—is embodied in the character and idiom of a distinctly lower class in order to triumph over the less noble, more licentious ethic of the *chronique scandaleuse* that had given the term "novel" a pejorative connotation in early eighteenth-century England. Squire B., like Lovelace after him, represents the degradation of the romance tradition that came in with the Restoration. Pamela and Clarissa represent a revival of romance values and motifs in a new social and, even more important, a new psychological realm. Where Defoe's heroes and heroines must adapt to the loss of value by means of extraliterary structures, Richardson's heroines force their lower- and middle-class literacy to express values hitherto reserved for other genres. "O, my good girl," Squire B. taunts Pamela, "you are well read, I see; and we shall make out between us, before we have done, a pretty story in romance."[38] The irony of the novel is that this remark is finally true.

Thus rather than founding a new species of writing, Richardson gives the novel a different dialectic. The fabulous and noble actions of chivalric adventure are internalized in the emotions and the will of an adolescent girl. Romance is assimilated to the novel by being located in the character's unconscious and by being dramatized as the deep structure of an unliterary surface. With *Pamela*, the novel assumes the form of mythopoeic assertion. It stands apart from the neoclassical canon, but does so now more independently than the older forms of the novel like the picaresque and the Quixotic, which exist as ironical qualifications of traditional genres. In Richardson the novel appropriates, and hence transvalues, romance. In the following century the place of the Richardsonian novel is considerably complicated by the more pervasive reevaluation of romance in romanticism, romance becoming, in fact, the basis for a countercanon to the neoclassical. I shall explore this question further in a later chapter. But the novel also continued its promotion of the more ironically uncanonical, and both the picaresque and *Don Quixote* continued to provide exemplary models for this dialectical redefinition of the new.

7

Displacement as Signification

Is what we call "obeying a rule" something it would be possible for only *one* man to do, and to do only *once* in his life?—This is of course a note on the grammar of the expression "to obey a rule."

It is not possible that there should have been only one occasion on which someone obeyed a rule. It is not possible that there should have been only one occasion on which a report was made, an order given or understood; and so on.—To obey a rule, to make a report, to give an order, to play a game of chess, are *customs* (uses, institutions).

To understand a sentence means to understand a language. To understand a language means to be master of a technique.

Wittgenstein, *Philosophical Investigations*

"*Tristram Shandy* is the most typical novel of world literature."[1] This assertion by Viktor Shklovsky, a paradoxical *mot* characteristic of the strengths and limitations of Russian Formalism, is a challenge that few of Sterne's critics have taken seriously. In Shklovsky's analysis, *Tristram Shandy* is novelistic in the way it confounds our expectations about the novel, but the nature of the novel itself remains highly abstract and completely unhistorical in his account. Ian Watt suggests that Sterne somehow managed to combine the divergent realisms of Richardson and Fielding, but he goes on to say much the same thing as Shklovsky when he claims that *Tristram Shandy* is "not so much a novel as a parody of the novel," a "*reductio ad absurdum* of the novel form itself."[2] This is certainly a point of departure for considering *Tristram Shandy* as a novel but it hardly begins to broach the subject of the place of Sterne's novel in a historical series of such texts. Most other commentators have preferred to consider the book as something other than a novel: as philosophy,[3] as satire,[4] as an exercise in rhetoric or another of the liberal arts.[5] "Technically, *Tristram Shandy* presents such a strange case that one hesitates to class it as a novel at all," writes Henri Fluchère.[6] The only way in which its status as a novel is generally allowed is by reference to certain experimental modernists—Proust, Gide, Joyce, or Beckett, a view in which self-consciousness is seen as peculiarly modern and in which

Sterne appears as oddly ahead of his time. One of the aims of this study is to dispel such simple evolutionary assumptions about the history of this inherently unstable literary form.[7]

It is not easy to read *Tristram Shandy* as anything particular or discrete, to be sure. Every thing or kind of thing it might be is always changing into something else. It is a book, a conversation, a journey, a sermon, an autobiography, an encyclopedia, or as Yorick suggests, a story about a cock and a bull, which as an ending to nine volumes of narrative makes it the first shaggy-dog story as well. Every frame that might contain the story seems to be identified, brought into play, and discarded. The very name of the hero is a multiple oxymoron. Both "Tristram" and "Shandy" point in a number of different semantic directions: sadness, valor, courtly love, craziness, and a light alcoholic drink.

Nevertheless, at a certain historical distance from this protean text one can discern the features of the novel as it had existed in Europe for the past two hundred years. It is a "life" like the Spanish picaresque *vidas*—*Lazarillo de Tormes, Guzmán de Alfarache, La Vida del buscón*. It supplements events and incidents with "opinions" which by their piecemeal and eccentric presentation become detached from the rule of doctrine or system. *Tristram Shandy* is novelistic in the way it attributes its many allusions and quotations to particular characters; they are the intellectual property of Walter Shandy, Uncle Toby, or Tristram. As in most novels there is the intermediary presence of character and consciousness. These conventions of novelistic selfhood, however they are manipulated, are the frame through which we perceive the action and the ideas. Consciousness is focused on other selves, in their ambiguously public and private identities—Yorick, Corporal Trim, the Widow Wadman—and on small or incidental physical objects—a bowling green, a sash-weight, a cloak, a hot chestnut. While Sterne borrows from the repertoire of classical and neoclassical satire, *Tristram Shandy* is a novel and not a satire in the way it subverts rather than validates the notion of cultural norms. Eccentric selves and trivial things are defended rather than prosecuted in their autonomy.

In a long view of the novel, therefore, one that considers the sixteenth century as well as the twentieth, we can see that *Tristram Shandy* is deceptive in its self-confessed novelty. It is idiosyncratic for the most part in the way it treats the novel's staple of innovation, the contemporary life story relating specific transactions between psychological selves and a material world. Such innovation, by privileging the self, allows new narrative codes to infringe on the codes of traditional literary representation. What we find in the case of Sterne, in fact, is the tendency of the novel, or the reception of the novel by a reading public, to become itself a matter of literary convention and norm. It is the stabilization of the novel in mid-eighteenth-century England, I would argue, that leads Sterne to his redoubling of the novelistic effort. Yet Sterne's project, as he signals at the beginning and end of his extended narrative, is also a particular tribute to the precedent of Cervantes's *Don Quixote*.

The reputation of *Don Quixote* in England had undergone a radical change in the two decades preceding the first volumes of *Tristram Shandy*. Before 1742, as we have seen, when Fielding's *Joseph Andrews*, "Written in Imitation of the Manner of Cervantes," and a learned preface to *Don Quixote* by William Warburton both appeared, Cervantes's novel had been regarded as a jest-book, a burlesque, or at best a satire. But with Fielding and Warburton, the peculiar literary ironies and the ambiguous idealism of Cervantes's hero began to be more widely appreciated; *Don Quixote* began to be read as a novel and as an important precedent for the "new species of writing" that was appearing on the English literary scene. The respectful imitation of Cervantes rapidly became a literary fashion in England, and *Don Quixote* was increasingly accommodated to an expanded literary canon. Marivaux's *Pharsamon ou, Don Quichotte Moderne* was translated in 1749. Charlotte Lennox's *The Female Quixote* appeared in 1752, accompanied by a favorable notice by Fielding in the *Covent Garden Journal*. Sarah Fielding, Henry's sister and fellow novelist, praised "that strong and beautiful human nature represented in *Don Quixote*'s madness in one point and extraordinary good sense in every other."[8] Hester Piozzi reports a more extravagant, though significantly qualified opinion of Dr. Johnson's: "After Homer's Iliad, Mr. Johnson confessed that the work of Cervantes was the greatest in the world, speaking of it . . . as a book of entertainment."[9]

Johnson's more well-known pronouncement on *Don Quixote* appeared in 1750. "Very few readers, amidst their mirth or pity, can deny that they have admitted visions of the same kind; though they have not, perhaps, expected events equally strange, or by means equally inadequate. When we pity him we reflect on our own disappointments; and when we laugh, our hearts inform us that he is not more ridiculous than ourselves, except that he tells what we have only thought."[10] In Johnson's balance of views there are potentially conflicting elements. On the one hand, there is the vision of *Don Quixote* as a general human model and as close to the classical genres in its perfection. On the other hand, there is a sense of strong subjective identification; Quixote is not a mirror of grand generality, but of our *own* disappointments; we are informed by our *own* hearts of the ridiculousness of our unconfessed desires. This same tension can be found in other contemporary responses to *Don Quixote*, less well-integrated than Johnson's, as in the anonymous "Essay on the New Species of Writing." The author identifies Fielding as "our English Cervantes," and announces his desire to regulate this new literary kind—"to put a stop to the unbounded liberties the Historians of this comic stamp might otherwise indulge themselves." The author takes the Preface to *Joseph Andrews* at face value, and credits Fielding rather than Cervantes with setting forth the "Laws which should ever after be deemed sacred by all that attempted his manner." Yet in a swerve from his neoclassical principles, he also criticizes those who do not "follow the bent of [their] own Genius," and claims that "a tolerable Original is greatly preferable to the best Copy."[11]

In the midst of this contradictory revaluation of *Don Quixote*, and of the novel as a literary form, stood Tobias Smollett, who provides the clearest example of the kind of novelist Sterne refuses to be. Smollett was both a translator and an imitator, in the best Augustan sense of the word, even though the material he was operating on was beyond the bounds of the Augustan canon. He translated Lesage's picaresque novel *Gil Blas*. Then he wrote *Roderick Random*, announcing *Gil Blas* as its model although specifying a correction of its "plan" in order to allow for a deeper emotional sympathy with the hero.[12] Lesage himself had already of course translated, imitated, and regularized the Spanish picaresque. Smollett then published a translation of *Don Quixote*, in 1755, and began publishing a *Quixote* imitation, *Sir Launcelot Greaves*, in 1760. There is no certain evidence, as Arthur Cash puts it, that Sterne actually read the novels of Smollett, or of Fielding or Richardson, but "we can hardly doubt that he did so."[13] We can also hardly doubt Sterne's awareness of the growing tendency of the English novel, in the decade after Fielding's and Richardson's greatest innovations, to normalize and institutionalize itself in the literary system. The definition of the novel that Smollett offered in the Preface to *Ferdinand Count Fathom* in 1753 is a prime instance of the trend:

> A Novel is a large diffused picture, comprehending the characters of life, disposed in different groups, and exhibited in various attitudes, for the purposes of an uniform plan, and general occurrence, to which every individual figure is subservient. But this plan cannot be executed

with propriety, probability or success, without a principal
personage to attract the attention, unite the incidents, un-
wind the clue of the labyrinth, and at last close the scene by
virtue of his own importance.[14]

First the assertion of a "uniform plan," then the assertion of a "principal personage": on a level of significant generality, Smollett bal-
ances the demands of the part and the whole. The radical imbalance
of *Tristram Shandy*, the continual victory of part over whole or "the
triumph of slight incidents over the mind" (322) as Tristram puts it,[15]
all make particular sense as a reaction against the norms of the
"novel" (Smollett's preface is one of the first times in English that the
word is used in its modern sense) now beginning to be established.[16]
   The gap between Smollett's theory and his practice is of course
noticeable. Roderick's adventures are notably "random," and it is
difficult to see any uniformity in the characteristically episodic picaresque plot. To some extent, Smollett was responding in *Ferdinand
Count Fathom* to criticism of *Roderick Random* for its lack of uniformity, as also in the matter of the chapter titles, for which he was
criticized in "An Essay on the New Species of Writing."[17] But even
in *Roderick Random* Smollett provides a structure and a focus for his
story, in his concern with the organic form of the body. Roderick's
adventures turn again and again on the norm of the human frame.
His survival depends on the strength and resiliency of his physical
constitution, which in turn insures the final triumph of his emotionally healthy mind. *Mens sana in corpore sano* is the protocol of Smollett's version of the picaresque. The physical violence of *Roderick
Random* and other novels of Smollett is a function of this corporeal
aesthetic, as literary decorum is identified with the propriety of the
body in an oddly literal fashion. Again, Sterne's cultivation of a
much more delicate kind of physicality or "sensibility" may be seen
as a reaction to Smollett's fondness for physical assault and battery.[18]
It is similar to Sterne's later opposition, in *A Sentimental Journey*, of
sentimental traveling to Smollett's peripatetic "spleen." The health
and wholeness of the body are explicitly denied in *Tristram Shandy*.
The physical frame, like every other frame, is always in the process of
coming apart and the narrative is deliberately valetudinarian rather
than robust.
   Since Smollett's *Quixote* novel, *Sir Launcelot Greaves*, appeared
almost simultaneously with the first two volumes of *Tristram Shandy*,
in January of 1760, it is difficult to argue that Sterne is reacting
directly to Smollett in the matter of Cervantes. Nevertheless, the
contrast between the two novels in their reception of *Don Quixote* is

141

revealing. Smollett attempts a formal regularity of plot and character, in the manner of Fielding rather more than of Cervantes. He places a particular emphasis on the preservation of a sound mind in a healthy body, a preservation threatened by time spent in a madhouse. But Smollett also treats the precedent of *Don Quixote* with a curious literalism. Sir Launcelot Greaves is not a Quixote figure in the sense that Parson Adams is, a character unwittingly analogous to Cervantes's hero in his parallel literary delusions. He is a man driven mad by love for a young woman who then dresses up as Don Quixote in order to advertise Sir Launcelot's despair. There is a gap between his private emotional state and his public role. He is an amateur chivalric hero, who by his very amateurism stands above the narrow and deforming professionalism of the doctors, lawyers, sailors, and squires who populate his adventures. Smollett treats Don Quixote in the manner of the contemporary "fancy painting," which depicts the Tragic Muse as a costume for a Mrs. Siddons. The art itself is representational; it is the subject who is playfully dressing up, for the time being.[19]

It is easy to dismiss *Sir Launcelot Greaves* as a novelistic failure. But it is interesting to see how the novel attempts to resolve the conflicting ideas about *Don Quixote* current in England in the 1750s. Cervantes's novel was still recognized as a satire and a parody of chivalric literature, but it was also seen, increasingly, as a sympathetic portrayal of the chivalric state of mind. This state of mind could be located in the reader, as we have seen, but it could also be discovered in the author himself, especially as it was only in this period that the romantic circumstances of Cervantes's captivity and resistance in Algiers became widely known in England.[20] Smollett makes the latter distinction in the "Life of Cervantes" prefixed to his translation of *Don Quixote* in 1755: "Notwithstanding all the shafts of ridicule which he hath so successfully levelled against the absurdities of the Spanish romance, we can plainly perceive from his own writings, that he himself had a turn for chivalry: his life was a chain of extraordinary adventures, his temper was altogether heroic, and his actions were, without doubt, influenced by the most romantic notions of honour."[21] It is such a distinction that Smollett tries, however clumsily, to make in *Sir Launcelot Greaves:* the heart of a profound romantic is quite literally encased in the trappings of a ludicrous madman. In fact, we are never given a satisfactory explanation of Greaves's motives in playing out the Quixotic scenario.

Sterne's treatment of Cervantes's novel provides a strong contrast.

Literally, *Don Quixote* is hardly to be seen in *Tristram Shandy*. There is a lengthy though indecisive comparison of Rocinante to Yorick's horse in the first volume, ending in a personal tribute to "the peerless knight of *La Mancha*, whom, by the bye, with all his follies, I love more, and would actually have gone further to pay a visit to, than the greatest hero of antiquity" (22). There is also a poignant evocation in the last volume of the spirit of humor, "who erst didst sit upon the easy pen of my beloved CERVANTES." In this latter case, the emphasis is strongly on the spirit of the author rather than on the letter of the text: "Thou who glided'st daily through his lattice, and turned'st the twilight of his prison into noon-day brightness by thy presence —— tinged'st his little urn of water with heaven-sent Nectar, and all the time he wrote of *Sancho* and his master, didst cast thy mystic mantle o'er his wither'd stump, and wide extended it to all the evils of his life" (628). (Sterne adds a footnote to explain Cervantes's loss of his hand.) At the level of translation and imitation on which Smollett operates, *Don Quixote*, as a text, is scarcely discernible in Sterne. Elsewhere in the novel, and in Sterne's letters, it is invoked mainly in the form of an adjective made from the author's proper name, "Cervantick."

Sterne's image of *Don Quixote* is not unimportant; it is simply a good deal more figurative than Smollett's. It appears to be Sterne's reaction against the increasing normalization and literalizing of *Don Quixote* as a precedent. Sterne's reception of Cervantes's work involves a paradoxical displacing of the precedent, away from the explicit form and content of *Don Quixote* altogether. In place of "dearer Cervantes," in fact, one can more easily see "dear Rabelais," or the useful Robert Burton, Sir Thomas Browne, and other Renaissance compilers from whom Sterne borrows chapter and verse. In place of one novel we find a scattering of *centos*, "books of quotation and allusion, on a very large scale, to all conceivable elements of their culture," as Rosalie Colie describes them.[22]

To say that *Don Quixote* is Sterne's point of departure for such encyclopedic allusions to previous encyclopedists may seem like an unwarranted privileging of the novelistic text. However, there are several figurative levels on which *Tristram Shandy* functions as a reinterpretation of *Don Quixote*. The most obvious figurative level is the level of character constituted by the main protagonists, Walter Shandy and Uncle Toby. Corporal Trim is a Sancho figure to Toby's Quixote—the more literal-minded servant to his master's obsession—but the Quixote role itself is distributed and divided

143

between Walter and Toby: each is a partial, domesticated, and largely immobilized version of Cervantes's hero. They are Don Quixote in retirement, a pastoral scale-model of the "Cervantick" original.

In Cervantes's novel, Don Quixote offers a paradoxical combination of "arms" and "learning." In his several set speeches on this Renaissance topos, he defends the profession of arms against the profession of letters as the more honorable calling of the two. Yet Quixote's own conception of military service is derived solely from his reading; his chivalry is a private renaissance of outmoded customs of combat. Quixote's arms are embodied primarily in Toby, the fanatic of fortifications, while his learning, his encyclopedic knowledge of literary precedent, is embodied in Walter Shandy, the master of outmoded *paideia*. Of course Toby's arms have a bookish dimension to them—he has "almost as many more books of military architecture, as Don *Quixote* was found to have of chivalry" (89), Tristram says—even though he must finally escape from books to physical models in order to cure his wound. More importantly, the self beneath Toby's soldier's role is exceptionally humane. His arms are defensive rather than aggressive; the man who would repel the French cannot bear to kill a fly. Conversely, Walter's humanism is continually on the attack. He argues for victory and is apt to wound his brother in direct assaults on Toby's *idée fixe*: "I wish the whole science of fortification, with all its inventors, at the devil; ——it has been the death of thousands, ——and it will be mine, in the end," he says at one point (113), only to apologize profusely when Toby silently turns the other cheek. Walter's intellectual systems are fortifications themselves, "institutes," as he calls them, designed to surround and defend the physical and psychic well-being of his offspring. But they are continually assuming the offensive with regard to other characters. Sterne transposes the active chivalric mode of *Don Quixote*, itself already radically transposed from *Amadis of Gaul* and the other chivalric romances, into the passive-aggressive interactions of personality. That the eroticism of this new family romance is remarkably attenuated is a further indication of its Quixotic source. The Widow Wadman provides a more immediate Dulcinea, but she is brought on only late in the game.

Walter Shandy upsets the Quixotic balance on the side of books and ideas, Uncle Toby tips the scales in the direction of exercises and concrete objects. Walter is a more intellectual, Toby a more physical Quixote, even though each recreates the literary paradox of learned arms and armed learning. More ambiguously Quixotic is the figure of Yorick, who inhabits the story on a different level of characterization and presides over the text most notably through his lamented absence. In a sense, he is a more unified and balanced Quixote figure than Walter or Toby, at least as long as he is able to retain his horse. Sterne makes the comparison explicit in connection with Yorick's and Quixote's modesty (22). But because of the demands on his horse occasioned by the midwife and because of the cruel satires directed against his more amaible humor, his figure recedes early on in the narrative into the famous black page. Yorick is Don Quixote in an elegiac mode, the Quixote of the last chapter of Cervantes's Second Part, whose death leaves the company around him deprived of their sustaining fiction. " 'Oh, don't die, dear master!' answered Sancho in tears. 'Take my advice and live many years. For the maddest thing a man can do in this life is to let himself die just like that, without anybody killing him, but just finished off by his own melancholy' " (*Don Quixote*, p. 937).

Of course, as Yorick's name and lineage show, Sterne is also transposing *Don Quixote* onto *Hamlet*. The hero of the novel becomes the jester of the play—the jester who only appears on stage in the form of a memento mori. Turgenev was to suggest that Don Quixote and Hamlet were opposing archetypes of the moral self, but for Sterne they are, on the aesthetic level, curiously interdependent, even though their arms and their learning, to pose the comparison in Renaissance terms, point them in opposite directions. Thus, as far as Yorick is concerned, we might say that there is a displacement within the displacement: *Don Quixote* is displaced by *Hamlet*, but Hamlet, the tragic hero of melancholia, is displaced by Yorick, the jester against death. The counterpoint between tragedy and comedy in Shakespearean drama is represented in a new novelistic key. It is interesting that Hamlet says in his brief tribute to Yorick in the play, "He hath borne me on his back a thousand times"; the jester is also a father figure—the last of many—for the hero in his tragic rites of passage before he attains his brief majority. While it does not seem possible to fix the intertextual play of identities with any finality, Sterne does suggest an intriguing series of literary transpositions on this level of the older generation in the novel.[23]

A last level on which *Don Quixote* appears as a text informing *Tristram Shandy* is the level of the younger generation, Tristram the author-narrator himself. Here the relationship is the most figurative. What is taken over from Cervantes is the formal principle of inclusiveness itself. Sterne redefines Cervantes's critical encyclopedia of the literary system as a critique of the system of culture as a whole.

In *Don Quixote* the multiple forms of literature are brought up against the unwritten data of human perception. In *Tristram Shandy* the multiplicity of culture is brought up against the uncivilized impulses of human nature. We find in Sterne a play not simply with literary forms and genres but with a broad spectrum of the arts and sciences: rhetoric, painting, music, sculpture, historiography, mechanical engineering, geography, physics, thermodynamics, medicine. The novel becomes not just an ad hoc poetics as in *Don Quixote* but an ad hoc *paideia*, a "cyclopedia of arts and sciences" as Tristram calls it (122) of its own. *Tristram Shandy* is an eccentric and subversive document in the movement in later eighteenth-century England that Lawrence Lipking has called "the ordering of the arts." New attempts were being undertaken by contemporaries of Sterne like Reynolds, Burney, Warton, and Johnson to organize the productions of culture in a historical as well as an ideal fashion, precisely because of the loss of authority of the older order of Renaissance humanism, which writers like Cervantes, as well as Burton and even Sir Thomas Browne, could take for granted.[24] Sterne's encyclopedia is of course decidedly unsystematic, and there is no reason to deny the influence of Rabelais, Burton, Browne, or even Swift on Sterne's eclectic and unproportioned assemblage. But the way these cultural entries are channeled through the errancy of a particular character indicates the special connection with *Don Quixote*.

> Now ride at this rate with what good intention and resolution you may, ——'tis a million to one you'll do some one a mischief, if not yourself——He's flung——he's off——he's lost his seat——he's down——he'll break his neck——see! ——if he has not galloped full amongst the scaffolding of the undertaking criticks! ——he'll knock his brains out against some of their posts——he's bounced out! —— look——he's now riding like a madcap full tilt through a whole crowd of painters, fiddlers, poets, biographers, physicians, lawyers, logicians, players, schoolmen, churchmen, statesmen, soldiers, casuists, connoisseurs, prelates, popes, and engineers——Don't fear, said I——I'll not hurt the poorest jack-ass upon the king's high-way. (298)

Sterne is neither anatomizing a particular subject, like Burton or Browne, nor satirizing a deforming methodology, like Rabelais. He is rather, like Cervantes, representing a new type of narrative by an elegiac gathering of the old. The novelty of the "life" is figured, in a kind of narrative metalepsis, by the antiquarian nature of the "opinions." For Sterne, however, the scope of history has been considerably enlarged and the depth of the past has become more profound since the example of Cervantes.

John Ferriar, the first to document what he considered Sterne's lack of originality, observed that what Sterne was apparently satirizing was largely over and done with. "Rabelais derides absurdities then existing in full force, and intermingled much sterling sense with the grossest parts of his book; Sterne, on the contrary, laughs at many exploded opinions and forsaken fooleries, and contrives to degrade some of his most solemn passages by a vicious levity."[25] We should not condemn Sterne for this comic antiquarianism; nor, on the other hand, should we unduly praise him, as Hermann Meyer does in drawing a similar contrast between Sterne and Burton: "Burton is a humanist who has faith in culture. For him the *topos* is a venerable, indeed a sacrosanct matter. . . . For Sterne, classical education has collapsed; he sees the cultivation of *topoi* exposed as an empty cultural fraud."[26] What we should mark instead is the extent to which *Tristram Shandy* stands outside the system of humanistic culture, and the way it uses the very decline and fall of that culture to dramatize its own innovation. Where Fielding is still working within the Augustan neoclassical framework, liberalizing and politicizing its revival of Greek and Roman literary forms, Sterne steps outside neoclassicism altogether and shows the essential futility of its attempts to reanimate the ruins of the ancient world. The death of the classic—which is of course Sterne's interpretation, not an inexorable fact of literary history—is a means, curiously displaced, of representing the rebirth of the novel—a form of literature that for Sterne and his contemporaries began with Cervantes. To try to revive *Don Quixote* directly, in the manner of Smollett, would be to play into the hands of death itself.

Instead, Sterne creates his own fictive order of succession: *Tristram Shandy* is a novel which will succeed itself, becoming its own cause in suprahistorical fashion. Tristram promises the reading public a series of sequels for the rest of his (or Laurence Sterne's) natural life, two volumes a year. "I swore it should be kept a going at that rate these forty years if it pleased but the fountain of life to bless me so long with health and good spirits" (479). Ginés de Pasamonte, the literary *pícaro* in *Don Quixote*, said his book could not be finished because his life was not yet over. Tristram Shandy reverses the equation. Like Scheherazade, his life cannot end until his story is over, and the calculus of futility that he laments in Volume IV—"at this rate I should live 364 times faster than I should write"—is really a

147

source of satisfaction. His primary life *and* opinions become a secondary life *of* opinions: "I perceive I shall lead a fine life of it out of this self-same life of mine. . . . I shall never overtake myself" (286). The narrative conceit is even given a philosophical sanction in a passage Sterne borrows from Locke: *"so we estimate the existence, or the continuation of the existence of ourselves, or any thing else commensurate to the succession of any ideas in our minds, the duration of ourselves, or any such other thing co existing with our thinking"* (190). The faster we change our minds, the longer we live.

The most appropriate term for this illogical but pervasive attitude in the novel is "displacement"; this, in effect, is the protocol of *Tristram Shandy* as a novel. As I have been arguing with earlier examples of the novel, the protocol of a novel defines both an internal and an external set of relationships of the text. "Displacement" in *Tristram Shandy* governs not only the intertextual relations of the book with one of its main precursors, *Don Quixote*, but also the way it situates itself in its own historical moment. The book is quite literally a displacement of Sterne's own life, from his identity as the Reverend Laurence Sterne to his identity as "Tristram Shandy," which was deliberately planned to launch Sterne from his Yorkshire parsonage onto the "great world" of London and the Continent. The persona of Tristram is displaced in turn by other personae like "Yorick," who assumed authorship of Sterne's earlier sermons in *The Sermons of Mr. Yorick* and who took off from the ongoing project of *Tristram Shandy* in *A Sentimental Journey*. In a particularly immediate way, Sterne aimed at living in his readers' imaginations. At the same time, Sterne displaces the reader from *his* habitual role and stance—challenging him ("Sir"), cajoling her ("Madam"), continually upsetting his or her narrative expectations. We are accused of reading too idly, of reading too carefully, of being too literal or too metaphorical, or too vulgar or too refined. The reader is brought into the text as an interlocutor, only to have her opinion rebuked, or their opinions divided. "——How could you, Madam, be so inattentive in reading the last chapter? I told you in it, *That my mother was not a papist.*—— Papist! You told me no such thing, Sir. Madam, I beg leave to repeat it over again" (56). "——What would your worships have me to do in this case? ——Tell it, Mr. *Shandy*, by all means. ——You are a fool, *Tristram*, if you do" (207). "The reader" becomes a succession of the personal pronouns that linguists call "shifters."

The typographical eccentricities, so often commented upon, are a further displacement and resituation of our perceptual engagement with the text. The famous black page—actually two black pages (33–

34)—appears as a drastic rearrangement of the conventional black border that appears around Yorick's "epitaph and elegy":

| Alas, poor YORICK! | (32)

This inscription—itself of course a comically displaced quotation from Shakespeare—is freed from its typographical frame as it is "read over with such a variety of plaintive tones" by passersby. It becomes a vocal performance:

Alas, poor YORICK!

The page is then overwhelmed by the funereal margin; delineation is total and cancels itself out.[27] We do not cease to "read" *Tristram Shandy* at this point—we know very well what this undifferentiated inking of the page signifies—but we are forced momentarily to read the text elsewhere, on a different semiotic level from most of the rest of the book. Similarly, with the white pages on which we are invited to sketch our cautious fantasy of the Widow Wadman (470–71), the blankness is not without meaning, but the production of meaning is suddenly transposed into a less specifically encoded space, which requires new responsive techniques.

Here we begin to talk about the intratextual organization of the novel, although as we shall see, Sterne calls the distinction between "internal" and "external" relationships of a text into question. On virtually every level of significance in *Tristram Shandy*, displacement appears as the governing principle, the modus operandi of the narrative. Such an assertion is a dangerous one to make about a story inhabited by Walter Shandy, about whose intellectual activities Tristram wryly observes, "It is the nature of an hypothesis, when once a man has conceived it, that it assimilates every thing to itself as proper nourishment" (151). "To look for the 'law' of *Tristram Shandy* is one of the least promising enterprises in criticism," Sigurd Burkhardt writes.[28] But a recognition that the protocol of *Tristram Shandy* is precisely not a law but rather a method of eluding laws is a necessary point of departure. Sterne in fact exaggerates the legalism of literary procedures so as to dramatize his own a-legality: "is a man to follow rules——or rules to follow him?" (281). His great disorder is not without a counterorder of its own. The best way to demonstrate this protocol of displacement is to reexamine some of the traditional topics—the *topoi* or commonplaces—of commentary on the novel.

The "world" of *Tristram Shandy* is a world that has lost its coherence. It is not a sheer anarchy, but a plurality of worlds displacing one another in the narrative sequence. Tristram glosses the term "world" in discussing the midwife's reputation: "a small circle described upon the circle of the great world" (11). The small circle is generally eccentric to the large one but it is also superimposed upon it, and the geometry is a paradigm for the spatial relations in the text. The novel is written in a "bye-corner of the kingdom" (3), yet it launches Tristram in mind and body upon the country, and even the Continent, as a whole. Shandy Hall is the locus of Mr. Shandy's retirement from the great world of London, although he binds himself to having his children born in the city. The rooms of the house dramatize an intricate series of displacements between indoors and outdoors, upstairs and downstairs, especially as Tristram is in the process of being born. The scene of the birth itself is displaced for us as readers from Mrs. Shandy's womb to Dr. Slop's heavily knotted green bag, from which he produces not the effectual forceps but the ineffectual squirt. Uncle Toby's bowling green is a displaced and delayed theater of war, and the "place" of Uncle Toby's wound is comically transposed from geography to anatomy by the Widow Wadman, as far as one can tell from her response. "——You shall see the very place, Madam; said my uncle *Toby*. / Mrs. *Wadman* blush'd" (623). Any situation in the novel is subject to a resituation, and the transitions are notoriously abrupt. Don Quixote told Sancho that there were adventures of islands and adventures of crossroads. In Sterne the crossroad is the adventure itself. Thus Tristram implores the powers that enable a man to tell a story "that wherever, in any part of your dominions it so falls out, that three several roads meet in one point, as they have done just here, ——that at least you set up a guide post, in the center of them, in mere charity to direct an uncertain devil, which of the three he is to take" (207). His wish is an obvious displacement of his desire to remain at a crossroads forever.

The time scheme of *Tristram Shandy* is similarly disarranged. The history of one object or event is continually giving way to the history of another object or event, in a way that explodes the model of causal explanation and scrambles the sequence of chronology. Like his contemporary, Hume, Sterne demonstrates that our ideas of cause and effect are a matter of custom rather than a function of logic,[29] and his narrative surprises are designed to spring us free of this fallacy of anticipated form. In Chapter 8 of Volume II, Tristram offers an elaborate justification of his apparent violation of the "unity, or rather probability, of time" (103) in his account of the appearance on the scene of Dr. Slop. It might appear to the hypercritic, he says, that

Dr. Slop had returned too quickly after Obadiah had been sent to fetch him, and he advances the argument that reading time is the true measure of acting time in the novel. But this correlation of time schemes is collapsed by the addition of another temporal fact, introduced *ab extra:* Obadiah happened to collide with Dr. Slop sixty yards from the stable. Thus, as John Traugott observes, there is no real coordination of different levels of temporality in the novel; all times appear as some kind of present.[30] And yet every present moment, if only by virtue of the medium of the printed book, is also already a part of history when the reader perceives it: "——that observation is my own; ——and was struck out by me this very rainy day, *March 26, 1759,* and betwixt the hours of nine and ten in the morning" (64). The very tense of the verb betrays the inevitable displacement of writing it down. Tristram's search for origins, his desire "to come at the first springs of the events I tell" (66) in his story, discovers not the locus of a linear beginning truly prior to the end but a peripheral event which is engagingly beside the point.

The strategy of displacement is of course a response to the vision of history as a decline and fall that Sterne shares with a contemporary like Gibbon. It does not conceive of the genetic creativity of history that was envisioned by Herder and the later romantics, in spite of their professed admiration for Sterne.[31] *Tristram Shandy* represents time by place, one might say, and the novel's candid embrace of the secondary, the derivative, and the unoriginal depends on the narrative's potential for commuting from one position to another. It is a preromantic rather than a postromantic discovery of *différance,* to use Jacques Derrida's Sternian play on spelling—a distinction that is also a deferment.[32] Even Tristram's famous flight from death in Volume VII, the most existential confrontation with time in the book, takes the form of a geographical journey to the warmer South. By a kind of composition of place, Tristram is able to recapitulate here an earlier journey as well, one that he has made with his father and uncle. "——Now this is the most puzzled skein of all——for in this last chapter, as far at least as it has help'd me through *Auxerre,* I have been getting forwards in two different journies together, and with the same dash of the pen" (515).

This leads to a third common topic in criticism of Sterne, the question of personal identity. As I have already noted, "Tristram Shandy" is a displacement of "Laurence Sterne," one that Sterne was always eager to acknowledge as correlative with himself. Several critics suggest that the problem with "Yorick" as a mask is that he is too proximate in professional role and emotional temper to Sterne's more immediate self-image.[33] Yorick gives way early in the novel to Walter and Toby, although he is brought back in again in the later volumes. Tristram's apparent preoccupation with this family friend has led some critics to suppose that he is Tristram's real father,[34] and Yorick's own ancestry shows how fraught a genealogy can be with fictitious begettings. What is more problematic and more interesting to speculate on is the way Tristram gives birth in the novel to his own father and uncle as characters. His narrative consciousness never attains the determinate identity of a character but delivers instead, in maieutic fashion, the displaced identities of two relatively fixed humorous characters. It lingers on the older generation as the proper substance of its own life and opinions. Tristram has an undeniable rhetorical presence as narrator, yet as an actor in the drama of the Shandy household he is always offstage or waiting in the wings.

A further displacement of the question of identity can be seen in the way the characters of Walter and Toby are sketched. Our attention is diverted from the original self to the model or toy with which it is characteristically occupied. Tristram rejects the idea of a transparent "*Momus's* glass, in the human breast" (74) and acknowledges the opacity of the mind in its bodily wrapping. After a catalogue of possible indirections for arriving at the image of another self, he offers his own approach to character through the hobbyhorse. The very terms of his description show the characteristic displacement from the great to the trivial, from the body-soul conjunction to something else.

> A man and his HOBBY-HORSE, tho' I cannot say that they act and re-act exactly after the same manner in which the soul and body do upon each other: Yet doubtless there is a communication between them of some kind, and my opinion rather is, that there is something in it more of the manner of electrified bodies, ——and that by means of the heated parts of the rider, which come immediately into contact with the back of the HOBBY-HORSE. ——By long journies and much friction, it so happens that the body of the rider is at length fill'd as full of HOBBY-HORSICAL matter as it can hold; ——so that if you are but able to give but a clear description of the nature of the one, you may form a pretty exact notion of the genius and character of the other. (77)

The center of a character's identity is to be deduced from his eccentricities, his nature from his avocation. And the entire procedure is couched in a series of physical analogies: by their playthings ye shall know them. The relevance of game theory to the novel has been ably demonstrated recently by Richard Lanham,[35] yet most of the games in *Tristram Shandy* are versions of solitaire.

Other examples of the workings of displacement in the novel could be adduced, ad nauseam if not ad infinitum. The relationship of digression to the supposed main plot of the book is another main case in point. Yet the *logic* of displacement, the way in which the protocol might make a new sense as well as delight by its nonsense is something that remains to be considered. One plays a game for diversion, but also, if the game is played at any length, for mastery. Blake was to create his own system in order not to be enslaved by another man's; in Sterne the equation is reversed. The manifest desire to escape from a predetermined order contains a latent desire to assert a control of one's own. That Sterne did not finally control his life by his elaborate fictional strategy is obvious. We hardly need James Work's final elegiac footnote to his edition of *Tristram Shandy*, "Sterne did not live to continue the book" (647). There is also evidence, from Volume VI of the novel onward, that the game of displacement was becoming more difficult for Sterne to maintain in its own terms. Biological time threatens to overtake fictional time in Volume VII as "Tristram" is pursued by "Death," and in Volumes VIII and IX the story makes its most massive digression, leaping back well before the time of Tristram's conception into the matter of Uncle Toby's amours. The spirit of pathos begins to make inroads on the spirit of jest, from the story of the death of Le Fever and the catastrophe (for Uncle Toby) of the Peace of Utrecht in Volume VI to the invocation of the maimed and imprisoned Cervantes and the story of Maria's madness in Volume IX. Over what might the author be said to have achieved control?

Some categories that Sterne found particularly intriguing as a novelist, as several generations of critics have observed, are derived from the philosophy of Locke. Yet Sterne effects important rearrangements of Locke's system, most notably in Locke's attempt to adjudicate the relationships among the order of ideas, the order of words, and the order of things, or as Locke calls them, "substances." Locke posits a hierarchy of these three orders in which ideas are supreme, substances or things act as the source of ideas (that is, of the "simple" ideas derived from sensation), and words are firmly subordinated to ideas and substances. Words do not refer to things directly, Locke insists, but to *the ideas in the mind of him that uses them, how imperfectly soever or carelessly those ideas are collected from the things which they are supposed to represent.*[36] Locke is

153

fighting a battle on two fronts. On the one hand, he is attempting to discredit the notion of ideas as innate; on the other hand he is trying to control what he recognized as the arbitrariness of the linguistic sign. But as his imaginative and philosophical followers were to discover—Berkeley, Hume, and Jonathan Edwards, for example—Locke's logical premises often admitted of radically different conclusions.[37] Hume developed Locke's epistemology in the direction of a cognitive skepticism. Berkeley took it in the direction of a metaphysical idealism. Edwards developed it into an affective theology of grace. Sterne, transposing Locke's argument into the more ironic discourse of the novel, came up with a practical semiotics. The mastery that Sterne achieves is a mastery of the sign, based on Locke's profound but occluded insight into the sign's arbitrary nature. In fact, Sterne anticipates twentieth-century semiotics in a number of fascinating ways, even though he has no interest in theoretical formulations per se.[38] He upsets Locke's equilibrium of ideas, words, and things by apportioning them out, as ruling passions, among three main figures in the novel. He gives language an ultimacy in Tristram and shows the limitations of concepts and substances in Walter and Toby.

In Walter Shandy, Sterne creates a philosopher who insists on the primacy of the notion. Walter's theories multiply the complexity of what Locke called "complex ideas"; they ruthlessly subordinate the claims of things and the claims of words to the rule of conceptual abstraction. The substance of the nose is comprehended by an institute of ideas about the nose. The influence of a proper name, in what amounts to a parody of Locke's concept of the "nominal essence," is subjected to an institute of ideas about names. The Lockean concern with education becomes the hyperideational *Tristrapaedia*. It is not that Walter believes in innate ideas but that he would protect the *tabula rasa* of his offspring's mind with a host of intellectual defenses.

Walter Shandy is also an ironic victim of the only "association of ideas" in the strict Lockean sense, in the whole novel, when his wife associates the idea of intercourse with the idea of her husband winding the clock.[39] Everywhere else his theories are subject to *dis*sociation in the minds of others, the dismemberment of the rigid anatomy of his thought by Toby or Bridget or someone else mistaking his meaning. In fact, the phenomenon is one that Freud specifically calls "displacement" in *Wit and Its Relation to the Unconscious*. "I propose to designate it as *displacement* [*Verschiebung*]," Freud says,

154

"for its most essential element, the deviation of a trend of thought, consists in displacing the psychic accent to another than the original theme."[40] When Walter Shandy uses the word "Siege" in a discussion of truth Uncle Toby suddenly pricks up his ears, the word obviously receiving a different psychic accent in his mind. Walter foresees the danger of displacement in Toby's unwitting wit and quickly drops the metaphor. But he is still outmaneuvered by his brother: "'Tis a pity, said my father, that truth can only be on one side, brother *Toby*, ——considering what ingenuity these learned men have shown in their solution of noses.—— Can noses be dissolved? replied my uncle *Toby*" (239). However well-guarded, Walter's philosophical assault on truth is thwarted by the unruly medium of language.

Toby likewise finds his well-being threatened by the imprecision of words. The deeper he gets into books of fortification in an effort to come to terms with his wound, the more bewildered he becomes. Tristram begins to explain his problem with a lengthy excursus into Locke's analysis of mental obscurity and confusion. But he then announces that imperfect ideas are not the source of Toby's problem at all: "'Twas not by ideas, ——by heaven! his life was put in jeopardy by words" (87). In Walter's case, words undermine the intellectual articulation of a subject; in Toby's case words frustrate his control of the physical. The resolution of Toby's impasse is suggested by the still more physically minded Corporal Trim, who proposes a shift from words to things, from a verbal to a physical medium of representation. "I think, quoth Corporal *Trim*, with humble submission to your Honour's better judgement, ——that these ravelins, bastions, curtins, and hornworks make but a poor, contemptible fiddle faddle piece of work of it here upon paper, compared to what your Honour and I could make of it, were we in the country by ourselves, and had but a rood, or a rood and half of ground to do what we pleased with" (95–96). Walter's system of ideas is solipsistic and a priori. Toby's system of substances is communal and after the fact. But both are retreats from the field of language into a realm that seems more susceptible to their outmoded rage for order.

The articulation of Toby's theater of war is based on the model of mechanics—and on the mechanics of model-making. Instead of the random connections of one word with another, Toby and Trim achieve what theoreticians of models call an isomorphism, a matching of parts and functions between the original and the replica, a matching that tries to banish chance. As Sigurd Burckhardt has convincingly argued, the mechanistic figures of *Tristram Shandy* should not be too easily dismissed as ironically metaphorical. "Engines and devices pervade the whole novel; they are second only to sex in supplying the metaphorical substance, and even sex appears a good deal of the time in the metaphor of the engines and mechanics of war."[41] Sterne is in part exploiting the rhetoric of eighteenth-century pornography, as in the lubricious hydraulics and thermodynamics of Cleland's *Fanny Hill*, but in the case of Toby, the character who embodies the spirit of mechanism in the novel, the metaphor is reversed. Sex is merely a distraction from the model machinations of war, a displacement which Toby on the whole resists. The fleeting connections of human parts are of less interest to him than the more permanent and reliable conjunctions of walls and ditches, ravelins, half-moons, bridges, hinges, wheels, and sash-weights, even if Trim is not quite as loyal to the colors. Nevertheless, since the mechanical model is ultimately faithful to the historical conduct of Marlborough's campaigns, its reassuring linkages are ultimately doomed by the Peace of Utrecht. This is a chronological event from which the story of Uncle Toby's amours in Volumes VIII and IX simply retreats. The belated erotic interest gives Toby's war games a new lease on life, but only in a still greater retrospect, reflecting on a more distant past.

Tristram, the physical and spiritual offspring of this older male generation, is the victim of theories and physical objects on one level of the narrative, but on another level, the ultimate level of narration itself, he inhabits the realm of language. This is the only realm in which he is at home. The ambiguity and ambivalence of words, a threat to the father and the uncle, are a consolation to the child. From Tristram's point of view, which of course determines our point of view as readers all along, Walter's ideas and Toby's things are simply aberrant cases of language, comically incongruous levels of signification. The very displacement of meaning that their contrasting projects represents is in fact a key to Tristram's practical understanding of language *as* displacement. The meaning of language, especially in the form of a printed text, is neither "here" nor "there," as the etymology of "text" implies. "*Text* means *Tissue*," Roland Barthes observes, "but whereas hitherto we have always taken this tissue as a product, a ready-made veil, behind which lies, more or less hidden, meaning (truth), we are now emphasizing, in the tissue, the generative idea that the text is made, is worked out in a perpetual interweaving."[42]

In another context and in a more systematic fashion, Barthes distinguishes between connotative and denotative systems of signs. An ordinary semiotic system relates a set of signifiers to a set of signifieds, but in these "staggered systems," as Barthes calls them, the signifying relationship is more complex. In the connotative system, signifier *and* signified—the sign as a whole—become themselves a signifier for a higher level of concept. In the denotative system, the sign is analytically divided and the signifier alone becomes the "meaning" of a lower order of significance. It seems to me that in the operations of Walter Shandy and Toby, Sterne has intuited this linguistic differential. In Barthes' terminology (and from Tristram's point of view) the systems of Walter and Toby are staggered systems of language, connotative and denotative linguistics respectively.

The connotative system, as Barthes explains it, is one "whose plane of expression is itself constituted by a signifying system." Thus Walter Shandy takes the totality of language, sound-image and concept, as the vehicle for his higher order of conceptualization. The plane of content, the higher order signified itself, is difficult to define in this case, as Barthes notes; it "is at once general, global and diffuse, . . . a fragment of ideology." This is precisely the situation in Walter Shandy's hyperbolic assertions of meaning beyond ordinary meaning. Words in general become for him a sign of the pre-eminence of ideas per se. The denotative system or "metalanguage," as Barthes calls it, is one in which the original sign itself becomes the content or meaning for a new semiotic operation, as in the creation of a special scientific language to analyze phenomena that ordinary language cannot distinguish. Toby's models and physical games function in this way. They act as a more reduced and specific set of references, correcting what is for Toby a deficiency in merely verbal representation. A physical replica of a bridge cannot be misappropriated by irrelevant contexts in the way that the sound-image "bridge" can.[43] The structure of *Tristram Shandy* has perhaps proved so fascinating and yet so elusive for literary critics for this very reason: that it exposes a primary structure of signification. This is another point at which we may think of Sterne as redoubling the playful analysis of Cervantes. Where *Don Quixote* interrupts the unfolding of literary stories to reveal their essential duplicity, *Tristram Shandy* interrupts the process of language itself, to show the inherent displacement of "meaning" that even denotative reference involves.[44] The interruptions are so frequent and so various in Sterne that a "primary" representational context is never established. The narrative remains radically suspended between points of reference.

Thus when Sterne plays with the meaning of the word "nose,"

Chapter Seven

insisting that "by that word I mean a Nose, and nothing more, or less" (218), he is not indulging in a pun, properly speaking. Rather he is calling into question the identity of the verbal sign, by showing how easily a new signified may attach itself to an old signifier. "Here are two roads, . . . a dirty and a clean one, ——which shall we take?" The reader is beguiled into displacing the concept arbitrarily bound to the sound-image—guided, of course, by what Sterne considers a common hobbyhorse of the human race, the topic of sexuality. The displacement is even more arbitrary in the case of "whiskers," or the *"petite canulle."* The "improper" meaning ("penis") is not accessible in the general semantics of English (or French), as it would be in the case of a pun, where one sound-image is bound to more than one meaning. It is true, of course, that such word play does have common roots in the situation semantics of the double entendre, found in certain types of joke.

Sexuality in Sterne is in fact radically linguistic, in a way that anticipates the heterodox Freudianism of Jacques Lacan, where the structure of the unconscious is identified with the structure of language. The lack of consummation in the sex of *Tristram Shandy*, and even more, the ambiguous fantasies of circumcision and castration, suggest Lacan's theory of the phallus as the signifier par excellence—a signifier whose function as such depends on the fantasy of its removal, that is, upon the castration complex. Sterne's insight is of course inchoate compared to Lacan's detailed articulation of the problematic of sexual desire and linguistic expression. But the basic economy of Lacan's analysis—that the closed system of a binary opposition of presence and absence may be opened by the introduction of a third mediating term, a sign that is both present and absent—is something that Sterne uncovers *avant la lettre.*[45]

As in the game of displacement of Freud's grandson, the *"Fort! Da!"* of *Beyond the Pleasure Principle* that Lacan finds so important in the discovery of the symbolic order, the game of displacement in *Tristram Shandy* shows a mastery of signs, an ability to manipulate the prior conditions of significance. The "rules" of the game appear purely arbitrary, and the novelty of the novel seems without precedent. Nevertheless, compared even with his contemporaries like Christopher Smart, or with his admirers of the next generation like Goethe, Sterne experiments with language and the meaning of meaning in a curiously circumscribed fashion. *Tristram Shandy* remains a discernible novel in the historical sequence of novels beginning in the sixteenth century nowhere more than in its refusal of a religious or metaphysical burden.[46] It is a burden that was soon taken up in France by Diderot, in explicit imitation of *Tristram Shandy* in *Jacques Le Fataliste,* and would later be taken on, in a more programmatic fashion for the *"Roman,"* in the German romantic movement, with Goethe, Richter, the Schlegels, Schiller, and Novalis. Sterne's influence in Germany was considerable if diffuse.[47] In *Wilhelm Meister, Hamlet* would become a new ur-text for the novel, more significant than *Don Quixote,* and the novel would become a chronicle of the formation of the self rather than a story of its displacements and dissolution. But in *Tristram Shandy* itself, the play of significance is limited to the secular and the perceptual realms. Behind the crumbling institution of literature, the institution of religion remains secure.

Indeed, it seems to be Sterne's assurance about the Word of God that allows his experiment with the words of men its free play. In this respect, Yorick plays the important role of Tristram's godfather—or symbolic father, as Lacan would say. He is the spiritual sponsor of Tristram's initiation into language, where the spirit is always guaranteed its liberation from the letter. Yorick's sermon in Volume II subjects a parting exhortation, supposedly from Paul ("Pray for us: for we trust we have a good conscience, in all things willing to live honestly") to Paul's own hermeneutic principle of the letter and the spirit.[48] Yorick does not "abuse the Apostle," as Doctor Slop anticipates he will, but he does use Paul's words deliberately out of context to refer the Lockean semiotic to a higher authority. In this religious sphere, order and balance are allowed to prevail. The Letter to the Hebrews, from which the sermon's text is taken, is the most closely reasoned book of the New Testament, and the sermon itself, actually preached and published some ten years earlier by Sterne, is a model of logic, proportion, and clear definition of terms. The performance of the text here is of course interrupted by Shandean antics and analyses, and it only enters the novel between the pages of Stevinus, one of Uncle Toby's quixotic books of armaments. But it has its own beginning, middle, and end ("FINIS"), and it indicates quite explicitly a fixed ethical and religious position beyond the innumerable aesthetic displacements that the novel effects. The sermon, in other words, signals another cultural system, still coherent for Sterne, in which self-consciousness is termed "conscience." It shows that this capacity for self-analysis and self-judgment is too unreliable to be institutionalized: "remember...that your conscience is not a law" (140). It insists on the subordination of human judgment in certain matters to the higher authorities of God and reason, who have provided the indivisible "tables" of religion and morality that conscience must "call in" and "consult" (132). This is one cultural system that Sterne's novel refuses to incorporate and subsume.

The novelty of Tristram as author is thus underwritten by the traditionalism of Yorick as preacher. Yorick's voicing of "the short and decisive rule which our Savior hath left us" (140) ultimately sanctions Tristram's flouting, in print, of "any man's rules that ever lived" (8). One might argue that Sterne is repressing an insight into the potentially infinite regression of his own irony, that he arbitrarily exempts certain texts and contexts from the endless play of semiotic displacement. Yet this is only to say that, like Kierkegaard after him, Sterne was a literary ironist who refused to consider literature as a total or self-sufficient institution—even as he might be said to have greatly expanded its possibilities. For Kierkegaard, the established church no longer provided a reliable resolution of the problems of secular consciousness; the relationship of man and God could only be one of a profound inwardness and an absolute otherness. But for Sterne, the religious way out remained comically immediate, as evidenced in the following exchange between Walter and Toby:

> But I say, *Toby*, when one runs over the catalogue of all the cross reckonings and sorrowful *items* with which the heart of man is overcharged, 'tis wonderful by what hidden resources the mind is enabled to stand it out, and bear itself up, as it does against the impositions laid upon our nature.
> ——'Tis by the assistance of Almighty God, cried my uncle *Toby*, looking up, and pressing the palms of his hands close together—— ... That is cutting the knot, said my father, instead of untying it. ——But give me leave to lead you, brother *Toby*, a little deeper into this mystery (277–78).

Sterne does not actually take this way out in *Tristram Shandy*. We are led deeper into the mystery rather than higher into the available resolution. But because of this resolution at a higher level, already formulated by Sterne as parson, every mysterious depth can become a new significant surface, as the plane of content is displaced, again and again, onto the plane of expression. It was Kierkegaard who argued for the essential relationship of the comic perception to the religious, who said that "the comic apprehension evokes the contradiction or makes it manifest by having in mind the way out, which is why the contradiction is painless."[49]

Like earlier novels, English and European, *Tristram Shandy* brings to light the contradictions of history, literary and otherwise. Tendencies that seem innovative, in view of later developments, coexist with tendencies that appear conservative, even reactionary. Georg Lukács was particularly aware of such contradictions in the works of the great realists of the nineteenth century, and he went as far as to identify them as the essence of realism in the novel. "This ruthlessness towards their own subjective world-picture is the hallmark of all great realists, in contrast to the second-raters, who nearly always succeed in bringing their own *Weltanschauung* into 'harmony' with reality, that is, forcing a falsified or distorted picture of reality into the shape of their own world view."[50] But as I have tried to show in this interpretation of Sterne's novel through its protocol of displacement, a novel does not merely submit to the historical process, which is after all, to a large extent, an affair of texts and signifying structures in the first place. A novel presents its own version of the historical process of which it is a part, including a version of its placement in a series of texts that it is aware of resembling. It was only after Sterne that historic*ism* became the dominant paradigm for Western European society, a paradigm in which all cultural forms were conceived as existing along a coordinating temporal axis. One might also venture that it is only after Lukács, the most authoritative modern exponent of Hegelian and Marxian history, that literary critics are coming to understand the original perception of novelists that history itself is no more than a tissue of texts. As *Don Quixote* demonstrates, it is a tissue that is continually torn and rewoven, by readers both idle and energetic. And the texts themselves, as Quixote forces us to realize, are only as unified or integral as the discontinuous but communal fabric of human desire can make them.

8

PICKWICK PAPERS *and* VANITY FAIR

The Renascence of Convention

I

Without making any boast of it Sancho Panza succeeded in the course of years, by devouring a great number of romances of chivalry and adventure in the evening and night hours, in so diverting from him his demon, whom he later called Don Quixote, that his demon thereupon set out in perfect freedom on the maddest exploits, which, however, for lack of a preordained object, which should have been Sancho Panza himself, harmed nobody. A free man, Sancho Panza philosophically followed Don Quixote on his crusades, perhaps out of a sense of responsibility, and had of them a great and edifying entertainment to the end of his days.

Franz Kafka, *The Great Wall of China*

The influence of the earliest Spanish examples of the novel was never absolute. The history by example that has been sketched out here from the sixteenth to the eighteenth century does not claim to be exhaustive or definitive of the variety of novelistic texts and types that appeared in the first two hundred years of this new species of writing. Nevertheless, during this time *Don Quixote* and the picaresque continue to be paradigmatic of the way that the bulk of European novels situate and define themselves within the larger literary culture, ironically displacing the established rules and values of a professedly classical tradition.

In the course of the eighteenth century, however, and for the two hundred or so years following, the novelistic critique of the literary status quo also takes another basic form. The new paradigm is part of the more general cultural shift of romanticism, and it involves a new valuation of the older vernacular tradition of romance. *Don Quixote* uses the vernacular romances as an impertinent challenge to the authority of Aristotelian rules and regulations. *Moll Flanders* uses romance elements as a means of flouting the Augustan hierarchy of genres. But in the novels of Richardson, of Rousseau, and of Goethe and Scott, romance motives begin to enter the domain of the novel with a new authority. In this new paradigm, the novel no longer functions as a displacement of the official literature but as a re-generation of the unofficial. In this new form of the novelistic critique "literature" is no longer conceived as a specific conservative institution, to be infiltrated and unsettled by types of writing that have been excluded from its perimeters. "Literature" is rather expanded to include any of the oppressive or falsifying fictions by which a society has kept human consciousness in bondage. This is the more generalized adversary against which the new form of novel takes its stand; the underlying vitality of the imagination is to be rescued from the moribund conventions which have held it captive. In this form of the novel, the romance tradition is not an exposure of literature's inherent weakness, but a revelation of its latent strength.

As long as the literary system of neoclassicism was firmly enough established, the novel could take a stand on the periphery and ironically call this centrality into question. But as the system itself began to lose its authority, through incursions from many different quarters, the novel in its more romantic form could also claim a new centrality for its peripheral operations. The problem of terminology here is a difficult one. As I noted in the first chapter, the distinction between "novel" and "romance" which began to be made in England in the eighteenth century has no equivalents in the other European languages, where cognates of "romance" have continued to designate older classical and vernacular types of idealizing narrative as well as the newer, antithetical series of "lives," "adventures," and "histories." Even in English, despite such distinctions as Clara Reeves's that "the Romance in lofty language, describes what never happened nor is likely to happen.—The Novel gives a familiar relation of such things, as pass every day before our eyes," critics continued to interchange the terms well into the nineteenth century.[1] And writers of prose fiction have continued to adopt and adapt narrative formulas of an idealizing or archaizing nature up to the present day.

Nevertheless, there is a clear historical distinction to be made between narratives which operate for the most part within the codes of the older romances—for example, Mlle de Scudéry's *Astrée*—and narratives which transform these codes and transpose them into other arenas of discourse and action, such as Richardson's *Pamela*.[2] It is a distinction between an extension of romance tradition itself and a reorganization of romance elements within the already established alterity of the novel. That such a reorganization of romance elements within the novel occurs in the course of the eighteenth century in Europe is undeniable. It seems to occur most gradually in France, where the hold of neoclassicism was the strongest, and most abruptly in England, where the advent of the novel was both delayed and explosive. In Germany, in spite of individual exceptions like the picaresque *Simplicissimus,* the novel only became an important form of literature during the widespread revival of romance tradition in the second half of the eighteenth century. And it is in Germany that the romanticizing paradigm of the novel received its fullest and most independent elaboration.

A generic distinction between romance proper and the romanticized novel should also be maintained, in spite of a tendency in Anglo-American criticism to give the two terms parity in categorizing the novels of the nineteenth century.[3] It is a large-scale distinction parallel to the one between satire and the novel described in Chapter 3. As I noted in considering the romances of classical antiquity, romances differ from novels in the way they transcend the historical conditions of human experience. Such transcendence is difficult to measure in any precise fashion, but it involves the appeal to a supernatural authority beyond the psychological and social accommodations in which the novel deals. Romance may present beings more powerful than the human, events caused by divine or demonic agency, or what Peter Brooks has termed the "moral occult" of the more popular melodramatic mode.[4] But the codes to which it appeals have the force of religious testament, requiring assent of a more than rational nature. As Fredric Jameson puts it, "romance . . . is dependent for its emergence on the availability of a code of good and evil which is formulated in a magical, rather than a purely ethical, sense. This code finds its expression in a vision of higher and lower realms in conflict."[5]

Thus where satire invests literary codes with the authority of the law, romance attributes to its narrative formulas the authority of sacred myth, even as the idea of the sacred becomes diffuse and fragmentary in the modern period. Apart from both these forms of authority stands the more tentative and individualizing protocol of the novel. The "partial magic" of the novel, where enchanters are merely the alibis of an ingenious hero's learned imagination, is different from the fuller, deeper magic of romance that requires the reader to suspend his disbelief—whether temporarily, in an act of what Coleridge calls "poetic faith" or more enduringly, as in the antiquarian and utopian persuasions required in the fiction of William Morris.

It is not my purpose here to adjudicate the territorial boundaries of this distinction, although it seems to me that in prose fiction after

1750 there are many more novels that incorporate strong romance elements than there are romances pure and simple. What I do want to insist is that within the romantic novel the sacred, the supernatural, and the occult are deprived of their transcendent authority. Their sacred myths are subject to a Higher Criticism which returns them to the realm of human history, psychic as well as social. Walpole's *Castle of Otranto*, Hölderlin's *Hyperion*, and Mary Shelley's *Frankenstein* remain within the romance mode. Balzac's *Peau de Chagrin*, Bronte's *Wuthering Heights*, and Hawthorne's *Scarlet Letter* are examples of the romanticized novel, their supernatural elements notwithstanding.

As far as the novel in general is concerned, this romanticizing alternative does represent a significant departure from the examples of *Don Quixote* and the picaresque. As a historical phenomenon, the regeneration of romance within the novel may be traced back as far as Madame de Lafayette and *La Princesse de Clèves*, but it was in the novels of Richardson—*Pamela*, *Clarissa*, and *Sir Charles Grandison*—that this alternative to the Quixotic and the picaresque was expressed with something like the exemplary force of the earlier novels. From *Clarissa* proceed a number of eighteenth-century epistolary and confessional novels of erotic intrigue and sentimental resistance: Diderot's *La Religieuse*, Rousseau's *La Nouvelle Héloïse*, Goethe's *Sorrows of Young Werther*, Laclos's *Les liasons dangereuses*. The impact of Richardson on the nascent American novel has been vigorously described by Leslie Fiedler, and his importance for Jane Austen, through the mediation of Fanny Burney, has been affirmed by a number of critics.[6]

It would take another whole book to assess the way later novels actually engage Richardson's texts, and there are of course many other examples of the romanticized novel that are equally if not more influential in the nineteenth century: Goethe's *Wilhelm Meister* and the *Bildungsromane* which follow its educational pattern, Scott's *Waverley* and the form of the historical novel, the panoramic urban novels of Balzac's *Comédie Humaine*, the reclusive Gothic novels of a variety of authors. One might even mention here the morally strenuous novels of Leavis's "Great Tradition," with Jane Austen at their head. As Brooks argues for the case of Henry James, "The Gothic quest for renewed contact with the numinous, the supernatural, the occult forces of the universe, leads into the moral self."[7] Nevertheless, we may use one notice of Richardson here to indicate briefly a major highway not taken as this exemplary history follows *Don Quixote* and the picaresque into the nineteenth century.

In his *Éloge de Richardson* of 1762, Diderot exclaims about the supremacy of Richardson's novels over more factual history. "Oh Richardson! I would dare to say that the truest history is full of lies and that your novel is full of truths. . . . From this point of view I would dare to say that often history is a bad novel, and that the novel, as you have made it, is a good history."[8] In this conceit of history as a "bad novel" we can see the way the romanticized novel no longer conceives of itself merely in opposition to a classical canon of literature; the critique is now extended to the superficial and conventional representation of society in all kinds of writing: official histories (as in *War and Peace*), parliamentary reports (as in *Hard Times*), antiquarian genealogies (as in *Tess of the d'Urbervilles*).

It is true that in this alternative paradigm the dialectic between "novel" and "literature" appears to be collapsed, but it is more accurate to say that it has been overlaid with different ideologies, ideologies that are presented as "merely literary" within a particular novel's multiple fields of discourse. The "literature" that novels of this sort react against is the *dictionnaire des idées reçues*, the literature of official platitudes and conventions of the modern social order. It is a different sort of establishment from the neoclassical canon, but it involves a no less arbitrary restriction of the possibilities of prose fiction. It is a literature that thinks of itself as natural rather than conventional. It has mistaken itself for life, and the novel must expose its deficient ontology.

"For a multitude of causes unknown to former times are now acting with combined force to blunt the discriminating powers of the mind, and unfitting it for all voluntary exertion to reduce it to a state of almost savage torpor. The most effective of these causes are the great national events which are daily taking place, and the encreasing accumulation of men in cities, where the uniformity of their occupations produces a craving for extraordinary incident which the rapid communication of intelligence hourly gratifies. To this tendency of life and manners the literature and theatrical exhibitions of the country have conformed themselves."[9] This indictment of the written order of the modern *Gesellschaft* by Wordsworth is as appropriate to the romanticizing novel (in spite of Wordsworth's subsequent jibe at "frantic novels") as it is to the "Poetry" he is seeking to define and defend. In fact, in this new paradigm one finds the novel closely aligned with the more traditional literary forms of poetry and drama, as these have been transvalued by romanticism. One might say that in regenerating the romance tradition the novel has moved closer to the older genres, but one could as easily say that

166

poetry and drama have moved in the direction of the novel in their reaction against neoclassical norms.

Mikhail Bakhtin speaks of literature becoming "novelized": "In an epoch where the novel reigns supreme, almost all other genres are to a greater or lesser extent 'novelized': drama (for example Ibsen, Hauptmann, and all naturalist drama), epic poetry (for example "Childe Harold" and especially Byron's "Don Juan"), even lyric poetry (an extreme example is Heine's lyrical verse)."[10] I would explain this novelization not simply as the result of an influence exerted upon poetry and drama by novels, but as the result of a broader cultural shift—away from a public, centralized, and hierarchical conception of literature toward a more private, more centrifugal, and more egalitarian conception. Romanticism in literature might be said to be an exploration of the power of otherness: otherness in nature as opposed to culture, in the supernatural as opposed to the merely natural; in the unconscious self, in the ancestral past, in the mysteries of the "Imagination." The novel, with its own traditions of cultural estrangement, enters into a complex exchange with the more stable and conservative literary forms. The empirical differences between the novel and poetry or drama are still clear enough, but on a theoretical level one might say that romanticism is the novelization of neoclassical literary culture.

Thus in turning to nineteenth-century novels in the series of the Quixotic and the picaresque, we enter on different historical ground, a terrain in which the earlier examples of the novel survive but only under the sedimentary pressure of more recent exemplary instances. A geological model is more appropriate than a biological one here. A particular fault line, allowing one to see the different strata superimposed, as it were, is presented at the beginning of Scott's *Waverley*, where the author bids an explicit farewell to *Don Quixote:*

> From the minuteness with which I have traced Waverley's pursuits, and the bias which these unavoidably communicated to his imagination, the reader may perhaps anticipate, in the following tale, an imitation of the romance of Cervantes. But he will do my prudence injustice in the supposition. My intention is not to follow in the steps of that inimitable author, in describing such total perversion of the intellect as misconstrues the objects actually presented to the senses, but that more common aberration from sound judgement which apprehends occurences indeed in their reality, but communicates to them a tincture of its own romantic tone and colouring.[11]

167

In the novels I shall consider hereafter the Quixotic and the pica-resque are still close to the surface, but they are subject to the later folding and faulting of the novelistic field. In the present chapter I shall consider novels by Dickens and Thackeray, in the next chapter novels by Melville and Twain. What is particularly interesting in these nineteenth-century reenactments of *Don Quixote* is that they also turn out to be reenactments of the picaresque novel that *Quixote* originally counterbalanced and subsumed. Don Quixote is superim-posed upon Ginés de Pasamonte—and vice versa—in a simultaneous revival of the rogue. In Defoe, Fielding, Smollett, and Sterne, these two paradigms of the novel are perceived as formally, even neoclassi-cally, distinct. There is little mixing of the two antithetical modes, even in the works of a novelist like Smollett who deliberately culti-vates both. But with *Pickwick Papers, Vanity Fair, The Confidence-Man,* and *A Connecticut Yankee,* in complex and differing ways, the originally contrasting novelistic types become a dialect within a par-ticular text. Such internalizing of the earlier opposition seems due to a number of historical changes. The presence of the many eighteenth-century variations on the Spanish novels helped erode the formal and thematic distinctions between the Quixotic and the picaresque, particularly the more romantic and idealizing picaresque of Lesage's *Gil Blas.* This process was furthered by the tendency of nineteenth-century criticism to isolate individual characters from their genres and plots, as in the investigation of Shakespeare's heroes and heroines out of literary context. Most important was the enormous growth of alternative types and kinds and series of novels already alluded to, which could only make the original distinctions less distinct.

In the case of *Pickwick Papers,* Dickens's first novel, the re-semblance with the exemplary *Don Quixote* has often been noted.[12] As we shall see, Dickens's imitation of Cervantes is also an imitation of Fielding, Smollett, Sterne, and others. The influence of the Quix-otic model is more conducive to exuberance than to anxiety and it seems to be an influence that Dickens only gradually realized in the course of the early serial installments. But within the first number, the quixotic Samuel Pickwick has already met his picaresque antiself in Alfred Jingle, and the ground of their opposition has been pre-pared in the near-duel of mistaken identities between Mr. Winkle and Dr. Clammer. Pickwick is a Quixote without appreciable literary delusions. His benevolence is often misguided and naive but it is the product of spontaneous emotions rather than of a particular course of reading. Pickwick's theory of tittlebats and his antiquarian paper on the elusive inscription "+/ BILST/ UM/ PSHI/ S.M./ ARK" (137) show traces of Cervantes's literary critique as expanded by Sterne.[13] But for the most part Pickwick's Quixotic nature is purely ethical; he is, as Dostoevsky noted, a portrait of a thoroughly *good* man. It is in Jingle's picaresque presence and absence that the uncertainty of the aesthetic is brought into play. Jingle is a strolling actor, one who impersonates a wide variety of social and literary types. His shorthand syntax delivers persuasive fragments of reported experience without committing itself to the verifiability of a declarative statement. As an eminently theatrical character, he is perhaps the first of a series of picaresque figures in the nineteenth and twentieth centuries whose deceptions are specifically linked to the calling of the artist.[14]

As the episodes of *Pickwick Papers* accumulate and the loosely episodic plot of the novel, so different from Dickens's later intricate plots, develops, the opposition between Pickwick and Jingle becomes both literal and symbolic, particularly as it focuses on the institution of marriage. Pickwick's benevolent bachelorhood is counterpoised by Jingle's fortune-hunting marital deceptions; Jingle's deceptions are in turn reflected in Pickwick's conviction and imprisonment for breach of promise to Mrs. Bardell. There are of course numerous other antagonisms and oppositions in the novel, but a great many of them cluster around these characterological poles. Pickwick's forgiveness of his adversary and Jingle's conversion at the end have their precedents in both novelistic traditions. But the complementary pairing of the chivalric naif and the delinquent is an important reintegration of *Don Quixote* and the picaresque on Dickens's part.

The most original and imaginative element of *Pickwick Papers,* as critics of all persuasions tend to agree, is the character of Sam Weller, "the novelist-poet within the novel," as Steven Marcus has called him.[15] The similarities and differences between Sam Weller and Sancho Panza have often been noted, but what is most vital in Sam's servant role in the novel is the way it mediates between the Quixotic and picaresque alternatives. It seems no accident that Sam makes his first appearance in the novel at a moment of confrontation between Pickwick and Jingle, when the "hero" has tracked the "villain" down at the White Hart Inn. In response to his readers' immediate signs of approval, Dickens was able to capitalize for the rest of the novel on the centrality of this inspirational intercessor.

In Cervantes, Sancho is essentially an understudy to Don Quixote, a low-style parallel to Quixote's chivalric delusion rather than a sharp-witted alternative to his master's madness. But for Dickens, this master-servant formula was also available in the picaresque—in Gil Blas's Scipio, Roderick Random's Strap, in Peregrine Pickle's Tom Pipes—and Sam has an instinct for survival that Sancho lacks. He shares in Pickwick's ethical dream, if only in his unshakable loyalty to his master and his unflagging participation in his fortunes. Sam will have himself prosecuted by his father in order to join Pickwick in the Fleet. He will defer his own romance until his wife-to-be can also enter into Pickwick's service. Yet he is also a shrewd and cynical judge of the performances of others, not always successful in countering their plots but rarely taken in by their pretensions to virtue. He is also, as several critics stress, a brilliant storyteller and imaginist, with a native artistic ability that Pickwick so notably lacks. His Wellerisms, his defining habit of speech in a novel where character is idiolect, are just the reverse of Sancho's proverbs. They reinvigorate the purely conventional phrase in a simile of outlandish violence. "There; now we look compact and comfortable, as the father said ven he cut his little boy's head off to cure him o' squintin'" (384). As in this brief exemplum delivered in the midst of the Dingley Dell Christmas, Sam redeems the Pickwickian ceremonies of innocence from their always threatening loss of emotional force. But as these similes remain comic and unmotivated, Sam redeems the pragmatic energy of living by one's wits from the inherent cruelty and selfishness of Jingle's career as trickster.

Sam is less important as a character in his own right than as a new possibility of relationship among the various ethical and aesthetic stances of other characters. As picaro-Sancho he relates the avuncular Quixote of Pickwick to the paternal blend of rogue and naif in his natural father, Tony Weller. He finds his own servant counterpart in Job Trotter, the knave of the doleful countenance who serves the knave as more amiable humorist. Sam is at the nexus of the legal and spiritual relationships which become the generative structures of so many of Dickens's later novels: master and servant, parent and child, guardian and protégé, all of them subject to infinite permutations and reversals. It is here that we can see quite literally how Dickens's novels were to outgrow the Quixotic and picaresque armature on which *Pickwick Papers* was constructed. Even within *Pickwick* itself, one can observe the pressures of other novelistic prototypes that had emerged in the romantic era. In particular, one can see how the more current forms of the *Bildungsroman* and the Gothic, the novel of education and the novel of terror, begin to impinge on the anachronistic models.

In *Wilhelm Meister's Apprenticeship* Goethe includes the Gothic as a counterfiction within his exemplary novel of education in much the same way that Cervantes incorporates the picaresque in *Don Quixote*. Along with the story of Wilhelm's aesthetic and moral education there are the haunted and haunting figures of Mignon and the Harper, whose Italian and incest-ridden origins signal their Gothic mode. In them, the world of the imagination is lyrical, frankly supernatural, and above all traumatic. They are in bondage to the past, fixated in a primary fantasy which they can only repeat. In the case of Wilhelm Meister himself, the world of imagination lays itself out in a series of phases through which his maturing mind may pass. From the puppet shows of his boyhood to the prolonged engagement with Shakespeare's *Hamlet* and to the moral allegories of the secret society of the Tower, Wilhelm inhabits a succession of literary fictions which are not so much rejected as outgrown. Where Don Quixote assimilates other literary genres to his own chivalric scenario by a process of endless analogy, Wilhelm Meister recapitulates a succession of literary genres (mainly dramatic) in his psychological development. Cervantes's picture of the old man as idle reader becomes a portrait of the young man as creative artist—even though Wilhelm must finally transcend the social role of artist in the course of his apprenticeship.

A similar contrast might be drawn between the Gothic novel and the picaresque. The half-outsider is replaced by the romantic outcast, exchanging ironic ambiguity for the stylized psychomachy of good and evil, benevolence and revenge. The picaro offers to an unsuspecting society its own mores in the form of fictions. The Gothic villain reflects a nightmare inversion of society's dream of moral perfection, an image of the dark compulsion that underlies its hope for freedom. This is not to say that either *Don Quixote* or the picaresque simply evolve into these other fictional forms, or that the earlier counterfictions are simply replaced by the later. Rather it is to remind ourselves that this history of the European novel in the nineteenth century—and from this point on the American novel as well—had begun to assume other broad dialectical forms. A classic example of the interaction of these two exemplars is provided by a later Dickens novel like *Great Expectations* where the counterfictions of *Bildungsroman* and Gothic novel dominate Pip's autobiographical narrative. His education and apprenticeship is continually jeopardized—indeed, is stood on its ideological head—by the recurrent Gothic scenes that fixate his supposedly developing mind. There is the graveyard school where he first comes to consciousness, Magwitch with his story of the "'orrible young man" who would eat Pip's liver, Miss Havisham's Satis House with its attempt at a chronological "arrest," and the multiple hauntings of Pip by his own and other people's pasts in London. *Great Expectations* has often been seen as a *Bildungsroman*, but it is a novel of *Bildung* unable to free itself from Gothic *Schauer*. Each new alternative or alternate self that the novel produces turns out to be haunted in a new way.

In *Pickwick Papers*, these possibilities do loom on the horizon. Gothic elements surface most clearly in the interpolated tales. In *Don Quixote* the interpolated stories are spots of freedom, recreative spaces in which a wide range of generic alternatives are explored. In *Pickwick Papers*, they are a locus of compulsion, in which madness, crime, misanthropy, and revenge appear again and again, the return of a literary if not of a psychological repressed. And these Gothic motifs may be traced beyond the tales themselves, until they reveal, as Christopher Herbert puts it, "imaginative passageways connecting Pickwick's carefree England with the subterranean Gothic realm."[16]

Nevertheless, these elements are more or less contained by the primary model of the picaresque: on the literal level of the action, the villain is subordinate to the rogue, the misanthrope to the cynical half-outsider. The effort at containment is particularly overt in Chapter LIII, where Dickens has Job Trotter, the picaro's picaresque servant, unexpectedly claim Dismal Jemmy, the teller of the first Gothic tale in the novel, as his brother. Less awkward and more successful are Dickens's efforts to avoid the fictional form of the *Bildungsroman*. Pickwick is both old and young, a figure who "retains all his former juvenility of spirit" (801) up to the very last page of the novel. He is both before and beyond the possibility of education and development. Even the younger members of the club over which Pickwick presides, such as Snodgrass and Winkle, are allowed to avoid significant growth or change. Pickwick outdoes even Don Quixote in avoiding the pressures of mutability, for his narrative ends not with repentance and death but with a promise of his perpetual ceremonial presence.[17]

The apparent efficacy of *Quixote* as a precedent for the never-to-be-repeated transcendence that has often been ascribed to *Pickwick Papers* raises questions about Dickens's understanding of Cervantes. Steven Marcus has called *Pickwick* "the greatest of Dickens' mysteries,"[18] and I would argue that some of its strangeness and singularity can be traced to *Don Quixote*—to its reception history in the early nineteenth century, first of all, and secondly to its peculiar place in Dickens's own imaginative biography.

In the literary culture of romanticism, as we have seen, the novel

enjoyed a new position of eminence, but it was often elevated beyond its prosaic foundations. Friedrich Schlegel defined the novel as
"the Romantic book," but in doing so he tended to make the novel
over into poetry. Cervantes' *Roman* is compared not with the novels
of his successors and imitators but with the poems of Dante and the
plays of Shakespeare. For the art of imaginative prose itself, Schlegel
professed a low regard, and both he and his brother spoke of *Don
Quixote* as a "chivalric poem" or "romantic poem." Goethe, whose
conception of the novel was less polemical and more concrete,
nevertheless construed *Don Quixote* in philosophical terms, as a dialectic between reality and "the idea." And Schiller managed to regard Don Quixote as the prototype of his own romantic hero Karl
Moor, "the strange Don Quixote whom we abhor and love, admire
and pity."[19]
  Much of the English romantic reception of Cervantes's novel follows the German lead, directly or indirectly. Wordsworth's reading
of Cervantes produces the dream of the Arab "semi-Quixote" recorded in Book V of *The Prelude,* which transforms the novelistic hero
into a wish-fulfilling preserver of "poetry and geometric truth."[20]
Coleridge lectured on Don Quixote as "a substantial living allegory,
or personification of the reason and the moral sense, divested of the
judgment and the understanding."[21] And Charles Lamb performs a
similar rescue of Cervantes from the realm of the everyday and the
prosaic—that is, from the novel he inhabits—in the *Essays of Elia:*

> Deeply corporealised, and enchained hopelessly in the
> grovelling fetters of externality, must be the mind, to
> which, in its better moments, the image of the high-
> souled, high-intelligenced Quixote—the errant Star of
> Knighthood, made more tender by eclipse—has never pre-
> sented itself, divested from the unhallowed accompani-
> ment of a Sancho, or a rabblement at the heels of Rosinante.
> That man has read his book by halves; he has laughed,
> mistaking his author's purport, which was—tears.[22]

  Lamb's scorn for what he sees as the reading public's preference
for Sancho over Quixote measures the distance Dickens stands from
these romanticizing and idealizing extremes of Cervantes. The un-
hallowed accompaniment of Sam Weller is precisely what brings
Samuel Pickwick to life. But there is a more subtle romanticizing of
Cervantes in William Hazlitt's *Lectures on the English Comic Writers*
which shows the line of interpretation that Dickens did take. It is a
reading that assimilates *Don Quixote* to the great English novels of

the previous century rather than distancing it as a monument of the imagination. At the same time, Hazlitt's approach allows a romantic "tincture," as Scott would call it, to color the novels of Fielding, Smollett, Richardson, and Sterne, as these are cordoned off from contemporary novelists and the "disorder" of recent times. Cervantes—and Lesage as well—are accorded the standing of honorary Englishmen; they "may be considered as having been naturalized among ourselves," and are described in much the same terms as the novelists "of native English growth."[23] Hazlitt notes the pathos and nobility of Quixote as hero, but he perpetuates an essentially eighteenth-century judgment on him: "an enthusiast of the most amiable kind; of a nature equally open, gentle, and generous." He mentions the "instinct of imagination" in Cervantes, but insists on novels in general as "authentic documents" of "past manners and opinions." *Joseph Andrews* is "a perfect piece of statistics in its kind."[24] On the other hand, this earlier age of the novel is subtly idealized and memorialized. "It is remarkable that our four best novel-writers belong nearly to the same age," Hazlitt writes, when "there was a general spirit of sturdiness and independence, which made the English character more truly English than perhaps at any other period." Hazlitt does for Georgian England what Scott was doing for the Scottish Highlands, yet in a way that did preserve the heritage of Cervantes.[25]

This is approximately the optic on *Don Quixote,* and on the picaresque as well, that Dickens adopts in *Pickwick Papers.* A specific debt to Hazlitt is not certain, but it is clear that Dickens either set out to recreate, or decided in the course of the early installments of the novel to recreate, the Quixotic and picaresque complex found in the novels of Fielding, Smollett, and Sterne—with of course the contributing precedents of later novelists like Goldsmith and a number of lesser comic and satiric writers of the early nineteenth century who continued to work this vein of sentiment and humor. *Don Quixote* is subsumed as a primary text to the secondary episodes, incidents, and characters of *Joseph Andrews, Roderick Random, Tristram Shandy,* and other eighteenth-century texts. It is from these intermediary sources, as several generations of influence studies have pointed out, that Dickens borrows numerous frames on which to hang his own novelistic imaginings at this point of departure in his career.[26]

The borrowings occur on a number of different levels, but the most obvious of them occur on the level of situation or predicament. A particular character type is placed in a particular embarrassing circumstance. Thus Pickwick in his nightclothes in the bedroom of the fiancée of Peter Magnus is a reprise of the similar bedroom farce with Parson Adams and Mrs. Slipslop in *Joseph Andrews*. The rough justice Pickwick and Sam receive from Mr. Nupkins is an elaboration of the prejudicial treatment of Parson Adams and Joseph Andrews by the fox-hunting justice of the peace. The comic duel between Mr. Winkle and Dr. Slammer is based on a similar encounter in *Peregrine Pickle*. And in a more serious vein, Pickwick's self-confinement in the Fleet, which occasions Dickens's first exploration of the prison as an image of society, has a clear precedent in Smollett's *Sir Launcelot Greaves*, when the latter-day Quixote visits the King's Bench prison and encounters the curious folkways of this "microcosm or republic in miniature"—its factionalism and vengeances, its economics and acts of charity—from within. Several of the prison characters in *Sir Launcelot Greaves*, in fact, closely resemble inhabitants of the Fleet in *Pickwick Papers*, especially the man who after nine years and the death of all his friends has become "naturalized to the place." [27]

Such borrowings are of interest to us not as signs of literary influence, in a generative model of literary history, but as indications of the way Dickens creates his own precursors, in Borges's paradoxical phrase—recreates them for his own symbolic purposes. In the first place, Dickens elaborates richly on the incidents that he reenacts. What occurs in two short chapters in *Sir Launcelot Greaves* takes eight long chapters in *Pickwick Papers*, and the variations on the theme of imprisonment are considerably more numerous and complex. Secondly, the incidents themselves are a form of allusion to an age of innocence, the golden age of Georgian culture that Hazlitt describes in his lecture "On the English Novelists," when the national identity was supposedly secure and virtue supposedly a publicly shared ideal. The old English customs and ceremonies and observances of which Pickwick is the novelistic embodiment have their naive and cruder form in the novels of Fielding and Smollett. Mr. Pickwick *is* the eighteenth-century novel, from a nostalgic nineteenth-century point of view. He is *the* Quixotic amiable humorist, one who verges on a confrontation with more contemporary forms of novel and society but who manages to vindicate his old-fashioned principles and preserve his amiability intact.

The cultural mythos of *Pickwick Papers* happens to converge here with Dickens's own biographia literaria. In a well-known passage in *David Copperfield*, which Dickens confided to Forster was "literally true," David recalls his boyhood reading in "a small collection of books in a little room up-stairs." The novels he mentions (although there were in fact many others) are *Roderick Random, Peregrine Pickle, Humphrey Clinker, Tom Jones, The Vicar of Wakefield, Don Quixote, Gil Blas*, and *Robinson Crusoe*, with the addition of the more exotic *Arabian Nights* and *Tales of the Genii*. [28] David is not simply an idle reader of these texts but an active recreator of their characters and incidents. He recalls his "impersonation" of Tom Jones and Roderick Random, and his projection of the settings of the novels onto his own surroundings: "Every barn in the neighborhood, every stone in the church, and every foot of the churchyard, had some association of its own, in my mind, connected with these books, and stood for some locality made famous in them." [29]

Thus Dickens's attitude toward the Quixotic and picaresque novels of the eighteenth century is energized by recollections from early childhood; indeed, this may be the primary source of his interpretation. Yet the fixation on early reading is itself a common romantic theme, as in the process described by Wordsworth in Book V of *The Prelude*, [30] or by Scott, interestingly enough, in the experience of reading *Gil Blas*: "Few have ever read this charming book without remembering, as one of the most delightful occupations of their life, the time which they first employed in the perusal; and there are few also who do not occasionally turn back to its pages with all the vivacity which attends the recollection of early love." [31] It is not simply that Dickens remembers his early reading of these novels, but that he makes the experience symbolic of the powers of a child's imagination—even as children are notably absent from his first novel. Dickens was to recur to this notion of novel-reading as a definitive stage of existence in a piece he wrote in 1853 entitled "Where We Stopped Growing": "Our growth stopped, when Don Quixote might have been right after all in going about to succour the distressed, and when the priest and the barber were no more justified in burning his books than they would have been in making a bonfire of our own two bedroom shelves. When Gil Blas had a heart, and was, somehow or other, not at all worldly that we knew of." [32] *Pickwick Papers* is a benevolent and idealized form of such an arrest of imaginative development.

Dickens recreates the Quixotic and the picaresque not merely out of sentimentality or nostalgia, however. He gives a new definition to these earlier examples of the novel; they belong in *Pickwick Papers* not to the self in its past existence but to the community in its ongoing present. This is the difference between Wordsworth's Quixote figure and Dickens's, between the solitary Arab riding across a desert plain and the "corporate identity," as William Axton puts it, of

Pickwick and his followers.[33] The "first ray of light" which illuminates the hero in the novel proceeds from an "entry in the Transactions of the Pickwick Club" (1). Pickwick is hardly an individual, subject to the pressures of socialization and alienation; he is much more, a priori, the "General Chairman" of a duly constituted fraternity. The first appearance of Sam Weller is literally out of the "woodwork of an old London inn, "once the headquarters of celebrated coaches in the days when coaches performed their journeys in a graver and more solemn manner than they do in these times" (118)—in other words, a nexus of traditional English transport and hospitality.

The road and inn motif of the Quixotic and the picaresque becomes in *Pickwick Papers* a primary sign of social interconnectedness. Movement on the road and a hospitable reception at various points along the road are pervasive issues in the novel, the unifying concerns of the loosely episodic plot. Like the horse that Pickwick encounters on his first sally, the corporate identity of the hero is only vital when in motion or in harness. "'He always falls down when he's took out o' the cab,' continued the driver, 'but when he's in it, we bears him up werry tight, and takes him in werry short, so as he can't werry well fall down; and we've got a pair o' precious large wheels on, so ven he *does* move, they run after him, and he must go on—he can't help it'" (7). The novel begins with the formation of a "Corresponding Society of the Pickwick Club," and Pickwick is immediately set in motion, in a continual series of leisurely posts and wild rides. At the end of each stage is a sustaining bed and board, in which the simple rituals of hospitality are acted out—well or badly. It is only in his tours of the social heterocosm of the Fleet that Pickwick loses his essential mobility and essential welcome, and he is forced to retire to his room. But when Mrs. Bardell arrives in prison and provides an altruistic reason for Pickwick to free himself, he resumes his intercessory travels.

An important figurative dimension of this literal concern with energetic movement and refreshment is suggested by a remark of Tony Weller, Sam's literal father and a coachman by profession:

> 'A coachman's a privileged indiwidual,' replied Mr. Weller, looking fixedly at his son. ' 'Cos a coachman may do vithout suspicion wot other men may not; 'cos a coachman may be on the wery amicablest terms with eighty mile o' females, and yet nobody think that he means to marry any vun among 'em.... A reg'lar coachman's a sort o' connectin' link betwixt singleness and matrimony.' (735)

The symbolic action of the novel, in fact, might be called alternative rites of passage, a series of ceremonial observances by characters in the novel which are both more social and less binding than the holy estate of matrimony. "Ceremony" is a word used frequently in *Pickwick Papers*, along with its cognates "custom," "observance," "solemnity," and its meaning in common usage—"a thing done in a formal or ceremonious way"—captures precisely the precarious stability of such heightened activities in the novel. The ceremonies that Pickwick presides over or participates in are not the sacred and fixed observances of ritual, but more fluid secular occasions, "other Sports," as the heading of Chapter XXVIII puts it, "which although in their way, even as good Customs as Marriage itself, are not quite so religiously kept up in these degenerate times" (374). They correspond to what a contemporary folklorist terms "enactments":

> heightened events experienced in such anticipated and conventionally framed ways that participation is both potentiated and encouraged. Activities become more unreal yet more real at the same time; unreal because of the felt departure from the ordinary toward the more heightened, self-conscious and stylized behaviors of named and framed activities-in-common; more real because the events take the motives and scenes of the everyday and bring them into some new perspective, allowing us to see them as part of some larger patterns of existence.[34]

In his succeeding novels, Dickens moves increasingly to a vision of social life as dominated by malign institutions, reified and alienating structures against which the more humble orders of the family and the household can offer little resistance: Dombey and Son, Chancery, the Marshalsea Prison. But in *Pickwick Papers*, except for the shadow of the Fleet, the evils of society tend to be those of isolated misanthropic individuals, who can be countered, if not reclaimed, by the benevolent regeneration of social ceremonies. The central ceremony, of course—one of continuing importance for Dickens and for Victorian society—is the Christmas celebrated at Dingley Dell, an extended and extensive observance that surrounds and eclipses the marriage of Bella Wardle and Trundle. "And numerous indeed are the hearts to which Christmas brings a brief season of happiness and enjoyment. How many families, whose members have been dispersed and scattered far and wide, in the restless struggles of life, are then reunited, and meet once again in that happy state of companionship and mutual good-will, which is a source of such pure and unalloyed delight" (374).[35]

This is a strain in Dickens which has not been highly valued in the twentieth century, but it is an explicit example of a view of life in society that informs all of Dickens's writing and is an unavoidable fact of fictional life in *Pickwick Papers*. One might make this phenomenon more strange and more acceptable to modern tastes by calling Dickens an intuitive anthropologist of the English middle classes, an observer who maps the outlandish structures of kinship, exchange, eating, and speech that underlie the familiar social surface. The comic integrity of all these strange relations in *Pickwick Papers* is based on the fact that they can all be read, at a level of felt abstraction, as variations on the ceremonial sense of life. As modern anthropologists have shown us, the most commonplace of social activities, the meal, is structured by formalized (or formalizable) "sequences" and "sets," coordinate axes along which various categories (drinks, dishes, courses, utensils, guests) are combined with one another and within which a range of substitutions may occur.[36] Dickens's genius is first of all to envision such a shared language of social intercourse in his novels, and then to present, in easily decipherable forms, a broad and continuous spectrum of possible statements using that language.

The meal, in fact, is a primary form of social behavior in *Pickwick Papers*, although the language of food it uses may be an eccentric idiolect of Victorian gastronomy. A particularly suggestive ceremonial statement of eating and drinking can be found in an otherwise unnotable chapter, Chapter LV, "Mr. Solomon Pell, assisted by a Select Committee of Coachmen, arranges the Affairs of the elder Mr. Weller" (769). The chapter opens with Tony Weller announcing the discovery of his late wife's will in the teapot. This leads to a discussion of the opposition between tea, hypocritically consumed by the members of the Temperance Society of which Mrs. Weller was a member, and alcoholic spirits, which are synonymous with true fellowship and celebration. When the Wellers seek out the legal counsel of Mr. Pell, their message finds him at a solitary meal, "regaling himself, business being rather slack, with a cold collation of an Abernathy biscuit and a saveloy" (771). He joins the Wellers at a public house and proceeds to consume several glasses of rum; when he offers his condolences to Tony Weller he draws out his handkerchief, "but he made no further use of it than to wipe away a slight tinge of rum which hung upon his upper lip" (772). Table manners replace the funereal observance. Pell is finally informed that there is business behind the drink, but when the group finally sets out to the stockbrokers' to cash in the "funs" left by Mrs. Weller, "it was a kind of festive occasion" and they agree to "a drop o' beer," "a little bit o' cold beef," and "a oyster" (774). The diminutives and singulars of the description are of course a polite understatement. The lunch ends with a toast, offered first to "the funs" (converted to pleasure by the inadvertent pun), then to Mr. Pell for his help in transferring the funds (completely noninstrumental), and finally to the assembled company itself, in a mute gesture by a nameless mottled-faced gentleman. "It is impossible to describe the thrilling effect produced by this striking ceremony," the author reports. (778).

When the party then moves on to business, to the office of Wilkins Flasher, Esquire, of the Stock Exchange, it encounters still further statements in the language of food and drink. First there is the conversation of Flasher and the young gentleman betting on the method of suicide of the recently ruined Boffer, and another wager on who will buy up Boffer's fine port. Then there are the ham sandwiches being consumed by the clerks.

> 'Wot are they all a eatin' ham sangwidges for?' inquired his father.
> ''Cos it's their dooty, I suppose,' replied Sam, 'it's a part o' the system; they're alvays a doin' it here, all day long!'
> Mr. Weller and his friends had scarcely a moment to reflect upon this singular regulation as connected with the monetary system of the country. . . . (779)

After the exchange is complete, the "umpires" all partake of a "dram" and the Wellers return home—to their pub.

The point of all this eating and drinking is that it socializes a potentially dehumanizing business, the conversion of Mrs. Weller's estate into hard cash. The lawyer's otiose representation of the Wellers, as receptive to a free glass as to financial reward, bridges the essential gap between the two systems of value, the communal and the capitalistic. To drink a health to the business is to spiritualize the mercenary system of legal advocacy; to eat ham sandwiches is to corporealize the purely abstract consumption of other people's means. The grotesque wagering of the brokers over the death of Boffer, a man who used to give "capital dinners" is only a reminder of the antagonism between ceremony and business. As Mary Douglas puts it, "the ordered system which is a meal represents all the ordered systems [of a culture] associated with it. Hence the strong arousal power of a threat to weaken or confuse that category."[37] What happens on a small scale in this chapter occurs on a larger scale throughout the novel: the triumph of the ceremonial spirit over the alienating letter of the law. Pickwick is financially independent and so avoids the constraints of the cash nexus. But his principles do become entangled in the anachronistic fictions of English common law.[38] He is never vindicated within the system of the law, but he does achieve a release from the system in the ceremonial opportunities offered by the elopement of Winkle and Arabella Allen. Pickwick is not to make a match, for the marriage is already a fait accompli, but he is invited to mediate between this match and the hostile opposition of the parents. Upon this self-liberation by the master of ceremonies in the novel, the still more versatile *servant* of ceremonies begins the celebration. "[Sam's] next proceeding was, to invest his whole stock of ready money, in the purchase of five-and-twenty gallons of mild porter: which he himself dispensed on the racket ground to everybody who would partake of it; this done, he hurra'd in divers parts of the building until he lost his voice, and then quietly relapsed into his usual collected and philosophical condition" (666).

The ceremonial forms that anthropology presents as cultural fact the novel, of course, represents as literary fictions. Dickens does not imitate Victorian manners and morals so much as stylize and recreate them, as a more simplified and heightened system of signs. In this overtly semiotic strategy Dickens may be compared with Sterne, who along with Fielding and Smollett is often cited as one of his eighteenth-century precursors. Like *Tristram Shandy*, *Pickwick Papers* restructures the social and psychological worlds into idiosyncratic forms of exchange and communication. But in one important respect the semiotics of *Pickwick Papers* is opposed to the semiotics of *Tristram Shandy*. *Pickwick* is centripetal and combinatory in its system of signs. It seeks for the common denominators that underlie individual self-consciousness, that will bring an increasingly fragmented society together in spite of itself, and that will offer the individual self a sustaining identity within the network of its relations. *Tristram*, as we have seen, is a centripetal quest of endless substitutions, a flight from coherence and a narrative in which the integral sign is continually exposed to comic disintegration. Self-consciousness in Sterne is a virtually automatic reflex and identity is only of interest as a point of departure. Thus Dickens shifts the accent of the novel from the private to the public, and the fiction of the "self" is resubordinated to the fiction of "society." The fictive status of both categories, in each case, is crucial, however, and is only underlined by the common reference to *Don Quixote*.

Thus the original literary status of Don Quixote's imaginary world has changed for Pickwick into a more nebulous yet more socially pervasive "spirit of fiction." This was the title of an anonymous piece that appeared in *All the Year Round*, the review of which Dickens was editor, in 1867, defending the kind of romantic realism of which Dickens was now the acknowledged master. "In the course of about thirty years," the writer claims,

> most things become mythical; fancies and feelings mingle in the records, and ideas are gradually substituted for facts. . . . The tendency to this has, indeed, produced a natural reaction, and the State Paper Office is now under the process of being ransacked, in order to ascertain from actual data the precise statement of the facts as they actually occurred and were regularly documented. Unfortunately, however, these data themselves are infected with the prevailing disease, and myths are even to be found in figures of arithmetic. . . . The spirit of fiction mingles with our daily life, and interferes in its most serious concerns.[39]

This infiltration of history by the literary imagination reverses the dialectic of Cervantes, in which the claim that literary fictions are historically verifiable is simultaneously made and confounded. As "the spirit of fiction," or as the observance of ceremonial occasions, literature is rendered less separate and distinct as a cultural institution. But literature is also given a wider currency and a potentially more powerful role in the cultural order as a whole. In a subtle but unmistakable way, *Pickwick Papers* shows the Victorian novel in the process of becoming an institution in its own right, an institution over which both Dickens and then Thackeray were to preside for many years.

II

The judge, when he sent me to prison, said that I had behaved like a woman without any moral sense. "I noticed," he said, and the paper printed it all, "that several times during the gravest revelations of her own frauds and ingratitude, Mrs. Monday smiled. . . . I am forced to conclude that she is another unhappy example of that laxity and contempt for all religious principle and social obligation which threatens to undermine the whole fabric of our civilization."

Joyce Cary, *Herself Surprised*

In his novel of 1853–55, *The Newcomes*, Thackeray wrote a Quixotic novel. Like Pickwick, Colonel Newcome is an eighteenth-century version of the Cervantes hero; Quixote himself is mentioned in the company of Addison and Steele's Sir Roger de Coverley and Richardson's Sir Charles Grandison, "The Finest gentlemen in the world," as Colonel Newcome calls them.[40] The gentility that Thackeray attributes to Don Quixote contrasts with the benevolence of Dickens's version, and it is symptomatic of a less direct engagement on Thackeray's part with the example of Cervantes. In a letter of 1853 Thackeray mentions that he has been reading *Don Quixote* but merely exclaims, "What a vitality in both those two characters! What gentlemen they both are! I wish Don Quixote was not thrashed so very often."[41] The more immediate and important precursor for Thackeray, the earlier novelist with whom he was most centrally concerned in defining his own art of fiction, was the eighteenth-century figure of Fielding. The preoccupation with Fielding existed before and after the publication of *Vanity Fair*. "The compliment that Thackeray had earlier regarded as the greatest of his life, that he was the 'Fielding of the nineteenth century,' became a mere truism," Gordon Ray writes.[42]

To complicate matters further, the Fielding on whom Thackeray fixes is not the imitator of *Don Quixote* so much as the novelist who deals, satirically, with the eighteenth-century picaresque. Thackeray frequently cites *Jonathan Wild,* Fielding's mock-heroic criminal biography, as a preferable alternative to the so-called "Newgate novels" of the 1830s, and in his own early experiments in fiction, *Catherine* and *Barry Lyndon,* he transforms Fielding's satire into much more novelistic narratives of roguery and deception. The uncertainties of authorial judgment on the protagonists of these books are more reminiscent of *Moll Flanders* and *Roderick Random* than of *Jonathan Wild the Great*. In addition, Thackeray fastens on a biographical tradition that Fielding was an unfortunate rake, and creates an image of "Harry Fielding" as a picaresque character in his own right. "He had ruined his constitution, had acquired habits that his resolution could not break through, and was paying with gout and a number of other ills the price of his debaucheries as a young adventurer on the town, and his dissipations as a country gentleman."[43] Later biographers of Fielding have pointed out indignantly that this image is in large measure fictitious, and Thackeray admits in a letter that it is partly a projection of his image of himself as a young man.[44] In view of all these complications, it is not unreasonable to speak of a "Fielding complex" in Thackeray's art.

A major element of this complex is Thackeray's attraction to and repulsion from the novel itself, in its potential lowliness and amorality. The novel is a literature with a decided social stigma. The deliberate invocation of *Don Quixote* in *The Newcomes* can be seen as a reaction against a novelist who has become identified with a picaresque low-life. " '*Tom Jones*, sir; *Joseph Andrews!* sir,' [Colonel Newcome] cried, twirling his mustachios. 'I read them when I was a boy, when I kept other bad company, and did other low and disgraceful things, of which I'm ashamed now. Sir, in my father's library I happened to fall in with those books; and I read them in secret, just as I used to go in private and drink beer, and fight cocks, and smoke pipes with Jack and Tom, the grooms in the stable.' "[45]

Colonel Newcome's genteel Quixotism is of course not definitive of Thackeray's attitude toward a writer he had adopted as his "model" since his undergraduate days at Cambridge.[46] But they do dramatize one side of an ambivalence that can be seen in his remarks on Fielding from at least 1840 onwards, well before he had become an established novelist and an eminent Victorian man of letters. Quite simply, Thackeray is disturbed by immoral actions both in the works and in the life. A milder version of his censure can be seen in Scott's essay on Fielding in *The Lives of the British Novelists*, and a more violent extreme in the writings of Charlotte Brontë, who would only allow, in her dedicatory preface to *Jane Eyre*, that Thackeray resembled Fielding "as an eagle does a vulture."[47] In his review of an edition of Fielding's works of 1840 Thackeray is a good deal less severe than in his lecture on "The English Humourists" in 1851, but the tension between aesthetic and ethical judgment is persistent, as in the qualification which precedes his early praise of *Tom Jones*. "Moral or immoral," Thackeray writes, "let any man examine this romance as a work of art merely, and it must strike him as the most astonishing production of human ingenuity."[48] Nor is the aesthetic judgment always favorable. He writes in a letter that *Joseph Andrews* "gives me no particular pleasure for it is both coarse and careless, and the author makes an absurd brag of his twopenny learning upon wh. he values himself evidently more than upon the best of his own qualities."[49] (Like many critics, Thackeray was caught in the trap Fielding lays in the Preface to *Joseph Andrews*.) On the whole, he is more comfortable with the clearer polarization of virtue and vice in novels like *Jonathan Wild*, where "no reader is so dull as to make the mistake of admiring, and can overlook the grand and hearty contempt of the author for the character he has described,"[50] and *Amelia*, about which he waxes lyrical on a number of occasions and about which he concludes, "*Amelia* perhaps is not a better story than *Tom Jones*, but it has the better ethics."[51]

It would be easy to conclude from these divergent opinions that

Thackeray was hopelessly inconsistent or indecisive in his attitude toward the literary past, that he confuses morality with respectability and novels with moral essays. More to the point would be to notice that these opinions about Fielding are local and occasional and that they are often used as instruments in a larger polemic. For example, Thackeray's famous attack on the character of Tom Jones in his lectures of 1851 seems at least partially addressed to an earlier critical comparison of Thackeray and Fielding made by John Forster. In his review of *Vanity Fair* in 1848, Forster had written, "If Mr. Thackeray falls short of Fielding, much of whose peculiar power and more of whose manner he has inherited or studiously acquired, it is because an equal amount of large cordiality has not raised him entirely above the region of sneering, into that of simple uncontaminated human affection."[52] Thackeray in 1851 roundly condemns not only Tom Jones but Fielding as well for his "evident liking and admiration for Mr. Jones;... here in Art and Ethics, there is a great error."[53] That Thackeray is responding to Forster here is suggested particularly by his citation of a phrase from Forster's review—"Fielding purifies the air by a hearty laugh from Tom Jones"—which Thackeray refers back to Charles Lamb.[54] Indeed, almost every reference to Fielding in Thackeray's writing is aimed at some actual or imagined antagonist. When Fielding is approved of, it is because he is better than the writers of the present age (the praise of *Jonathan Wild* is aimed at the Newgate novelists, including Dickens), because he is beyond the contemporary reading public ("Since the author of 'Tom Jones' was buried, no writer of fiction among us has been permitted to depict to his utmost power a MAN.... Society will not tolerate the Natural in our Art"),[55] or better than the satirists (now including Cervantes) whose "settled sneer or laugh is unintelligible to thousands, who have not the wit to interpret the meaning of the vizored satirist preaching from within."[56] When Fielding is disparaged it is generally for qualities that render Thackeray liable to criticism himself, or to invidious comparison. "I wonder whether that is true about Mr. Fielding?" he wrote to Bryan Waller Procter in 1853. "I think he had brutalized his life and his intellect suffered by the bad women's company he kept: but haven't we sometimes laughed at Macready for being jealous of the memory of Garrick?"[57] The Fielding of the nineteenth century admits that he is capable of resenting the Fielding of the eighteenth.

Again, we may seem to have come up with a purely negative conclusion about Thackeray as a critic—that as a writer he is jealous of both contemporaries and precursors. But if we suspend moral or psychological judgment, we may see such attitudes as the sign of a pervasive structure in Thackeray's writings. Consider, for example, the following passage from *The Paris Sketch Book*, prefatory to a review of some popular French fiction:

> I am sure that a man who, a hundred years hence, should sit down to write the history of our time, would do wrong to put that great contemporary history of Pickwick aside, as a frivolous work. It contains true character under false names; and, like Roderick Random, an inferior work, and Tom Jones (one that is immeasurably superior), gives us a better idea of the state and ways of the people, than one could gather from any more pompous or authentic histories.[58]

The description here is informed, in a thoroughgoing way, by the principle of rivalry. English novels are introduced as a rather more enduring commodity than the French novels to be discussed. But within this example there is a further rivalry (as old as *Don Quixote* and of particular importance in Thackeray's later novels) between the novel and historical writing. The ostensibly "frivolous" *Pickwick Papers* shows up professional histories as "pompous."[59] There is finally the double discrimination among Smollett, Dickens, and Fielding, in which the simple inferiority of *Roderick Random* is topped by the "immeasurable" superiority of *Tom Jones*. Literature becomes an arena not of pleasure or profit but of contest; the adversary relationship is more important than the rules of the game.

In order to avoid the kinds of judgment on Thackeray's moral character of psychic health that such an observation might entail—and that have generally dogged the heels of Thackeray scholarship—I would like to appeal again to an anthropological perspective. The term "symmetrical behavior" has been coined by Gregory Bateson in the analysis of social behavior in alien cultures and subcultures, as a means of describing such a principle of thoroughgoing emulation. "If, in a binary relationship, the behaviors of A and B are regarded (by A and B) as *similar* and are linked so that the more of a given behavior by A stimulates more of it in B, and vice versa, then the relationship is 'symmetrical' in regard to those behaviors," Bateson writes. He mentions the stockpiling of armaments, the acquisition of status symbols, and athletic emulation as examples of simple symmetrical relationships.[60] This is not to say that *Pickwick Papers* itself was stimulated by an ambition to outdo *Roderick Random* or that it stimulates competiton retroactively in *Tom Jones*. Rather as these books enter into the field of Thackeray's imagination they engage

one another in symmetrical relationship. One can see a closely analogous phenomenon in *Barry Lyndon*, the picaresque novel that Thackeray wrote in 1844 in emulation of *Jonathan Wild*, in a passage that
defends the institution of gambling. The analysis of "play" here is
even self-conscious of the symmetrical behavior of its own apolo-
getics:

> In later times a vulgar national prejudice has chosen to cast
> a slur upon the character of men of honour engaged in the
> profession of play; but I speak of the good old days of
> Europe, before the cowardice of the French aristocracy (in
> the shameful Revolution, which served them right)
> brought discredit and ruin upon our order. They cry fie
> now upon men engaged in play; but I should like to know
> how much more honourable *their* modes of livelihood are
> than ours. The broker on the Exchange who bulls and
> bears, and buys and sells, and dabbles with lying loans,
> and trades on state secrets, what is he but a gamester? The
> merchant who deals in teas and tallow, is he any better?
> His bales of dirty indigo are his dice, his cards come up
> every year instead of every ten minutes, and the sea is his
> green table.[61]

Barry Lyndon continues until he has brought all the professions and
the middle classes into the same sporting arena.

In the original magazine version, "The Luck of Barry Lyndon,"
which Thackeray later altered when he republished the book as *The
Memoirs of Barry Lyndon, Esq.*, there was a footnote by the putative
editor of Lyndon's papers insisting that this self-defense of a gambler
is "quite unsatisfactory; for to prove that others are rogues (and such
possibly there may be in the recognized professions), is by no
means to disprove his own roguery, and so the question stands
exactly where it did previously."[62] The comment was later omitted,
but it provides an instructive contrast between Thackeray's imaginative methods and those of his acknowledged model, Fielding. Instead of using a framing irony as Fielding does in *Jonathan Wild*,
where the more humane norm is signaled by the exaggerated violation of humane values, Thackeray as editor simply parries the thrust
of Thackeray as hero and the "question stands exactly where it did
previously." *Jonathan Wild the Great* is contained by the inverse code
of the mock-heroic and by the palpable control of the plot on the part
of the author that Thackeray spoke of as Fielding's "literary providence."[63] The contrasting term that Thackeray eventually hit on for
his own authorial stance and framework, of course, is "vanity."

Literary providence overlooks the fictional world from a position of ethical and ontological security; Fielding's self-consciousness as author never erodes his self-confidence as gentleman, able to take the measure of his characters and to deal out appropriate rewards and punishments. Literary vanity, on the other hand, is a leveling perspective. Social and ethical honor are called into question everywhere, and the author is involved in the same problematical realm of derivative values that his characters inhabit.

Thackeray's peculiar consciousness of himself as author, in other words, involves him in a fundamentally symmetrical relationship with his own literary creation. Imitation turns out to be a process that works in both directions. The process is most brilliantly and precariously defined in *Vanity Fair*. Here the novelistic author rivals the historian in his mirroring of English social life; the subtitle, "A Novel Without a Hero," may be taken as a jibe at Carlyle's herocentric vision of history.[64] But the author also finds his own ontological ground compromised in his artistic representation. "The world is a looking-glass, and gives back to every man the reflection of his own face," the author says in Chapter 2 (19).[65] But as Roger Wilkenfeld has shown in a close analysis of the retrospective preface to *Vanity Fair* "Before the Curtain," the images of mirror, of curtain, and of reading itself, are thoroughly two-sided. "The model of Vanity Fair is so constituted that one is either within it or without it and to become its reader is also to become its inhabitant and to become an inhabitant is to displace a 'moral' with a 'mood.'"[66] It is not so much a question of epistemology in Thackeray as a question of behavior. The author may be aesthetically omniscient—"for novelists have the privilege of knowing everything," he wryly observes (31)—but this knowledge does not carry with it an ethical superiority or privilege. It can only compete for the reader's attention with the actions and actings-out of the alter egos it has imagined.

To say that Thackeray's author in *Vanity Fair* is in competition with the characters of the novel is on the face of it absurd. The concept of symmetrical behavior must be understood here as a structure of thought rather than as simple motivation. What is at issue is the question posed long ago by Gordon Ray of Thackeray's "responsibility" as a novelist. According to Ray's argument, in the course of writing *Vanity Fair* (and in the course of working out his guilt at the mental collapse of his wife) Thackeray dramatized a newly acquired sense of social and moral responsibility; he did this primarily through the role of the author that is so evident in the novel. Thus in a type of ethical conversion he abandoned his earlier aesthetic detachment and Bohemian stance. The epochal nature of this change has been questioned by other scholars,[67] and Thackeray's success in dramatizing a coherent moral vision has been questioned from a number of points of view. "I am not trying to say that Thackeray has no moral vision, or that his moral vision does not enter the novel. I think it *does* enter but I am fairly sure it does not *control* the world of the novel," Ann Wilkinson, one of the more perceptive the Thackeray's recent critics, writes.[68] My own claim is that Thackeray's vision as author, moral and aesthetic, is imaginatively dependent on the visions of the fictional characters it presides over.

Thus I would say that Thackeray is responsible in *Vanity Fair* largely in the sense of being answerable to other imagined behaviors, and answerable for those behaviors to a variety of imagined challenges and objections. His answers often take the form of a forestalling rephrasing of the question. Thus in the famous scene in Chapter 53, when Rawdon Crawley discovers Becky and Lord Steyne in their compromising tête-à-tête and draws *his* conclusions, the author still responds to the question of the French maid, "Mon Dieu, Madame, what has happened?" with a reflection on the question rather than an immediate revelation. "What *had* happened? Was she guilty or not? She said not; but who could tell what was truth which came from those lips; or if that corrupt heart was in this case pure? All her lies and her schemes, all her selfishness and her wiles, all her wit and genius had come to this bankruptcy" (517). The author gives us certainties ("that corrupt heart") which are too general for "this case." He offers the figurative term "bankruptcy" which subtly shifts the question of value from morals to economics, but he declines the opportunity to define the nature of Becky's offense more specifically. The economic framework implicitly leads the author back to the French maid, who deals with Becky's fallen jewelry like a rapacious creditor. Yet we learn later that the seizure is in considerable excess of what might be reckoned as properly hers. The author is less an arbiter of essential character than a broker of reputations specific to the moment, an agent of exchange who can only describe the value of one set of appearances by implicit comparison with another set. When we learn of "a lady very like" the French maid later living in Paris, keeping a milliner's shop and enjoying the patronage of Lord Steyne (527), we realize that the essential mimicry of the plot will never provide a standard by which one particular act can be separated definitively from its symmetrical doubles.[69]

From this vantage point, the often-noted resemblances between

Becky and Amelia, the twin heroines at ostensibly opposite moral poles, can be seen as an important feature of the novel. Amelia in and of herself would not seem to be included in patterns of symmetrical behavior. She exemplifies rather an opposite type of behavior, which Bateson terms "complementary." In complementary relations "the behaviors of A and B are *dissimilar,* but mutually fit together" in dependent fashion.[70] As examples of this complementarity Bateson mentions relationships of dominance and submission and exhibitionism and spectatorship, and these terms are as good as any for describing the relations of George Osborne and Amelia on the one hand and Amelia and William Dobbin on the other. Yet Amelia's ability to play one role in the relationship with Osborne and the opposite role in the relationship with Dobbin shows that her dependence is easily reversible, and even the final accommodation between Amelia and Dobbin is only possible in terms of another reversal—that she become a little "parasite" to his supporting "oak tree," in the famous image. In spite of her complementary features, Amelia is still part of a larger network of symmetries in the novel, many of which she actively if unconsciously fosters. She is concerned that her son live up to the image of his father. She prefers the miniature portrait of her dead husband to the life-size presence of her would-be suitor. And she is only finally freed to pursue her own interest with Dobbin by Becky's revelation about George Osborne—that Amelia had in fact lost his affections to Becky, her rival, before his death. She is jolted into action by Becky's crude but vital comparisons: " 'Couldn't forget *him!*' cried out Becky, 'that selfish humbug, that low-bred cockney-dandy, that padded booby, who had neither wit, nor manners, nor heart, and was no more to be compared to your friend with the bamboo-cane, than you are to Queen Elizabeth!' " (658). (Thackeray does not allow the theatrical Becky the last word here, however, for he has Amelia upstage her in the revelation that she has written to Dobbin already.) Even when Amelia and Dobbin are living happily ever after, Amelia can't help sighing to think that Dobbin is "fonder" of his daughter than of his wife.

More important than Amelia's belated awakening is the consciousness of the author, in which the parallel careers of Becky and Amelia are compared, explicitly and implicitly, from the start. The author continually speculates on the relative merit and relative interest of his two feminine leads, and in these different scales of value the honors are generally divided between the two characters. The author's narrative speculations in fact take a similar form to the existential speculations of Becky Sharp herself. Becky risks financial and moral capital in order to be seen to advantage in society. The author risks the reader's patience and confidence in order to present his vision of a society based on the taking of advantage. The author's innumerable questions in the novel, his openly admitted surmises and his considerations of what might have been the case had the course of events been slightly different, reduplicate on the plane of storytelling the picaresque adventures that Becky Sharp is acting out. It is a standard observation about *Vanity Fair* that Thackeray is fascinated by Becky's aesthetic vitality in spite of his moral disapproval. But the observation might also be reversed: Becky's recurrent protestations of morality show a remarkable sympathy on her part with the kind of anxious respectability shown by the author himself. Thus at the very end of the novel she all but joins the "Manager of the Performance" with her own booth in Vanity Fair—a Vanity Fair masquerading as the Celestial City. "She busies herself in works of piety. She goes to church, and never without a footman. Her name is in all the Charity Lists. The Destitute Orange-girl, the Neglected Washerwoman, the Distressed Muffin-man, find in her a fast and generous friend. She is always having stalls at Fancy Fairs for the benefit of these hapless beings" (666).

Vanity Fair thus places the moral certainties that is ostensibly pursues in a compromising position. Like the society it describes, the text of the novel is a context where ethical positions are subtly undermined by aesthetic resemblances between one kind of behavior and another. In extending the lack of ethical privilege to his own authorial vision, Thackeray perceptibly distances himself from the moral certitudes of so many English novelists, including Fielding and Dickens as well as Austen, Eliot, and Lawrence in their different ways. What Thackeray stands apart from is the myth of emotionally shared values, within whatever social unit might be regarded as fundamental. In this respect, Thackeray seems less English and more Continental, closer to the myth of moral skepticism and worldliness represented by such French novelists as Stendhal and Flaubert, in whom irony is freed from its rhetorical grounding in communal values and drifts more freely among isolated individuals and alienated social groups.

In fact, the pervasive rivalries and symmetrical maneuverings of *Vanity Fair* lend themselves quite well to the influential analysis of certain nineteenth-century European novelists recently proposed by

René Girard, an analysis of novelistic behavior according to a model of "triangular desire." In *Deceit, Desire, and the Novel,* Girard demonstrates a pattern of action based on reaction in such novelists as Stendhal, Flaubert, Dostoevsky, and Proust; "triangular desire" is his term for a derivative passion modeled on the rivalry between one self and another. He traces the structure from its external form in *Don Quixote* and the openly Quixotic *Madame Bovary* to an internalized form in other novelists and novels. Some of his remarks on Stendhal are particularly suggestive in this context:

> Stendhal uses the word 'vanity' (*vanité*) to indicate all these forms of 'copying' and 'imitating.' The *vaniteux*—vain person—cannot draw his desires from his own resources; he must borrow them from others. Thus the *vaniteux* is brother to Don Quixote and Emma Bovary. . . . [But] a *vaniteux* will desire any object so long as he is convinced that it is already desired by another person whom he admires. The mediator is here a *rival,* brought into existence as a rival by vanity, and that same vanity demands his defeat. The rivalry between mediator and the person who desires constitutes an essential difference between this desire and that of Don Quixote or of Emma Bovary. . . . The mediation begets a second desire exactly the same as the mediator's. This means that one is always confronted with two *competing* desires. The mediator can no longer act his role of model without also acting or appearing to act the role of obstacle.[71]

In its general theoretical power, Girard's analysis could easily be extended to Thackeray and *Vanity Fair,* not to mention other nineteenth-century novels concerned with problems of symmetry and rivalry—for example, Goethe's *Elective Affinities,* Lermontov's *A Hero of Our Time,* or Hawthorne's *Blithedale Romance.* Triangular desire seems to operate particularly in those novels where social relations are redefined by a psychological will to power. Some more specific discriminations would be in order in the case of *Vanity Fair,* however, and it is by modifying the terms of Girard's persuasive analysis that I would like to expand on the interpretation of Thackeray's novel here.

First of all, the object of desire is by no means as clear in *Vanity Fair* as it is, for example, in *The Red and the Black.* The game of emulation per se is of more importance than the particular stakes, whether these are financial, social, or erotic. Neither Becky nor Amelia is able to take possession of George Osborne in any significant way. Becky and

Rawdon are able to live as well on "nothing a year" as other characters are on more substantial incomes. The object in Thackeray often functions as the occasion for the mirroring of one behavior by another, as a means of generating or regenerating the excitement of the competition. This is certainly the role of the money in the wistful remark of old Mr. Osborne about old Mr. Sedley after the latter's death. "Look at your poor grandfather, Sedley, and his failure," Osborne tells young George. "And yet he was a better man than I was, this day twenty years—a better man I should say by ten thousand pounds" (588). The victor uses the object as a way of recapturing a rivalry that is over and done with. Thus "vanity" in Thackeray is continually being deprived of its passional or intentional nature. It is always declining from its connotation of grasping "pride" (as in Juvenal) to the connotation of retrospective "emptiness" as in Ecclesiastes.

It is the success of this emptying out of affect which finally distinguishes Thackeray as author from any of his characters. The triangle of desire becomes a triangle of disengagement or renunciation of desire. In Girard's analysis of Stendhal and others, the appetite of one, character for an object is deflected through the appetite of another character for that object—and vice versa. In our reading of Thackeray, the spectacle of one character and another in competition for a goal gives way to the spectacle of an author observing the behavior of one character and another, recognizing that neither side has ultimate stability or substance. The novelist periodically adopts the perspective of wisdom and denies that novelty is possible. "Vanity of Vanities, saieth the Preacher. . . . and there is no new thing under the sun." There is no Jamesian consolation of the value of art in Thackeray's narrative detachment. Artistry is part of the problem of rivalry rather than an independent solution. It is only in a consciousness of death, it would seem, the final negation of all the other oppositions that consciousness keeps putting forth, that one can find release from symmetrical striving. Yet even in one of the most deeply elegiacal passages of the book, when he dwells on the death of John Sedley, the author cannot resist elaborating alternatives, *two* visions of the end.

> Which, I wonder, brother reader, is the better lot, to die prosperous and famous, or poor and disappointed? To have, and to be forced to yield; or to sink out of life, having played and lost the game. . . . Which of these two speeches, think you, would be the best oration for your own funeral? Old Sedley made the last; and in that humble

frame of mind, and holding by the hand of his daughters, life and disappointment and vanity sank from under him. (586–87)

Such residual religiosity, borrowed from a tradition of Judeo-Christian wisdom literature that generally avoids recourse to the consolations of an afterlife, is certainly minimal in *Vanity Fair;* it is a vanishing point of the novel's vision more than a perspective.[72] But it does provide cultural support for a recurrent scene in Thackeray's writing: the retrospective vision of social distinctions after their eventual collapse. It is a vision that subtly undermines the ethical imperatives of Victorian culture, and subtly reestablishes the amorality or premorality of art. Bunyan's unambiguous "Vanity Fair" is subject to two connotative displacements; "vanity" becomes "emptiness," "fair" becomes "beautiful." Point of view, the perspective of the historically alienated half-outsider, becomes more important than moral position within the society itself.

This observation leads to a second specific distinction I would make in applying to Thackeray the dialectic of desire proposed by René Girard. It is not so much in reference to *Don Quixote* that *Vanity Fair* may be understood as in reference to the picaresque novel. In fact, the derivative appetites and bogus acquisitions described in picaresque novels from *Lazarillo de Tormes* onward seem a much clearer precedent for the internal mediation of desire than the *Quixote* itself. Girard's typological analysis is historically one-sided, and it is through a picaresque redaction of Fielding that Thackeray arrives at the symmetrical ethos of his fiction. One could even argue that Thackeray reconstitutes something like the original structure of the Spanish picaresque when he learns to attack the morally respectable middle of Victorian culture from the double vantage point of religious transcendence and social degradation—even though it is finally social class and classification that concerns him rather than any more exalted or more alienated determinants of value.

The opposition of Thackeray and Dickens as mid-century Victorian novelists has been described in many ways, not the least of which is temperamental. Even before the Garrick Club affair that formalized their adversary relationship, one finds Thackeray in his remarks on Dickens imagining the two of them as rivals. He was particularly inclined to the competitive view after the success of *Vanity Fair,* and when Dickens published *David Copperfield* Thackeray referred to himself as "the other Author." "It pleases the other Author to see that Dickens who has long left off alluding to his the OA's works has been copying the OA, and greatly simplifying his style and foregoing the use of fine words. By this the public will be the gainer and David Copperfield will be improved by taking a lesson from Vanity Fair."[73] It is perhaps an oversimplification to say that the opposition could also be seen as a revival of the older opposition between the Quixotic and the picaresque. Yet the difference between the ceremonial collectivity of fictions in Dickens and their competitive divisiveness in Thackeray, the difference between Dickens's emphasis on the altruistic consumption of fictions and Thackeray's emphasis on their egotistical making, does owe something to both novelists' engagement with these earlier examples of the novel. One might say, most concisely, that they read Fielding in historically contrasting fashion, Dickens reading Fielding as the genial imitator of Cervantes, Thackeray reading him as the more cynical *and* sentimental critic of the picaresque, in *Amelia* as well as in *Jonathan Wild*.[74]

Support for this latter interpretation is provided by Thackeray himself in his lecture "Charity and Humour." Here Thackeray acknowledges Dickens as the contemporary heir of the spirit of humor in Fielding—a Fielding who, for this particular occasion, has been forgiven and socially redeemed. "A lax morality in many a vital point I own in Fielding, but a great hearty sympathy and benevolence; a great kindness for the poor; a great gentleness and pity for the unfortunate; a great love for the pure and good; these are among the contributions to the charity of the world with which this erring but noble creature endowed it."[75] The humorist in Fielding is distinguished from the satirist—"Many more persons are sickened by *Jonathan Wild* than can comprehend the satire of it"[76]—and in the name of human kindness the humorist is greatly to be preferred.

This celebration of humor and the Dickensian "feast of love and kindness," however, leaves Thackeray's own position as a novelist ambiguous, as usual. He avoids identification with the "settled sneer" of satire, partly by reiterating his earlier denunciation of Swift, "the professional hater of his own kind." And he hesitantly recommends a *"Vanity-Fair* party" in the politics of contemporary humor. But he is forced to admit that he "has lately been described by the London *Times* newspaper as a writer of considerable parts, but a dreary misanthrope" and that his own daughters read Dickens's novels "ten times for once that they peruse the dismal preachments of their father."[77] As a novelist in his own right, Thackeray openly complains at his exclusion from the fictional communion. The tone here is more than one of self-mockery and self-pity. It is the cultivated dissonance of a novelist for whom the harmonies of the publicly accepted forms of the novel had become—or had always been—suspect. "Humour" and "satire," as well as "history," were the terms under which the novel had established itself in mid-nineteenth-century England, and Thackeray instinctively refused the security of all three. Although he continued as a major figure in this Victorian literary confession of faith, he could neither believe in its doctrines nor be happy in his unbelief.

9

THE CONFIDENCE-MAN *and* A CONNECTICUT

YANKEE IN KING ARTHUR'S COURT

The Novel, the Original, and the New

I

What, exactly, have the errors of exegesis and philosophy done in order to confuse Christianity, and how have they confused Christianity? Quite briefly and categorically, they have quite simply forced back the sphere of paradox-religion into the sphere of aesthetics; and in consequence have succeeded in bringing Christian terminology to such a pass that terms which, so long as they remain within their sphere, are qualitative categories, can be put to almost any use as clever expressions. If the sphere of paradox-religion is abolished, or explained away in aesthetics, an Apostle becomes neither more nor less than a genius; and then—good night Christianity!

Kierkegaard, "Of the Difference Between a Genius and an Apostle"

One of the recurrent topics in the interpretation of American literature is its distinctive features *as* a literature. American literature clearly proceeds from the European, yet it also seems peculiarly different. Two major historical factors are obvious. American literature is marked by the "literary consequences of Puritanism," in Larzer Ziff's phrase, to a degree that no European literature ever was.[1] The relative independence of colonial and early national culture gave the Calvinist imagination a special cultural breeding ground in the New World. On the other hand, partly because of the Puritan suspicion of traditional European concepts of literature and partly because of the exigencies of life in a land of only rudimentary European civilization, American literature is also marked by its delayed development; it only came into its own and flourished during the romantic period of European literary culture. "It is no mere coincidence that American literature came of age in the Romantic era as a Romantic literature," William Spengemann argues. "What we normally think of as American literature (in distinction from literature written in America) emerged with the validation of America's own native literary tradition by European Romanticism. Emerson's essays, Hawthorne's tales, *Moby-Dick*, *Walden*, and *Song of Myself* express the American writer's recognition that Romanticism was saying something he had long known but had hitherto felt diffident about saying because Neoclassical regulations forbade: that the world America was continually remaking must be seen not from the unmoving center of the Old World but from the places where the world was being continually made anew."[2]

In this context, American literature can be seen as a further stage in the decentering of the European literary tradition that I have been considering in this study of the novel. Another way of putting it would be to say that American literature is a "novelization" of European literature on a broad scale—hardly an independent literary culture of its own, but a displacement and a resituation of traditional concepts of imaginative writing that had prevailed in Europe. To the brute facts of geographical and then political displacement must be added the cultural revolutions of Reformation and romanticism, in their special American forms, that validated and consolidated this historically momentous shift. With romanticism, one might say, European literary culture becomes theoretically novelistic; with American literature, the novelization is both theoretical and practical. The national dream is hardly of a great epic poem or drama; it is a dream of the Great American Novel. In a sense, the claims made for the novel by Henry James could only have been made by an heir of the American Renaissance.

This gross phenomenon of cultural history was subject to any number of different evaluations, to be sure. James's own famous lament about the absences of culture that the American writer had to face is a case in point: no state, no king, no court, no aristocracy, no clergy, no palaces, no cottages, no ivied ruins, etc. The secondary quality of American culture and society can easily be perceived as a lack. Thus in *Blackwoods* in 1819 one finds a passage that strikingly anticipates James's view. The United States "contains no objects that carry back the mind to the contemplation of early antiquity; no mouldering ruins to excite curiosity in the history of past ages; no memorials commemorative of glorious deeds, to call forth patriotic enthusiasm and reverence; it has no traditions and legends and fables to afford materials for romance and poetry...."[3] On the other hand, the poverty of traditional culture may just as easily be seen as a wealth of new possibilities. The London *New Monthly Magazine* proclaimed for American literature in 1820, "The elements of noble material are certainly at hand."

> The division of the country into separate states, and the consequent variety of individual character—the emigra-

tions to the back-settlements—the rencontres with the savage tribes—the collisions between the habits and sentiments of the remoter and more central districts—the multiplicity of religious sects—the developments of the republican character in its progressive stages of refinement—all this, and much more, added to the magnificent aspect of the country, with its gigantic mountains and primeval forests, and wide savannas and majestic rivers, must furnish such stores for romantic, pathetic, comic, and descriptive representations, as it would be vain to look for in the now-exhausted resources of the parent country.[4]

Where these divergent evaluations of the American situation agree is in the lack of a definite literary tradition or literary history, however broadly conceived. These views are of course symptomatic as well as diagnostic of the situation, but their bearing on a specifically American sense of the novel is important. The novel in America was faced with reinventing itself, in a way that the Victorian novel in England, with its ability to hearken back to eighteenth-century precedents, was not. Where Dickens and Thackeray might look back to Fielding and Smollett for a familiar set of models and motives, novelists like Melville and Twain were forced to be novelists all over again, at their greater cultural distance from the European past. American novelists were confronted with a need to be more original on the one hand, to reach back behind discredited traditions to more archetypal sources of authority, while on the other hand to be more novel in the common sense of the word, more new-fashioned or newfangled in their evocation of a brave New World. These obligations are of course implicit and ideal, but they do characterize the dual program of the tremendously creative period of American literature that has been called the American Renaissance. "Our age is retrospective," Emerson complains in *Nature*. "It builds the sepulchres of the fathers. It writes biographies, histories, and criticism. The foregoing generations beheld God and nature face to face; we, through their eyes. Why should we not also enjoy an original relation to the universe?" Yet this general desire for first things is translated immediately into a specific desire for latest things: "The sun shines to-day also. There is more wool and flax in the fields. There are new lands, new men, new thoughts."[5]

Emerson, of course, was not a novelist, and the outlines of this peculiar turn of the novel can be seen in the broader aspects of the culture, both in Puritanism, in its English and American forms, and in romanticism, in its different European varieties. The Puritan imagination vested the power of originality in the Christian God, who revealed himself first and foremost in the Bible, his Word. Yet this imagination also reinforced the significance of the contemporary life of the individual, in its very plainness and factuality, as an important element in God's providential plan. The scriptural heightening of everyday life is evident in an individual allegory like *Pilgrim's Progress* (which Coleridge read "with the same illusion as we read any tale known to be fictitious, as a novel"),[6] but it is more pervasive in the typological thinking of the American Puritans, where the biblical figure was to be literally fulfilled in the national history. The mediating ideals of humanist culture were continually overturned by what Sacvan Bercovitch calls the "federal eschatology" of Puritan historical writing.[7] In the course of the breakdown of the New England theocratic society, this traditional typological exegesis of the Bible, with its insistence on the priority of Scripture, was effectively reversed; the primary meaning was shifted from the biblical text to the events of secular history themselves. The power of the "original" was increasingly assumed by the example of the "new." Even while referring to different spaces within the cultural system, the *original* and the *new* were closely interdependent, well before the novel as a form of imaginative literature was at all important in American society.

The romantic concern with originality and novelty is most conveniently illustrated by Coleridge, who like the Puritans had little interest in prose fiction per se. Throughout his poetry and critical prose, Coleridge is fascinated with the idea of the source, a locus of originality and origination. He meditates on mythological and religious sources in "Kubla Khan," on psychological and ethical sources in "The Rime of the Ancient Mariner" and "Christabel," on philosophical and literary sources in the *Biographia Literaria*. At the same time, he deliberately places the immediacy of inspiration at a distance, in the contingencies of personal existence and the hesitancies of reflective thought. The vision of Mount Abora is dissipated by the person on business from Porlock; the Imagination is akin to Genesis, yet it seems only productive in an alienated "Secondary" state. Coleridge's closest American counterpart is perhaps Poe, in whom vatic originality and ratiocinative novelty similarly alternate with one another, blending archetypal sources with detectable traces while bypassing the ordinary, the conventional, and the merely traditional in the process. Poe's review of Hawthorne's *Twice-Told Tales* uses precisely these terms, originality and novelty, even as it tries, with a tortuous logic, to adjudicate between them.[8]

Thus an application of my theory of the novel to American fiction of the mid- and later nineteenth century must take account of the way this hitherto largely alternative literary kind emerges in the midst of a general literary culture that self-consciously validated the strange, the extravagant, the original, and the new. It is not so much that the American novelist had no solid or specific social structure to imitate as that he had no widely shared sense of a literary tradition either to oppose or transcend. The force of literary novelty was dissipated by its very pervasiveness. The differences between English and American fiction in the nineteenth century, often debated, may be best understood in these terms. Richard Brodhead argues persuasively that for Hawthorne and Melville the "novel form is insistently a mixed medium" as compared with the "unifying and homogeneous narrative mode" of English novelists like Dickens and George Eliot.[9] Yet it is surely a question of the levels and terms on which the mixing of narrative media occurs and the degree to which the heterogeneity is stressed. Vanity Fair certainly mixes its narrative modes, from allegory to personal reminiscence. Yet these are most often referred to the impulses of a Fieldingesque "Author" and they are by no means as obtrusive or as ontologically disorienting as comparable shifts in The Scarlet Letter or Moby-Dick. Conversely, the novels of Cooper are formally homogeneous adaptations of the historical novels of Scott, but with a characteristic substitution of the geographical frontier for the historical past. Originality and novelty are displayed in The Deerslayer on the plane of content rather than on the plane of expression.

Melville's career as a novelist, which reached its peak in Moby-Dick and ended seven years later with The Confidence-Man, is a fascinating example of the special problematics of the novel in American culture. The expansive originality of Moby-Dick, its eclectic assimilation of the Bible, classical philosophy, modern anthropology, natural science, Shakespearean drama, travel narratives, and tall tales, proved to be a performance that Melville was unable to sustain. In an important though limited sense, Melville illustrates F. Scott Fitzgerald's dictum that the lives of American authors contain no second acts. What is especially curious is that in the novels after Moby-Dick— Pierre, Israel Potter, and The Confidence-Man—as well as in the shorter tales, Melville worked within increasingly conventional limitations of form. Why he should have imposed these more modest and recognizable external constraints on his writings is by no means clear. They certainly gained him no greater audience, and they are clearly inadequate to the apparent cognitive ambitions he continued to have for his art. But in *Pierre,* he produced an almost stereotyped inter-weaving of Gothic novel and *Bildungsroman;* in "Bartleby the Scrivener" he worked within the rhetorically limited form of the anecdotal magazine tale; and in *Israel Potter* he adopted the form of the historical novel (more from Thackeray than from Scott) with a perversely self-deprecating reliance on the factual framework of an actual autobiography published in 1824. This is not to say that the tone of these works does not radically change the significance of typical fictional form, or that Melville does not load every rift with symbolic ore. But it is to point out the increasingly *un*original surface structures which he used to express his imaginative depths, after writing what he himself recognized as his masterpiece.

The puzzling disjunction between form and meaning in Melville's fiction recalls his own romantic commentary on Shakespeare's plays: "In Shakespeare's tomb lies infinitely more than Shakespeare ever wrote."[10] The actual, formal artwork is held to be literally in-commensurate with the absolute vision, or vision of the absolute, that produced it. Such a hyperbolic theory of literature, which at least partially informs even *Moby-Dick,* has a long historical lineage, both classical and Judeo-Christian, as scholarship on the "sublime" has shown.[11] One can encounter such a notion most immediately before Melville in Emerson, for example in *The American Scholar:* "as the seer's hour of vision is short and rare among heavy days and months, so is its record, perchance, the least part of his volume. The discern-ing will read in his Plato or Shakespeare, only that least part, —only the authentic utterances of the oracle, —all the rest he rejects, were it never so many times Plato's and Shakespeare's."[12] What this attitude means for the novel, as this literary form assumes a metaphysical burden traditionally reserved for philosophy, religious discourse, and certain types of poetry, is that formal perfection becomes doubly irrelevant. The quest for origination superimposed on the novel's characteristic quest for novelty reduces still further the value of co-herence and proportion. Thus to recognize the symmetries of Mel-ville's later writing is to feel a disturbing sense of disproportion between visible form and inscrutable content, a sense that the pat-terning of the narrative is deeply overdetermined and irrelevant.

It is in this context, it seems to me, that any attempt to understand Melville's last novel must proceed. Whether the mood of *The Confi-dence-Man* is one of bitterness and despair or one of humor and acceptance is endlessly debatable, as is the question of the literary merit of the text within the Melville canon and in the larger un-canonical field of prose fiction.[13] But it can be recognized that *The*

Confidence-Man is a resolutely formal structure so arranged as to call into question the value and significance of form itself. Once the fundamental fact of this interrogation is seen, one may go on to try to specify the various terms in which it is carried out.

Some crucial terms in *The Confidence-Man*'s interrogation of form are presented in the last chapter of the book, in which "The Cosmopolitan Increases in Seriousness." This latest, or most dwelt upon of the figures in the novel who might qualify for the generic title of "*The* Confidence-Man" approaches the last in the series of interlocutors who might qualify as his prey or dupe—"a clean, comely, old man, his head snowy as the marble, and a countenance like that which imagination ascribes to good Simeon, when, having at last beheld the Master of Faith, he blessed him and departed in peace" (273).[14] The old man is reading a Bible and the Cosmopolitan sits down and waits.

> "Sir," said the old man, after looking up puzzled at him a moment, "sir," said he, "one would think this was a coffee-house, and it was war-time, and I had a newspaper here with great news, and the only copy to be had, you sit there looking at me so eager."
>
> "And so you *have* good news here, sir—the very best of good news."
>
> "Too good to be true," here came from one of the curtained berths.
>
> "Hark!" said the cosmopolitan. "Someone talks in his sleep."
>
> "Yes," said the old man, "and you—*you* seem to be talking in a dream. Why you speak, sir, of news, and all that, when you must see this is a book I have here—the Bible, not a newspaper?" (273)

This conflation or juxtaposition of "Gospel" and "news" is of course a staple of evangelical rhetoric, but it is also a polarity that runs through *The Confidence-Man* from its beginning, where the mute man holds up the blackboard quotations about "charity" from First Corinthians next to the placard announcing a reward for a mysterious imposter from the East. We are confronted all along in the novel with two ideal types of text: Scripture, whose authority is original and absolute (for some of the people some of the time), and the popular press, whose authority is its claim to immediate and empirical witness. The Gospel may be seen as an eternally contemporaneous good news, but the press may also be seen as the most modern emissary of God's truth. "The press still speaks for truth though impaled," says the Cosmopolitan, "in the teeth of lies though intrenched. Disdaining for it the poor name of cheap diffuser of news, I claim for it the independent apostleship of Advancer of Knowledge: —the iron Paul" (187–88). The tendency of the novel to evoke the Pauline Epistles, which appear to present the original Gospel witness at one remove, only complicates the dialectical reversals and relationships.

This opposition of textual types may be used to group the broad array of Melville's "sources" for *The Confidence-Man*—that is, the literary and cultural materials he alludes to directly or seems to presume an awareness of on the part of the reader. On the one hand are the syncretistic mythologies and religions that infiltrate the text, in the form of similes and allusions: Greek, Hebrew, Inca, Hindu, Buddhist, Egyptian, and so on. Melville is less interested in these mythologies in and of themselves than for the challenge they pose to biblical authority. The issue they raise in *The Confidence-Man* is similar to the issue to which Edward Casaubon sacrifices himself in George Eliot's *Middlemarch:* whether revealed religion can defend itself against the rising tide of historically discovered myth.[15] On the other hand is the broad contemporary literature of the American trickster and swindler that Melville clearly draws on, making his novel remarkably topical as well as unusually hermetic. The arrest of an actual "Confidence-Man" was reported in the Albany newspapers at the time Melville was writing the book, the same figure who had been apprehended previously in New York City while Melville was there in 1849. John Seelye has demonstrated the degree to which the theme of confidence-men and their deceptions was a lively literary concern of the American 1850s, and the Boston *Evening Transcript* remarked in its review of Melville's book,

> One of the indigenous characters who has figured long in our journals, courts, and cities is 'the Confidence Man'; his doings form one of the staples of villainy, and an element in the romance of roguery. Countless are the dodges attributed to this ubiquitous personage, and his adventures would equal those of Jonathan Wild. It is not to be wondered at, therefore, that the subject caught the fancy of Herman Melville. . . . He has added by his 'Confidence Man' to the number of original subjects—an achievement for the modern *raconteur*, who has to glean in a field so often harvested.[16]

The paradox of the American novel, the convergence of archetype and stereotype, the simultaneous quest for the earliest and the latest word, is posed by *The Confidence-Man* in a particularly stark fashion.

The mention of Jonathan Wild in the notice just quoted raises the question of a more intermediate range of reference in the text, Melville's possible evocation of the picaresque novel. To what extent can *The Confidence-Man* be interpreted in the series of European picaresque novels that we have been considering in this study? We know that Melville was familiar with both *Lazarillo de Tormes* and *Guzmán de Alfarache*,[17] but the plethora of native American trickster and delinquent narratives would seem to overwhelm these earlier texts as specific precedents. What we find, in fact, is a literary-historical uncertainty similar to the one we encountered in Defoe. The prevalence of subliterary or extraliterary models raises the question of whether a specifically literary, specifically novelistic history of the novel is possible, at least as far as the picaresque novel is concerned. Yet this uncertainty for the critic is an uncertainty endemic to study of the novel in general and the picaresque in particular. As a series of texts, picaresque novels are all along radically open to a variety of cultural analogues—criminal biographies, travel narratives, jestbooks, expressions of regional humor, folktales—which they frequently imitate, incorporate, and rework. In the case of *The Confidence-Man* there is an especially intriguing nonfictional precedent in the writings of Benjamin Franklin, whose manufactured proverbs and projected manufactures had already struck Melville as involved with duplicity and deception. *Israel Potter* records the meeting of Israel and Franklin, in which Israel concludes, "Every time he comes in he robs me . . . with an air all the time, too, as if he were making me presents."[18] After reading Melville, it is difficult to read Franklin's *Autobiography* without noticing how much it resembles a novel by Defoe.

There is an oblique allusion to the Spanish picaresque novel in the last chapter of *The Confidence-Man*, where a young boy appears, selling dubious safety devices, dressed in clothes "like the painted flames in the robes of a victim of *auto-da-fe*" and with teeth like those of "Murillo's wild beggar-boy's" (277). Nevertheless, it would be more accurate to say that Melville recreates a facsimile of the picaresque novel out of a wide range of narrative precedents rather than to speak of specific literary debts to earlier European models. On the other hand, it is interesting to note how much these very European models were being absorbed by the popular American imagination, as in an 1855 review of P. T. Barnum's *Autobiography*, where the reviewer saw Barnum as "the ideal 'Yankee,' in whom European prejudices find, gracefully combined, the attractive traits of a Gines de Passamonte, and a Joseph Surface, a Lazarillo de Tormes and a Scapin, a Thersites and an Autolycus."[19]

The European picaresque novel does not provide a significant paradigm for *The Confidence-Man*, then; it contributes some elements, but it does not seem to provide a real form or formula for Melville's complex creation. A British reviewer went as far as to say that it was not a novel at all, "unless a novel means forty-five conversations held on board a steamer, conducted by personages who might pass for the errata of creation, and so far resembling the Dialogues of Plato as to be undoubted Greek to ordinary men." Such a response is narrow-minded, but it is also revealing. It reminds us of the numerous narrative contingencies and descriptive details characteristic of the nineteenth-century novel that Melville has omitted or reduced to their abstract essentials. It also points to another of the cultural archetypes of originality that Melville invokes along with biblical revelation—the Platonic ideal of philosophy. The reviewer objects to this pursuit of the absolute not for its own sake so much as for the setting in which it is carried out—in a novel and on a steamer, in the midst of the mundane. "The isles of 'Mardi' were in Polynesia, not off the United States," he goes on to say. "Captain Ahab did not chase Moby-Dick in a Mississippi steamboat."[20] We have already argued that this paradoxical combination of the original and the new-fashioned is characteristic of the literature of the American Renaissance, and we have identified the form this paradox takes in *The Confidence-Man* as a combination of Scripture and journalism as models of the text. But the particular logic of this combination in Melville's novel, the protocol of its own double-edged novelness, is something we must consider at greater length.

Again, the last chapter provides one of the clearest emblems. When the Cosmopolitan engages the old man in conversation about the "good news," he asks the old man to settle for him some doubts he has had about a quotation he has recently heard from the Bible: "Believe not his many words—an enemy speaketh sweetly with his lips." As Frank Goodman finds the passage, in Ecclesiasticus, and reads on, he discovers more of this unwelcome wisdom counseling distrust. "Gall and wormwood it is to me, a truster in man; to me, a philanthropist," he says (275). The old man is surprised by these passages and asks to look for himself. He finally resolves Frank Goodman's difficulties with a visual demonstration. "'Ah!' cried the old man, brightening up, 'now I know. Look,' turning the leaves forward and back, till all the Old Testament lay flat on one side, and all the New Testament flat on the other, while in his fingers he supported vertically the portion between, 'look, sir, all this to the right is certain truth, and all this to the left is certain truth, but all I

hold in my hand here is apocrypha" (275). It is important to realize
that this demonstration is not "The Confidence-man's" but that of
his "victim." Prompted by a challenge to his own more optimistic
faith, the old man proudly shows that even within revelation itself
that which is "hidden and suspicious" still lies.[21]

This incident offers a physical model of the deeply dialectical
structure of the novel, where, among other things, the philosophical
dialectic of Plato is brought to bear on the religious substance of
things hoped for in the Judeo-Christian world. In his own conflation
of Hebraism and Hellenism, Melville continually exposes the inconsistency and contradiction in human attitudes and institutions.
Within an attitude of "faith" or "confidence" or "charity" lies an
attitude of "no trust," "suspicion," or "misanthropy." Yet beneath
these latter stances or positions a deeper ground of contrary belief
can also be revealed. Even the archetypal doubter, the Missouri
bachelor Pitch, who sticks to what he says, is eventually persuaded
to trust the man from the "Philosophical Intelligence Office" and hire
a boy to work for him. The distrustful logic of Pitch's attitude is
confounded by the analogic of this spokesman for confidence, whom
Pitch accuses of "punning with ideas." Although Pitch's suspicions
return as soon as the Philosophical Intelligence Office man has left the
Fidèle, they do so now in the mode of analogy which has been exposed as the basis of logic:

> Fain, in his disfavor, would he make out a logical case. The
> doctrine of analogies recurs. Fallacious enough doctrine
> when wielded against one's prejudices, but in corrobora-
> tion of cherished suspicions not without likelihood. Ana-
> logically, he couples the slanting cut of the equivocator's
> coat-tails with the sinister cast in his eye; he weighs
> slyboot's sleek speech in the light imparted by the oblique
> import of the smooth slope of his worn boot-heels; the
> insinuator's undulating flunkyisms dovetail into those of
> the flunky beast that windeth his way on his belly. (148)

Now as it happens, this passage occurs in Chapter 23, the exact
middle of the forty-five chapters of the book. It is unique in the novel
in that no figure of the Confidence-Man is present; we are presented
only with the interior monologue of an apostle of mistrust. In the
twenty-two preceding chapters we have encountered at least five
likely candidates for the role of the book's title, in an increasing order
of secularity and universality, from the lamblike mute to the loqua-
cious agent of the Philosophical Intelligence Office. In all their en-
gagements they reveal that the distrust of their apparent victims is

laced with credulity. In the last twenty-two chapters we will be given one "true" confidence man, the cosmopolitan Frank Goodman, who demonstrates in a series of encounters that a series of other would-be confidence men are in fact deeply involved in distrust. The image of the Apocrypha in between the two Testaments provides a suggestive model for this gross structure of *The Confidence-Man*, with Chapter 23 as the unauthoritative supplement between the two testaments of confidence. On the left-hand side are the several figures of the Confidence-Man, who are not so much "avatars," as criticism of the book has conventionally termed them, as prefigurations or prophets in the more familiar Christian typologies of the Old Testament. "When in former times God spoke to our forefathers, he spoke in fragmentary and varied fashion through the prophets," the Book of Hebrews says. "But in this final age he has spoken to us in the Son" (1:1). On the right-hand side of Chapter 23, there is the single figure of the Cosmopolitan, who whatever the substance of his role, appears as the fulfillment of the earlier figures' promises: as the Messiah or Christ. Frank Goodman takes no money, he preaches widely to anyone who will listen, his aim is apparently disinterested conversion rather than personal gain, even if this turning around is frequently a disorientation. "Indeed," he says to the obviously distrustful confidence man Charlie Noble, "our sentiments agree so, that were they were written in a book, whose was whose, few but the nicest critics might determine" (179).

Such an analogy between the structure of *The Confidence-Man* and the structure of the Bible is of course impossible to prove in any logical manner, though it is less historically implausible than some of the strange gods that Melville has been presumed by other critics to be following. The parallelism does not mean that the Confidence Man in his latest manifestation *is* Christ in any allegorical or doctrinally expository sense.[22] Rather it suggests that Melville was playing seriously with his own analogy, introduced in Chapter 33, "It is with fiction as with religion: it should present another world, and yet one to which we feel the tie" (207). The tie in this case is not so much between worlds or between characters as between texts.

As far as characters are concerned, it would be more accurate to say that the Cosmopolitan is a figure not of Christ but of Paul, not the Son of Man who announces that the kingdom of God is at hand but the Apostle who writes of the transformation of the Old Law into the New. Like the Old Law of justice becoming the New Law of charity in Paul's letters, the scriptural dispensation of charity becomes the novelistic dispensation of confidence in Melville's text. In the terms of Kierkegaard that I have used as an epigraph, the "apostle" becomes a "genius"—"quite an original genius" the reward poster in the first chapter suggests, in a phrase that echoes throughout the novel. With the exception of the lamblike man at the beginning, who may or may not be taken as a manifestation of "the" Confidence-Man, and with the exception of Charlemont, who appears only in an interpolated tale, a figure of Christ himself is conspicuously absent in *The Confidence-Man*. In *Pierre*, Christ is invoked repeatedly as an analogue for the suffering of the hero, and in spite of superficial treatments of the typology, Christ also plays an important analogical role in the later *Billy Budd*. But in *The Confidence-Man* it is not a comparison of figures that the novel solicits but a comparison of textual revelations.

The nature of this comparison is difficult to assess. To say that Melville was writing a parody of the Bible in *The Confidence-Man* would be an oversimplification. The tangential and oblique quality of the parallels creates a much more delicate and precarious kind of irony. It would also be too easy to say that Melville was satirizing certain tendencies of liberal or transcendentalist theology, which insisted on the humanization of Jesus and the Bible. There are clear statements of such a secularizing program in Emerson, Channing, and Theodore Parker,[23] and Melville does satirize certain aspects of Emerson and Thoreau in the characters of Mark Winsome and Egbert. But transcendentalism is criticized for failing to live up to its humanistic professions of faith rather than for these professions per se. And in the following passage from Thoreau one can see an approach to Scripture that is parallel rather than opposite to *The Confidence-Man*'s:

> The New Testament is an invaluable book [Thoreau writes], though I confess to having been slightly prejudiced against it in my very early days by the church and the Sabbath school, so that it seemed, before I read it, to be the yellowest book in the catalogue. Yet I early escaped from their meshes. . . . It would be a poor story to be prejudiced against the Life of Christ because the book has been edited by Christians. In fact, I love this book rarely, though it is a sort of castle in the air to me, which I am permitted to dream. Having come to it so recently and freshly, it has the greater charm, so that I cannot find any to talk with about it. I never read a novel, they have so little real life and

thought in them. The reading which I love best is the scripture of the several nations, though it happens that I am better acquainted with those of the Hindoos, the Chinese, and the Persians, than of the Hebrews, which I have come to last.[24]

Such a cavalier appropriation of the Bible, with its ironic insistence on the novelty of the reader's experience of it, is too close to Melville's own thematic to be a target. Thoreau's description of the New Testament as a work of imagination may provide a cultural context for Melville's more oblique revisionism, but it can hardly be taken as the object of his attack.

The Confidence-Man is neither parody nor satire of Scripture, I would argue, but a novelization of the Old and New Testaments, a project that both recapitulates earlier forms of a novelistic critique of literature and defies the traditional assurances of the novel itself. The dialectical balance of religious authority and secular authorship, of worldly and otherworldly witness, is virtually unique in the equipoise of its irony. Yet it also reenacts a subversion of the canons of literacy that we have been observing since the time of Cervantes. Thus *The Confidence-Man* is both the perfection and the dissolution of the novel, at least in the context of Melville's own literary career.

The dissolution of the novel that *The Confidence-Man* effects is the more evident side of the dialectic. As every reader has noticed, the conflict between authorities—the authority of divine revelation and the authority of the journalistic eyewitness report—undermines and invalidates the less absolute and the less immediate certainties that the European (and American) novel has customarily provided. Novels usually convey the pronouncements of an author with some definite knowledge of characters and events, even if this author is not omniscient. Novels also suggest that the identities of persons, places, and physical things are relatively fixed, even though certain crucial appearances may prove to be deceptive. But in *The Confidence-Man* the author asserts almost nothing without immediately qualifying or negating his pronouncement. Through equivocation, tautology, and conditional statement, his declarative sentences lose most of their declarative force, and the author is continually absolved from responsibility for value judgments. The whole book is, as the heading of Chapter 14 puts it, "Worth the consideration of those to whom it may prove worth considering" and its "worthiness" is largely manifest as "wordiness," as in the Black Guinea's dialectal pun.

In a similar fashion, the sense of referential identity usually supplied in novels by names, personality traits, furniture, architecture, and the like, is disconcertingly absent from *The Confidence-Man*. We have only the title and our novelistic expectations as grounds for assuming that *"The* Confidence-Man" is somehow one character rather than several, and, even if several, we have only circumstantial evidence that these spokesmen for confidence are in league with one another in any calculated way. When a referential locale for the ambiguous action and dialogue is occasionally provided, the description turns out to be riddled with uncertainty, with similes, double negatives, and speculative surmises, as in the description of the steamer itself:

> Pierced along its great white bulk with two tiers of small embrasure-*like* windows, well above the waterline, the Fidèle, though, *might at distance have been taken by strangers* for some whitewashed fort on a floating isle.
>
> Merchants on 'change *seem* the passengers that buzz on her decks, from quarters *unseen,* comes a murmur *as of* bees in the comb. Fine promenades, domed saloons, long galleries, sunny balconies, confidential passages, bridal chambers, staterooms plenty *as* pigeon-holes, and out-of-the-way retreats *like* secret drawers in an escritoire, present *like* facilities for publicity *or* privacy. Auctioneer *or* coiner, with equal ease, *might somewhere* here drive his trade. (7; my emphases)

Except for the brief catalogue of architectural features, described in the unspecific plural, the literal scene is simply overwhelmed by figuration and innuendo.

Such extreme deprivation of ordinary narrative assurances in *The Confidence-Man* is a function, as I have argued, of Melville's pursuit of a novelty both more profound and closer at hand than the European or American novel had hitherto provided within its cultural context. On the other hand, at a somewhat higher level of formal abstraction, *The Confidence-Man* does exhibit many of the distinctive features of a conventional novel in the European tradition. It has a central character (apparently) who lends his title, if not his proper name, to the book; it presents a gallery of secondary character types in social interaction and colloquial dialogue. Several of these distinctive features are rather more old-fashioned than any Melville had used in his earlier novels. The chapter headings and the interpolated tales recall the eighteenth-century novel, and it is hard not to think of Fielding in the three chapters (14, 33, and 44) in which the author steps back from his narrative and discusses the nature of his art.[25]

The most old-fashioned and the most important precedent of all for Melville's novel turns out to be *Don Quixote* itself, which Melville read and annotated in 1855, at a time when he was planning and writing *The Confidence-Man*.

Melville probably knew *Don Quixote* before this time, but his surviving copy is an 1853 edition of Jarvis's translation marked "H. Melville/ Sep 18. '55."[26] He had probably planned what turned out to be his last published novel earlier in that year, but it seems to have been only in February of 1856 that he was able to work on it exclusively, finishing it in July of that year.[27] Thus a close reading of Cervantes on his part coincided with his writing of his own novel, and although the annotations are cryptic and the parallels elusive, the biographical datum of Melville's engagement with *Don Quixote* provides an unusually specific basis for my historical interpretation. In effect, Melville does to the Christian Bible what Cervantes does to the chivalric romances: he displaces its concerns into a radically different textual field, investing it with a different, more problematic authority. In *Don Quixote*, I would argue, Melville found a model for writing his most formally perfect novel, even though with that achievement he concluded that the art of the novel was essentially unable to resolve his persisting metaphysical questions. In his subsequent ventures into lyric poetry and narrative verse he turned to a different literary kind, one in which the demands of novelty and originality, as well as the need for a reading public, were less extreme. *The Confidence-Man* in this interpretation is at once the triumph of the novel in Melville's career and the final frustration in that form of his persistently religious and philosophical imagination.

Melville made only two verbal comments in his copy of *Don Quixote*, but both are suggestive of this interpretation of his reading of Cervantes. The first is an annotation "Cid Hamet & c" with several page references.[28] It shows that Melville was more attentive than many nineteenth-century readers to the device of the Arab historian—that is to the apocryphal narrative form of *Don Quixote* as distinct from the authentic figure of the hero it presents. Unlike Dickens, for example, who appropriates the conception of an idealistic hero, Melville takes over, in his own fashion, the idea of authorial uncertainty. While he may have had Fielding in mind as an additional precedent, Melville interprets the Quixotic "Author's" authority in a radically different way from Fielding. In effect, he places Fielding's authorial self-confidence in question and undermines his ethical presumptions. If Fielding recasts Cide Hamete Benengeli in an ethical mold, as I have argued, Melville reconstructs him in thoroughgoing ironic fashion as a figure of the aesthetic. It is no longer a case of an "editor" doubting a "historian" with the problem of a "translator" in between, but a question of a potentially solipsistic author revolving abstract epistemological questions within his own mind, or at best displaying them for an invisible reader—"a certain voice which methinks I hear" (206)—who appears to raise objections in this dialogue of one.

The other verbal annotation Melville made was in response to a series of analogies that Don Quixote makes to a knight without a mistress: "like a tree without leaves, a building without cement, a shadow without a body that causes it." Punning with ideas, as *The Confidence-Man* puts it, Melville extends the list: "Or as Confucius said, 'a dog without a master,' or, to drop both Cervantes and Confucius parables—a god-like mind without a God."[29] The structure of this double analogy points to the two directions in which Melville projects his highly abstract image of Cervantes's novel: on the one hand, toward a baser, more degraded, sense of reality; on the other hand, toward a more sublime ideal of truth. The "dog without a master," which in fact turns up as a phrase in the mouth of the Black Guinea, the second *figura* of the Confidence-Man, suggests the more cynical and metaphysically forlorn picaresque series of tricksters in the first half of the novel. The "god-like mind without a God" suggests the more wistful and benevolent apostleship of Frank Goodman, the Cosmopolitan. This confidence man is not created in the image of God so much as recreated in the images of men: "a cosmopolitan, a catholic man; who, being such, ties himself to no narrow tailor or teacher, but federates, in heart as in costume, something of the various gallantries of men under various suns" (151).

The Confidence-Man thus reimagines the Quixotic knight-errant in two opposing images, sub- and super-human. The fact that a religious authority, Confucius, is invoked to support the first alternative and that the second alternative claims to speak the truth without "parable" only complicates the metaphorical translation. Many of Melville's other markings of *Don Quixote* show a similar dialectic of transcendental and descendental impulses at work. A number of passages that Melville singles out with a marginal line or notation of a page number turn out to involve the freeing of the galley slaves, where the chivalric Quixote meets his delinquent counterparts, including Ginés de Pasamonte. "Blockhead," Don Quixote says to Sancho in a passage Melville marked by a line in the margin, "it is not incumbent on knights-errant to inquire whether the afflicted, enchained, and oppressed whom they meet upon the road are reduced to those circumstances, or that distress, by their faults and their misfortunes. Knights-errant are bound to assist them merely as being in distress, and to regard their sufferings alone, and not their crimes."[30] But the idea of Quixote as a confederate of the criminal is balanced in Melville's markings by the idea of him as an ally of the saint. In a passage marked with an X that Melville apparently intended to comment on but did not, we find Don Quixote reacting to a painting of Paul's conversion that he encounters in a religious procession.

> When Don Quixote saw it represented in so lively a manner that one could almost say Christ was speaking, and Saint Paul answering, he said: "This is the greatest enemy the church of God our Lord had in his time, and the greatest defender it will ever have; a knight-errant in his life, a steadfast saint in his death, an unwearied labourer in the Lord's vineyard, a teacher of the Gentiles, whose school was heaven, and whose professor and master was Jesus Christ himself."[31]

Melville's is an admittedly unusual reading of Cervantes, although its religious dimensions were to be taken further in later treatments of the novel—in Dostoevsky's *The Idiot,* for example, or in Unamuno's *Our Lord Don Quixote.* The formal resemblances between *Don Quixote* and *The Confidence-Man* are hardly concrete or specific enough to speak of imitation and there is a major transvaluation of literary values in Melville's reworking of the Quixotic precedent. In *Don Quixote* the chivalric romances are errant texts, without any claims to authority outside Quixote's subversive madness. In *The Confidence-Man* the structural equivalent of the chivalric romances is the Bible, but its otherworldly errancy also speaks with the voice of an authority beyond the aesthetic, however much this other world is called into question. Nevertheless, it does seem that his encounter with *Don Quixote* provided Melville with a model of a novelistic irony on which he could repose in his extravagant double quest for originality and "news." The Old and New Testaments are both criticized and defended, in the same way that the chivalric romances are denounced and vindicated in *Don Quixote.* The notions that a particular body of writings is "realistic" or "unrealistic," that certain texts are "good" or "bad," and that certain doctrines in them are "correct" or "incorrect" are set forth, contradicted, and convoluted, until the apparent rhetorical purpose of the narrative is overwhelmed in the speculative complication. In *Don Quixote* the protocol of this confrontation of texts centers on the necessary interruption and interpolation that the experience of reading for entertainment involves. In *The Confidence-Man* the protocol revolves around the revelation of apocrypha—the paradoxical discovery of an unauthorized wisdom that is either hidden or spurious, or both.

In *Pierre*, Melville had expressed his own disillusionment with novels through the embittered persona of his hero:

> Like all youths, Pierre had conned his novel-lessons; had read more novels than most persons of his years; but their false, inverted attempts at systematizing eternally unsystemizable elements; their audacious, intermeddling impotency, in trying to unravel, and spread out, and classify, the more thin than gossamer threads which make up the complex web of life; these things over Pierre had no power now. Straight through their helpless miserableness he pierced; the one sensational truth in him transfixed like beetles all the speculative lies in them.[32]

Yet by the time of *The Confidence-Man*, five years later, Melville seemed more inclined to accept the "novel-lessons" for what they were worth, even at the price of laying aside the "sensational truth" that he had earlier used to pierce through them. The crux of *The Confidence-Man* as a novel, its own assertion or denial of its relative fictional value, seems to lie in the enigmatic Chapter 44, which subjects the recurrent phrase "quite an original" to critical speculation. In this chapter, the author appears to deny that his (latest) character is original, at least in the absolute sense with which he tries to invest the word. The very rhetoric of the phrase, with the colloquial irony of the adverb and the denial of singularity in the indefinite article, severely qualifies the notion of generative originality from the start, however, and the author has clearly taken the words "quite an original" out of their context in the preceding chapter, where they are used as hardly more than a disparaging cliché. Thus the phrase in which the term "original" is embedded acts on several fronts to deprive the word of its honorific connotations.

The equivocation about the originality of the Cosmopolitan as a figure and hence about *The Confidence-Man* as a novel is thus transmitted to the very definition of originality which purports to adjudicate the matter. The famous analogy of the original character with "a revolving Drummond light" takes a recent mechanical invention as its initial point of departure even as it reaches back to an archetypal source of origination: "so that, in certain minds, there follows upon the adequate conception of such a character, an effect, in its way, akin to that which in Genesis attends upon the beginning of things" (271).

This later analogy is swathed in qualifying phrases: "in certain minds," "there follows," "adequate conception," "in its way," "akin to that which." The very allusion "in Genesis" looks suspiciously like an allusion to the biblical text rather than to the cosmic event itself. In the following paragraph the distinction between the original character and other types—"new, singular, striking, odd, eccentric, and all sorts of entertaining and instructive characters"—seems to break down completely. We are told that the point in common between this uncommon phenomenon and the other phenomena, more common, is that they cannot originate in the author's imagination alone. "There would seem but one point in common between this sort of phenomenon in fiction and all other sorts: it cannot be born in the author's imagination—it being as true in literature as in zoology, that all life is from the egg." What this new female source conception refers to is difficult to see, but it effectively denies the (masculine) author the power to create *ex nihilo*.

The most subtle frustration of the will to origin that this chapter presents is in the examples of original characters that it puts forth: Hamlet, Don Quixote, and "Milton's Satan." As we have seen throughout this study, the originality of Don Quixote is highly derivative, more involved with renovation than with innovation—recreative rather than creative in any primary fashion. The same could be said, in a demonic sense, for Milton's Satan, who is first of all a belated redaction of the biblical and theological Adversary, and who secondly, in Milton's own account, is notable for his parodic imitations of the Deity. "Evil be thou my Good" is the classic statement of his innovation by inversion of a preexisting hierarchy. His revolt in Heaven is an attempt to rule in the place of Christ, his construction of Pandemonium is a mimicry of divine architecture, and his temptation of Adam and Eve is a negative response to a Creation already accomplished, an act not of founding but of usurpation. Even Hamlet, who is suspicious of all a prioris, spends most of his heroic agon in the play reacting to the commands and designs of others. The closest he comes to assuming his own initiative is his recognition that "The readiness is all"—that he can respond without delay to other people's plots.

What is suggestive in these examples is the way the novelistic figure of Don Quixote is mentioned in between the tragic example of Hamlet and the demonic example of Milton's Satan. *The Confidence-Man* is distinctive in its exclusion of the dramatic and poetic hero/villain/victims who figure so prominently in the earlier novels *Moby-Dick* and *Pierre*. In the second half of *The Confidence-Man* we only hear of this type at one remove, in the curiously interpolated tales of Colonel Moredock, Charlemont, and China Aster. Here we find the lineaments of Melville's heroes of adversity such as Ahab, Pierre, and Israel Potter: isolation from society, obsession with revenge and restitution, the need to be one's original self whatever the cost. These are the traits of the "dark truth" that Melville so admired in Shakespeare and Milton. But in the narrative proper of *The Confidence-Man*, for which these tales are merely exempla of the failure of confidence, we are given only the unheroic heroism of Cervantes, the sociable and ironic genius which displaces the problem of originality into the field of the novel. In a sense, Chapter 44 of *The Confidence-Man* is an elegy for the heroic characters who had finally absconded from Melville's vision, but it is also an acceptance, indirect and ironic, of the essentially quixotic nature of that literary ideal. The narrative eclipses and obscures these figures of visionary poetry and agonistic drama and reposes on a different kind of precedent, peculiar to the novel. *The Confidence-Man* is a testament of acceptance in several different senses of the phrase, but it is also the beginning of Melville's great refusal of the art of the novel, weakened only toward the end of his life by the tentative reconstructions of *Billy Budd*.

II

He was dressed in tin armour, which seemed to fit him very badly, and he had a queer-shaped little deal box fastened across his shoulders, upside-down, and with the lid hanging open. Alice looked at it with great curiosity.

"I see you're admiring my little box," the Knight said in a friendly tone. "It's my own invention."

Lewis Carroll, Through the Looking-Glass

Having just finished his novel *Tom Sawyer* in 1875, Mark Twain wrote to his friend William Dean Howells about the book completed and later books to come. "I have finished the story & didn't take the chap beyond boyhood," he said. "I believe it would be fatal to do it in any shape but autobiographically—like Gil Blas. I perhaps made a mistake in not writing it in the first person. . . . By and by I shall take a boy of twelve and run him on through life (in the first person) but not Tom Sawyer—he would not be a good character for it."[33] The association in Twain's mind of what was to be the *Adventures of Huckleberry Finn* with the picaresque novel *Gil Blas* in a convenient point of entry for considering Twain's aggressively native American art in a broader European context. *Huckleberry Finn* is the clearest

American example of a picaresque novel on the model of the earliest Spanish examples of this series: the first-person narrative of an orphan and part-time delinquent, moving in an episodic series of adventures through different social milieus and revealing their duplicity as well as his own. "The total view of the *pícaro* is reflective, philosophical, critical on religious or moral gounds," yet his reflections never attain the coherence or autonomy of a revolutionary critique of society. He remains, as Claudio Guillén puts it, a "half-outsider."[34]

Twain may have been speaking in this letter to Howells's European predilections, to be sure, but he may have been influenced by them as well. In an essay on *Lazarillo de Tormes* published in the 1890s, Howells wrote, "I am sure that the intending author of American fiction would do well to study the Spanish picaresque novels; for in their simplicity of design he will find one of the best forms for an American story. The intrigue of close texture will never suit our conditions, which are so loose and open and variable; each man's life among us is a romance of the Spanish model, if it is the life of a man who has risen, as we nearly all have, with many ups and downs."[35] Whatever the source of his inspiration, Twain came the closest to following this prescription of any American writer of his time.

But as many critics have observed, the picaresque adventures of Huck Finn are invaded by the Quixotic machinations of Tom Sawyer—explicitly identified with *Don Quixote* on a number of occasions. When Tom's gang attacks a supposed group of Spaniards and Arabs and it turns out to be a Sunday school picnic, Huck complains. "I didn't see no di'monds, and I told Tom Sawyer so. He said there was loads of them there, anyway; and he said there were A-rabs there, too, and elephants and things. I said, why couldn't we see them, then? He said if I warn't so ignorant, but had read a book called 'Don Quixote,' I would know without asking."[36] Tom's chivalric games impose on Huck's delinquent hazards, especially at the end on the Phelps's Farm where the literarily scripted "Great Evasion" takes over control of the more improvised and immediate escapes that Huck and Jim have already effected. Many critics of the novel have objected to this ending as an evasion of artistic responsibility of Twain's part, and it can easily be argued that Twain's Quixote is much less engaging here than Twain's picaro. But for the purposes of this study it is important to note the explicit doubling of the novelistic exemplars. One can observe a similar conflation or confusion in Howells as well. "The adventures of his rogue of a hero," Howells says of the author of *Lazarillo*, "who began life as the servant and accomplice of a blind beggar, and then adventured on through a most diverting career of knavery, brought back the atmosphere of *Don Quixote,* and all the landscape of that dear wonderworld of Spain, where I had lived so much, and I followed him with all the old delight."[37]

Howells modulates from *Lazarillo* to *Don Quixote* with a perceptible ease, through the idealizing perspective of reminiscence. His reading illustrates in advance the parable of Cervantes and the *Quixote* put forth by Borges, in which the reader's increasing historical distance from sixteenth-century Spain erases Cervantes's original opposition between literary and historically actual landscapes. But for Twain, as for Melville before him, the convergence of the two paradigms of the novel is more problematic and complex. In *Huckleberry Finn* the picaresque hero encounters not only his Quixotic antitype but his trickster prototypes as well: the King and the Duke. These professional rogues, more aggressive and self-serving in their deceptions and more involved in the pretensions of high style than Huck and Jim, invade the world of the raft midway through the novel. They implicate Huck and Jim in their confidence games. They sell Jim back into slavery. The innocent escapism of the initial picaresque mode becomes more vicious with the advent of these darker criminal figures—grown men who effectively destroy the possibility of boyish half-outsiderhood. At this point in the novel Huck is born again as Tom Sawyer and Tom reappears as a militantly playful Don Quixote. Huck is pressed into service as his reluctant Sancho, and a boyhood framework is reimposed on a fiction which has explored the more dangerous intermediate terrain between boy and man.

This is not an idle allusion to Cervantes, as Arturo Serrano-Plaja has shown. "Twain was perhaps the first to see how much of the world of children there is in Don Quixote. And so we have his 'correction' of Cervantes' book: A child, doing childish things is much more consistent than an adult who acts like a child."[38] The final revelation that Tom knew all along that Jim had been set free in Miss Watson's will is simply the final stage of reversion to Cervantick boyishness. As this conclusion unmans Jim at the same time that it frees him, it is one that many readers find disturbing, and the humanistic cost of the Quixotic illusion is even clearer in Twain's later novels. Hank Morgan says of Sandy's Quixotic vision of the hogs as princesses in *A Connecticut Yankee,* "I was ashamed of her, ashamed of the human race" (246).[39]

More than many nineteenth-century readers—certainly more than

Howells—Twain seems to have read out the darker, more negative aspects of *Don Quixote*, the satiric and debasing implications of the hero's illusionistic quest. Such implications are of course more evident in Cervantes's Second Part, as we have seen—in the adventure of the enchanted boat where "Don Quixote and Sancho went back to their beasts and to their beast-like existence" (661), or in the "bristling adventure" (Chap. 68) where they are trampled by hogs.

In effect, Twain recreates the older eighteenth-century reading of *Don Quixote* as a satire, the reading made proverbial by Byron in *Don Juan* that "Cervantes smiled Spain's chivalry away." Yet like Byron, Twain sees the melancholy side of this victory of the imagination over itself and records it elegiacally.[40] In *A Connecticut Yankee in King Arthur's Court* Twain recreates this version of the Quixotic project all over again. He will laugh away the chivalry of sixth-century England and along with it the recidivist feudalism of nineteenth-century England, the French *ancien régime*, and the American South, the last of which feudalisms, Twain claims, was largely inspired by Sir Walter Scott. "A curious exemplification of the power of a single book for good or harm is shown in the effects wrought by *Don Quixote* and those wrought by *Ivanhoe*," Twain had written in *Life on the Mississippi*. "The first swept the world's admiration for the medieval chivalry silliness out of existence; and the other restored it."[41] Yet even as Twain corrects and readjusts the *Quixote* model in *A Connecticut Yankee*, we still find a number of elements that suggest the countervailing model of the picaresque. Instead of being represented in different characters, as in *Huckleberry Finn*, these models are now superimposed in the single contradictory figure of Hank Morgan, the practical Yankee, devoid of poetry, who nevertheless exchanges his historical existence for a historical dream.

Twain had apparently anticipated a sequel to *Adventures of Huckleberry Finn* when he had Huck plan "to light out for the Territory ahead of the rest." As Eugene McNamara points out, Twain tried to use the more Western setting adumbrated here in the abortive *Huck Finn and Tom Sawyer Among the Indians*, and he attempted at least two other sequels as well.[42] But these derivative "second parts" never came to completion, and Twain's next published work took up the picaresque along with the Quixotic in quite a different way. The picaro figure is now more like the confidence men of *Huckleberry Finn*: adult, intellectually superior, and aggressive, the victim finally of his own skills and ambitions. Morgan's literary genealogy runs back to the social and mechanical manipulations of Franklin and Defoe as well as to the showmanship and salesmanship of the popular mid-nineteenth-century literature of the confidence man that Melville was drawing on. Morgan is not appreciably related to the figure of the young orphan, servant of many masters struggling to evade the cruelties of the economic world, the figure of the Spanish picaro that Twain had hearkened back to in Huck Finn. In other words, Twain emphasizes in A Connecticut Yankee different elements in the widely branching series of picaresque novels from the elements he had emphasized in Huckleberry Finn.

The different emphasis seems due in part to Twain's templating of the rogue with the idealist. The picaro and the Quixote figure become patterns for one another and this entails important variations in the latter as well as the former. Where Tom Sawyer is Quixote as a hyperimaginative child, Hank Morgan is Quixote as a hardheaded, scheming adult. In a brilliant reversal of Cervantes's polarities, Twain makes the actual, contemporary, materialistic world of Morgan's nineteenth century into a visionary fiction within the world of King Arthur's sixth-century court. Morgan's historical knowledge, obviously derived from books as well as from his own experience, becomes equivalent to Quixote's chivalric romances. It is a world encoded in Morgan's mind, resisted by other characters and even perceived by the reader as belonging to another order of existence. In a subsidiary role, Merlin emerges as the literal embodiment of the evil enchanter, Quixote's fictive antagonist. The narrative frame of the novel of course reverses this dialectic. In the opening "Word of Explanation" and the "Final P.S. by M.T." we see Morgan as an enchanting and deluded old man, dreaming of a past which is at best an unprecedented memory. But in the forty-three chapters of Morgan's own narrative and the one chapter of Clarence's we lose touch with the common ontology of the nineteenth-century present, wander like Alice "through the looking glass," and wonder like Alice "Which was the dream?"

In this undermining of historical being Twain had not yet reached the metaphysical and cosmic scope of The Mysterious Stranger, where "there is no God, no universe, no human race, no earthly life, no heaven, no hell. It is all a Dream, a grotesque and foolish dream. Nothing exists but You. And You are but a Thought.—a vagrant Thought, a useless Thought, a homeless Thought, wandering forlorn among the empty eternities."[43] This demonic idealism, a doctrine propounded by the Jobean and Faustian Satan of the tale, is a deliberate collapse of Twain's earlier novelistic oppositions, which still obtain in A Connecticut Yankee. Yet A Connecticut Yankee has gone well beyond the more controlled oppositions of Huckleberry Finn. The controlling Quixotic scenario in the earlier novel gives way to a more problematic version of *Quixote* in the later one, a version of *Quixote* in which the old and the new, the literary tradition and the individual talent for invention, are brought to bear on one another in ironic and mutually destructive fashion. The past is made vividly present and the present is relegated to a visionary future. The contrast of epochs that Twain claimed was his intention in the novel becomes, as Charles Holmes calls it, a "reversible interplay, in which each set of terms acts progressively upon the other, so that by the time the conclusion is reached both schemes of value have been thoroughly undercut."[44]

Twain's use of the example of Cervantes is a distinctive one. Except for the one episode where Sandy envisions the hogs as princesses, to Hank Morgan's disillusionment and disgust, there is little of the appropriation of character and incident that one would call imitation. As scholars have shown, Malory's *Morte D'Arthur* on the one hand and Lecky's *History of European Morals* on the other are much more visible sources for the specific events and attitudes that Twain recreates in his novel.[45] Like Sterne and like Melville before him, Twain tends to engage Cervantes obliquely, reimagining the premises of the earlier novel rather than trying to reproduce its effects. When Howells compared *A Connecticut Yankee* to *Don Quixote* in his review of 1890, he did so on the unspecific basis of "the same humorous largeness" of the two authors.[46] It is true that humor is an important element in Twain's irreverent series of exchanges between past and present, almost an end in itself. Nevertheless, the quality or tone of that humor is very different from the more subtle and compassionate irony of Cervantes.

There is a revealing passage about humor at the beginning of *A Connecticut Yankee* that suggests the peculiar ethos of Twain's own project. Before Morgan has rescued himself from his initial captivity, he watches the effect of Merlin's storytelling on the company of the Round Table. In the flat repetition of his one self-glorifying tale Merlin puts his whole audience to sleep, in what the reader recognizes as a verbatim repetition of Malory on the part of Twain. Then Sir Dinadan the Humorist begins to tell jokes, and in contrast to Merlin has his listeners in continuous laughter. Only the page Clarence and Morgan himself remain disengaged. "I think I never heard so many old played-out jokes strung together in my life," Morgan says. "It seemed peculiarly sad to sit here, thirteen hundred years before I was born and listen again to poor, flat, worm-eaten jokes that had given me the dry gripes when I was a boy thirteen hundred years afterward. It about convinced me that there isn't any such thing as a new joke possible" (54). This denial of the creative possibilities of joking is of course a joke itself, in the American tradition of the tall tale and the put-down, and when Clarence calls Sir Dinadan's jokes "petrified," Morgan reasserts the creative power of American humor. "I said 'petrified' was good; as I believed, myself, that the only right way to classify the majestic ages of some of those jokes was by geologic periods. But that neat idea hit that boy in a blank place, for geology hadn't been invented yet. However, I made a note of the remark, and calculated to educate the commonwealth up to it if I pulled through. It is no use to throw a good thing away simply because the market isn't ripe yet" (54–55).

Twain is ringing the changes on the idea of novelty and conventionality in humor here. Morgan moves from the position that all jokes are conventional and lacking in originality to a plan for creating the audience to appreciate the novelty of his own single wisecrack. Yet his own joke is derived from another person's somewhat conventional jibe. The word "invented" seems important here, as it calls up the whole technological and scientific dimension of Morgan's future role and suggests the basic extravagance of his various schemes of progress. As with his more serious ventures, Morgan can envision expending enormous amounts of energy for the sake of communicating a particular ingenious "effect." The commonwealth will be educated until it can "get" the joke, until it can appreciate the inventive intelligence of the man responsible for it. This passage is of course overtly comic in its extravagance, less serious than many of Morgan's other projects in its willingness to sacrifice ideological consistency to the effective moment. But as any number of critics of the novel have pointed out, this sacrifice of general ideology to specific effect occurs throught A Connecticut Yankee, on similar or on different levels. The most notorious example is Morgan's flip decision to have Morgan Le Fay's musicians hanged, following suit after she has the composer of "what seemed to be the crude draft or original agony of the wail known to later centuries as 'In the Sweet By-and-By'" done away with. "It was new," Hank Morgan explains, "and ought to have been rehearsed a little more" (203). Immediately after this witty execution, we find Hank Morgan switching to a different emotional and ideological level, deploring the cruelty of Morgan Le Fay's dungeons and torture chambers.

Rather than lament Twain's inconsistency of intention or affect, I would single out this mechanism of humorous invention and inventive humor as a key to understanding the novelistic quality of A

Connecticut Yankee. In the first place it characterizes quite accurately the later novel's relationship to its earlier models, both to *Don Quixote* and the series of the picaresque. Twain's fiction is a "new joke" spun out from the premises of the Quixotic and the picaresque, a comic "stretcher," as Morgan calls one of the chivalric tall tales of the Round Table. It attempts to revive the old stories not by respectful imitation but by a deliberate play on the reader's capacity for spontaneous emotional response. The response may be one of anger or pity as well as of laughter and derision, depending on the way the author manipulates the reader's attitude toward the victim. The hanging of the musicians evokes a contempt for their skill while suppressing any sympathy for their emotional condition. The torture of the "native young giant of thirty years or thereabouts" (209) evokes a sympathy for the victim's emotional state (reinforced by the reported reaction of his wife, "a poor young creature, her face drawn in anguish, a half-wild and hunted look in her eyes"). Our contempt is directed toward the royal pleasure and the royal conscience which has been "trained" (again a criterion of skill) to enact this form of punishment.

Like Dickens, Twain thus alternates disconcertingly between satiric and romantic modalities in his novel, but he does so even more abruptly, in response to the demands of the local narrative performance, and in a more extreme fashion. In *Pickwick Papers*, the focus is on the integration or disintegration of the community or group. In *A Connecticut Yankee*, the focus is on the scapegoating of the individual by the institution, in the pathetic mode, or the scapegoating of the institution by the individual, which is generally comic. But the vital element in Twain's novel is the ability of the individual performer to take a conventional, institutional situation and make it new in the feelings of his audience. It is less the art of comedy than the art of the comedian.

The showmanship of Hank Morgan is closely related to the showmanship of Mark Twain, as author, as performer, and even as promoter of the inventions of others, like the Paige typesetter.[47] It is a form of invention which invests all value in the "effect." If the audience responds, as the sixth-century characters so often do to Morgan's spectacular productions, then the revival has been a success. If they fail to respond, as the mass of society refuses to respond after the church's institutional interdiction, the value of the enterprise is destroyed completely. There seems to be no middle ground between success and failure on which the performer can rest. That the issue is not simply one of narrative craft but one from which Twain draws

224

philosophical conclusions is indicated by passages like the following:

> Training—training is everything; training is all there is *to* a person. We speak of nature; it is folly; there is no such thing as nature; what we call by that misleading name is merely heredity and training. We have no thoughts of our own, no opinions of our own; they are transmitted to us, trained into us. All that is original in us, and therefore fairly creditable or discreditable to us, can be covered up and hidden by the point of a cambric needle, all the rest being atoms contributed by, and inherited from, a procession of ancestors that stretches back a billion years to the Adam-clan or grasshopper or monkey from whom our race has been so tediously and ostentatiously and unprofitably developed. And as for me, all that I think about in this plodding sad pilgrimage, this pathetic drift between the eternities, is to look out and humbly live a pure and high and blameless life, and save that one microscopic atom in me that is truly *me*: the rest may land in Sheol and welcome for all I care. (217)

The issue is framed here in a way that makes it peculiarly relevant to the root question of the American novel: can the affect of the "new" be identified with the generative power of the "original"? The imaginative structure of *A Connecticut Yankee* dramatizes this quest. Morgan is a representative man of the nineteenth century, with the freshness of its vulgarity and the innovative potential of its technology. "Unquestionably, the popular thing in the world is novelty," he proclaims as he introduces the "cow-boy business" into the chivalric tournament (502). "If there weren't any quick new-fangled way to make a thing, I could invent one—and do it as easy as rolling off a log," he boasts as he introduces himself to the reader (20). The sixth century in which he lands is not traditional European society so much as European society in its primitive and original state. Morgan compares himself at one point to Joseph in Egypt, and goes on: "I stood here, at the very spring and source of the second great period of the world's history; and could see the trickling stream of that history gather, and deepen and broaden, and roll its mighty tides down the far centuries" (96). The sense of the primitive is reinforced by the frequent comparisons of this early European aristocracy to American Indians on the one hand and to children on the other. Morgan's power in this situation is "colossal," as he claims, and his identity is unprecedented. "I was a Unique; and glad to know that

225

that fact could not be dislodged or challenged for thirteen centuries and a half, for sure" (96).

The paradox of Morgan's uniqueness, as he himself recognizes here, is that it is primarily situational.[48] In the context of the nineteenth century he is thoroughly conventional, a "Yankee of the Yankees" whose superintendency of the Colt arms factory is hardly a mark of distinction. It is only when he is placed in King Arthur's court that his stereotypical newfangledness becomes a matter of radical individuality. Furthermore, his powers of genuine invention are limited to minor conveniences like the miller gun. What occupies most of his energies is the re-invention of the nineteenth century in the sixth, the reproduction and promotion of inventions with which he is already familiar. The inventor is thus conflated with the promoter, yet the inventor also continues to be identified with the creator in a more absolute sense. Thus Morgan jokes about "the creators of this world—after God—Gutenberg, Watt, Arkwright, Whitney, Morse, Stephenson, Bell" (420).

The paradox of Morgan's position is complicated by the fact of its dependence on an institutional definition for its success. As he tries to institutionalize his anachronistic advantage, Morgan effectively undermines its very basis. If successful, he would simply transform the Old World archetype into the New World stereotype. There is no possibility of a synthesis or combination of the two, since Twain divides his ontology between these two necessarily separated historical epochs. Morgan's confessed desire to run for president of the future republic and Sir Launcelot's adventures in the newly created stock market only give a preview of an impending imaginative collapse. It is only by bringing on a bigger and more threatening antagonist, the church, that Twain can play his dialectic of novelty and originality out to the end. The only resolution is a standoff between survivors, and this standoff is implicit in the definition of the dialectic from the start. When Morgan becomes "the Boss" he describes how his attitude toward the court mirrors the court's attitude toward him: respect for man and disrespect for the office, and vice versa. "I didn't charge for my opinion about them, and they didn't charge for their opinion about me: the account was square, the books balanced, everybody was satisfied" (103).

As a number of commentators have observed, the balancing of accounts cannot be conducted in terms of specific characters or institutions. Morgan is not a hero, nor is Arthur a villain; Morgan is not all-powerful and Merlin is not totally incompetent. The Round Table betrays itself, and even the church shows inconsistencies in its role of *Infame*, as Morgan complains. "Something of this disagreeable sort was turning up every now and then. I mean, episodes that showed that not all priests were frauds and self-seekers, but that many, even the great majority, of these that were down on the ground among the common people, were sincere and right-hearted, and devoted to the alleviation of human troubles and suffering" (215). Both men and offices continue to interchange what appear to be their essential attributes. Such exchanges of identity, which fascinated Twain in so many of his stories, even turn up in the passage from Malory quoted at the beginning of *A Connecticut Yankee*, in which Sir Launcelot exchanges armor and reputations with Sir Kay.

"Self," then, is not a stable category in *A Connecticut Yankee*, once it has been stripped of its environment of "training." What selfhood a character does possess is not so much an identity as a capacity for defining its situation, of organizing as well as being organized by its surroundings. George Carrington's useful description of *Huckleberry Finn* is even more applicable to Twain's subsequent novel: "the world . . . is a situational world, and man in that world is situational man. The term 'character,' referring to a fixed structure of traits, is irrelevant and misleading; men are groups of potentialities that respond to situations."[49] Nevertheless, in *A Connecticut Yankee* the number of different situations is not unlimited. The powers of invention of Hank Morgan and the other potential selves tend to produce situations of two basic types. One of these is the feudal situation of Arthur's court, a hierarchical definition of the social group as an institution, with its chief officer (whether King or Boss) and its gradations of rank, whether these are based on merit or on birth. One of Morgan's proudest democratic accomplishments is the re-creation of West Point, and the analogy between Morgan as captain of industry and Arthur as the monarch of chivalry is an ironic variation of Carlyle's *Past and Present*.

The other situation basic to the novel might be called the federal situation, in which egalitarian relations among members of a group are emphasized, in which participation is voluntary and only partial, in which a man can at least appear to be an individual by virtue of holding part of his allegiance or action in reserve. The federal situation is not limited to the historically "progressive" forces in the novel. It can be seen among the knights of the Round Table in their good-natured brotherhood, or between Arthur and Morgan when they travel incognito, making brief alliances with the commoners en route. "There it was, you see," Morgan says after one of these encounters. "A man *is* a man at bottom. Whole ages of abuse and oppression cannot crush the manhood clear out of him. Whoever thinks it a mistake, is himself mistaken. Yes, there is plenty of good enough material for a republic in the most degraded people that ever existed . . . if one could but force it out of its timid and suspicious privacy, to overthrow and trample in the mud any throne that ever was set up and any nobility that ever supported it" (390–91).

This passage stands in opposition to the pessimistic passage cited earlier on "training" being everything. Paradoxically, however, the federal ideology here employs a rhetoric of violence and coercion, while the conclusion of the feudal passage—that institutions determine all—leads to a resolution of peaceful coexistence—"to look out and humbly live a pure and high and blameless life" (217). Neither situation is a stable one, and neither can refrain from declaring itself absolute. Yet in the alternating assertions of the narrative, one can see that the federal ideology needs the feudal for its definition of itself, both as an antagonist and as an instrument. The Yankee needs the imperial role of "the Boss" to carry out his democratic reforms, and his antagonism toward the church recalls the antagonisms of the medieval Holy Roman emperors. Conversely, Arthur needs the confederate institution of the Round Table to maintain his feudal command, and it is Lancelot's robber-baron activities on the stock exchange that precipitate the breakdown of this brotherhood and the end of Arthur's reign.

The logic of this interdependence can be understood most broadly in terms of Twain's peculiarly novelistic vision of society and history. The category of the new—whether it is a new piece of fiction, a new joke, or the New World—depends in this vision upon its opposition to the category of the old: literary tradition, the repetitious nature of oral humor, the more stratified world of European society. The major difference between *A Connecticut Yankee* and *Huckleberry Finn* is that the opposition is much stronger, more hostile and belligerent, in the later novel, if only because it is more internalized, within each important character and each important institution. In *Huckleberry Finn* both the feudal and the federal ideologies are dramatized in Huck's relation to Jim—Jim as runaway slave and Jim as boyhood companion—but this ambivalence is held in check by its projection onto other, simpler characters. The King and the Duke are falsely and maliciously feudal; Tom Sawyer is feudal in a benignly and finally chivalrous way. But in *A Connecticut Yankee* Morgan's democratic dream becomes a nightmare because it is so closely bound up with his autocratic command of the historical world, a world in which there is finally little substantive otherness. The historical and geographical space between the feudal and federal structures, which are cognate for Twain with the oppositions of North and South, America and England, post- and prerevolutionary France, the nineteenth century and the sixth century, has collapsed into a more purely psychological realm, which can locate itself both everywhere and nowhere. The historically grounded realities of life on the Mississippi become the imaginary compulsions of Camelot—and Hartford. Hank Morgan ends his life in a state of redoubled homelessness. He becomes exiled from the past that had previously exiled him from the present, and neither time nor place retains its identity.

What *A Connecticut Yankee* dramatizes is not a stable contrast between the new and the old, but an unstable reaction between the new and the original. The new set of relations must break down an original set of relations in order to manifest its novelty. *The Confidence-Man* exposes a meretricious novelty at the heart of every original act, until the novel and the original can no longer be distinguished. *A Connecticut Yankee* tries to appropriate the original power of society (as Twain conceives it) by a performative act of inventive genius. This act aims not at destroying the power of the original order but at converting it, transforming a causal coercion, where one person physically compels another to obey him, into an effective egalitarianism, where the performer wins the imaginative assent of his audience. Thus the new order of things looks back to the original order as a source of energy. In spite of Morgan's desperate proclamation at the end of the novel that "all political power has reverted to its original source, the people of the nation" (544), Twain is implicitly reversing Rousseau's famous dictum. Man is born in chains and everywhere he is set free. The state of nature here is not one of liberty and equality but one of hierarchical power and coercion—a power that the more enlightened state of culture paradoxically required for its progress.

A classic instance of this interdependence can be seen in one of Twain's most overtly didactic chapters, "Sixth-Century Political Economy." In a discourse on the relativity of wages and prices, Morgan tries to convince the blacksmith Dowley of the superiority of a free market, a discussion which speaks directly to the contemporary political issue in America of protectionism versus free trade. Morgan's logic is perfect, but Dowley is unable to grasp it. In revenge, and in order to demonstrate his superiority in a more forceful way, Morgan leads Dowley into a trap by implicitly threatening to have him imprisoned in the stocks for paying higher wages himself than the law allows. The world-be federalist invokes a feudal institution as a weapon in his own project of economic and legal reforms. The effective result is that he and King Arthur are attacked and end up as slaves.

Thus the federal order that Morgan would reconstitute keeps borrowing from the feudal order to energize its development. The Connecticut Yankee needs King Arthur's court, without which he would revert to a stereotypical existence. Twain's insight into American culture here is shrewd, suggesting how the myth of civilized progress entails a countermyth of primitive regression. Like Melville, Twain shows a spirit of cosmopolitan fraternity grounded in a structure of Indian-hating, although Twain is less successful than Melville in ironically transcending this negative basis. One can see in *A Connecticut Yankee* most starkly the way in which American literature is peculiarly unstable as a literature. The predominantly novelistic models of the Quixotic and the picaresque slide imperceptibly off into the predominantly political structures of feudalism and federalism. A similar type of slippage of cultural systems can be seen in *The Confidence-Man*, away from the literary categories toward the religious and the social. It is not that the American novel is somehow deficient in its representation of society, as Lionel Trilling and others have claimed. It is rather that the boundaries between literary and social systems, between literary and religious systems, or between social and religious, are less institutionally distinct than in the case of the older, more stable European cultures.

A literary history of the novel that considers American examples must therefore recognize the degree to which the heterogeneous and heterodox mode of the novel is endemic to American culture, at least by the middle of the nineteenth century. A corollary of this recognition is the recognition that historical examples like *Don Quixote* and the European picaresque novel are particularly contingent, as opposed to necessary, models—still more so for American novelists than for their European counterparts. For Dickens and Thackeray the Spanish models had already been well assimilated to the eighteenth-century English novel. For both Melville and Twain, the Spanish models themselves are merely pretexts for narrative elaboration and rationales for narrative choice. They do not provide anything like the constraint of generic rules or the guarantee of traditional value. As Pierre Menard, Borges's fictive "author of the *Quixote*," puts it, "the *Quixote* is a contingent book; the *Quixote* is unnecessary."[50]

230

The same is all the more true of the picaresque novel in American literature, which Howells can simply call a "romance" and which a decade later, in one of the pioneering studies of the Spanish type, F. W. Chandler can call the "romance of roguery." For Chandler, the Spanish picaresque had numerous successors in Europe but it was his view that in English letters a different kind of rogue literature grew up independently, drawn from native sources. The picaresque novel itself was only significant as an evolutionary link between older types of narrative and the modern novel, or as Chandler put it, "between the old story for the story's sake and the new story of the ethical life."[51] As we have seen throughout this study, the history of the novel cannot be so easily delimited into evolving phases or species. Neither, as we have also seen, can it be endowed with a teleology independent of the purposes of individual authors and communities of readers. *Don Quixote* and the picaresque are enabling examples for Melville and Twain, but they are not a necessary element of what Henry James imagined as the American writer's "complex fate."

10

FELIX KRULL *and* THE SOT-WEED FACTOR

The Modernity of the Archaic

I

Tradition is a matter of much wider significance. It cannot be inherited, and if you want it you must obtain it by great labour. It involves, in the first place, the historical sense, . . . a perception, not only of the pastness of the past, but of its presence; the historical sense compels a man to write not merely with his own generation in his bones, but with a feeling that the whole of the literature of Europe from Homer and within it the whole of the literature of his own country has a simultaneous existence and composes a simultaneous order.

T. S. Eliot, "Tradition and the Individual Talent"

In 1954, at the age of eighty, Thomas Mann published what was to be his last novel, the *Confessions of Felix Krull, Confidence Man.* The book is often regarded as a curious ending to Mann's career as one of the great modern novelists. A recent study of Mann calls it a "coda" to his more serious oeuvre. "True, Mann's last work *Felix Krull* has given much delight. But its best scenes had been written long before; Mann considered its themes suspended and surpassed by *Joseph* before he returned to it. Completing it struck him as somehow unworthy, a mere pastime after his real task, *Doktor Faustus.*"[1] Yet the very idea of returning to an earlier and less philosophically ponderous story was something that attracted Mann particularly once he had finished *Doctor Faustus* in 1947. He had written almost a third of what was finally published as the "Memoirs of the First Part" by 1913, and he continued to think of it as a much longer novel even as he interrupted work on it—first to write *Death in Venice*, then to take up another "brief interlude" to the *Confessions, The Magic Mountain.*[2] He published the nine chapters of Book One in 1922 as *Felix Krull: The Book of Childhood*, and added six chapters of Book Two to another publication in 1937, at a time when he was turning all his attention to the four *Joseph* novels. In 1943 he considered returning to the story he had abandoned three decades earlier, and in regard to which all his other works now seemed "interpolations." Mann again suspended this resumption of *Krull* in favor of his magnum opus, *Doctor Faustus,* but even as he did so he noted an "inner kinship of the Faust subject with this one (the motif of loneliness, in the one case mystic and tragic, in the other humorous and roguish)."[3] Finally, in 1951, he wrote to Erich Kahler that he had begun to write more of Krull's confessions. "I have actually resumed on the selfsame page of Munich manuscript paper (from Prantl on Odeonsplatz) where I stopped at that time, unable to go on."[4]

It seems more appropriate, therefore, to look at Mann's last novel not as a coda to his career but as a possibility envisioned early in his imaginative life, a possibility to which he keeps imagining he will return and to which, toward the end of his life, he eventually does. Even in 1954, his attitude toward *Felix Krull* stresses its potential for continuity. It is a novel that will never be complete, he says; it is rather an expanding fragment in which "one can always write further and invent further stories, a framework on which one can hang anything possible."[5] The idea of an unbroken line of development between the old and the new seems to fascinate the older Mann particularly. He says he is curious to know whether anyone will detect a break in style between the early material and the more recent,[6] and he finds a precedent for this self-revival in Goethe, whom he had always taken as a model. "I have just been reading Barker Fairley's excellent *Study of Goethe,*" he writes in 1947. " 'He was often able to recover a former mode and complete a work that belonged to the past.' I can do that too."[7] Mann's *imitatio* Goethe is itself a means of connecting the new with the old, and the resumption of the early Krull story is an attempt on Mann's part to realize once again his vision of individual progress as a simultaneous regress into tradition and the past.

It is in this context that I would place the question of *Felix Krull*'s relationship to the historical series of the picaresque novel. All the evidence suggests that Mann's awareness of *Felix Krull* as a picaresque novel belongs to the later rather than the earlier period of composition. In 1911 he conceived of it as a parody of Rousseau's *Confessions* and Goethe's *Dichtung und Warheit,* modeled with conscious irony on an obscure confidence-man's autobiography, Georges Manolescu's *Prince of Thieves,* which Mann had read in 1906. It was only after he had studied the great seventeenth-century German picaresque novel *Simplicius Simplicissimus,* in the course of his Reformation researches for *Doctor Faustus,*[8] that he began to think of his story in the broader historical context of the *Schelmenroman.* In 1947, for example, he wrote to Hermann Hesse, "What would you think if I were to amuse myself in my old age by expanding the Felix Krull fragment into a full-length picaresque novel?"[9] And it was apparently only in 1951 that he considered the connections of *Felix Krull* with the Spanish precursors of the German novels of roguery. Oskar Seidlin, an emigré scholar at Ohio State University and a boyhood friend of Mann's son Klaus, had sent Mann a copy of his article "Picaresque Elements in Thomas Mann's Work," in which Seidlin made lengthy comparisons between the *Krull*-fragment and *Lazarillo de Tormes*.[10] Mann wrote back, expressing his thanks and saying that although he had lately mentioned *Simplicissimus* as the most distant prototype for *Felix Krull*, "now it is not the most distant. Your learning shows me behind it further 'scenery of rolling hills' and the pleasure with which I notice it proves to me how indispensable to me it is and always was: the new and the authorized from afar, one could say—the surprisingly traditional."[11]

We can see here an intriguing example of the way a novelistic type or series is constellated retrospectively as well as prospectively in an author's imagination. The relationship of the early *Krull*-fragment to the precedent of the picaresque is not unlike the relationship of *Lazarillo* itself to the novels that followed it half a century later. An initially isolated example is perceived retroactively as belonging to a larger community of texts. This is a process to which Mann himself was particularly sensitive, as when he noticed "correspondences" between his *Joseph* novels and the Greek novel as described by Karl Kerényi. "Altogether, there is something marvelously enticing and mysterious in the world of 'correspondences' [*Beziehungen*]," he wrote. "The word itself has for a long time enchanted me, and what it signifies plays a pre-eminent role in all my thinking and artistic activity. Since reading your book, I have no doubt that a relationship born of inner necessity and intuition will reveal itself between my Joseph epic, particularly its third, Egyptian volume, and the Greek novel of late antiquity, with its oriental influences."[12] A more skeptical view might question the "inner necessity and intuition" of the relationship but, from the perspective of the novelist and the novel, this is the model of historical relatedness that is established. *Felix Krull* is an intuitive picaresque novel, Mann would argue, which only in the course of its development comes to consciousness of its historical roots. In a similar fashion, Mann writes to Kerényi twenty years later of the recently published *Confessions of Felix Krull, Confidence Man: The Early Years*, "I was not aware, God knows, of undertaking a Hermetic novel when I began with this forty years ago. I had no other intention than yet another impersonation and parody of art and artist. It was only in the course of the subsequent continuation that certain associations . . . found their way in, and the name of the god arose."[13]

To the affiliations of *Felix Krull* with the picaresque novel Mann adds—or adduces—affiliations with a picaresque myth. What is important in both these notions of implicit relationship is the idea of reaching back to an earlier, more primitive, narative form. That the *Schelmenroman* was a primitive form of the later *Bildungsroman* was a commonplace of German historical criticism; it is echoed by Mann when he refers to *Simplicissimus* as "the naive and unreflective epic."[14] The ethos of Mann's belated cultivation of the picaresque is precisely that of a return to novelistic origins. Critics have noted that *Felix Krull* attaches itself to the *Bildungsroman* as well as to the picaresque, but this "double novel," as Karl Ludwig Schneider has called it,[15] is better seen as a deliberate atavism, a conscious reversion to type. The *Bildungsroman* as the German and the Goethean form of the novel par excellence, had long been a formal preoccupation of Mann's. *The Magic Mountain* was conceived as "a kind of *Bildungsroman* and Wilhelm Meisterade," "an attempt to revive the *Bildungsroman*," and a "parody" "of the German *Bildungsroman* on the basis of tuberculosis."[16] In *Felix Krull* Mann evolves a rather different approach. This eminently civilized, "emancipated" form of the novel is traced back to its primitive roots.[17]

There are, to be sure, certain features of Grimmelshausen's *Simplicissimus* which are specifically reflected in Mann's novel, features that distinguish both novels from the Spanish examples of the picaresque that we have considered earlier in this study. There is a degree of eroticism in *Simplicissimus* and *Felix Krull* that is alien to the Spanish novels; the seduction of Felix by Madame Houpflé, a.k.a. Diane Philibert, who insists on seeing Felix as the god Hermes, is a fairly close rendition of the erotic adventures of Simplicius in Paris, where he is engineered into playing the mythological role of Orpheus to a lustful Eurydice.[18] There is also the peculiar fairy-tale quality of the protagonists' miraculous good fortunes. "I thought I was practically married to Lady Luck (or at least was so close to her that even the worst must turn out to my advantage)," Simplicius says at one point.[19] Felix is simpleminded and Simplex is fortunate in a way that is quite different from the sharp wits and hard luck of most of the Spanish picaros most of the time. A final point of similarity that distinguishes the two German picaros is the cosmological framework within which both are placed. Simplicius undertakes a journey to the center of the earth in Book Five, in which he learns the alchemical secrets of the universe. In a more theoretical vein, Felix learns from Professor Kuckuck about the evolution of organic life and discovers in a museum of natural history his privileged place in the succession of species. Such cosmic significance, however ironically presented, is alien to the careers of Lazarillo, Guzmán or Pablos.

Nevertheless, the question of influence and imitation is most profitably seen in *Felix Krull* as part of a larger pattern of achieved relationship, a protocol acted out in the composition of the novel but also reflected in its narrative dynamics. This is the pattern of returning to an earlier level of experience, not for the sake of the earlier level but as a means of bringing forth a later, more advanced one. In a phrase Mann uses in *Doctor Faustus*, it is "a regression full of modern novelty."[20] In this paradoxical model of development, a being can advance or move beyond its immediate condition to a more complex level of organization only by reverting to a previous, less differentiated mode of existence. The "advance" is always problematic, but to the extent that the "return" can be enacted in the mind, the form and substance of the simpler mode can be used to revitalize and heighten the spirit's reflection. It is this deeply typical modernist project that *Felix Krull* tries to enact, though in a more oblique and subtle form than in some of Mann's earlier work.

All "confessions" involve a return from the present to the past, but the most overt ploy of Felix Krull as relater of his life is to engage the reader's desires in his own experiences. "Sympathetic reader," he exclaims in a typical transition (247).[21] His rhetorical stance is both awkward and inviting. He reveals the poverty of his narrative resources, but transforms this very poverty into a promise of plenitude and riches. Krull pretends at times "to be writing primarily for my own amusement and only secondarily for the public," but as he goes on to develop this typical diarist's conceit he turns it into an invitation to the reader to contribute his own fantasies to the text.

> Dreamer and idler! I hear the reader addressing me. Where are your adventures? Do you propose to entertain me throughout your whole book with such fine-spun quiddities, the so-called experiences of your covetous idleness? No doubt, until the policeman drove you away, you pressed your forehead and nose against the big glass panes and peered into the interior of elegant restaurants through the openings in the cream-coloured curtains—stood in the mixed, spicy odours that drifted up from the kitchen through cellar gratings and saw Frankfurt's high society, served by attentive waiters, dining at little tables on which

stood shaded candles and candelabra and crystal vases with rare flowers? So I did—and I am astounded at how accurately the reader is able to report the visual joys I purloined from the beau monde, just exactly as though he had his own nose pressed against that pane. (77)

The reverse apostrophe here, where the reader addresses the author, is reminiscent of *Tristram Shandy*, but where Sterne attempts to disconcert the reader and free him from his conventional expectations, Mann attempts to draw the reader into the narrative's seductive typicality—the typicality of daydream and wish-fulfillment, where stereotypes are reinvested with the power of desire. Felix apologizes periodically for "anticipating" the future in his narrative, but such disingenuous disclaimers merely help create the sense of pleasurable expectation. "Of Schimmelpreester I shall say no more in this place. Later on, at the end of my exacting career, he was to intervene in my destiny decisively and providentially..." (20; ellipsis in the original). The will to pleasure deliberately circumvents fearful suspense. "I shall pass quickly over the first confused days following our arrival in Frankfurt, for it pains me to recall the distressing role we were obliged to play in that rich and resplendent centre of commerce, and I should be afraid of earning the reader's displeasure by a circumstantial account of our situation" (68). The characteristic pain and humiliation of the picaro, described at length in *Simplicissimus* as well as in the Spanish novels, becomes a deliberate cultivation of the pleasure principle. "The reader will learn of this step with approval and a feeling of relief," Felix says when he tells of depositing some of his dubiously gotten gains in a checking account (180). His greatest strength as a confidence man is the self-confidence of his narcissistic youth. It is a youth which is immediately recapturable for Krull, and he models the reader's reaction for him at the beginning of Book Two. Admitting that he had abandoned his memoirs for some time and has even doubted their appeal for a reader, Felix reports: "Today, however, my eye chanced to fall on the composition in question; once more and not without emotion I ran through the chronicle of my childhood and early youth; aroused, I continued to spin out my reminiscences in imagination; and as certain striking moments of my career appeared vividly before me, I was quite unable to believe that incidents which exercise so enlivening an effect on me could fail to entertain the reading public as well" (53–54).

It is common in critical discussions of the novel to speak of Felix Krull as a portrait of the artist, but it would be more accurate to call him a representation of the preconditions of artistic activity—at least according to certain modern psychological theories. Freud had much earlier written on "Creative Writers and Day-Dreaming" and Felix's story is a perfect example of the daydream as the primal activity *behind* aesthetic creation. The ordinary daydreamer hides his fantasies, Freud says, because these would repel us. "But when a creative writer presents his plays to us or tells us what we are inclined to take to be his personal daydreams, we experience a great pleasure, and one which probably arises from the confluence of many sources." Freud admits that the technique of overcoming our natural repulsion is mysterious, but speculates on two methods in this "essential *ars poetica*."

> The writer softens the character of his egoistic day-dreams by altering and disguising it, and he bribes us by the purely formal—that is, aesthetic—yield of pleasure which he offers us in the presentation of his phantasies. We give the name of an *incentive bonus*, or a *fore-pleasure*, to a yield of pleasure such as this, which is offered to us so as to make possible the release of still greater pleasure arising from deeper psychical sources. In my opinion, all the aesthetic pleasure which a creative writer affords us has the character of a fore-pleasure of this kind, and our actual enjoyment of an imaginative work proceeds from a liberation of tensions in our minds. It may even be that not a little of this effect is due to the writer's enabling us thenceforward to enjoy our own daydreams without self-reproach or shame.[22]

Such an identification of aesthetic and psychoerotic experience has often been taken as dangerously reductive by artists and critics, but it is this very reductiveness that makes it applicable to the fictional contract of *Felix Krull*. In the character of his confidence man, Mann dramatizes a particular stage of consciousness, which, in a certain psychological ideology, is conceived as genetically prior to aesthetic consciousness. More importantly, the genetic fallacy, as it might be called, is oriented in Freud as well as Mann not toward the creative process but toward the dynamics of audience response. The axis of causality is shifted from the author to the reader. It is not that the artist purifies his own daydreams so much as that he suspends the censoring consciousness of his audience. As Felix says of the metamorphosed ugliness of the actor Müller-Rosé, "What unanimity in agreeing to let oneself be deceived. Here quite clearly there is in operation a general human need, implanted by God Himself in human nature, which Müller-Rosé's abilities are created to satisfy."

Like Freud, Mann transforms an epistemological problem into an economic one: "life's economy, which this man is kept and paid to serve" (28). Representation is not a question of mimetic fidelity to an object outside the system of art, but of meeting the passional demands of a perceiver who is an integral part of the system. As a function of the economy, Felix's deceptions of others turn out to be remarkably benign and inconsequential. He pretends to play the violin; he steals candy; he avoids the draft; he "robs" and "seduces" a woman whose literary imagination takes over the definition of the encounter; he impersonates a marquis who is actively collaborating with the impersonation. Krull's picaresque victims are actually his co-conspirators, and the ultimate collusion, Mann shows, is that of the reader himself.

Thus *Felix Krull* carries out a psychological subversion of the elevation and dignity of art, a regression to an ordinary state of half-consciousness which both enables and challenges the more developed aesthetic judgments and discriminations. In one sense, we realize that Mann is only dramatizing this regression through a consummate artistry of his own, but in another sense we recognize that he is putting into question the system of civilized values on which the career of the artist—his own included—rests. If literary creation is grounded in daydreaming, can its beauties be distinguished from triviality and degradation? If the moral values of art are imposed on a basis of amoral fantasy, does the recognition of this antithetical base revitalize these values or dissolve them?

It is interesting to compare Mann's narrative articulation of this problem with some closely related discursive statements by Karl Kerényi and C. J. Jung, both of whom published essays on the "trickster" figure in the same year that the expanded *Felix Krull* appeared.[23] For Jung, the figure of the trickster appears anywhere and everywhere in human culture, "in picaresque tales, in carnivals and revels, in sacred and magical rites, in man's religious fears and exaltations."[24] All these manifestations constitute a "psychologem," an "archetypal structure of extreme antiquity," and in Jung's version of psychoanalysis this structure is both socially "collective" and morally "inferior." As such, it continues to have a compensatory or stabilizing function for the "highly developed individual," who can preserve his higher level of consciousness by regarding the lower mythic level, even if he does not fully comprehend the myth.

> From this point of view we can see why the myth of the
> trickster was preserved and developed: like many other

myths, it was supposed to have a therapeutic effect. It holds the earlier low intellectual and moral level before the eyes of the more highly developed individual, so that he shall not forget how things looked yesterday. We like to imagine that something which we do not understand does not help us in any way. But that is not always so. . . . Because of its numinosity the myth has a direct effect on the unconscious, no matter whether it is understood or not.[25]

Jung's version of the trickster's effect is more normative and sanitary than Mann's, at least in the portion of Mann's novel that he was able to complete. Krull is not so easily contained within the category of the "lower," either in intellect or morals, and his appeal to the reader's unconscious is much less profound and much more calculating than, in Jung's view, the appeal of the trickster is to the unconscious of the highly developed individual.

There is a similar kind of theoretical containment in Kerényi's analysis of the trickster figure, although a more discriminating one than in Jung. Kerényi is at pains to distinguish the trickster hero, as in the Winnebago Indian myths he is considering, from "the trickster god who contains him"; this god is most evident in the Greek myths of Hermes that Kerényi had earlier studied at length. In contrast to Jung, Kerényi asserts that the traits of the divine trickster "are not *just* psychic realities. They are the world around us, and, at the same time, a world revealed to us by Hermes."[26] The trickster divinity transcends and stabilizes the trickster hero, even though he overturns the merely social conventions of order. The god is "the timeless root of all the picaresque creations of world literature, ramifying through all times and countries, and not reducible to a merely literary entity"; he is "a being who is exalted above the petty limitations of mortal tricksters."[27]

Again, Mann's procedure seems the reverse of this mythologizing of the picaresque. The mythological attributes of Krull as a Hermes figure are obvious, and have been analyzed in convincing detail by scholars,[28] but it is clear from the ironic tone of the novel that the human character is more a parodic reduction of the godhead than a symbolic incarnation of it. The divine role of Psychopomp translates not into the *Seelenführer* or guide of souls of Kerényi but into a *Phantasiesteigerunger,* a heightener of the imagination. It is the superficially literary fancy of Madame Houpflé that provides Felix with his mythological label, and when he tries to capitalize on this meager bit of information in his later conversation with Professor Kuckuck, the figure of the deity is casually assimilated to the organic perfection of the human race. " 'Oh, Hermes,' he replied. 'An elegant deity. I won't take coffee,' he said to the waiter. 'Bring me another bottle of Vichy. An elegant deity,' he repeated. 'And the golden mean of human stature, neither too large nor too small' " (263). Mann alludes to Greek myth here, but he does so in a way that denies it as an ontological basis. Hermetic lore is simply another manifestation of the cult of earliness in the novel, which Mann ironically detaches from any substantive metaphysical ground. In a similar fashion, Felix reenacts the *Tiefenpsychologie* of Jung on a comically superficial level.

It is, of course, difficult to predict what the course of the novel would have been if Mann had been able to carry these *Confessions* further. His archives include a set of plans for six parts in all, including sections on Felix's world travels, his imprisonment, his marriage, and his flight to England.[29] It is possible that a higher and firmer moral framework might have developed in the course of these later parts. But it is more likely, as Mann's letter quoted earlier recognizes to be characteristic of the type of novel that *Felix Krull* had become, that the story would have remained a series of episodes, escaping any logical or ontological framework that might be erected around them. Mann does express the qualified belief that the book "despite all its looseness, all the misconduct it promotes, has a certain symbolic topicality which will not escape the brighter and more cultivated and will raise it in their eyes much above the reproach of idleness."[30] Yet such a raising of the novel's aspect is less recognizable as an ideological position communicated by the author than as a symbolic action rehearsed and performed by the narrator-hero himself. The "primitive" and "disordered" experience is repeatedly raised up by Felix Krull, who offers himself as the mediator between the lower and the higher realms—between the early, primitive, or inferior levels of consciousness and the later, civilized, or elevated ones.

This raising up or heightening of consciousness is of course a dominant concern of the *Bildungsroman* tradition, but *Felix Krull* repeatedly abridges what even Mann's own *Magic Mountain* presents as a gradual, evolutionary development.[31] "Education is not won in dull toil and labour," Felix asserts; "rather it is the fruit of freedom and apparent idleness; one does not achieve it by exertion, one breathes it in; some secret machinery is at work to that end; a hidden industry of the senses and the spirit, consonant with an appearance of complete vagabondage, is hourly active to promote it, and you could go so far as to say that one who is chosen learns even in his sleep" (70–71). Felix's waking apprenticeship becomes a mastery of somnolence: "at this time I devoted myself to sleep almost to excess" (71). It is not that he represents the world of dreams so much as that, daydreamer extraordinaire, he commutes between the dream level and the normal waking level of consciousness. He carries the aura of one level over into the other, as when he says of his theft of chocolates from the delicatessen, "it was the carrying over of my dream treasure into my waking life" (42).

Examples of this symbolic *translatio* are numerous in the novel. The most literal is perhaps Felix's role as lift boy or elevator operator in Paris, the most comic his role as seducer in Lisbon where his attentions are forcibly transferred from the daughter to the mother. "That was not choosing or acting like a man but like an infant," Senhora Kuckuck explains in claiming his sexual advances for herself. "Mature reason had to intervene before it was too late" (377). In any number of episodes, Felix contrives to represent himself as "some extraordinary being in between" (104): between light complexion and dark, between male and female, between social classes, between his own being and the being of others. Of his meeting with the prostitute Rozsa he writes, "It was without introduction, this conversation, it was without polite conventions of any sort; from the very beginning it had the free, exalted irresponsibility that is usually a characteristic only of dreams, where our 'I' associates with shadows that have no independent life, with creations of its own, in a way that is after all impossible in waking life where one flesh-and-blood being exists in actual separation from another" (109).

In his own person or character, then, Felix Krull is only interesting in the root sense of the Latin *inter esse*, to be between. His actions or ideas or phrases are not properly his; they are curiously derivative and are continually collapsing into banality in their own right. Krull is not simply a symbolic character; rather he has the character of a symbol, of a metaphoric vehicle which lends itself to any number of tenors beyond itself. Mann worried about slipping into the "philosophical ponderous" in this lighter, later work, into a vein of cosmic speculation that is characteristic of his earlier fiction. There are undeniably such intellectual overloadings of the narrative here, as in the discussion of cosmic and organic evolution that Felix has with Professor Kuckuck, but Felix's relationship to such matters is unique. He is neither the student of the ideas his novel expresses, like Hans Castorp, nor the demonic incarnation of them, like Adrian Leverkühn. He is rather the physical model for them, in much the same manner that he posed for his godfather Schimmelpreester in the costumes and attitudes of different historical periods. "He's a natural costume boy," his father would say (20).

There is, however, a peculiar sense of teleology in the repeated passages that Felix Krull makes between one phenomenological level and another. He does not synthesize the different stages so much as pass, at a level of parodic reflection, from one to another, and Mann's narrative remains strangely dynamic in spite of its self-consciousness and illusionism. The novel reveals a particular progression in the series of metaphorical leaps that it describes and performs. In Book One, the sphere of Felix's transactions is limited to games of mock-ascendancy within the family, to assertions of conscious control over the involuntary muscles, and to exercises and studies in the power of the entertainer to gratify his audience by physical deception. In Book Two, after "that truly cleansing catastrophe which is correctly called social ruin" (62), his sphere is broadened to international society. Felix passes between cities, between languages, and between social classes, exchanging the constraints of military service for a more figurative service which he claims as the definition of "true freedom" (101). It is in the middle of this second book that Krull's role of psychopomp or guide of the spirit receives its most virtuoso elaborations. It reaches out to embrace the act of seeing itself:

> What a wonderful phenomenon it is, carefully considered, when the human eye, that jewel of organic structures, concentrates its moist brilliance on another human creature! This precious jelly, made up of just such ordinary elements as the rest of creation, affirming, like a precious stone, that the elements count for nothing, but their imaginative and happy combination counts for everything—this bit of slime embedded in a bony hole, destined some day to moulder lifeless in the grave, to dissolve back into watery refuse, is able, so long as the spark of life remains alert there, to throw such beautiful, airy bridges across all the chasms of strangeness that lie between man and man! (79)

This was a passage Mann added in the 1950s to the otherwise completed Chapter IV already published in 1937; it is one indication of the still broader scope that he decided to attribute to his rogue's progressions.[32] Book Three begins with a further elevation of Felix's career in his fascinated description of Andromache, the circus acrobat who performs the *salto mortale* on the trapeze. Krull begins here to be less of a performer in his own right than the identifying audience of performances more spectacular and dangerous than his own. The philosophical stakes are raised as he considers Andromache in the larger context of the circus: "Magnificent animal bodies; and it is between animal and angel, so I reflected, that man takes his stand. His place is closer to the animals, that we must admit, but she, my adored one, though all body, was a chaster body, untainted by humanity, and stood much closer to the angels" (188).

The most philosophically extended and comically farfetched of the recapitulations of forward progress that Felix is made to enact in the novel is the history of the universe itself. In a series of exchanges that Mann adapted from a textbook in biology, a popular book on Einstein, and a display on evolution in the Chicago Museum of Natural History, Professor Kuckuck and Felix (masquerading as the Marquis of Venosta) develop a fantastic analogy between the career of the confidence man and the career of Being itself.[33]

> He would, however, give Man and me, the Marquis de Venosta, our due and not conceal what it was that distinguished Homo sapiens from all the rest of Nature, the organic and simple Being both, and which very likely was identical with the thing that had been added when Man emerged from the animal kingdom. It was the knowledge of Beginning and End. I had pronounced what was most characteristically human when I had said that the fact of Life's being only an episode predisposed me in its favour. Transitoriness did not destroy value, far from it; it was exactly what lent all existence its worth, dignity, and charm. Only the episodic, only what possessed a beginning and an end, was interesting and worthy of sympathy because transitoriness had given it a soul. But that was true of everything—the whole of cosmic Being had been given a soul by transitoriness, and the only thing that was eternal, soulless, and therefore unworthy of sympathy, was that Nothingness out of which it had been called forth to labour and to rejoice. (270–71)

The picaresque novel as the life and adventures of the universe. This cosmic expansion of the hero's regressive progress seems to be an ultimate analogy, which at the same time calls into question the very model of organic development on which the concepts of regress and progress depend. It seems as if "knowledge" (*Wissen*) is an irreversible movement forward in evolution, but then such spirituality is read back into everything, a totality which has been "given a soul" (*beseelt*) by its transience. At the end of the chapter Kuckuck tells Krull to dream of a stone that has lain in a brook for thousands and thousands of years. "Look upon its existence with sympathy, Being at its most alert gazing upon Being in its profoundest sleep" (271). Again, the implied phenomenology of the spirit is compromised, since the encounter between the extremes of being is to take place in dream, the medium of the unconscious.

It is difficult not to feel that Felix's career of "parodying nature," as he puts it earlier (37), has reached some kind of ultimacy here. The remaining chapters of Book Three, in which the evolutionary theme is played out in a visit to the museum and attendance at a bull fight, seem anticlimactic. Felix's inadvertent seduction of Senhora Kuckuck through her daughter is a return to the more circumscribed family romance of his own childhood. His ensuing travels around the world in the harmless but also rather limiting guise of the Marquis de Venosta do not promise a particularly exciting sequel. Nevertheless, such disappointment at a falling off of interest or excitement is precisely what Mann's last novel is attempting to capitalize on. Whatever turns its successive parts might have taken—and we know from the history of the picaresque novel what radical departures "second parts" may take—the extant First Part of *Felix Krull* keeps challenging the cultural assumption that maturity is best, that sublimity and pathos, particularly in art, are the most enduring of civilized values. Mann challenges the modern ideal of the novel as high art—an ideal he had labored as hard as any modern novelist to promote.

Mann's novelistic ambivalence toward the ascendancy of the novel is captured in his remarks on "Freud and the Future," with their paradoxically backward glance. "Infantilism—in other words, regression to childhood—what a role this genuinely psychoanalytic element plays in all our lives," Mann had written in his tribute to Freud in 1936.

> What a large share it has in shaping the life of a human being; operating indeed . . . as mythical identification, as survival, as a treading in footprints already made! . . . The artist in particular, a passionately childlike and play-possessed being, can tell us of the mysterious yet after all obvious effect of such infantile imitation upon his own life, his productive conduct of a career which is after all nothing but a reanimation of the hero under very different temporal and personal conditions and with very different, shall we say childish means.[34]

It is this sympathy with the primitive indignities of the artistic imagination that Mann so artfully deploys in *Felix Krull*, even as the myth of earliness and the earliness of myth are so universally expanded as to slip their ontological moorings. The break with tradition that the novel characteristically describes becomes a kind of *salto mortale* in *Felix Krull*, where the movement of regression prepares the way for a countermovement of free flight forward. Mann is able to "utilize the tremendous impetus thus gained to fly back" (187), but, as Felix says of Andromache, as in the trapeze performance, the interest lies in the unsecured space between the points of departure and arrival.

II

The Fielding novel, on the other hand, the pseudo-Shakespearian "comic epic" with its broad canvas, its emphasis upon reversals and recognitions, and its robust masculine sentimentality, turned out, oddly enough, to have no relevance to the American scene; in the United States it has remained an exotic, eternally being discovered by the widest audience and raised to best-sellerdom in its latest imported form, but seldom home-produced for home consumption.

Leslie Fiedler, *Love and Death in the American Novel*

Felix Krull is a peculiar transformation of the picaresque novel. It reinterprets the life of the rogue as a parable of mythic and reflexive consciousness—a story, as Mann ultimately suggests, of two modalities of modern art. Krull is more primitive than the artist by vocation, yet the contextual irony that attends upon his confession makes him more sophisticated than the vocational artist as well. He is alternately "before" and "beyond" the formalities of artistic expression, in an oscillation that cannot be fixed with any certainty. *Felix Krull* is characteristic of a great many modern novels in such a redefinition of the novel's cultural dialectic, and this ongoing historical study of the picaresque and the Quixotic must take account of still another far-reaching reformulation of the novel's project, a turn that the novel has taken in the twentieth century.

As I noted in Chapter 8, the early counterfictions of the Quixotic and the picaresque were overlaid in the course of the later eighteenth and early nineteenth centuries by other counterfictions such as the *Bildungsroman* and the Gothic, or the historical novel and the novel of urban panorama. These general types of fiction define another deep structure of narrative possibilities in the novel's ongoing tradition of the new. This is not to say that the later types and the subsequent structure ever become the exclusive concern of European and American novelists, but they do constitute a layer of texts, actual and ideal,

246

in the sedimenting of narrative possibilities. I have suggested a geological model of literary history, in which one stratum is laid down over another, but in which numerous extrusions also occur. The earlier textual layer of the Quixotic and the picaresque is exposed and accessible in a number of different places, but it is also subject to the pressures and distortions of the more recent assumulations of texts. Such a geological metaphor has its limitations, to be sure, but it seems truer to the vicissitudes of cultural history than the metaphor of organic growth. Individual texts and diachronic series of texts can and should be studied in and of themselves, but the succession of broader synchronic contexts, the deep imaginative structures of successive historical periods, must eventually be taken into account as well.

In the twentieth century, as many critics have argued, the European novel—along with its American counterpart—began to assume substantially different configurations. The change is of course not absolute; older and different forms of novel-writing continue to be deployed in relative innocence or deliberate avoidance of the modernist paradigms. The change is also recent enough that no common terms are readily available that might be used to characterize the modern redefinition of the novelistic project. Nevertheless, we may draw on our discussion of *Felix Krull* to suggest the following formulations. The modern novel continues to function in a dialectical or oppositional way, but it challenges literary convention anew, on two different fronts. On the one hand is the novel that opposes literary conventions of narrative with the deeper authority of the mythical archetype. One might call this the novel of ritual passage. On the other hand is the novel that attacks conventional formulas of storytelling from a radically experimental vantage point, the modern novel that flaunts its technical and technological self-awareness as a means of declaring its independence from any shared or received idea of order whatsoever. One might call this counterfiction the novel of free play.

Myth and self-consciousness are widely perceived as distinctive features of the modern novel, but the terms are in need of greater specification. The novel of ritual passage uses mythological elements, usually in syncretistic fashion, to adumbrate a master plot underlying the vicissitudes of contemporary culture. The movements of the characters, however random they appear on the surface, either conform or ironically fail to conform to some ritual charter that has guided other human movements in other times and places. Although the charter is rarely presented in its entirety, the mythic elements are signs of composite totality, a totality that purports, on an ideal level, to resist the historical forces of differentiation. The purest examples of this type of modern novel are perhaps the novels of D. H. Lawrence from *The Rainbow* onward. The relations of contemporary men and women are acted out on a composite mythological ground of Egyptian, Hebraic, Etruscan, Norse, Druidic, and Aztec elements—a ground which they can touch at certain ritually sanctioned moments but which they can never appropriate within their personal or inter-personal consciousnesses. The simple loss of self is never Lawrence's final solution; it is rather a renewal of the possibility of selfhood through some inchoate ritual of sacrifice. Lawrence is only one of a wide variety of twentieth-century novelists who anchor their fictive artifices in the preformations of myth and ritual.[35]

The novel of free play might be best represented by Sartre's early novel *Nausea*, which seems now, at a certain historical distance, to be the missing link between the exacerbated and ingenious novelties of the *nouveau roman* and the deconstructive self-consciousness of Proust and André Gide. Here the novel insists on an arbitrary artistry, an escape from predetermined patterns of discourse, including its own. New versions of the self are created through ironic reflection on older means of self-representation, a process which is forced to reject even its own previous statements.

> *Monday:*
> How could I have written that pompous, absurd sentence yesterday:
> "I was alone but I marched like a regiment descending on a city."
> I do not need to make phrases. I write to bring certain circumstances to light. Beware of literature. I must follow the pen, without looking for words.[36]

The fragment here declares its autonomy from the law of the whole, the medium assumes logical priority over ideological intent. Later novels of free play of course reject Sartre's relative sophistications as relatively naive. Robbe-Grillet denies the category of "self" altogether; Butor replaces the first with the second person pronoun. Declarations of a *"post*modernism" seem parochial or premature, if only because so much experimental fiction of recent decades still operates according to the premises of such early modernist movements as Dada and surrealism, assumptions that consciousness may be radically altered by the manipulation of the performative and physical media of art.[37]

248

Such a typology of the novel in the twentieth century as I am suggesting here is not intended to pass judgment on the value of particular novels. Like the *Bildungsroman* or Gothic forms, the novel of ritual passage and the novel of free play may be realized in narratives of astonishing freshness and power or in trite and formulaic ways. The typology simply describes, at a high level of abstraction, some constraints that distinguish the project of the twentieth-century novel, with its "regression full of novelty," in Mann's phrase, from the project of the novel in earlier periods. It also suggests a sense in which the two paradigms logically entail one another in the field of modern fiction as a whole. The impulse to liberation from the confines of conventional literary art—confines of "plot," "character," or "scene"—assumes its full significance only when seen in terms of the countervailing impulses to consecrate art at some higher or deeper level of revelation and to desecrate it in the profane immediacies of the writer's and reader's present. Indeed, in many individual texts, the two paradigms are equally evident—for example in Joyce's *Ulysses*. The voyage of Odysseus—interpreted by Joyce via Bérard as cosmopolitan myth rather than nationalistic epic—underlies the wanderings of Leopold Bloom and Stephen Daedalus; the references create the illusion of a culturally firm foundation beneath the accidents of contemporary urban traffic. But stylistic experimentation also creates the illusion of a freedom from any prior formal constraint. Joyce forges a radically different narrative instrument for each of the eighteen sections of the novel, and the virtuosity of the teller frequently overwhelms the immemorial qualities of the tale.

It is true that such mythopoeic and self-ironizing strategies are not limited to the modern novel alone. They can be found in earlier fiction—in Hölderlin's *Hyperion,* Mary Shelley's *Frankenstein,* Schlegel's *Lucinde,* Flaubert's *Bouvard and Pécuchet.* Yet one can argue that in spite of such isolated examples in the nineteenth century, such narrative modes do not become programmatic for the European novel until the century following. A more serious objection might be raised not about the term *modern* but about the term *novel.* "Ritual passage" and "freeplay" are hardly peculiar to prose fiction in the twentieth century. Indeed, in this period particularly, the significant distinctions between the anticanonical novel and more traditional literary forms become increasingly unclear. We might well agree with Bakhtin that modern literary culture has been "novelized" in a thoroughgoing fashion—still further than it had been in the case of American literature in the century preceding. Such a phenomenon seems especially evident in the modern vogue of the long, often fragmentary poem in free verse and with the spread of various naturalisms in the modern theater.

Nevertheless, on a more concrete level, the literary differential of the novel remains discernible in the modern period, in theory as well as in practice. Modern poetry still retains an imaginative commitment to the authority of the spoken word and the heard voice; modern drama still maintains a practical commitment to the auditory enactment and the visual scene. The numerous examples of formal and technical intercourse between novel and poem and between novel and play have complicated but have not obscured the novel's distinguishing radical of presentation: the familiarities and estrangements of the printed book. Furthermore, such local incursions on this historical distinction between prose fiction and poetic and dramatic forms are offset by a series of challenges from the new technologies of communication of the twentieth century: audio-recording and film. It is more characteristically against these recent sister arts of narrative rather than against the traditional literary genres—however antitraditional these may have become—that novelists feel the need to define their problematic form. In spite of a practical interest in "lyrical" prose styles and in spite of a theoretical concern with "dramatic" narrative modes, the twentieth-century novel seems more deeply animated by its confrontation with the form and content of film.[38]

These pressures on the modern novel from without are paralleled by what might be called another pressure from within. One of the most significant twentieth-century developments within the field of prose fiction and the printed book has been the proliferation of the modern short story. This form clearly has its origins in the supernatural tales, particularly German and American, of the early nineteenth century and in the more realistic stories of Gogol, Turgenev, Flaubert, and Maupassant later on. But it becomes an important phenomenon in the twentieth century, less and less confined to the periodical medium and occupying a place of honor in the careers of many of the most eminent modern novelists themselves: Joyce, Kafka, Lawrence, Faulkner, Mann.

Throughout its history, the novel's relationship to shorter forms of narrative fiction has been complex. As we have seen in the case of Cervantes and the collections or cycles of novellas like the *Decameron*, the longer narrative form of the novel has been seen as the culmination of the frame-tale structure in medieval and Renaissance storytelling, a new, existential framing in which an individual character and consciousness replace the storytelling group or company and in which stories are encountered in the flesh as well as heard. In the case of the modern short story and short-story cycle, it is as if the existential narrative frame of the novel has been dismantled. The modern short story is less a slice of life than a piece of a novel, shaped and pointed to give it an autonomy and wholeness of its own. If a collection like the *Decameron* is prenovelistic, a collection like Joyce's *Dubliners* is only comprehensible as a postnovelistic phenomenon. The "unity of effect or impression" that Poe originally identified as the ideological essence of the short prose form and that most commentators and practitioners have insisted upon since, in fact places the short story in direct opposition to the novel in the latter's diversity and its indeterminacy of effect. "Now, it cannot be said too emphatically that the genuine Short-story abhors the idea of the Novel," Brander Matthews wrote in *The Philosophy of the Short Story* in 1901. One consequence of this formal antipathy is that the short story has tended, much more than the novel, to set up its own canons and to conceive of itself as a form of high literary art.[39]

Thus in the literary system of the twentieth century, the position of the novel is challenged as much from within the field of prose fiction as, in the traditional opposition of poetry or drama, from without. Such a challenge is most ingeniously expressed in the exemplary short stories of Borges—as in "Pierre Menard, Author of the *Quixote*," which invokes the archetypal and exemplary novel of my study in the most direct and literal fashion of any of the successor fictions that I have discussed, but which also recasts it in the most pointedly antinovelistic way. Menard is a French symbolist poet, among whose surviving works is "an examination of the essential metric laws of French prose" and for whom *Don Quixote* is insignificant in comparison to "The Rime of the Ancient Mariner," "Le Bateau Ivre," and Poe's line "Ah, bear in mind this garden was enchanted!" Where Cervantes's project was accidental and relatively clumsy, Menard explains, his own project is impossibly exacting:

> My obliging predecessor did not refuse the collaboration of chance: he composed his immortal work somewhat *á la diable*, carried along by the inertias of language and invention. I have taken on the mysterious duty of reconstructing literally his spontaneous work. . . . To compose the *Quixote* at the beginning of the seventeenth century was a reasonable undertaking, necessary and perhaps even unavoidable; at the beginning the the twentieth, it is almost impossible. It is not in vain that three hundred years have

251

gone by, filled with exceedingly complex events. Amongst
them, to mention only one, is the *Quixote* itself.[40]

Borges ironically turns the tables on the novel, a literature of contingency and critique of tradition. Menard writes thousands of manuscript pages, his editor assures us, but leaves only two chapters and a fragment of a third of *Don Quixote* in "his" (identical) version.

What Borges dramatizes here is a new refutation of the novel, in which individuality and original ideas dissolve into a universality of thought. "Every man should be capable of all ideas," Menard writes, "and I understand in the future that will be the case." Or as Borges writes in his "Parable of Cervantes and the *Quixote*," "in the beginning of literature is the myth, and in the end as well."[41] The only vestige of the novel itself is Borges's specification of idle reading as the means of attaining this extraliterary mythic goal: "Menard (perhaps without wanting to) has enriched, by means of a new technique, the halting and rudimentary art of reading: this new technique is that of the deliberate anachronism and the erroneous attribution. . . . This technique fills the most placid works with adventure. To attribute the *Imitatio Christi* to Louis Ferdinand Céline or to James Joyce, is this not a sufficient renovation of its tenuous spiritual indications?"[42]

It is only in reference to such brief, pointed *Kurzprosa*, to use the German phrase, that it makes any sense to speak of the antinovel in modern literature. The example of Beckett provides an interesting parallel to that of Borges, the one a master of modern fiction who writes no novels at all, the other a novelist who, from *Murphy* to *How It Is*, progressively refines the novel out of existence. In the case of the latter-day modernism of John Barth, whose *Sot-Weed Factor* I have chosen as the last example in this exemplary history of the novel, the author's exposure to Borges and Beckett seems eventually to have had a significant effect. After one more long novel, *Giles Goat-Boy*, Barth turned to the short story and the short-story cycle as primary fictional forms. "I found the short story an unhospitable and unsympathetic genre during most of my writing life," Barth said in an interview in 1970. "I have become a convert to the short story recently. I found myself going from 800-page novels to 10-word stories, and now think the novel as queer and strange a genre as I thought the short story was."[43]

Nevertheless, before this formal change of heart, Barth did write a long self-conscious novel, self-consciously within the tradition or series of the Quixotic. Barth spoke of *The Sot-Weed Factor* (and *Giles*

Goat-Boy) as "novels which imitate the form of the Novel, by an author who imitates the role of Author," but he also noted that "if this sort of thing sounds unpleasantly decadent, nevertheless it's about where the genre began, with Quixote imitating Amadis of Gaul, Cervantes pretending to be the Cid Hamete Benengeli (and Alonso Quijano pretending to be Don Quixote), or Fielding parodying Richardson."[44] If anything, Barth shows a bias toward the earliest forms of the European novel in The Sot-Weed Factor—he speaks in the same essay of his "temper that chooses to 'rebel along traditional lines'"—and a nostalgia for a narrative self-consciousness that has not yet become an end in itself. "Oh God comma I abhor self-consciousness," one of the twin channels of stereo tape-recording says in the story entitled "Title" in Lost in the Funhouse.[45]

The Sot-Weed Factor is an overtly historical novel, but it is a historical novel redoubled. Eighteenth-century (and earlier) novelistic modes are used to relate a late seventeenth- and early eighteenth-century series of events. Fielding is the primary model—Barth said that he wanted to "make up a plot that was fancier than Tom Jones"[46]—but there are significant traces of Smollett, Defoe, Cervantes, and Rabelais also. There is a stylistic as well as a structural level of imitation, with Barth using a moderate facsimile of eighteenth-century English syntax and diction. Most importantly, Barth appropriates a number of historical documents in his fictional reconstruction. His hero, Ebenezer Cooke, is based on the elusive records of a historical personage of that name, author of the early eighteenth-century American poem "The Sot-Weed Factor" published in England in 1708 and in Maryland in 1731. Barth borrows narrative details of Cooke's verse satire as elements of his own plot, and he follows almost all the known data (admittedly scanty) about Cooke in tracing his hero's movements and associations.[47] To a lesser extent, Barth draws on John Smith's Generall Historie of Virginia, even as he undermines its authenticity with documents of his own invention—Smith's scurrilous Secret Historie and the Privie Journall of Henry Burlingame which further debunks Smith's self-debunking.[48] Finally, scholars of the period have shown the considerable extent to which Barth uses historical documents in the Archives of Maryland as a source of characters and events which one would otherwise imagine to be purely fictitious.[49]

Such extensive historical underpinning constitutes a curious reversal of the dialectic of Don Quixote, where archaic fictions are imported into a contemporary setting through the memory and perception of a single deluded reader. In The Sot-Weed Factor, an archaic historical foundation is provided for a work of fiction that is otherwise frankly contemporary in its concerns. We observed a similar reversal of the priority of fact over fiction in Twain's *Connecticut Yankee*, but Barth carries Twain's reversal a step further by denying both his characters and his readers any direct access to the mind or voice or text of the modern situation. We have no Hank Morgan to mediate between past and present. While historians may complain (as Alan Holder does) that Barth is playing fast and loose with American colonial history, the literary critic is more struck with the way Barth's art of fiction reaches out to historical documents for some sort of validation. This is quite different from Borges's project in "Pierre Menard," it should be noted, which aims at subverting the authority of a "historical" original; it is also quite different from Cervantes's device of the Arab historian, whose claims to truth are simultaneously undermined by his proverbial reputation for lying.[50] The surprise is that there is so much historical fact behind Barth's fiction.

For *The Sot-Weed Factor*, the colonial history of Maryland and the eighteenth-century history of the English novel provide a significant alternative to the resources of the novel in the twentieth century; as such, they function as an available mythology, not unlike the regional mythology of Faulkner's Yoknapatawpha County. As a native of Eastern Shore Maryland himself, Barth suggests at the end of the novel, he is heir-apparent to Ebenezer Cooke's literary estate. But the mythical past is a burden in Faulkner, and in Barth the situation is just the reverse. Instead of being doomed to the repetition of ritual patterns from the past, Barth's characters are given what one of them calls the "philosophic liberty . . . that comes from want of history" (181).[51] Barth's is a myth of alternatives rather than a myth of origins. Myth is appropriated by novelistic self-consciousness and free play. The protocol of *The Sot-Weed Factor*, the narrative formula by which a great majority of the available narrative codes are processed, is the recognition, enabling and disenabling, of alternative routes. As one of the novel's proverbs puts it, with leering double entendre, "there's more ways to the woods than one" (66).

The epigraph from Leslie Fiedler suggests the point of the Quixotic form of the novel for Barth, in its Fieldingesque redaction. The form is significant precisely for its general irrelevance to the dominant strain of American fiction, whether this dominant strain is held to be Richardsonian and Gothic, as in Fiedler's argument, or realistic and socially engaged, as Barth seems to assume in some of his own critical pronouncements.[52] The "Fielding novel" is exotic and cosmopolitan, unresponsible to its native audience's demands for relevance. This apparent alterity is what gives it its liberating appeal. There are of course earlier American novelists who have cultivated the Quixotic form in much the same fashion, as a cosmopolitan corrective for provincial prejudices: Brackenridge, Melville, and even, to some extent, Twain. But in *The Sot-Weed Factor* the Quixotic and Fieldingesque form is only one of a number of countercultural assertions that Barth is trying to make. The figure of an "American Adam," widely regarded in academic criticism as an archetype of American literature, is explicitly evoked in Ebenezer Cooke's militant innocence, but in Barth's hands it is an archetype with a difference. Cooke is an English-educated young man exposed to a native American corruption. His final discovery is that innocence is itself the Original Sin. " 'That is the crime I stand indicted for,' [Ebenezer] replied: 'the crime of innocence, whereof the Knowledged must bear the burthen. There's the true Original Sin our souls are born in: not that Adam *learned*, but that he *had* to learn—in short, that he was innocent' " (788). Barth offers a self-conscious alternative to R. W. B. Lewis's *American Adam*, just as he offers a ribald alternative to the legend of Pocahontas, "One of our few, true native myths, . . . a magical and moving explanation of our national origins," as Philip Young has put it.[53] Pocahontas's stubborn virginity in the novel is a gross physical counterpart of Ebenezer's moral commitment to chastity. One can even seen the emphasis on the Catholic culture of colonial Maryland as an alternative to Perry Miller's influential views of the importance of Puritanism in American intellectual history. Barth offers a different errand into the wilderness, a conspiracy of the Church Universal and "the One True Faith" (373) in which the identities and the real motives of the arch-conspirators can never be finally determined. (The supposedly virtuous Lord Baltimore and the supposedly villainous John Coode have only appeared in the novel in Burlingame's impersonations of them.) Moral and religious programs are thoroughly obscured in the endless plots and counterplots of Catholic worldliness, and the final irony, according to Barth, is that the province is secured only after the later Lords Baltimore have turned Protestant.

The posture of opposition underlies a number of the forms and themes in *The Sot-Weed Factor* and the structure of the narrative is most fruitfully approached as an ingenious multiplication of alternatives. Thus we have two contrasting redactions of a Quixote figure in the novel. The more obvious one is Ebenezer Cooke, who is Quixotic in the tradition of Joseph Andrews: idealistically virginal (in partial imitation of his sister) and precariously involved in the possibility of incest. More faithful to Cervantes than Fielding was in some respects, Barth provides Ebenezer with his own Sancho-esque servant and has him end in disenchantment with his highly literary ideals. But there is also the figure of Henry Burlingame III, Ebenezer's sometime tutor, who is Quixotic in the tradition of Melville's Confidence-Man: a dubiously sinister and benevolent player of many roles, a self-confessed cosmopolitan, a putative savior of American civilization. In some respects, Cooke and Burlingame exchange their different Quixotic attributes in the course of the novel. Ebenezer must give up his procrustean identity as "a Poet and a Virgin" for a more flexible vision of experience. Burlingame must give up his protean manhood and admit the limitations of his imaginative freedom. He discovers his biological forebears and a cure for his physical impotence in the same historical document, his grandfather's *Privie Journall.*

These central characters of the novel are not presented in isolation but in a series of shifting triangular relationships which further complicate their positions. The superficially labyrinthine plotting of the novel generally proceeds according to this pattern: one agent confronts two competing objects of desire. Burlingame desires both Anna and Ebenezer Cooke; Ebenezer desires both his sister Anna and the prostitute Joan Toast. The prohibitions against homosexuality and incest only seem to add to the interest of the alternatives. Anna is faced with a choice between Ebenezer and Henry, Joan Toast with a choice between Ebenezer and John McEvoy, her protector and pimp. Burlingame himself has been the contested third party in an erotic triangle involving Isaac Newton and Henry More. An illegitimate half-sister of Ebenezer and Anna turns up in Maryland who has lived, alternately, with the Indians Cohunkowprets and Quassapelagh, who turn out, in their turn, to be the half-brothers of Henry Burlingame III. *Und so weiter.* There seems to be no character in the novel who is not involved in at least one such situation of divided loyalties.[54]

This bifurcating logic is evident in many aspects of the novel. It is dramatized in Barth's rendition of an eighteenth-century anthithetical style—for example, as the novel begins:

> In the last years of the seventeenth century there was to be found among the fops and fools of the London coffee-houses one rangy, gangling flitch called Ebenezer Cooke, more ambitious than talented, and yet more talented than prudent, who, like his friends-in-folly, all of whom were

supposed to be educating at Oxford or Cambridge, had
found the sound of Mother English more fun to game with
than her sense to labor over, and so rather than applying
himself to the pains of scholarship, had learned the knack
of versifying, and ground our quires of couplets after the
fashion of the day, afroth with *Joves* and *Jupiters,* aclang
with jarring rhymes, and string-taut with similes stretched
to the snapping-point. (13)

The prose is a dance of alternatives, redoubled in the central chiasmus ("more ambitious than talented, and yet more talented than prudent"). It is not aimed at the reader's judging one course better than the other—as, for example, in the rhetoric of the Augustan heroic couplet—so much as at the reader's admiring the sheer plenitude of choice. Another archaic device, the Rabelaisian catalogue or list, is similarly adapted to Barth's own purposes. Ebenezer is confronted with sixteen different types of notebook as he tries to begin his poetic career, a series of choices displayed in a sixteen-line column in the text (124–25). A French whore and an English whore exchange epithets for their common profession for some seven continuous pages (466–72); Ebenezer and Henry Burlingame engage in an extended rhyming contest to determine who will ride and who will walk behind a flatulent horse (404–7).

The confrontation of alternatives takes place on broader thematic levels as well. The polymorphous bawdiness of the novel is organized around a contrast of genital and anal sexuality ("There's more ways to the woods than one") and the vocation of art itself is infected with the disease of alterity, from Ebenezer's choice of a "double essence," as he calls it (191), of virgin *and* poet to his opium vision of a twin Mount Parnassus. "The most important thing, of course, was to choose the proper mountain in the first place, but since by no amount of inquiry could he gain any certain information, Ebenezer at length chose arbitrarily and began to climb with the rest" (480). The biological motif of twinship, represented in Ebenezer and Anna, is given cosmic elaboration in the "Layman's Pandect of Geminology," a Shandean *paideia* prepared by Burlingame as Anna's tutor when he guesses her secret passion for her brother. "When first I guessed her trouble, long ere she saw't herself, we launched a long and secret enquiry into the subject of twins—their place in legend, religion, and the world. 'Twas my intent by this investigation not so much to cure Anna's itch—which I was not at all persuaded was an ailment—as 'twas to understand it, to see it in's perspective in the tawdry history of the species, if we might, and so contrive the most enlightened way to deal with it" (520). The either/or form and the list converge here in a catalogue of ambivalent filiations.

This obsessive cultivation of alternatives and dilemmas gives *The Sot-Weed Factor* a certain thinness of specification, even by the standards of the Quixotic novels with which it invites comparison. The historical data over which the author presides so archly are largely inaccessible to the reader. This only adds to the sense that whatever the stakes of a supposedly crucial decision in the novel, the particular value of the choice lies beyond the speculative field in which the problem of choice is set up. The relativity of value for the speculative intelligence is of course a theme that Barth addresses explicitly in *The Sot-Weed Factor* as well as in earlier novels, but it is also an imaginative problem which he seems unable to transcend himself, perhaps because of the way he characteristically defines it. The terms of the dilemma Barth participates in as well as describes can be seen with particular clarity in an essay he wrote seven years after the publication of *The Sot-Weed Factor*. In "The Literature of Exhaustion" Barth tries to draw a distinction between avant-garde experimentalism in art and a more traditional notion of artistic achievement—art which does something with its chosen medium, however technically up to date that medium may be. "I suppose the distinction is between things worth remarking—preferably over beer, if one's of my generation—and things worth doing," Barth writes.[55] But it is precisely this contested term "worth" that refuses to discriminate between the two conceptions of aesthetic activity. "Things worthy remarking" in *The Sot-Weed Factor* are only things that have value in the realm of action: political intrigue, sexual conquest, the making of history as opposed to the making of literature. "One must needs make and seize his soul, and then cleave fast to't, or go babbling in the corner; one must choose his gods and devils on the run, quill his own name upon the universe, and declare, 'Tis *I*, and the world stands such-a-way!' One must *assert, assert, assert*, or go screaming mad. What other course remains?" (365). This notable declaration of Burlingame's is not to be taken as Barth's final word in the novel, but it does show how the ideal of action for its own sake tends to arrogate all value to itself in the novel's affirmative mode. On the other hand, the things worth doing only seem to achieve *their* worth by virtue of their being remarkable—"things that almost anyone can dream up and discuss but almost no one can do," as Barth says of genuine artistic achievement in "The Literature of Exhaustion."[56] Deeds, including literary deeds, only seem worth doing when they can surprise the would-be observer of them and persuade him of the impossibility of his ever doing likewise. The reader becomes a spectator rather than a participant, and a polarity is again set up that renders intermediate values worthless.

The alternatives underlying the vision of alternatives in Barth's imagination appear to be two conflicting definitions of literary art: literature as an act of the will and an assertion of the self versus literature as the vicarious inactivity of the mind, an immobilized contemplation of possible courses of action. Barth presents his hero's (actual) satiric poem "The Sot-Weed Factor" as both things and yet neither. The poem ironically becomes a historical act in that it eventually helps convince would-be colonists that Maryland must be a place of some civilized culture to have produced such a literary work. But it also becomes a purely personal piece of speculation, in that Ebenezer disavows his vocation as a poet and writes nothing further for thirty-four years. Although he continues to think, "none of his later conceptions struck him as worthy of the pen" (804). Like Cooke's poem, Barth's novel imagines for itself no mediating function; it emerges as a technical medium shared by doing and thinking about doing, two mutually exclusive systems of cultural value. The appropriate icon of the novel is provided by the pages of the manuscript of John Smith's privately aggrandizing *Secret Historie*, which have inscribed on their versos the publicly incriminating journal of the 1691 Maryland Asembly.

To recognize this deeply structured dilemma is not to condemn Barth as a novelist but to discover once again how difficult novels are to evaluate by any settled standards of literary worth. The difficulty stems in part from the way novels reconstruct, in the broad and paradoxical texture of the printed book, fragments of a culture's ideology that often remain relatively separate and/or unexamined in the culture at large. Novels are frequently an affront to the canons of criticism as well as to the canons of literature, and the academic critic is particularly hard put to find a cultural vantage point from which to assess the collisions of form with form in a novel that belongs to his own immediate cultural moment, academic and otherwise. Nevertheless, the following comparison may help to place *The Sot-Weed Factor* within the broader literary space of the novel that this study has been concerned to map out across several centuries. Of all the particular novels that I have taken up, *The Sot-Weed Factor* seems closest to *Vanity Fair* in the quality of its aesthetic dissonance.

Both *Vanity Fair* and *The Sot-Weed Factor* aspire to the condition of the "Fielding novel" at the same time that they notably lack the assurance of Fielding in his authorial role. Both novels are written out of an allegiance uneasily divided between the claims of aesthetic perception and the claims of the ethical (or unethical) act. *Vanity Fair* apologizes for its sympathy with artful surfaces, *The Sot-Weed Factor* apologizes for its nostalgia for valid historical deeds and events; though the polarities are different, the resulting tensions are similar. Both Thackeray and Barth present apparently opposing pairs of heroines and heroes whose overt differences betray unresolved identities between them. From opposite sides of the fence, the principle of rivalry in *Vanity Fair* and the principle of alternative choice in *The Sot-Weed Factor* reveal the same complicity between the duplicitous and the single-minded.

It may be that in its resistance to traditional literary codes of resolution and closure the novel is fated to produce some of its most interesting examples in those books whose claims to unequivocal literary merit are most debatable. One of the sources of the ambivalence in both Barth and Thackeray as novelists is a somewhat rigid conception of the institution of literature itself, a deferential attitude toward literary propriety, moral at its base, to which they are unwilling to submit their own writings. The literary and extraliterary elements are seen in this view as necessarily in conflict with one another. The novelty of the novel is thus discordant and unsettling, since neither the traditional elements nor the newly discovered or newly imported elements are capable of asserting a tonal or atmospheric control. Much of Twain's novel writing assumes this posture as well, where the flouting of felt conventions is carried with a sense of unease or guilt. Both the humor and the pathos are frequently aggressive in their excess, since the attempted resolution of conflicting value claims is perceived as a threat to the integrity of the community and the integrity of the self.

In contrast are novelists like Cervantes and Fielding, for whom the conflict of old and new values is conceived from a position in the middle. The apparent ultimacies of a quarrel of the ancients and the moderns are perceived as secondary phenomena, capable of being resolved in a separate peace. Such a difference between harmonious and discordant versions of the novel's orchestration of cultural forms is by no means a function of historical development alone, with later novelists discovering more discord than harmony. If my reading of *The Confidence-Man* is correct, Melville was able to make the transition from an antithetic to a synthetic mode in the course of a single brief career. Thomas Mann provides the most salutary example of a modern for whom the cultural contraries of the novel are less antagonistic than propitious, productive of higher levels of resolution.

"Man is the lord of counter-positions," Hans Castorp comes to realize in *The Magic Mountain;* "they can only be through him, and thus he is more aristocratic than they."[57] For Barth, on the other hand, men are grotesquely suspended between the longing for unity and the need for division, like his Siamese twins in *Lost in the Funhouse* who petition the King of Siam for relief from their condition: "To be one: paradise! To be two: bliss! But to be both and neither is unspeakable."[58] From *Don Quixote* to the present neither the vulgar definition nor the aristocratic has been able to assume hegemony over the novel for very long.

11

Novel and History

It is impossible to imagine what a novelist takes himself to be unless he regard himself as an historian and his novel as history. It is only as an historian that he has the smallest *locus standi*. As a narrator of fictitious events he is nowhere; to insert into his attempts a back-bone of logic, he must relate events that are assumed to be real.

Henry James, "Anthony Trollope"

The series of novels that I have studied in the foregoing account, from *Don Quixote* and the Spanish picaresque to novels of the mid-twentieth-century United States, may not seem to provide a particularly authoritative or exhaustive literary history. Such history by example is not necessarily a history as example. My study of novels in the line of the Quixotic and the picaresque does not account for the transition from one text to another with any general causal explanation. The reasons why later novels hearken back to *Don Quixote* and/or the Spanish picaresque are admitted to be various, deriving as much from the exigencies of a given writer's career or the dynamics of the contemporary literary context as from any special power or logic that inheres in the earlier texts. Nor does my history provide anything like a continuous narrative of development. It does not fill in the large chronological gaps betwen the precursors and the subsequent examples. There is no discussion of *Gil Blas* as a picaresque novel, of *The Idiot* as an imitator of the matter (rather than the manner) of Cervantes, or of numerous other Quixotic and picaresque fictions from *Le Berger extravagant* to *The Adventures of Augie March*. Finally, to complete this list of disclaimers, my history has glanced only briefly and schematically at the alternative types and series of novels that branch out from, or spring up independently of, these earliest lines of succession.

Nevertheless, I do claim for this history of the novel a paradigmatic value. It shows in particular instances how the novel is historical and how it is not. The account is intended to be both more general and more specific than the continuous explanatory narrative that historians of other institutions (including literary genres) have led us to expect, if only because these are the levels on which novels establish significant historical relationship with one another. The account is

262

more general in considering a succession of novels in the light of a theory of the novel. The idea of how one novel "follows" another is derived from an idea of the novel's self-definition, its claims for itself as a cultural event. The account is more specific in considering the way one complex narrative interacts with another complex narrative or group of narratives; the self-definition of the novel is respected here as well. This history of the novel claims to be exemplary, in other words, in allowing the novel in the abstract and particular novels in the concrete their own authority as intentional documents, intead of imposing on them a form of description and argument that overrides their ambiguous essays at innovation.

The intentionality that I am claiming for the novel, in the face of more disingenuous critical formalisms which, I would argue, simply displace or disguise this essential historical notion, is not a simple matter. It is the product of intersecting intentions: of the novelist, of the novel as a particular kind of writing, and of the shifting formalities of the larger cultural context. It is an intentionality that can only be reconstructed from its effects—the effects of the texts on the changing community of its readers. Cervantes can hardly be said to have intended the European novel as it later developed; the Spanish Counter Reformation certainly did not envision the popular secular fiction that would emerge from its harsh critique of literary humanism. But in exploiting the resources of the printed book—cognitive, social, and economic—the works that this author and this subculture produced initiated a mode of symbolic experience that displaced the authority of the text from its producers to its consumers. The plurality of present readers and the futurity of later readerships were recognized as active determinants of a novel's meaning and value, and the narrative became distinctly open-ended in the process of its own transmission and survival. Jonathan Swift satirized this new open-endedness of literature, both cause and effect of the emerging novel, when he dedicated *A Tale of a Tub* to "Prince Posterity": "For altho' *Your Highness* is hardly got clear of Infancy, yet has the universal learned World already resolv'd upon appealing to Your future Dictates with the lowest and most resigned Submission: Fate having decreed You sole Arbiter of the Productions of human Wit, in this polite and most accomplish'd Age."[1] Yet Swift's attempt to reaffirm a more fixed and traditional standard of cultural authority could only take its place beside the novels of Defoe and the subsequent "new species of writing" in the literary marketplace. As I have suggested throughout this study, the novel is a thoroughly dialectical form based on a fundamental paradox of the printed book: its mass privacy. Over and over again, the community of traditional literary forms and values is subjected to the double dislocation of this mechanical reproduction of art. On the one hand, a privacy of the silent reading experience inevitably open to personal and idiosyncratic response in spite of the concurrent publication in notices and reviews of more settled and more educated judgments. On the other hand, a publicity of circulation, with an audience as potentially extensive and indeterminate as literacy itself. This peculiar technology of communication on which the novel was originally based, itself continually reaching out to new masses and in toward new privacies, has provided a continual impetus for the more ideological levels of the novel's ongoing critique of literary tradition.[2]

Don Quixote and the earliest Spanish picaresque novels function for later generations of novelistic texts on both the different levels of this history. On the general level they provide charters of novelistic innovation, founding documents in the novel's break with tradition and its equalization of literary and nonliterary forms. But as this break and this equalization are always partial and relative, Don Quixote and the picaresque have also functioned as models of a more specific sort—as precedents for the unprecedented, frameworks for the breaking of frames, pretexts for the retextualizing of cultural imperatives. It is significant that as models they are curiously provisional, "without authority," in the Kierkegaardian phrase, particularly in comparison with comparable models of poetic or dramatic form. For Fielding, Don Quixote is a mock neoclassical norm; for Mann, the picaresque is the novel at its most primitive. It is also significant that the Quixotic and the picaresque constitute not a single precedent for the novel but a double one, antithetical at its inception. Don Quixote's overcredence in literary fictions and the picaro's lack of faith in the fictions of the social order are contrasting versions of a common problem, and for later novels a cultivation of the one often involves a coming to terms with the other, as we have seen with certain English and American novels of the nineteenth century.

Finally, as the historical layers of intertextuality accumulate between the "earliest" and the "latest" example of a series, the shape and length of the succession is often reenvisioned. For Thackeray, the Quixotic series begins with Fielding rather than with Cervantes; for Barth it reaches back through Fielding and Cervantes to Rabelais. In the case of Felix Krull, in spite of Mann's belated recognition of Lazarillo, the picaresque proceeds from the German Simplicissimus, even as it is also projected back into classical mythology and the Homeric hymns. The historical relation between successor and precursor is a dialectical one, if only because the successor text recreates the series in its own image.

What this means is that novels are—among other things—readings of earlier novels, readings of particular texts and more generalized series of texts as well as readings of the much broader cultural field of narrative precedents and possibilities. Generally speaking, such historical self-reflexiveness is common to all literary texts—perhaps even to all cultural artifacts. But in the case of the novel, the reflexiveness puts special emphasis on the fictive, self-made quality of the authorizing past. A "tradition" of the novel is a story of the novelist's own choosing and devising, merely one of the many plots that struggle against one another for recognition in the text. The authority of a particular book may be absolute on one level of reading—as with the authority of *Amadis of Gaul* for Don Quixote—but there are always other levels of reading, suggested within the text and enabled beyond it, on which its authority becomes ironically relative. Against Ortega's dictum cited in the first chapter that "every novel bears *Quixote* within it like an inner filigree, in the same way as every epic poem contains the *Iliad* within it like the fruit its core," one might pose Borges's novelistic claim about the *Iliad* itself in its translations. "What are the many translations of the *Iliad*, from Chapman to Magnien but different perspectives on an object in motion, a long, experimental game of omissions and emphases? . . . To presuppose that any [such] recombination of elements is necessarily inferior to its original is to presuppose that rough draft 9 is necessarily inferior to rough draft H. Of course there can be nothing but rough drafts. The concept of the 'definitive text' belongs only to religion or fatigue."[3] As a half-outsider, ironically situating itself in the interstices of culture between a literary past and an extraliterary present (or vice versa, as the case may be), a novel reads out the conflicting codes according to protocols of its own fabulation. The particularity of individual texts may capture the imagination of subsequent novelists, but these two are immediately subject to the novel's experimental and recombinatory process.

Thus a history of the novel is a problematic undertaking, since the form is in itself only ambivalently and evasively historical. This particular study offers itself as exemplary in a final sense of the word because it tries to reinforce this awareness. As I have noted throughout, the influence of *Don Quixote* and the picaresque is no more all-pervasive than their authority is absolute. They merely define the most extensive series of rereadings of the novel by the novel in European and Westernized literary history. One could construct similar exemplary accounts for other historically significant texts: for *Clarissa* and its successor novels of physical violation and moral judgment (as F. R. Leavis and Leslie Fiedler have suggested in their radically different fashions), for *Wilhelm Meister* and the series of *Bildungsromane* (from Carlyle's *Sartor Resartus* to David Storey's *Saville*, to take only English examples), for *Madame Bovary* and the modernist novels of point of view and confusion of distance, for *Ulysses* and its contemporary mythographic-encyclopedic imitators, and so forth. Some of these studies have been undertaken already, yet most of them avoid reflecting on the peculiarities of a history of the novel per se, a form of literary expression so deeply and ambiguously involved with the materials of history itself. For this is the other side of the novel's evasion of its own historicity: its pretension, as Henry James shrewdly observes, to be a history in its own right. Novels aspire to embody history rather than to participate in it, and in comparison with other literary forms, historical dramas and Pound's *Cantos* notwithstanding, they have had more abundant resources for supporting this ambition. As a conclusion to this study and a way of returning to some of the issues raised in the first chapter, I would like to consider at greater length this competition and resemblance between the novel and history writing.

The term *history* is ambiguous in its modern usage, as Hegel reminds us: "History combines in our language the objective as well as the subjective side. It means both the *historiam rerum gestarum* and the *res gestas* themselves, both the events and the narration of the events."[4] Yet for most practicing historians the ambiguity is logically resolved by distinguishing between events and the narration of events on the basis of the intervening evidence. History writing, or the rhetoric of history, as J. H. Hexter calls it, is based on an "overriding commitment of historians to fidelity to the surviving records of the past."[5] The written history has no immediate access to the *res gestas*, but must reconstruct them from the available documentation of the past. The historian interprets the written record (though it may be supplemented with other types of artifactual evidence) and attempts to translate from this primary documentation to actions and events. The actions and events—political, military, artistic, economic—are themselves subject to further interpretation. They are not the final meaning of the written account but are themselves construed as signs of underlying intentions or forces or even laws.[6] The difference between the historian and the chronicler is that for the

266

latter the chain of reference usually stops short of this ulterior significance. The historian constructs a narrative in such a way that his own
text refers through intermediary documents to the events that they
record, and through the events to the forces, ideational and material,
of which these events are the most probable expression.

The novel resembles the historical narrative in many respects, not
the least of which is its traditional commitment to narrative explanation. As Louis O. Mink has argued, both history and literary storytelling appeal to a "configurational" mode of understanding, where
phenomena are accounted for not by the application of theoretical
laws nor by the arrangement into systems of classification but by the
construction of persuasive sequences, stories of happenings with
beginnings, middles, and ends.[7] Some historians and literary critics
have gone further and argued that works of formal history can be
best understood as operating according to literary and rhetorical
models. One of the most forceful of these scholars, Hayden White,
goes as far as to claim that "historical discourse shares more than it
divides with novelistic discourse."[8]

Nevertheless, as White himself reveals in a telling analysis of
Michel Foucault, another antihistorical historian, such an interpretation of historical narrative is essentially "grounded in poesis." "To
transform prose into poetry is Foucault's purpose, and thus he is
especially interested in showing how all systems of thought in the
human sciences can be seen as little more than terminological formalizations of poetic closures with the world of words, rather than
with the 'things' they purport to represent and explain."[9] Such a
subversion of historical representation by literary analysis passes
over the very ground on which the novel stakes its ambiguous claim.
One might paraphrase Sidney (who was paraphrasing Aristotle) and
say that, while the novel is more historical than literature, it is also
more literary than history. The novel locates itself *between* literature
and history as cultural institutions.

Thus the novel evades the classifications and undermines the norms
of poetics, but it also evades and undermines the referential imperatives of history. Novels play "literature" and "history" off against
one another as codified forms of written discourse. They reopen
poetic closures by appealing to the more random plots of supposed
historical phenomena. But they also foreclose historical reference.
They betray the surviving records of the past to the logics of literary
coherence—the logics of plot, of character, of point of view, and of
their more particular protocols of narration. Since the novel also
challenges the validity of *merely* literary categories, such coherence

may seem more honored in the breach than the observance. But it still functions as an expectation of the novel's narrative form, deflecting historical writing from its goal of correspondence.[10]

The opposition between the novel and history writing may be described more precisely in terms of the referential or representational function of the text. Novels are pseudohistorical, in the sense that they raise the question of documentation. They do this openly and ironically, as in the case of *Don Quixote* and the manuscript of the historian Cide Hamete Benengeli which unexpectedly becomes the basis of the text; or subtly and persuasively, as in a novel like *Moll Flanders*, which begins, "My True Name is so well known in the Records, or Registers at *Newgate*, and in the Old-Baily, and there are some things of such Consequence still depending there, relating to my particular Conduct, that it is not to be expected that I should set my Name, or the account of my Family to this Work."[11] From the obvious example of the epistolary novel to the surreptitious case of Henry James's "reflectors" and "centers of consciousness" reading the signs of social intercourse and exchange, the novel has characteristically imitated the reliance of critical historiography on surviving records. But where history infers from the record to extratextual phenomena, agents, and events, novel-writing turns this referentiality back upon itself. In the novel, the world offers itself up as a series of textual records—fragmentary or complete, reliable or duplicitous, literal or figurative. The reader is referred to an extratextual "reality" or "truth" only to be referred back to the compendious textuality of human experience, which the book he is holding seeks to elucidate and control.

Thus the "illusion of life" that the novel is traditionally said to promote is really an illusion of reference to life. The disturbing effect of the more abrupt violations of this illusion—Thackeray calling his characters puppets, Trollope confessing the invention of his plot—shows the extent to which this illusion of reference must be intertained intially if the novel is to play its dialectical role. A *locus standi* must be created, in James's phrase, if only to provide the novelist with an Archimedean point from which to move the institution of literature off its foundations. Yet it is also true that the most realistic and unselfconscious of novels depends on the ambiguity of experience as recorded, even if the record is as immediate and evanescent as visual or aural perception. Even such raw sensory data in a novel are already processed, already shaped in a *re*-presentation of the world.

For example, in Joyce's *Portrait of the Artist as a Young Man,*

Stephen Daedalus registers the following impressions: "the fellows were practicing long shies and bowling lobs and slow twisters. In the soft grey silence he could hear the bump of the balls: from here and from there through the quiet air the sound of cricket bats: pick, pack, pock, puck." From the sports slang of the initial phrases, transcribing the diction of the group, to the unconscious rhyme of "there" and "air," the elements of Stephen's hearing become more personal and more elegantly patterned, until they realize their formalization in an overtly poetic simile: "like drops of water falling softly in a brimming bowl." Yet this translation of sensory data into poetic inner speech only prepares the way for an undermining of the process. As reference doubles back upon itself, deflecting correspondence into coherence, the patterns of coherence become fixed and inert, corresponding only to the perceiver's desire. Verbal icon becomes symbolist cliché and achieved form becomes merely an element in a field of data requiring new formalization. Later on in the novel Stephen's villanelle "Are you not weary of ardent ways" emerges as a parody of his power of verbal mimesis, the flesh becoming word in the process of his daydream: "Her nakedness yielded to him, radiant, warm, odorous and lavishlimbed, enfolded him like a shining cloud, enfolded him like water with a liquid life: and like a cloud of vapour of like waters circumfluent in space, the liquid letters of speech, symbols of the element of mystery, flowed forth over his brain."[12] The world may exist to end in a book, as Mallarmé claimed, but for the novelist this book keeps revealing its bookishness and falling back into a more worldly perspective.

The semiosis of experience that novels characteristically effect is thus not always explicit. It need not depend on a found manuscript or a written letter. But it does aspire to the status of a written text, even as it interferes with writing's referential function. In Dickens's *Great Expectations*, to take another common example, a whole prototextual sign language is generated simply by attention to the physical detail of hands. Fingers point, in the flesh and as road signs; hands grasp, whether in friendship, oppression or hypocrisy (Pumblechook's "May I?"); Pip is brought up "by hand," Jaggers washes his hands from the taint of the law, convicts are handcuffed to one another. The resemblance of Estella's wrists to Molly's establishes their crucial relationship as mother and daughter. Handwriting is a form of communication and deception. Compeyson, the arch-villain of the novel, is a master forger and a manipulator of his fellow man. "Let *him* make a tool of me afresh and again? . . . No, no, no," Magwitch cries. When Pip tells Jaggers that he knows Estella's parentage, Jaggers tells him that rather than reveal the secret, "you had better—and would much sooner when you had thought well of it—chop off that bandaged left hand of yours with your bandaged right hand, and then pass the chopper on to Wemmick there, to cut *that* off too."[13] These manual markers in the novel are not simply metaphors, a pattern of imagery in the traditional sense where literal phenomenon and figurative expression are relatively distinct. They are rather an example of the physically literal world shaping itself into rudimentary patterns of meaning, creating a primitive version of language which characters may speak and—occasionally—comprehend. They are part of the represented world presenting itself back as a text.[14]

Looking back to *Don Quixote* and the Spanish picaresque novels, one might say that they present the ambiguities of the world *sub specie textus* in a cruder and more explicit fashion, that later novels greatly refine and expand their more obvious strategies of reflexive reference. But it is important to recognize that novels are never absolute nor prescient in their retroverse historical method. They react as much as anything to the local historiography of their cultural moment. Bruce Wardropper has shown how *Don Quixote* is in part a critique of the credulities of Renaissance history-writing in Spain, a comic reflection on the difficulty serious historians had in separating fact from fiction in the body of historical writings. Wardropper cites a particular forgery by Miguel de Luna, the official Arabic interpreter to Philip II, who "claimed to be merely a translator of a work written in the 8th century by Albucácim Tárif, a Moor alleged to have access to King Roderick's archives."[15] And as I have already noted in the second and third chapters, *Lazarillo* and *El Buscón* make ironic commentary on the popular Renaissance biographical genre of the *homo novus*, the self-ennobled man of lower birth who makes his mark in aristocratic society. Later versions of the novelistic critique of history are numerous. Fielding speaks ironically of "those Romance-Writers who intitle their Books, the History of *England*, the History of *France*, of *Spain*, &c.," who agree in matters of geography and chronology but who contradict one another wildly in ethical judgments of individual figures.[16] *Vanity Fair* bankrupts the Carlylean vision of history as hero-worship, "the everlasting adamant," as Carlyle put it, "lower than which the confused wreck of revolutionary things cannot fall."[17] *The Sot-Weed Factor* stands the Virgin Land school of American history on its head and thumbs its nose at modern historiography in general; in Chapter 18 of Part III, "The Poet Wonders Whether the Course of Human History is a Progress, a Drama, A

Retrogression, a Cycle, an Undulation, a Vortex, a Right- or Left-Handed Spiral, a Mere Continuum, or What Have You. Certain Evidence in Brought Forward, But of an Ambiguous and Inconclusive Nature."[18] This is to say nothing of more deep-rooted and searching rejections of the authority of history in *The Red and the Black, War and Peace,* or *Absalom, Absalom!*[19]

The term "historical novel," then, is something of a redundancy, comparable to the redundancy of "nouveau roman": a local or specific reaffirmation of an inherent proposition of the novel from its beginnings. Yet the term is also something of a contradiction, since, unlike the earlier forms of romance, the novel is "sensitive to its origins in historiography and aware of the need to handle its claim to historical accuracy with massive doses of irony."[20] The irony of Scott, with whom, one critic suggests, "the 'historical novel' as a serious literary mode began and ended,"[21] is not always obvious. But the historical imagination that Scott evokes, through the medium of oral sources and written documents, is often an impassioned and prejudicial vision that leads to social disaster. There is a quiet rebuke to romantic histories of the folk in the epigraph to *The Heart of Midlothian:* "It is mighty well, said the priest; pray, landlord, bring me those books, for I have a mind to see them. With all my heart answered the host; and going to his chamber, he brought out a little old cloke-bag, with a padlock and chain to it, and opening it, he took out three large volumes and some manuscript papers written in a fine character." The passage is from Chapter 32 of the First Part of *Don Quixote;* it introduces the reading of "The Tale of Foolish Curiosity." As a novelist, Scott uses a narrative method that plays one partisan school of historical explanation off against another. The "veracity and the authenticity of [the] historical narratives" is a result of the conflict between more credulous fictions of the past and more rapacious visions of the future.[22]

To say that the novel has always imitated the methods of written history while controverting historical truth into aesthetic structure is to grant novels a kind of parity with written history. Fictive narratives of individual and collective becoming and factual accounts of similar processes are seen as making continual incursions on one another, at least in the cultural systems of the West. This view may seem ahistorical itself, but it is not intended as such. It merely suggests that historical interpretation of the novel needs to be more *broadly* historical than it has generally been, not limited to the very units and metaphors of development that novels themselves have appropriated from historical discourse. The novel does not "rise" like the middle classes, though many novels do present versions of this historical masterplot. The novel does not grow, mature, and lapse into senility, though the vitality of the form does seem to fluctuate in particular national cultures at particular times.

Most importantly, there is no real evidence to suggest that the novel is about to disappear or to use its materials up. Such a view has been widely held at times, and is stated most authoritatively for the twentieth century by Ortega y Gasset: "In short, I believe that the genre of the novel, if not irretrievably exhausted, has certainly entered its last phase, the scarcity of possible subjects being such that writers must make up for it by the exquisite quality of the other elements that compose the body of a novel."[23] Yet this model of decadence is obviously conceived in collusion with many twentieth-century novelists themselves—Proust, Mann, and Joyce, for example—as well as with modern historians like Spengler and Toynbee. Contemporary novelists continue to talk about the death of the novel—an American has even published a work of fiction with this title[24]—but if nothing else the adoption of this originally European form by numerous other countries and continents of the modern world has given it a wider currency and new valuation.[25] The British novel may be languishing at present, the (North) American novel may be undergoing a crisis of purpose, but novels from Japan and Latin America seem remarkably energetic and inventive. One of the most notable phenomena of literature in the last half-century has been, in the words of a Soviet scholar, "the process of penetration of the literature of certain countries into the literary worlds of other countries. . . . This process is developing both in scale and intensity and in social significance."[26] The novel has been able to move most easily across these political and linguistic barriers, and such interpenetration is by no means limited to contemporary texts. Through new translations and new editions, increasingly inexpensive and widely distributed in the paperback revolution, the novel's history has become more synchronically available to readers and writers than ever before.

Against this thesis of the novel's essential implication in the writing of history it might be argued that since the later eighteenth century, all forms of European literature have come to embody this historical antagonism and aspiration. From Wordsworth's history of his own poetic growth to Pound's history of world culture, from the historical plays of Goethe and Schiller to those of Brecht and Peter Weiss, poetry and drama have also been deeply involved in the imaginative reconstruction of self and society in their tormented temporal becoming. Such an observation, however, merely shifts the discussion to a higher level of generality and abstraction, on which novels and other types of literature do have many features in common. One might as well ascend to a higher level still and observe that the novel is simply one form among many in the transformation of Western culture from a traditionalizing basis to a modernizing one. From the reassertion of classical and biblical authority in the Renaissance and Reformation to the contrary emphasis on an *un*authorized modernity in the Enlightenment and beyond, the novel has been one particular manifestation of our culture's paradoxical adjudication of the conflicting claims of past and present. As Paul de Man notes, "modernity and history relate to each other in a curiously contradictory way that goes beyond antithesis or opposition. If history is not to become sheer regression or paralysis, it depends on modernity for its duration and renewal; but modernity cannot assert itself without being at once swallowed up and reintegrated into a regressive historical process."[27] Literature in its older poetic and dramatic modalities constitutes one series of ways in which this contradiction is explored, expressed, and repressed anew; the novel, in its seemingly newer performative space of the printed book, constitutes another series. A recognition of the common ground (or groundlessness) that many cultural expressions in the West have shared in the last several centuries should not lead us to disregard the more specific and concrete differences between one form of expression and another. The claim of this study has never been for the novel's absolute uniqueness but for its distinctive features in the historical field of possibilities.

To return to these more concrete considerations and the question of the novel's future, I might take up again the notion that the novel is currently being supplanted by film—that a new medium of imaginative storytelling is taking over this function of the printed book, or at least luring away the novel's available audience. It may well be that in the distant future this new technology of communication, perhaps in conjunction with other explosive technologies like the computer, will radically reorganize the system of the arts, just as the printing press transformed the artistic system based on the old scriptorium. Nevertheless, as the history of writing and literacy alone shows, the consequences of a particular technology of communication are only gradually absorbed by cultures and societies.[28] And as the history of the novel itself shows, the creation of a new art form does not necessarily entail the destruction of an older one. The advent of the novel has hardly spelled the end of poetry and drama, though both these older forms have been increasingly affected by the novel's presence.

This is apparently what is happening in the twentieth century: film has exerted a cultural pressure on the novel which has impelled it in new formal and thematic directions. The new techniques of visual narrative have been appropriated by novelists from Joyce to Robbe-Grillet, and the economic production and distribution of novels have been significantly restructured by the intermediate form of the screenplay. Nevertheless, such influence is part of a circular process. Eisenstein claimed that the cinematic methods of D. W. Griffith were derived in large part from Dickens, and novels past and present have been a particularly rich source of story for film production. The fact that producers now buy the screen rights to many more novels than are actually made into films provides an important economic stimulus to the literary marketplace. And the production of a film or film series for television is often tied in with the publication or republication of a book. The reissue of *Tom Jones* or *Women in Love* in conjunction with recent cinematic versions may strike some readers as an unnecessary popular promotion of established classics, but along with the reissue of such more neglected texts as Trollope's Palliser novels or Thackeray's *Barry Lyndon*, it hardly argues for an antagonism between the two media.[29] As one novelist has put it, "I don't see why the novel should go bankrupt thanks to the visual media. The enormous expansion of the visual media does create problems for the written word, for any literary genre; but in the case of the novel it poses the problem precisely: what can you say only through the medium of the novel? . . . This in itself brings the novel back to an elementary position in which it has to become everything to become itself."[30]

The novelist in question here is the contemporary Mexican author Carlos Fuentes, and it is with a brief discussion of one of his most recent works that I would like to bring this study to a conclusion. Many of my scholarly historical arguments find a striking—and unanticipated—novelistic parallel in what will serve as a final example in this exemplary history of the novel. The novel is entitled *Terra Nostra:* it is a book I discovered only at the very end of my own research and writing, in the course of pursuing a reference to a lecture Fuentes gave in 1975 called "Cervantes, the Founding Father," which was later expanded and published with the title of *Don Quixote, or The Critique of Reading*.[31] In the lecture Fuentes referred to a novel he had been working on for the last six years; it was published in Spanish in 1975 and in English translation in the year following.

While a reviewer's enthusiastic comparison of Fuentes with Milton, Tolstoy, and Proust seems excessive,[32] his novel is nevertheless an ambitious and intriguing piece of work—"quite an original," in Melville's ambiguous phrase.

Terra Nostra is, as the polyphonic narrator says to himself at the end of it, "a transposition of the historic past into a future that will have no history."[33] It begins in Paris in 1999, in the midst of worldwide revolution and disaster, but after some thirty pages it leaps back into what Fuentes calls "the least realized, the most abortive, the most latent and desiring of all histories: that of Spain and Spanish America" (771). The primary focus of the kaleidoscopic narrative is the building of the Escorial by Philip II, and it is from this monomaniacal dead center, as Fuentes presents it, that a series of other historical and geographical projections proceed: back to Palestine at the time of the Crucifixion, back to Tiberius on the island of Capri in the first century of the Roman Empire, over to Renaissance Venice, and—most importantly—across to Mexico at the time of its European discovery and conquest. There are briefer visions of Mexico at the time of Maximilian and at the moment of an imagined U.S. invasion, with a return to Paris in 1999 some six months after the time of the opening chapter.

The novel shows both an extreme fidelity to the historical record and a flagrant violation of it. Fuentes borrows heavily from the work of modern historians: from Norman Cohn on revolutionary millenarianism in the Middle Ages, from Frances Yates on the Renaissance theaters of memory, from Americo Castro on the mixture of Christianity, Judaism, and Islam in Spanish culture, and from a number of other scholars whom he freely acknowledges.[34] But he also takes great liberties with the most elementary of historical facts. His Philip II is the son rather than the grandson of Philip I; the all-important figure of Charles V is simply elided. Elizabeth, the Virgin Queen of England, is made Philip's wife (rather than rejecting his offer of marriage), and although she has no sexual relations with her husband she is by no means virginal. Both Columbus and Cortez, the discoverer and the conqueror of the New World, are embodied in a mythic voyager called simply the Pilgrim. More interestingly, a whole series of historical events and movements are faithfully enough reconstructed or alluded to, but are collapsed into a rather brief chronological period—if one is still inclined to think in terms of a temporality independent of the novel's violent dislocations of it.

The range of historical reference and pseudoreference in Terra Nostra is thus immense, and factual characters freely mingle with fictional ones—fictional characters of Fuentes's own invention, such as the revolutionaries Ludovico, Simon, and Pedro, but also those appropriated from earlier literary texts, such as Celestina, Don Juan, and Don Quixote of La Mancha. It is difficult to decide at first what holds the proliferating plots and histories together, and in an important sense the novel deliberately aims at overthrowing all authoritative structures of order, literary as well as historical. Nevertheless, at the risk of oversimplifying an extremely complex narrative, I would observe the following rudiments of a protocol or master plot for the novel. *Terra Nostra* is concerned with the reappropriation of the earth—"our earth," as the title claims—by the human multitudes who inhabit it. Felipe II, El Señor, is the central figure of oppression in a struggle between monolithic imperialism and a pluralism unto anarchy. The one insists on the singleness of political power, the unity of religious belief, the purity of race; the other asserts a diversity of authority, of thought, and of ethnic group. The forces of pluralism are not merely a Marxist proletariat, although there are (anachronistic) elements of this class represented, but a variety of cultural perspectives—social, artistic, religious, scientific, and economic—to which Fuentes gives a pointedly political representation.

Symbolically, this conflict is frequently expressed in the arithmetical or "arithmythic" form, as the novel has it (603), of unitary, binary, and ternary groupings. "Binaries differentiate. Ternaries activate. . . . three is the creative number," Ludovico is instructed by the Cabalistic Ancient (528–29). Earth emerges as the third, creative term between Heaven and Hell; on earth, between life and death, is the creative medium of memory. "Life. Death. And the memory that blends them into a single flower of three petals" (477). These heretical trinities proliferate in the novel, not simply opposing the form of oneness but actively dispersing it. Thus there are three illegitimate pretenders to the throne of Spain (each with twelve toes and a red cross on his back): the Idiot Prince, Don Juan, and the Pilgrim. There is the tripartite imperium of Rome, Spain, and Paris (the last, we are told, the "capital of the third age" [577]); there is the polymorphous perversity of the sexual relations in the novel, where heterosexual domination is undone in scenes of bisexuality and a startling instance of androgyny at the very end. Like the millenarian Adamites it describes from time to time, the novel aims at a pluralistic reappropriation of the human body as well as of the earth.

Such a *combinatoire* has obvious affinities with contemporary structuralist analysis, and Fuentes seems to owe a large debt to the New World mythological studies of Claude Lévi-Strauss. In fact, his extended narrative of the Pilgrim and his enemy brother Smoking Mirror is a reworking of the Quetzalcoatl and Texcatlipoca myths quite close to a Lévi-Straussian analysis of this material proposed earlier by Octavio Paz.[35] The critique of traditional European schemes of history in this novel is particularly energized by the anti-historical polemic of Lévi-Strauss and contemporary structural anthropology. In a genuine tour de force, Fuentes presents Cortez's conquest of Mexico as the dark underside of the myth of the Plumed Serpent. The Pilgrim/Quetzalcoatl is forced to review his actions during twenty days that have been hitherto inaccessible to his memory.

> A cane of lights: each mirror glittered and every gleam was a terrible scene of death, slashed throats, conflagration, frightful war, and in each I was the protagonist, I was the white, blond, bearded man on horseback, armed with a crossbow, armed with a sword, a cross of gold embroidered upon his breast, I was that man who set fire to temples, destroyed idols, fired cannons against the warriors of this land armed only with lances and arrows, I was the centaur who devastated the same fields, the same plains, the same jungles of my pilgrimage from the coast, my mounted troops trampled whole towns, cities were reduced to dark ashes by my wrathful torches. . . . (469)

Terra Nostra's mythmaking is of course not unique as such. It participates in the mythopoeic form of the modern novel that we have called the novel of ritual passage. Fuentes looks to literary forebears like Lawrence and Faulkner as well as to more scientific students of myth.[36] In this case particularly, the opposition between myth and history is mediated by a third term—the novel in its own history. In centering his narrative in sixteenth-century Spain, Fuentes is also focusing on the origins of the novel as a literary form. He makes some allusions to the Spanish picaresque novels, in the name "Guzman" given to El Señor's chief huntsman and courtier, in the proto-picaresque bawd Celestina, who undergoes several protean changes of shape, and in a minor character, Catilinon, identified as a "rogue from the streets of Valladolid" ([4]). Yet these allusions are never focused in a coherent figure or text; it is with Cervantes and *Don Quixote* that *Terra Nostra* is most literally and extensively engaged. We encounter Cervantes himself as "the Chronicler," we meet Quixote and Sancho and the galley slaves. Most importantly, we witness the creation of *Don Quixote* as the archetypal novelistic text: *"Don Quixote,* written by everybody, read by everybody."[37]

Terra Nostra's appropriation of *Don Quixote* occurs in three more or less separate stages. The first is a vision of Cervantes as the Chronicler, a naive but dangerously heretical writer attached to the court of Felipe II. The Chronicler's fate is described and imagined by Julian, a priest and painter who is the Chronicler's friend but ends up betraying him. The heresies that the Chronicler naively conjures up are first a pastoral poem in praise of a young Semitic sodomite named Mihail-ben-Sama, who is also Queen Isabel's lover. In the Chronicler's poem the young man becomes a "hero not of purity but of the impure, hero of all horizons, hero of all beliefs" (238). Because his sponsorship of the relation between Mihail and Isabel is threatened with exposure, Julian reveals to Felipe some other manuscripts of the Chronicler, heretical alternative versions of the Gospels. As Julian describes them, "in one instance the most Pure Virgin, Our Lady, admits adultery with an anonymous camel driver; in another Our Lord Jesus Christ declares that he is a simple political agitator of Palestine; and, in the most evil of these examples, our St. Joseph declares himself criminally responsible not only for having betrayed our Sweet Jesus but for having built as well the cross that served as the rack of torture that redeemed our sins" (239–40). Felipe is not as horrified as Julian expects him to be—in fact he keeps the manuscripts for his own purposes—but he does send the Chronicler to the galleys for his offenses. This fictitious Cervantes ends up historically in the battle of Lepanto, maimed hand and all, having written a final story out of the many he has been able to imagine. It is the story of "a battered beetle, an insect lying overturned on its hard armor-plated back, waving its numerous legs" (235) and turns out to be the text of Kafka's "The Metamorphosis."[38]

The second stage of this bizarre reimagining of Don Quixote brings forward Don Quixote himself, here a character occupying the same historical time and space as the other characters of the novel. Celestina the peasant girl first meets Don Quixote after he has been tossed in a blanket, and he mistakes her for Celestina the bawd. Ludovico meets Quixote sleeping in a windmill by himself—Sancho has deserted his master for the governorship—and takes him along on a pilgrimage of the three dreaming youths that he is leading at this point. Quixote reveals his secret history—that in his youth he was really Don Juan, that he seduced Dulcinea and killed her father, and that he was responsible for Dulcinea's death. Now, as the old Don Alonso, he encounters the galley slaves and invites the youth currently serving as Don Juan to continue living his life for him. We finally learn that Don Quixote has told the three dreaming youths in succession all fifty (as Fuentes counts them) of his adventures as the

Knight of the Mournful Countenance. (Fuentes provides a marvelous one-paragraph synopsis of Cervantes's novel.) But these fifty adventures are multiplied by twenty different points of view "and each story contained as many others" (604). The ultimate proliferation, as the painter Julian reveals to Felipe, is that these adventures have been "reproduced on paper, in hundreds and at times thousands of copies, thanks to a strange invention recently brought from Germany, which is a very rabbit of books." Felipe, who believes that only what is written is real but that this reality should be his sole possession, is appalled at the "infinite sum of the readers of this book, for . . . the book is never without a reader, the book belongs to everyone" (605).

The final phase of the appropriation reassembles the disjecta membra of *Don Quixote*. In the chapter entitled "The Confessions of a Confessor" we hear Julian telling the Chronicler the "facts" of Felipe II's reign and charging the Chronicler with recording them truthfully in a history. But even as he dutifully writes a historical account, the Chronicler finds himself diverted from his purpose.

> I thought then about the knight Ludovico and his sons had met in the windmill and I began to write the story of a hidalgo from La Mancha who continued to adhere to the codes of certainty. For him nothing will be in doubt, but everything would be possible: a knight of faith. That faith, I said to myself, would originate in reading. And that reading would be madness. The knight would persist in the unique reading of the texts and would attempt to transmit that reading to a reality that had become multiple, equivocal, and ambiguous. . . .
>
> I paused at this point and decided, audaciously, to introduce a great novelty into my book: this hero of mockery and hoax, born of reading, would be the first hero, furthermore, to know he was read. At the very time he was living his adventures, they would be written, published, and read by others. A double victim of reading, the knight would twice lose his senses: first, as he read, second, upon being read. . . . But as object of reading, he begins to conquer reality, to infect it with his insane reading of himself. And this new reading transforms the world, which begins more and more to resemble the world wherein are narrated the knight's adventures. The world disguises itself: the enchanted knight ends by enchanting the world. . . . The knight will continue to live only in the book that recounts his story; there will be no other recourse to prove his own

existence, it will not be found in the unique reading life
gave him, but in the multiple readings life took from him
in reality, but granted him forever in the book . . . only in
the book. (668–69)

The reader of this study will recognize certain similarities between
Fuentes's interpretation of *Don Quixote* and the interpretation of the
novel presented in these pages. Fuentes's images of Cervantes as a
revolutionary heresiarch and of Cervantes's novel as an anarchist
changeling are more fantastic than many versions of *Don Quixote* and
the picaresque. But his images are also more deeply involved with
the literal text and with the historical milieu of this exemplary novel.
Fuentes dramatizes Cervantes's critique of reading in a more overtly
political fashion than I, in my literary-historical account, believe is
tenable. It would, however, be churlish to deny the complementarity
of his artistry and my theorizing at this particular point in space and
time. A history of the novel cannot itself stand outside history. It can
only reflect on a cultural dynamic of which it is a part. This is a lesson
that the novel since *Lazarillo* and *Don Quixote* has taught and taught
again: the facts of history and the fictions of literature are finally kept
apart only by the consensus of their readers. In the novel, and in
critical discussions of the novel, these opposing modes of discourse
keep collapsing into one another. The consensus of readers is continually being dismantled and reformed, in a way that we have come
to realize as exemplary of our bibliophiliac condition.

Notes

Chapter One

1. See especially the six articles from *Novel* collected (along with a shorter version of this chapter) in *Towards a Poetics of Fiction*, ed. Mark Spilka (Bloomington: Indiana University Press, 1977); *Zur Poetik des Romans*, ed. Volker Klotz (Darmstadt: Wissenschaftliche Buchgesellschaft, 1965); Robert Scholes, *Structuralism in Literature* (New Haven: Yale University Press, 1974), pp. 59–141; and Jonathan Culler, *Structuralist Poetics* (Ithaca: Cornell University Press, 1975), pp. 189–238.

2. See Michael Holquist and Walter Reed, "Six Theses on the Novel—and Some Metaphors," in *New Literary History* 11 (1980), 413–23.

3. E.g., Roland Barthes, "An Introduction to the Structural Analysis of Narrative," *New Literary History* 6 (1975), 237–72; Tzvetan Todorov, *The Poetics of Prose*, trans. Richard Howard (Ithaca: Cornell University Press, 1977).

4. *Literature as System: Essays Toward the Theory of Literary History* (Princeton: Princeton University Press, 1971), p. 376.

5. A distinction might perhaps be made between "poetics" without any article preceding it, which as René Wellek suggests "in a wide sense is identical with theory of literature" ("Closing Statement," in *Style in Language*, ed. Thomas A. Sebeok [Cambridge, Mass.: MIT Press, 1960], p. 411, and "*a* poetics" with the definite article, which is a particular kind of discourse about literature. "Poetics" per se is a general field of collaborative scholarly investigation; "a poetics" is a specific example of a genre of literary criticism. The distinction, finally, amounts to one between scientific and humanistic usage.

6. *The Spirit of the Letter* (Cambridge, Mass.: Harvard University Press, 1965), pp. 345 ff.

7. *Literature as System*, p. 127. Guillén has been referring here to Poggioli.

8. See Edith Kern, "The Romance of Novel/Novella," in *The Disciplines of Criticism*, ed. Peter Demetz, Thomas Greene, and Lowry Nelson, Jr. (New Haven: Yale University Press, 1968).

9. Forster, *Aspects of the Novel* (New York: Harcourt Brace, 1927), pp. 14–15; Frye, *Anatomy of Criticism* (Princeton: Princeton University Press, 1957), p. 304; Freedman, "The Possibility of a Theory of the Novel," in *The Disciplines of Criticism*, p. 65. Freedman does go on to offer a unifying definition of the novel, but his terms become overly general and abstract.

10. "Partial Magic in the *Quixote*," *Labyrinths*, ed. Donald A. Yates and James E. Irby (New York: New Directions, 1964), p. 193.

11. "Irrelevant Detail and the Emergence of Form," in *Aspects of Narrative*, ed. J. Hillis Miller (New York: Columbia University Press, 1971), p. 75.

12. *The World of Don Quixote* (Cambridge, Mass.: Harvard University Press, 1967), p. 3.

13. I adopt this term from Alvin Kernan, who uses it (with no particular reference to the novel) in "The Idea of Literature," *New Literary History* 5 (1973), 31–32, 38–40.

14. *Middlemarch*, ed. Gordon Haight (Boston: Houghton Mifflin, 1956), pp. 43–44.

15. *Meditations on Quixote*, trans. Evelyn Rugg and Diego Marín (New York: W. W. Norton, 1961), p. 162.

16. The impact of romanticism on the novel is discussed in a more general way in chapters 8 and 9.

17. *The Lyrical Novel* (Princeton: Princeton University Press, 1963).

18. *Culture and Society, 1780–1950* (London: Chatto and Windus, 1958). Williams discusses only English writers, but his analysis also bears on the broader European context.

19. Alfred Schlagdenhauffen, cited in *Dialogue on Poetry and Literary Aphorisms*, trans. Ernst Behler and Roman Struc (University Park, Pa.: Pennsylvania State University Press, 1968), p. 10.

20. *The Theory of the Novel*, trans. Anna Bostock (London: Merlin Press, 1971), p. 14.

21. *Studies in European Realism*, trans. Edith Bone (London: Hillway Publishing, 1950), pp. 152–53. Cf. Graham Good, "Lukács' *Theory of the Novel*," *Novel* 6 (1973), 183–84.

22. *The Craft of Fiction* (New York: Scribner's, 1921), p. 22.

23. *European Literature and the Latin Middle Ages*, trans. Willard Trask (New York: Pantheon Books, 1953), p. 247 (cited by Guillén in *Literature as System*).

24. *Literature as System*, p. 390.

25. Indeed, some novelists—Cervantes, for example, or Dostoevsky— profess a great respect for poetry if not poetics, for the orderly, the harmonious, and the classical in literature, a profession that seems curiously at odds with their own creative practice. The problem of intention that such apparent inconsistency raises—the conflict between genre and individual genius, precedent and theory, theory and practice—will emerge in some of the following chapters. Although my argument here may seem to suggest it, I by no means believe that the literary etiquette of the novel as a form acts as the sole determinant of a particular novel's ethos.

26. See especially Alexander Parker, *Literature and the Delinquent: The Picaresque Novel in Spain and Europe, 1599–1753* (Edinburgh: Edinburgh University Press, 1967), and chapters 2 and 3 of the present study.

27. For an excellent discussion of the Italian background of this controversy and its informing presence in *Don Quixote*, see Alban K. Forcione, *Cervantes, Aristotle, and the Persiles* (Princeton: Princeton University Press, 1970) and chapters 2 and 4 above.

28. See Culler's chapter "Poetics of the Novel" in his *Structuralist Poetics* and Scholes's "Toward a Structuralist Poetics of Fiction" in his *Structuralism in Literature* for general surveys of this critical movement.

29. "Linguistics and Poetics," in *Style in Language*, ed. Sebeok, p. 350. Todorov also cites Valéry as a source for his use of the term "poetics," but admits (in "Valéry's Poetics," *Yale French Studies* 44 [1970], 65–71) that structuralist poetics ignore Valéry's emphasis on the creative activity of the artist. Culler more persuasively redefines Valéry's poetics of authorial expression as a poetics of reader response (p. 117), but in doing so he under-

mines the systematic and (for the structuralist) scientific status of the term.

30. Todorov's essay appears in *Qu'est-ce que le structuralisme?*, ed. François Wahl (Paris: Editions du Seuil, 1968); Barthes' essay originally appeared in *Communications* 8 (1966), 1–27. Cf. Todorov's "Structuralism and Literature," in *Approaches to Poetics*, ed. Seymour Chatman (New York: Columbia University Press, 1973), and Genette's "Critique et Poetique," in *Figures III* (Paris: Editions du Seuil, 1972).

31. *Figures III*, p. 11.

32. *S/Z*, trans. Richard Miller (New York: Hill and Wang, 1974), p. 12.

33. *S/Z*, p. 5. Kristeva describes the novel as a "closed text" in its surface structure but as an open one on deeper transformational levels. See esp. pp. 42 ff. in *Le Texte du roman*, Approaches to Semiotics 6, ed. Thomas A. Sebeok (The Hague: Mouton, 1970).

34. *S/Z*, p. 5.

35. *S/Z*, p. 188.

36. The most relevant texts here are P. N. Medvedev/M. M. Bakhtin, *The Formal Method in Literary Scholarship: A Critical Introduction to Sociological Poetics*, trans. Albert J. Wehrle (Baltimore: Johns Hopkins University Press, 1978), and the forthcoming translation of Bakhtin's essays on theory of the novel, *The Dialogic Imagination*, by Michael Holquist and Caryl Emerson, to be published by the University of Texas Press. The earlier-translated and better-known studies by Bakhtin, *Problems of Dostoevsky's Poetics*, trans. R. W. Rotsel (Ann Arbor, Mich.: Ardis, 1973), and *Rabelais and His World*, trans. Hélène Iswolsky (Cambridge, Mass.: MIT Press, 1968), depend on and elaborate this methodology. For a discussion of the problem of Bakhtin's collaborators and/or pseudonyms, see Holquist's article on Bakhtin in vol. 2 of the *Modern Encyclopedia of Russian and Soviet Literature* (Gulf Breeze, Fla.: Academic International Press, 1978).

37. *The Formal Method*, p. 30.

38. "Epos and Novel," in *The Dialogic Imagination*. I am indebted to Michael Holquist and Caryl Emerson for permission to quote from their forthcoming translation.

39. Gary Morson, "The Heresiarch of *Meta*," *PTL* 3 (1978), 407.

40. In addition to *The Formal Method* and *The Dialogic Imagination*, see V. N. Vološinov, *Marxism and the Philosophy of Language*, trans. Ladislav Matejka and I. R. Titunik (New York and London: Seminar Press, 1973). For a glimpse of the legacy of Bakhtin being carried on in contemporary Soviet semiotics, see the "Theses on the Semiotic Study of Cultures (as Applied to Slavic Texts)" by B. A. Uspensky, V. V. Ivanov, V. N. Toporov, A. M. Pjatigorski, and Ju. M. Lotman, in *Structure of Texts and Semiotics of Culture*, Slavistic Printings and Reprintings 294, ed. Jan Van Der Eng and Mojmír Grygar (The Hague: Mouton, 1973).

Chapter Two

1. *The History of the English Novel*, 10 vols. (New York: Barnes and Noble, 1950; first pub. 1924). Other examples of this phylogenetic approach are J. J. Jusserand, *The English Novel in the Time of Shakespeare* (London: T. Fisher Unwin, 1890), and Margaret Schlauch, *Antecedents of the English Novel, 1400–1600* (Warszawa: PWN-Polish Scientific Publishers, 1963). The organic metaphor behind this kind of history is made almost parodically explicit in

Richard Church's *The Growth of the English Novel* (London: Methuen and Co., 1951), which begins, "The English novel is a sturdy plant whose taproot plunges deep through the centuries," and whose first four chapters are entitled "The Seed-Bed," "The First Cotyledons," "Secondary Leaves," and "The Tree Takes Shape."

2. *An Introduction to the English Novel*, 2 vols. (London: Hutchinson University Library, 1951), I, 11.

3. Bakhtin, "Epos and Novel," trans. Holquist and Emerson. Hegel says very little about the novel per se, but his charecterization of "Epic Poetry" directly informs Lukács's, and Hegel's general discussion of "The Formal Independence of Individual Characters," particularly the section entitled "Dissolution of the Romantic Form of Art," more obliquely anticipates what Lukács says about the novel as a biographical and a negative form. See Hegel's *Aesthetics: Lectures on Fine Art*, trans. T. M. Knox (Oxford: Clarendon Press, 1975), I, 573–61, and II, 1040–1110. The contrast between epic and novel is characteristic in German discussions of the novel, as in Friedrich von Blankenburg's *Versuch über den Roman* (1774).

4. *The Rise of the Novel* (Berkeley: University of California Press, 1957), p. 9.

5. Ibid., p. 32.

6. Ibid., p. 33.

7. Ibid.

8. See E. C. Riley, "Who's Who in *Don Quixote?* or An Approach to the Problem of Identity," *Modern Language Notes* 81 (1966), 113–30, and Paul Turner, "Novels, Ancient and Modern," *Novel* 2 (1968), 15–24. Diana Spearman debunks some of the literary sociology behind Watt's argument in *The Novel and Society* (London: Routledge and Kegan Paul, 1966).

9. *The Theory of the Novel*, p. 40.

10. Ibid., p. 56 (my emphasis).

11. Ibid., pp. 103, 101.

12. Ibid., pp. 129–30.

13. "Epos and Novel," trans. Holquist and Emerson.

14. Ibid.

15. Ibid.

16. Cf. Coleridge, in "The Education of Children": "The common modern novel, in which there is no imagination, but a misereble struggle to excite and gratify mere curiosity, ought, in my judgment, to be wholly forbidden to children. Novel-reading of this sort is especially injurious to the growth of the imagination, the judgement, and the morals, especially to the latter, because it excites mere feelings without at the same time ministering an impulse to action" (*The Portable Coleridge*, ed. I. A. Richards [New York: Viking Press, 1950], p. 402).

17. *Beginnings: Intention and Method* (New York: Basic Books, 1975), p. 81.

18. It is interesting in this regard to consider Roland Barthes' virtuoso reading of Balzac in *S/Z*. See Michel Butor's denial of the essential difference between "the so-called 'Balzacian' novel" and the contemporary experimental novel, in "Balzac and Reality," *Inventions*, ed. Richard Howard (New York: Simon and Schuster, 1968).

19. "Literary History as a Challenge to Literary Theory," *New Literary History* 2 (1970), 11, 9. Cf. Paul de Man's call for "a literary history that would

not truncate literature by putting us misleadingly *into* or *outside* it, that would be able to maintain the literary aporia throughout, account at the same time for the truth and the falsehood of the knowledge literature conveys about itself, distinguish rigorously between metaphorical and historical language, and account for literary modernity as well as for its historicity" (*Blindness and Insight* [New York: Oxford University Press, 1971], p. 164).

20. " 'Don Quixote and 'Moby Dick,' " in *Cervantes Across the Centuries*, ed. M. J. Benardete and Angel Flores, 2d ed. (New York: Gordian Press, 1969), p. 227. Some recent attempts to place *Don Quixote* in an ongoing tradition of the novel include René Gerard, *Deceit, Desire, and the Novel*, trans. Yvonne Freccero (Baltimore: The Johns Hopkins University Press, 1965); Harry Levin, "The Quixotic Principle," in *The Interpretation of Narrative: Theory and Practice*, ed. Morton Bloomfield (Cambridge: Harvard University Press, 1970); Robert Alter, *Partial Magic: The Novel as Self-Conscious Genre* (Berkeley: University of California Press, 1975); and Marthe Robert, *The Old and the New: From Don Quixote to Kafka*, trans. Carol Cosman (Berkeley, University of California Press, 1977).

21. Ralph Freedman, "The Possibility of a Theory of the Novel," p. 75. Recent studies of the picaresque include Robert Alter, *Rogue's Progress*, Harvard Studies in Comparative Literature 26 (Cambridge: Harvard University Press, 1964); Alexander Parker, *Literature and the Delinquent;* Stuart Miller, *The Picaresque Novel* (Cleveland: Case Western Reserve University Press, 1967); Claudio Guillén, "Toward a Definition of the Picaresque," *Literature as System;* Ulrich Wicks, "The Nature of Picaresque Narrative: A Modal Approach," *PMLA* 89 (1974), 240–49; and Barbara Babcock, " 'Liberty's A Whore': Inversions, Marginalia, and Picaresque Narrative," *The Reversible World: Symbolic Inversion in Art and Society* (Ithaca: Cornell University Press, 1978). A good bibliographical survey is provided by Wicks, "Picaro, Picaresque: The Picaresque in Literary Scholarship," *Genre* 5 (1972), 153–216.

22. Borges, "Kafka and His Precursors," *Labyrinths*, p. 201. Leslie Fiedler, for example, still refers to *Don Quixote* as a "Mannerist proto-novel" ("The Death and Rebirth of the Novel," in *The Theory of the Novel: New Essays*, ed. John Halperin [New York: Oxford University Press, 1974], p. 192), while Diana Spearman, in spite of her insight into its antecedent realism, insists on calling the Spanish picaresque novel a "tale" (*The Novel and Society*, pp. 108–9). The most lucid historical treatments of the Spanish origins of the novel to date are Parker's *Literature and the Delinquent* (which, however, tends to see the later European picaresque novels as a falling off from the Spanish achievement) and Dámaso Alonso's broad but stimulating essay "The Spanish Contribution to the Modern European Novel," *Cahiers d'histoire mondiale* 6 (1961), 878–97. Alonso emphasizes the double heritage of the picaresque and *Don Quixote* via Fielding and Lesage.

23. I quote from Michael Alpert's translation in *Two Spanish Picaresque Novels* (Harmondsworth, Middlesex: Penguin Books, 1969), p. 23. All further quotations from *Lazarillo* give page numbers in parentheses from this edition.

24. *Two Spanish Picaresque Novels*, trans. Alpert, p. [83]; all further quotations are from this edition. On the authorship of this preface, see p. 66 above.

25. Thus both Walter Starkie and J. M. Cohen render Cervantes's "Desocupado lector"; Samuel Putnam makes it a present participle: "Idling reader." All further quotations are from Cohen's translation, in the Penguin Classic edition (Baltimore, Md., 1950).

26. McLuhan, *The Gutenberg Galaxy* (Toronto: Toronto University Press, 1962); Ong, *The Barbarian Within* (New York: Macmillan, 1962), and *Rhetoric, Romance, and Technology* (Ithaca: Cornell University Press, 1971); Eisenstein, "Some Conjectures about the Impact of Printing on Western Society and Thought: A Preliminary Report," *Journal of Modern History* 40 (1968), 1–56, and "The Advent of Printing and the Problem of the Renaissance," *Past and Present* 45 (1969), 19–89. The quotation is from Eisenstein, "The Advent of Printing and the Protestant Revolt: A New Approach to the Disruption of Western Christendom," in *Transition and Revolution*, ed. Robert M. Kingdon (Minneapolis: Burgess Publishing Co., 1974), p. 263. These articles are the basis of Eisenstein's book, *The Printing Press as an Agent of Change*, 2 vols. (Cambridge: Cambridge University Press, 1979).

27. "The Preliteracy of the Greeks," *New Literary History* 8 (1977), 369–91. H. J. Chaytor, *From Script to Print* (Cambridge: W. Heffer and Sons, 1945), p. 138, suggests that the incunabula period in Spain, the period during which printed texts were scarce, lasted some thirty or forty years longer than the conventional European terminus of 1500.

28. *The Interpretation of Cultures* (New York: Basic Books, 1973), p. 451.

29. See, for example, Walter Ong, "The Writer's Audience Is Always a Fiction," *PMLA* 90 (1975), 9–21, and Roland Barthes, *The Pleasure of the Text*, trans. Richard Miller (New York: Hill and Wang, 1975). To describe the place of Jacques Derrida's "grammatology" in such a sensibility is beyond the scope of this chapter.

30. Henri Hauser, *La Naissance du Protestantisme*, ed. G. Dumezil (Paris: Presses universitaires de France, 1962), p. 58; cited by Eisenstein, "The Protestant Revolt," p. 249.

31. See Hugh Trevor-Roper, *The Crisis of the Seventeenth Century: Religion, the Reformation, and Social Change* (New York: Harper and Row, 1968), pp. 34 ff. Antonio Dominguez Ortiz, *The Golden Age of Spain, 1516–1659*, trans. James Casey (New York: Basic Books, 1971), pp. 241 ff., notes a "fashion for politico-moral treatises" in Spain beginning about 1600, to which Cervantes seems to be responding ironically.

32. See Henry Thomas, *Spanish and Portuguese Romances of Chivalry* (Cambridge: Cambridge University Press, 1920), pp. 147–55.

33. "The Problem of the Renaissance," pp. 24–26.

34. Cf. Chaytor, *From Script to Print*, p. 10: "as readers were few and hearers numerous, literature in its early days was produced very largely for public recitation; hence, it was rhetorical rather than literary in character, and rules of rhetoric governed its composition." As Robert Kellogg observes, these rhetorical rules and the ethos of an oratorical performance continued to inform a good deal of Renaissance literature. "The oration, both actual and as a model for literary works, constitutes a medium of discourse intermediate between a purely oral, bardic tradition and one in which through the medium of the written book an author can address a solitary reader" ("Oral Literature," *New Literary History* 5 [1973], 62).

35. In a sense, Cervantes is appealing to an older, medieval conception of

"the anonymity and ambiguity of authorship," as E. P. Goldschmidt puts it, but he does so with a Renaissance consciousness of "literary fame and intellectual property" (*Medieval Texts and Their First Appearance in Print* [London: Bibliographical Society, 1943], pp. 92, 116.

36. "Don Quijote's Metaphors and the Grammar of Proper Language," *Modern Language Notes* 95 (1980), 276.

37. For a reading of Lázaro as the ultimate object of irony, see Stephen Gilman, "The Death of Lazarillo de Tormes," *PMLA* 81 (1966), 149–66; for a reading of Lázaro as ironist throughout, see R. W. Truman, "Lázaro de Tormes and the 'Homo Novus' Tradition," *Modern Language Review* 64 (1969), 62–67, and chapter 3, above.

38. Forcione, *Cervantes, Aristotle, and the Persiles*, pp. 11–48. Cf. Bernard Weinberg, *A History of Literary Criticism in the Italian Renaissance* (Chicago: University of Chicago Press, 1961), pp. 954–1073.

39. Forcione, *Cervantes, Aristotle, and the Persiles*, pp. 106–7. Cf. P. 165: "In large part the position of Cide Hamete concerning literary theory is one of negation. He is articulately aware of an adversary, the Horatian-Aristotelian dogma of the Renaissance, and he continually subjects it to a ridicule, which in its mildness comes from a position of unshaken superiority." E. C. Riley, *Cervantes' Theory of the Novel* (Oxford: Clarendon Press, 1962) analyzes much of the Aristotelian background, but does not pay as much attention to Cervantes's ironic treatment of it.

40. Paraphrase in Thomas, *Spanish and Portuguese Romances*, pp. 174–75; Parker, *Literature and the Delinquent*, pp. 19 ff.

41. J. H. Elliott, *Imperial Spain, 1469–1716* (London: E. Arnold, 1963), pp. 238–39.

42. *Illuminations*, ed. Hannah Arendt, trans. Harry Zohn (New York: Harcourt, Brace and World, 1968), p. 223. Benjamin is writing primarily of the effect of photography and cinema on the visual arts, but is here generalizing. Cf. McLuhan's analogy between the medieval secondhand book trade and the contemporary art market for old masters' paintings (*Gutenberg Galaxy*, p. 249).

43. Cf. Hiram Haydn, *The Counter-Renaissance* (New York: Scribner's, 1950), esp. Chapter 1, "Renaissance Humanism." The rest of Haydn's book describes the many forms that the breaking up of this tradition took in intellectual history.

44. Cf. C. S. Lewis, *English Literature in the Sixteenth Century* (Oxford: Oxford University Press, 1954), p. 21: "It is largely to the humanists that we owe the curious conception of the 'classical' period in a language, the correct or normative period before which all was immature or archaic and after which all was decadent. . . . When once this superstition was established it led naturally to the belief that good writing in the fifteenth or sixteenth century meant writing which aped as closely as possible that of the chosen period in the past. All real development of Latin to meet the changing needs of new talent and new subject-matter was thus precluded; with one blow of 'his Mace petrific' the classical spirit ended the history of the Latin tongue. This was not what the humanists intended."

45. *The Literary Mind of Medieval and Renaissance Spain* (Lexington: University of Kentucky Press, 1970), p. 20.

46. *European Literature and the Latin Middle Ages*, p. 268. One should

perhaps add here Dámaso Alonso's reminder to Curtius and others that a corollary of this anticlassical temper is the circumstantial and detailed "realism" of much medieval Spanish literature, which of course provides an important precedent for the realism of the later novel; see "The Spanish Contribution," pp. 883–84.

47. *Imperial Spain*, p. 219.

48. *The Golden Age of Spain*, pp. 216–17.

49. Thomas, *Spanish and Portuguese Romances*, p. 178. Cortés also wanted to have all copies of the chivalric romances in Spain collected and burned. On the other hand, Melchor Cano reported in 1564 the case of a Spanish priest who believed that the exploits of Amadis and other heroes were true, on the grounds that nothing printed with the sanction of church and state could be false—an argument later advanced by Don Quixote (Thomas, pp. 152–53; *Don Quixote*, p. 440).

50. "Incarnation in Don Quixote," in *Cervantes Across the Centuries*, p. 169. Cf. Said on the paradoxical importance and insignificance of written texts in Arabic-Islamic culture vis-à-vis the Koran (*Beginnings*, pp. 199–200).

51. "Inquisition" would be "Inquisición" or "Santo Oficio"; Cervantes uses "escrutinio," more literally translated by Putnam as "scrutiny."

52. The phrase is from Erasmus's *Adages*, quoted by Eisenstein, "The Problem of the Renaissance," p. 51. There was, however, a great flood of mystical writing printed in Spain after 1559, "almost a literary mass-movement," as A. G. Dickens calls it (*The Counter Reformation* [New York: Harcourt, Brace and World, 1969], p. 25). This type of literature, with its emphasis on ecstatic transcendence of the world through inner experience, might be seen as the imaginative obverse of the novel. It is also true that proscribed books were printed in other countries and smuggled into Spain.

53. See Parker, *Literature and the Delinquent*, pp. 10–13. But the psychological effects of the dramatic economic collapse of Spain in the 1590s should not be ruled out entirely; see Elliott, *Imperial Spain*, pp. 279 ff.

54. *Imperial Spain*, pp. 305–6. Cf. Fernand Braudel, *The Mediterranean and the Mediterranean World in the Age of Philip II*, trans. Siân Reynolds (New York: Harper and Row, 1972), II, 725–34, on the "bankruptcy of the bourgeoisie." "In Spain what was vanishing had hardly existed in the first place.... Insufficiently urbanized, the Peninsula was obliged to entrust essential commercial functions to intermediary groups unable to identify with the true interests of the country yet playing a vital part in the economy" (p. 726).

55. *The Rogue*, trans. James Mabbe, The Tudor Translations, Second Series (London: Constable and Co., 1924), IV, 127. Castro's thesis that the picaresque expresses the resentment of the *conversos* or converted Jews is plausible in the case of Alémán, who was of Jewish ancestry, but seems a secondary factor to the more pervasive *ressentiment* of the mercantile middle class, which happened to include a fair number of *conversos*; see *The Structure of Spanish History*, trans. Edmund L. King (Princeton: Princeton University Press, 1954), pp. 564–70.

56. *Literature as System*, p. 144.

57. *Pour une sociologie du roman* (Paris: Gallimard, 1964), pp. 23, 26 (my trans.).

58. *Rhetoric, Romance, and Technology*, p. 34.

59. *Idea and Act in Elizabethan Fiction* (Princeton: Princeton University Press, 1969), p. 45.

60. *Sidney's 'Apologie for Poetrie,'* ed. J. Churton Collins (Oxford: Clarendon Press, 1907), p. 8.

61. *The English Reformation* (London: B. T. Batsford, 1964), pp. 307, 332.

62. *Middle-Class Culture in Elizabethan England* (Chapel Hill: University of North Carolina Press, 1935), p. 5.

63. See Frank Wadleigh Chandler, *The Literature of Roguery* (Boston: Houghton Mifflin, 1907), I, 197–98. Gabriel Harvey, Nashe's literary antagonist, claims to have received a copy of *Lazarillo* from Spenser, who was a friend of Nashe's (Chandler, I, 62). Fredson Bowers is the only English scholar to have argued for the generic identity of *The Unfortunate Traveller* with the Spanish picaresque, but he admits many of the differences of mood and matter that I go on to argue here; see "Thomas Nashe and the Picaresque Novel," in *Humanistic Studies in Honor of John Calvin Metcalf,* University of Virginia Studies, vol. I (Charlottesville: University of Virginia Press, 1941).

64. *Shorter Novels: Elizabethan* (London: J. M. Dent & Sons, 1929), pp. 265, 274. Cf. Davis, *Idea and Act,* p. 218: "The relation between the hero-narrator and his imagined audience, established in the easy reciprocal mockery of this induction, is kept alive throughout the book by all those means of establishing the immediacy of spoken discourse . . .: by Jack's pose as the audience's drinking companion, by his sudden questions to the audience, imagined interlocutions, calling attention to direct hits, and so forth."

65. *Shorter Novels,* p. 291.

66. Ibid., p. 285.

67. See Chandler, *The Literature of Roguery,* I, 59–70, 87–119, and Claudio Guillén, "The Anatomy of Roguery" (Ph.D. diss., Harvard University, 1953). For a discussion of the case of Rabelais, see the openings of chapters 3 and 4 above.

68. The arguments, respectively, of Paul Turner, "Novels, Ancient and Modern," Robert Scholes and Robert Kellogg, *The Nature of Narrative* (Oxford: Oxford University Press, 1966), p. 57, and Arthur Heiserman, *The Novel before the Novel* (Chicago: University of Chicago Press, 1977), pp. 3–4.

69. Gareth Schmeling, *Chariton,* Twayne's World Author Series (New York: Twayne Publishers, 1974), p. 28.

70. *Chariton's Chaereas and Callirhoe,* trans. Warren E. Blake (Ann Arbor: University of Michigan Press, 1939), p. 78.

71. *The Greek Romances of Heliodorus, Longus, and Achilles Tatius,* trans. Rowland Smith (London: George Bell and Sons, 1901), p. 110.

72. Cf. Ben Edwin Perry, *The Ancient Romances: A Literary Historical Account of their Origins* (Berkeley: University of California Press, 1967), p. 57: "In the big world of Alexandrian times there were sharply defined strata in society and intellectual aptitude which had not existed in the old city-state. . . . the lowly romance of love and adventure [was] meant for a reading public composed of young or naive people of little education, most of whom presumably lived in small towns or rural districts, rather than at Athens or in other cities, and would seldom be near a theater."

73. As Goethe said of *Daphnis and Chloe,* "The entire work manifests the highest art and culture" (*Conversations with Eckermann;* quoted by William E. McCulloh, *Longus,* Twayne's World Author Series [New York:

Twayne, 1970], p. 106). For a good account of the relation of these later romances to the rhetoric of the Second Sophistic, see Schmeling, *Chariton*, pp. 25–30.

74. P. G. Walsh, *The Roman Novel* (Cambridge: Cambridge University Press, 1970), p. 56. Walsh gives an extensive analysis of the literary allusions in both the *Satyricon* and the *Metamorphoses*.

75. *The Ancient Romances*, p. 90. It is interesting that Apuleius is also self-conscious about the medium of the papyrus—"this Egyptian paper written with a subtle pen of Nilotic reeds" (*The Golden Ass*, trans. Jack Lindsay [Bloomington: Indiana University Press, 1962], p. 31)—but as with his allusion to his own imperfect Latin, the joke seems to be at the expense of the humble materials rather than at the expense of high literature.

76. Lindsay, in his introduction to *The Golden Ass*, p. 18.

77. *The Greek Romances*, pp. 213, 478.

78. For an account of this sequel, which is included in many early editions and translations of *Lazarillo de Tormes*, see Chandler, *Romances of Roguery, Part I: The Picaresque Novel in Spain* (New York: Columbia University Press, 1899), pp. 205 ff. Alexander Scobie considers the possibility of the influence of Petronius and Apuleius on the Spanish picaresque but concludes that "the case is not a particularly strong one" (*Aspects of Ancient Romance and Its Heritage* [Meisenheim a Glan: Hain, 1969], p. 92).

Chapter Three

1. See Marcel Bataillon, *Erasme et l'Espagne* (Paris: E. Droz, 1937), pp. 652–53; Francisco Marquez Villanueva, "La actitud espiritual del *Lazarillo de Tormes*," *Espiritualidad y literatura en el siglo XVI* (Madrid-Barcelona: Alfarguana, 1968), pp. 67–137. Ann Wiltrout argues for the influence of one of Erasmus's satiric colloquies on *Lazarillo* in "The *Lazarillo de Tormes* and Erasmus' 'Opulentia Sordida,'" *Romanische Forschungen* 81 (1969), 550–64, and R. W. Truman suggests a confluence of motifs in "*Lazarillo de Tormes*, Petrarch's *De remediis adversae fortunae*, and Erasmus's *Praise of Folly*," *Bulletin of Hispanic Studies* 52 (1975), 33–53.

2. "'Liberty's A Whore,'" *The Reversible World*, p. 108.

3. *The Praise of Folly*, trans. John Wilson (1688) (Ann Arbor: University of Michigan Press, 1958), p. 141. Cf. 1 Cor. 3:18: "Make no mistake about this: if there is anyone among you who fancies himself wise—wise, I mean by the standards of the passing age—he must become a fool to gain true wisdom. For the wisdom of this world is folly in God's sight" (NEB).

4. The allusion to Cicero recalls an accusation that Cicero himself came from "low and obscure ancestors and from modest and unworthy parents," a piece of information retailed by Torquemada in Spain in 1553; see Harry Sieber, *The Picaresque*, The Critical Idiom (London: Methuen & Co., 1977), p. 15.

5. Gilman, "The Death of Lazarillo de Tormes," p. 161.

6. See in this regard Mikhail Bakhtin's broad and compelling study of Rabelais in the tradition of the folk carnival, *Rabelais and His World*. The more sparing, though still significant, folk elements of *Lazarillo* are noted in A. D. Deyermond, *Lazarillo de Tormes: A Critical Guide*, Critical Guides to Spanish Texts, no. 15 (London: Grant and Cutler, 1975), pp. 34–35, 81–87.

7. Bakhtin uses the term, for example. See also Barbara Babcock-

Abrahams, "The Novel and the Carnival World: An Essay in Memory of Joe Doherty," *Modern Language Notes* 89 (1974), 911–37; Alice Fiola Berry, "'Les Mithologies Pantagruelicques': Introduction to a Study of Rabelais' *Quart livre*," *PMLA* 92 (1977), 471–80; and Gabriel Josipovici, "A Modern Master," *New York Review of Books*, 24, no. 16 (Oct. 13, 1977), 34–37.

8. *Rabelais: A Study in Comic Courage* (Englewood Cliffs, N.J.: Prentice-Hall, 1970), p. 30.

9. *Mimesis: The Representation of Reality in Western Literature*, trans. Willard R. Trask (Princeton: Princeton University Press, 1953), pp. 277–78.

10. Greene claims, for example, that the term satire "shrivels up" before Rabelais (*Rabelais*, p. 10), and Bakhtin insists on the broader and more integral humor of Gargantua and Pantagruel as distinct from the narrow and disintegrating quality of satire in the seventeenth and eighteenth centuries (*Rabelais and His World*, pp. 59–144, passim). Ronald Paulson, on the other hand, argues for the essentially satiric nature of Rabelais and extends the term to the Spanish picaresque novel and *Don Quixote* as well; see *The Fictions of Satire* (Baltimore: Johns Hopkins Press, 1967), pp. 58–73, 80–86, 98–104. The theory of satire is only slightly less vexed than the theory of the novel.

11. *The Cankered Muse: Satire of the English Renaissance*, Yale Studies in English, vol. 142 (New Haven: Yale University Press, 1959), pp. 3–4.

12. Ibid., pp. 7–8.

13. See Leonard Feinberg, *Introduction to Satire* (Ames: The Iowa State University Press, 1967), p. 11: "In actual practice, satirists usually apply a standard not of morality but of appropriateness—in other words a *social* norm. It is a norm concerned not with ethics but with customs, not with morals but with mores; and it may be accepted by an entire society, or only one class of that society, or just a small coterie."

14. *The Resources of Kind: Genre-Theory in the Renaissance*, ed. Barbara K. Lewalski (Berkeley: University of California Press, 1973), p. 7; she is paraphrasing Claudio Guillén here. As Colie goes on to argue, the *mimesis* of Aristotelian genre theory was often interpreted to mean the imitation of the formal models themselves, or as Alexander Pope put it in his *Essay on Criticism*, "Learn hence for Ancient *Rules* a just Esteem; / To copy *Nature* is to copy *Them*."

15. *Le Texte du roman*, pp. 45 ff. Kristeva does not distinguish adequately, however, between the structure of the novel and the structure of satire ("la menippée").

16. See, for example, Parker, *Literature and the Delinquent*, pp. 28–31. Francisco Rico, on the other hand, regards *Lazarillo* and *Guzmán de Alfarache* as the prime examples of the picaresque novel and Quevedo's *El Buscón*, which Parker regards as the "zenith" of the picaresque, as a dead end; see *La novela picaresca y el punto de vista*, 2d ed. (Barcelona: Editorial Seix Barral, 1973), pp. 129 ff.

17. See Bataillon, Introduction, *Le roman picaresque* (Paris: Renaissance du Livre, 1931), p. 5.

18. *La novela picaresca y el punto de vista*, esp. pp. 45–55.

19. "The Death of Lazarillo de Tormes," p. 158.

20. Luke 16:28–31 (NEB). It is arguable that Lazarillo is an allusion as well to the Lazarus in John 11, who *does* arise from the dead and who does "bring

glory to the Son of God"—as well as precipitating the Crucifixion. But the parabolic nature of the story in Luke and the way in which Lazarus is seen as inferior to Moses and the prophets is closer to the spirit of the Spanish novel than is the dramatic and compelling miracle described in John. Some biblical scholars suggest that the Johannine episode may in fact be a reshaping of the Lucan parable, though the borrowing may have proceeded in the other direction; see the commentary on John 11 in the Anchor Bible, *Gospel According to John* (i–xii), ed. Raymond E. Brown, S.S. (Garden City, N.Y.: Doubleday, 1966), pp. 428 ff.

21. "The Death of Lazarillo de Tormes," p. 153. See also Richard Hitchcock, "Lazarillo and 'Vuestra Merced,'" *Modern Language Notes* 86 (1971), 264–66, and L. J. Woodward, "Author-Reader Relationship in the *Lazarillo de Tormes*," *Forum for Modern Language Studies* 1 (1965), 43–53, for different versions of this normative approach.

22. "Parody and Irony in the Self-Portrayal of Lázaro de Tormes," *Modern Language Review* 63 (1968), 605. Cf. Frank Durand, "The Author and Lázaro: Levels of Comic Meaning," *Bulletin of Hispanic Studies* 45 (1968), 89–101, esp. p. 100: "To acknowledge specific social or clerical criticism, clearly stated moral observations, is to accept the obvious; to limit one's conclusions to the fact that Lázaro feels he has reached the ultimate heights of success when he has, in fact, descended to the lowest moral depths, is to remain on the surface of the work at the easiest ironic level."

23. I owe this allusion to my friend Alfred MacAdam, now of the Spanish Department of the University of Virginia. The quotation, and the previous one as well, are from W. S. Merwin's translation, *The Life of Lazarillo de Tormes: His Fortunes and Adversities* (Garden City, N.Y.: Doubleday, 1962), p. 39.

24. See Chandler, *The Romances of Roguery*, pp. 205–9. But by 1620 Jean de Luna had "corrected and emended" this sequel, making the tuna-fish transformation a trick rather than a metamorphosis and in general reproducing quite effectively the realism and irony of the original.

25. "Genre and Countergenre: The Discovery of the Picaresque," *Literature as System*, pp. 135–38. An earlier version of this essay appeared in 1966.

26. *Literature as System*, pp. 146 ff. The publication of what amounts to a parody of the picaresque novel, *La Pícara Justina*, in the same year as the First Part of *Don Quixote* should be mentioned as a further element in the recognition process.

27. *Resources of Kind*, pp. 12, 115 (her italics). Colie argues that some genres are defined by subject matter alone, but this is simply an overextension of the term. As Alistair Fowler claims, "Strictly speaking, only motifs with a formal basis, such as the singing contest, are securely genre-linked," although Fowler admits that there is a tendency for "genre" to become a more loosely defined "mode" ("The Life and Death of Literary Forms," *New Literary History* 2 [1971], 203, 214). For a stimulating Marxist critique of genre theory, see Fredric Jameson, "Magical Narratives: Romance as Genre," *New Literary History* 7 (1975), 135–63.

28. A precedent for such sequels was provided by the chivalric romances (*Amadis of Greece* following *Amadis of Gaul*, *Orlando Furioso* following *Orlando Innamorato*). It is interesting that Cervantes ends the First Part of *Don*

Quixote with a line from *Orlando Furioso,* "Forse altri cantera con miglior plettro" ("Perhaps another will sing with a sweeter tone"), after promising to relate more of Quixote's adventures himself. He perhaps anticipated a worthier imitator than he got in Avellaneda. The idea of the novelist as "sole proprietor" of his fictional characters and terrain, as claimed by William Faulkner for his Yoknapatawpha County, has yet to be recognized by modern copyright law.

29. The endings of *Lazarillo* and Melville's *The Confidence-Man,* respectively—though modern editors of *Lazarillo* regard the promise of a sequel as the work of an interpolator.

30. *Literature as System,* pp. 71–106, passim.

31. *The Picaresque Novel* (Cleveland: Case Western Reserve University Press, 1967), p. 4.

32. "The Nature of Picaresque Narrative: A Modal Approach," *PMLA* 89 (1974), 240. Wicks does discriminate levels of generality and abstraction similar to Guillén's, however. And he advocates a hermeneutic circularity of interpretation, in which the reader moves from "the total picaresque fictional situation" (243) back to specific texts. Richard Bjornson's *The Picaresque Hero in European Fiction* (Madison: University of Wisconsin Press, 1977), which appeared too late for me to profit from in this chapter, proceeds under the aegis of Wicks's modal approach. It combines historical and critical commentary on a series of picaresque narratives from *Lazarillo* to *Roderick Random,* but avoids the question of the novel per se.

33. Sieber, *The Picaresque,* pp. 22–23.

34. Donald McGrady calculates that the moralizing alone makes up 13 percent of the First Part of *Guzmán* and 23 percent of the Second Part (*Mateo Alemán* [New York: Twayne Publishers, 1968], p. 74). Lesage's translation, Englished in turn by Motteux, is the clearest example of the paring away of the moralizing. On the other hand, translations like those of Barezzo Barezzi's Italian, Gaspar Ens's Latin, and even Mabbe's English add considerably to the so-called digressive material; see James Fitzmaurice-Kelly's introduction to Mabbe, *The Rogue,* pp. xxx–xxxvi, and Edmond Cros, *Protée et le gueux* (Paris: Didier, 1967), pp. 104–26. Cros, for his part, overemphasizes the moralistic commentary. He treats *Guzmán* not as a picaresque novel but as a rhetorical anatomy of beggary, not "The Life of Guzman de Alfarache" but "The Book of the Beggar" (*Le livre du gueux*).

35. The phrases are J. A. Jones's in "The Duality and Complexity of *Guzmán de Alfarache:* Some Thoughts on the Structure and Interpretation of Alemán's Novel," in *Knaves and Swindlers: Essays on the Picaresque Novel in Europe,* ed. Christine J. Whitbourne, University of Hull Publications (London: Oxford University Press, 1974), p. 44.

36. See Lawrence Lipking, "The Marginal Gloss," *Critical Inquiry* 3 (1977), 609–55, for a useful discussion of literary marginalia, esp. pp. 621–25 on the gloss in the Renaissance and its dependence on biblical commentary.

37. *Exemplary Stories,* trans. C. A. Jones (Baltimore, MD: Penguin Books, 1972), p. 205.

38. M. N. Norval, "Original Sin and the 'Conversion' in the *Guzmán de Alfarache,*" *Bulletin of Hispanic Studies* 51 (1974), 346–64.

39. Norval, "Original Sin," p. 363. He offers a detailed critique of

Alexander Parker's position (in *Literature and the Delinquent*) that Guzmán has been psychologically changed by his conversion, though one must acknowledge the theological ambiguity of any conversion experience.

40. *Literature and the Delinquent*, pp. 50, 46. The only English translation, in *The Spanish Libertines*, trans. Captain John Stevens (London, 1707), unfortunately simplifies the diction and strips down the plot. Marcel Bataillon shows that the parody was a roman à clef for the society of the Court at Madrid ("Recherches sur la *Pícara Justina*," *Annuaire du Collège de France* 59 [1959], 567–69, and 60 [1960], 416–20).

41. Leonard Brownstein, *Salas Barbadillo and the New Novel of Rogues and Courtiers* (Madrid: Playor, S.A., 1974), pp. 85–94. Brownstein notes that a laudatory poem by a friend compares *La hija de Celestina* to "los Poemas" of Heliodorus and Achilles Tatius.

42. See the critical edition of Fernando Lázaro Carreter, Acta Salmanticensia, Filosofía y Letras, vol. XVIII, no. 4 (Salamanca, 1965), pp. lxv–lxvii.

43. The term "counterfiction" is used in an article on *El Buscón* by Michele and Cecile Cavillac, "A propos du *Buscón* et de *Guzmán de Alfarache*," *Bulletin Hispanique* 75 (1973), 124. But I would like to reserve it for the more independent antithesis of *Don Quixote*, as a substitute for what Guillén calls "countergenre." Cf. T. E. May, "Good and Evil in the *Buscón*: A Survey," *Modern Language Review* 45 (1950), 321: "Pablos shows the old *pícaro* of literature undergoing a transformation basically similar to that suffered by the knight of romance in becoming incarnate in Don Quixote."

44. This is the conclusion of Lázaro Carreter in his critical edition, pp. xv n., lxxviii.

45. The insult is compounded in the Spanish by the use of the second person singular rather than the polite and proper "Vuestra Merced." Carreter includes a brief "Carta Dedicatoria" that appears in two of the manuscripts and that he considers more likely to be by Quevedo himself, which does use the polite mode of address. Nevertheless, the self-presentation is peculiarly evasive and the politeness elaborately self-effacing, especially as compared to Lazarillo's prologue, on which it is most likely based. It reads, in its entirety: "Having known your honor's desire to hear the various discourses of my life, in order not to leave room that someone else (as in other cases) may lie, I have wanted to send you this account, which I hope will be not merely a small relief for your sad moments. And because I intend to be long in the telling of how short I have been of good fortune, I will cease to be so now." I am indebted to my colleague Ramón Saldívar for help with the translation.

46. E.g., the miserly priest who keeps the bread from Lazarillo becomes Dr. Cabra, "the High Priest of Poverty and Avarice Incarnate" (94) who actually starves boys to death; the poor *hidalgo*, Lazarillo's third master, becomes Don Torribio Rodriguez Valligo Gomez de Ampuero y Jordan, the nobleman-beggar, whose honor consists in his patchwork clothing. See R. O. Jones, *The Golden Age: Prose and Poetry, A Literary History of Spain* (London: Ernest Benn, 1971), pp. 135–36.

47. The most obvious element of *Guzmán* that *El Buscón* rejects is the lower-class critique of aristocratic honor; others include the ideas of social mobility, moral self-scrutiny, the need for social reform, and the possibility of the picaro's conversion. The critique is detailed by M. and C. Cavillac,

who describe it as "une réaction *systématique* a l'encontre du modèle élaboré par Mateo Alemán avec la contribution abusive de Mateo Luján.... Son intention ne semble pas avoir été celle, positive, de rivaliser avec Alemán en fertilité d'invention et en puissance créatrice, mais bien celle, négative, de détruire la fiction alémanienne" ("A propos de *Buscón*," pp. 124–25). The fact that Quevedo does try to rival *Lazarillo* is perhaps a sign that he regards it as less of a threat than *Guzmán*.

48. *The Unity and Structure of Quevedo's Buscón*, Occasional Papers in Modern Languages, no. 1 (Hull: University of Hull Publications, 1965), p. 7. Cf. Parker, pp. 61.ff.

49. "Zur Kunst Quevedos in Seinem *Buscon*," *Archivum Romanicum* 11 (1927), 511–80.

50. *Literature and the Delinquent*, pp. 59–60.

51. May speaks of Pablos as the "shadow self" of Don Diego, and of Don Diego as the "conscience of Pablos, before which he is weaponless" ("Good and Evil in the Buscón," pp. 327–28). The doppelgänger effect is undeniable, although Quevedo's version of self-alienation is quite different from the nineteenth-century versions in such writers as Hoffmann, Gogol, Dostoevsky, and later in Kafka: the social definition of the self is both all-powerful and completely inaccessible, a kind of *societas abscondita*.

Chapter Four

1. Gustavo A. Alfaro, "Cervantes y la novela picaresca," *Anales Cervantinos* 10 (1971), 24. Alfaro provides a useful survery of the scholarship on this question.

2. For an informative discussion of these novellas as a critique of the picaresque of Alemán, see Carlos Blanco Aguinaga, "Cervantes and the Picaresque Mode: Notes on Two Kinds of Realism," in *Cervantes: A Collection of Critical Essays*, ed. Lowry Nelson, Jr. (Englewood Cliffs, N.J.: Prentice-Hall, 1969).

3. The allusion to Guzmán is noted by Guillén, among others, in "Genre and Countergenre: The Discovery of the Picaresque"; Guillén observes that "the success of Miguel de Cervantes' entry in the publishing race was so irresistible that *Guzmán de Alfarache*, the best seller, would not reappear until 1615, in Milan" (p. 146).

4. *Exemplary Stories*, trans. C. A. Jones, p. 9. I prefer Jones's translation of Cervantes's title (*Novelas ejemplares*) since it preserves the important distinction between novel and novella.

5. L. G. Salingar, "*Don Quixote* as a Prose Epic," *Forum for Modern Language Studies* 2 (1966), 56.

6. *Rabelais and His World*, p. 275.

7. "The Novel and the Carnival World," p. 914. Cf. Kristeva, *Le Texte du roman*, pp. 162–76.

8. *Gargantua and Pantagruel* appeared on the Spanish Index of Prohibited Books. According to two older studies of Rabelais's influence, there was no significant Spanish awareness of Rabelais in this period; see Jacques Boulenger, *Rabelais à travers les âges* (Paris: Le Divan, 1925), and L. Sainéan, *L'Influence et la réputation de Rabelais* (Paris: Librairie Universitaire J. Gambier, 1930).

9. *Gargantua and Pantagruel*, trans. J. M. Cohen (Harmondsworth, Middlesex: Penguin Books, 1955), pp. 37, 39.

10. The best discussion of this oral dimension of Rabelais, one which stresses the popular, antiliterary nature of his French vernacular, is Michel Beaujour's chapter "Maintenant Tu Parle Naturellement," in *Le Jeu de Rabelais* (Paris: L'Herne, 1969). See also Barbara Bowen, "Rabelais and the Comedy of the Spoken Word," *Modern Languge Review* 63 (1968), 575–80.

11. See 'Der Aufbau der Erzählung und des Romans" and "Wie Don Quijote gemacht ist," in *Theorie der Prosa*, trans. Gisela Drohla (Frankfurt: S. Fischer, 1966). My translation of the conclusion of the first of these chapters here has been improved by Michael Holquist's knowledge of the Russian.

12. "Three Versions of Don Quixote," *Modern Language Review* 68 (1973), 814.

13. The most careful account is that of F. W. Locke, "El Sabio Encantador: The Author of *Don Quixote*," *Symposium* 23 (1969), 46–61. Ruth El Saffar examines the interplay of author and character at length in *Distance and Control in Don Quixote*, North Carolina Studies in the Romance Languages and Literatures, no. 147 (Chapel Hill: University of North Carolina, Department of Romance Languages, 1975); her interpretation, in contrast to mine, argues that the narrative devices try to maintain the authority of the author over his text rather than to realize the power of the reader. The most useful discussion of the narrative structure remains that of E. C. Riley, *Cervantes's Theory of the Novel*, pp. 205–12.

14. *Labyrinths*, pp. 193–96.

15. This rhetoric of appearances is discussed at length by Predmore, *The World of Don Quixote*, pp. 57–83.

16. I am drawing here on the ideas of Renaissance culture put forward by Harry Berger, Jr., in "The Renaissance Imagination: Second World and Green World," *Centennial Review* 9 (1965), 36–78.

17. One of the few critics who argues for the unity of the First Part, and in a way that parallels my own interpretation, is Edward Dudley, "Don Quijote as Magus: The Rhetoric of Interpolation," *Bulletin of Hispanic Studies* 49 (1972), 355–68.

18. *Cervantes, Aristotle, and the Persiles*, p. 108.

19. See, for example, El Saffar, *Novel to Romance: A Study of Cervantes's Novelas ejemplares* (Baltimore: Johns Hopkins University Press, 1974), pp. 13–29, and René Girard, *Deceit, Desire and the Novel*, pp. 291–92.

20. *Don Quixote: An Introductory Essay in Psychology* (Oxford: Clarendon Press, 1935). The phenomenon was observed even earlier by Charles Lamb, who deplored the degradation of Quixote's quest that it implied; see "Barrenness of the Imaginative Faculty in the Productions of Modern Art," in the *Last Essays of Elia*, and p. 173 above.

21. *Cervantes's Theory of the Novel*, p. 214.

22. Cf. James B. Larkin, "Avellaneda versus Cervantes: Rival or Unwitting Accomplice?" *Papers on Literature and Language* 12 (1976), 246–59. "It is inconceivable that many of Cervantes's contemporaries reading the apocryphal *Quijote* could have perceived the work as anything but the travesty it was. Could Cervantes have been so naive as to be unaware of all this? Would he knowingly have afforded an obscure rival priceless publicity simply out of

personal pique over something that everybody was doing anyway?" (249).

23. For other readings of this intricately structured episode, see George Haley, "The Narrator in *Don Quijote:* Maese Pedro's Puppet Show," *Modern Language Notes* 80 (1965), 145–65; John J. Allen, "The Narrators, the Reader and Don Quijote," *Modern Language Notes* 91 (1976), 201–12; and El Saffar, *Distance and Control,* pp. 104–13.

24. Quotations are from Merritt Hughes's edition of *Paradise Lost* (New York: Odyssey Press, 1962).

25. Robert Kellogg, "Oral Literature," p. 62. The stylistic analyses of Stanley Fish in *Surprised By Sin: The Reader in Paradise Lost* (Berkeley: University of California Press, 1967) exaggerate the ethical character of the poem, but they do address themselves to this kind of performative model. It is of course true that the medium of the printed text complicates the oral model considerably.

26. I am following the admittedly controversial theories of Harold Bloom concerning the relationship of English romantics to Milton, beginning with his essay "Keats and the Embarrassments of Poetic Tradition," *From Sensibility to Romanticism: Essays Presented to Frederick A. Pottle,* ed. Frederick H. Hilles and Harold Bloom (New York: Oxford University Press, 1965), and continuing in *The Anxiety of Influence* (New York: Oxford University Press, 1973) and *A Map of Misreading* (New York: Oxford University Press, 1975).

27. It is interesting that the antiromantic version of literary tradition put forward by T. S. Eliot in the twentieth century disparages both *Paradise Lost* and *Hamlet* as authoritative models.

Chapter Five

1. The most useful studies of this complex reception history are Chandler, *The Literature of Roguery,* vol. I; Dale B. J. Randall, *The Golden Tapestry: A Critical Survey of Non-Chivalric Spanish Fiction in English Translation, 1543–1657* (Durham, N.C.: Duke University Press, 1963); Edwin Knowles, "Cervantes and English Literature," in *Cervantes Across the Centuries;* Maurice Bardon, *"Don Quichotte" en France au XVIIe et au XVIIIe siècle* (Paris: Librairie Ancienne Honoré Champion, 1931), vol. I; Esther Crooks, "Translations of Cervantes into French," in *Cervantes Across the Centuries;* W. M. Frohock, "The 'Picaresque' in France before *Gil Blas,*" *Yale French Studies* 38 (1967), 222–29; English Showalter, Jr., *The Evolution of the French Novel: 1641–1782* (Princeton: Princeton University Press, 1972). A good study of the assimilation of the Spanish picaresque in seventeenth-century Germany is Hans Gerd Rötzer's *Picaro—Landstörtzer—Simplicius* (Darmstadt: Wissenschaftliche Buchgesellschaft, 1972).

2. D'Aubignac, *Macarise, ou la reine des isles fortunées;* quoted in Stirling Haig, *Madame de Lafayette* (New York: Twayne, 1970), p. 148 n.

3. *The Evolution of the French Novel,* p. 31.

4. "The 'Picaresque' in France," p. 225.

5. See Showalter, *The French Novel,* pp. 32 ff.

6. *La Bibliothèque Française,* 2d ed. (1667) (Genève: Slatkine Reprints, 1970), pp. 57 ff.

7. The relevant texts are Lesage's adaptation of Avellaneda's sequel, *Nouvelles aventures de l'admirable Don Quichotte de la Manche* (1704), and *Gil Blas* (1715–35); Marivaux's *Pharsamon* (passed by censors 1713, pub. 1737);

and Robert Challe's *Continuation de l'histoire de l'admirable Don Quichotte de la Manche* (pt. I, 1695; pt. II, 1713). On Challe's authorship of this last text, see English Showalter, Jr., "Did Robert Challe Write a Sequel to *Don Quixote?*" *Romanic Review* 62 (1971), 270–82.

8. See C. C. Mish, *English Prose Fiction, 1600–1700: A Chronological Check-List*, rev. ed. (Charlottesville: University of Virginia Press, 1967), and Mish, "Best-Sellers in Seventeenth-Century Fiction," *Papers of the Bibliographical Society of America* 47 (1953), 356–73, which show that except for reprintings of Elizabethan favorites such as Sidney's *Arcadia*, Lyly's *Euphues*, and Lodge's *Rosalind*, and translations of Continental romances, there were very few English romances published until the end of the century.

9. See "Cervantes in England" and "*Don Quixote* Abridged," *Papers of the Bibliographical Society of America* 49 (1955), 19–36. The *Cambridge Bibliography of English Literature* does list a prose imitation of the *Quixote* for 1699, William Winstanley's *The Essex Champion*, and there is an early serious appreciation of Cervantes by Locke in 1690 in an Appendix to *An Essay Concerning Human Understanding*.

10. See especially W. Gückel and E. Günter, *D. Defoes and J. Swifts Belesenheit und Literarische Kritik* (Leipzig: Mayer and Müller, 1925), and Helmut Heidenreich, ed., *The Libraries of Daniel Defoe and Phillips Farewell* (Berlin: Selbstverlag, 1970). Heidenreich's introduction is a particularly valuable summary of the evidence.

11. Heidenreich, *Libraries*, p. xxvi.

12. *Daniel Defoe: A Critical Study* (Cambridge, Mass.: Harvard University Press, 1971), p. 96.

13. Gückel and Günter, *Defoes und Swifts*, p. 8.

14. The fullest discussion of this question to date is provided by Ronald Paulson's *Satire and the Novel in Eighteenth-Century England* (New Haven: Yale University Press, 1967), which however argues for the dependence of the novel on satiric precedent rather than for the parallelism of the two species of writing.

15. "Fiction and Society in the Early Eighteenth Century," in *England in the Restoration and Early Eighteenth Century*, ed. H. T. Swedenberg, Jr. (Berkeley: University of California Press, 1972), p. 59. See also G. A. Starr's Introduction to the Oxford English Novels edition of *Moll Flanders* (London: Oxford University Press, 1971), pp. xvi–xx, on the question of the novel's audience.

16. John J. Richetti, *Defoe's Narratives* (Oxford: Clarendon Press, 1975), p. 18.

17. See Starr, Introduction, pp. vii–xii, for some of these patterns. Richetti's recent reading of the novel draws on this latent romance material, though without reflecting on its origin.

18. *To the Palace of Wisdom: Studies in Order and Energy from Dryden to Blake* (New York: Doubleday, 1964), p. 267.

19. All quotations from *Moll Flanders* are from Starr's Oxford English Novels edition and give page numbers in parentheses.

20. *To the Palace of Wisdom*, p. 267.

21. *Rogue's Progress*, p. 57.

22. *Literature and the Delinquent*, p. 2.

23. "Some Notes Toward a History of Fictional Forms: From Aphra Behn

to Daniel Defoe," *Novel* 6 (1973), 131–32. Novak adduces further arguments for Defoe's awareness of the picaresque novel as well as the criminal biography.

24. *The Spanish Libertines* (London: Samuel Bunchley, 1707), p. A5. Cf. the English translator's preface to the 1708 version of *Guzmán de Alfarache*, which praises Bremond's French translation, from which it in turn is derived, for its reduction of the original: "all that was tedious in the Spanish is left out, all that was Pleasant kept in."

25. *The Spanish Libertines*, p. 4.

26. E.g. "my poor Mother going into a *Goldsmith's* Shop to purchase a Ring, by an odd Sort of Mistake, I don't know how, but it seems she walk'd off with a whole String of them" (London: J. Roberts, 1728), pp. 4–5.

27. *The Spanish Libertines*, p. 47.

28. *The Counterfeit Lady Unveiled and Other Criminal Fiction of Seventeenth Century England*, ed. Spiro Peterson (Garden City, N.Y.: Doubleday, 1961), p. 58.

29. See G. A. Starr, *Defoe and Spiritual Autobiography* (Princeton: Princeton University Press, 1965).

30. *The Counterfeit Lady Unveiled*, p. 99.

31. Daniel Defoe, *Tales of Piracy, Crime, and Ghosts*, ed. Carl Withers (New York, 1945), pp. 136–37. A few months after writing this pamphlet, Defoe wrote another version of Sheppard's life in the third person, which put the emphasis on the ingenuity of Sheppard's escapes from jail. One should compare Defoe's subtle reworkings of the genre with Swift's more openly revolutionary "Last Speech and Dying Words of Ebenezor Elliston," which rejects the idea of criminal repentance entirely; see *Irish Tracts 1720–1723 and Sermons, The Prose Works of Jonathan Swift*, vol. 9, ed. Herbert Davis and Louis Landa (Oxford: Shakespeare Head Press, 1948), pp. 35–41.

32. *Selected Poetry and Prose of Daniel Defoe*, ed. Michael Shugrue (New York: Holt, Rinehart and Winston, 1968), p. 226.

33. *The Counterfeit Lady Unveiled*, p. 98.

34. See Watt, *The Rise of the Novel*, pp. 240–42, for this and other views of Defoe on classical epic.

35. John Beadle, *Journal or Diary of A Thankful Christian* (1656), quoted by William Haller, *The Rise of Puritanism* (New York: Columbia University Press, 1938), p. 97.

36. See esp. Maximillian Novak, "Defoe's Theory of Fiction," *Studies in Philology* 61 (1964), 650–68.

37. "Notes Toward A 'Class Theory' of Augustan Literature: The Example of Fielding," in *Literary Theory and Structure: Essays in Honor of William K. Wimsatt*, ed. Frank Brady, John Palmer, and Martin Price (New Haven: Yale University Press, 1973), p. 148.

38. See in general Weber's *The Protestant Ethic and the Spirit of Capitalism*, trans. Talcott Parsons (New York: Scribner, 1930), and R. H. Tawney's *Religion and the Rise of Capitalism* (London: J. Murray, 1926). On Defoe in particular, the best discussion is still Hans A. Andersen's "The Paradox of Trade and Morality in Defoe," *Modern Philology* 39 (1942), 23–46.

39. *Novel and Romance, 1700–1800: A Documentary Record*, ed. Ioan Williams (New York: Barnes and Noble, 1970), pp. 68–69. Gildon was himself the author of a neoclassical poetics, *The Complete Art of Poetry* (1718).

40. *Hudson Review* 1 (1948), 70.
41. "Fact, Theory, and Literary Explanation," *Critical Inquiry* 1 (1974), 245–72. See also his "Defoe, Richardson, Joyce and the Concept of Form in the Novel," *Autobiography, Biography, and the Novel*, by William Matthews and Ralph W. Rader (Los Angeles: William Andrews Clark Memorial Library, 1973).
42. See Andersen, "Trade and Morality in Defoe," pp. 35–37.
43. Michael Shinagel's *Defoe and Middle-Class Gentility* (Cambridge, Mass.: Harvard University Press, 1968) shows the relevance of this class concept to Defoe's life and writings, but rather underestimates its problematic status in the novels.
44. My interpretation of Moll's use of contracts here owes much to the unpublished remarks of George Fayen.
45. "Since all Traditions must indisputably give place to the *Drama*, and since there is no possibility of giving that life to the Writing or Representation of a Story which it has in the Action, I resolved in another beauty to imitate *Dramatick* writing, namely, in the Design, Contexture, and Result of the Plot. I have not observed it before in a Novel" ("Preface to *Incognita* [1691]," in Williams, pp. 27–28). As Williams notes, Congreve is using the term "novel" largely in the sense of "novela," although he pushes it in the direction of realism in his distinction between "novel" and "romance."
46. See *Economics and the Fiction of Daniel Defoe*, University of California Publications, English Studies 24 (Berkeley: University of California Press, 1962).
47. "The Displaced Self in the Novels of Daniel Defoe," *ELH* 38 (1971), 571.
48. See Novak, *Economics*, pp. 13–15, on Defoe's official disapproval of financial speculation as a form of gambling, although Defoe's practice in this regard was hardly consistent.
49. *Defoe and Spiritual Autobiography*, pp. 155 ff.
50. "The Storyteller," *Illuminations*, pp. 100–101.

Chapter Six

1. There was a Spanish picaresque novel of this nature, Antonio Enriquez Gómez's *Siglo Pitagórico* (1644), but Fielding models his narrative on Lucian's satiric voyages, a classical precedent.
2. This is true, for example, of Robert Alter's otherwise useful *Fielding and the Nature of the Novel* (Cambridge, Mass.: Harvard University Press, 1968). Homer Goldberg's *The Art of Joseph Andrews* (Chicago: University of Chicago Press, 1969) is an important exception to this rule, but Goldberg goes too far in the other direction, claiming a generic regularity of the "comic romance" that extends from Cervantes through such French authors as Scarron, Lesage, and Marivaux.
3. "'Novel,' 'Romance,' and Popular Fiction in the First Half of the Eighteenth Century," *Studies in Philology* 70 (1973), 85.
4. *The Spectator*, ed. Donald F. Bond (Oxford: Clarendon Press, 1965), I, 154–57.
5. Charlotte Lennox's *The Female Quixote* was published in 1752.
6. Ethel Thornbury, *Henry Fielding's Theory of the Comic Prose Epic*, University of Wisconsin Studies in Language and Literature 30 (Madison, 1931),

p. 67. Thornbury ignores the importance of the romances themselves for Fielding's adaptation of "epic" rules to the novel.

7. Quotations are from "Monsieur Huet's Letter to Monsieur de Segrais... Upon the Original of Romances," in Samuel Croxall's *Select Collection of Novels* (London, 1722), p. v. On Huet's place in the Continental debate over the romances, see Forcione, pp. 51–55.

8. "Upon the Original of Romances," p. xxix.

9. Ibid., pp. xlviii, li.

10. In his rather skeptical survey, *Some French Influences on Henry Fielding* (Urbana: University of Illinois, 1932), Sidney Glenn considers that Huet is one of the more likely direct "sources" for Fielding's critical thought.

11. Arthur L. Cooke, "Henry Fielding and the Writers of Heroic Romance," *PMLA* 62 (1947), 993.

12. *Joseph Andrews,* ed. Martin C. Battestin (Middletown, Conn.: Wesleyan University Press, 1967). All further quotations are from this volume in the Wesleyan edition and give page numbers in parentheses.

13. Thus Goldberg claims "The manner of the Preface is entirely serious, without irony or facetiousness" (*The Art of Joseph Andrews,* p. 269 n.). The only published opinions that the Preface is to some extent ironic that I am aware of are the comments by Mark Spilka, "Fielding and the Epic Impulse," *Criticism* 11 (1969), 69; Leo Braudy, *Narrative Form in History and Fiction* (Princeton: Princeton University Press, 1970), p. 117; and Robert Alter, "Fielding's Style," *Novel* 1 (1967), 53.

14. "Samuel Richardson's Introduction to *Pamela,*" ed. Sheridan E. Baker, Jr., *Augustan Reprint Society Publication,* no. 48 (1954), pp. v–vi.

15. See, for example, John Clarke, *An Essay Upon Study,* 2d ed. (London, 1737), p. 250. Clarke uses the term "romance" to describe both *Télémaque* and *Don Quixote,* but admits that he has read very little of this genre.

16. *Tom Jones,* ed. Sheridan Baker (New York: Norton, 1973), p. 158.

17. In addition to discussions cited in the previous chapter, see A. P. Burton, "Cervantes the Man Seen through English Eyes in the Seventeenth and Eighteenth Centuries," *Bulletin of Hispanic Studies* 45 (1968), 1–15; E. A. Peers, "Cervantes in England," *Bulletin of Hispanic Studies* 24 (1947), 226–38; Walter Starkie, "Miguel de Cervantes and the English Novel," in *Essays by Divers Hands* 34 (1966), 159–79; and Stuart Tave, *The Amiable Humorist* (Chicago: University of Chicago Press, 1960), pp. 151–63.

18. "Postscript" to *The Odyssey, The Poems of Alexander Pope,* vol. X, ed. Maynard Mack (London: Methuen, 1967), p. 388.

19. *Memoirs of Captain Carleton,* in *Novels and Miscellaneous Works of Daniel Defoe* (London: George Bell, 1883), II, 406. This view, as Tave notes, p. 27, was sometimes used as an argument against satire; such is the thrust of Defoe's conclusion here. Fielding himself alludes to it in the *Covent Garden Journal*—see n. 24 below.

20. "A Supplement to the Translator's Preface, Communicated by a learned writer, well-known in the literary world," *Don Quixote,* trans. Jarvis (London: J. and R. Tonson, 1742). The identification of the author as Warburton is made by A. W. Evans, *Warburton and the Warburtonians* (Oxford: Oxford University Press, 1932), p. 292.

21. Thus Charles Perrault writes that antiquity "has nothing of the same

nature that it can oppose to *Don Quixote* and *Le Roman comique*" and he finds in these modern works "a wit that is finer and more piquant than all that of Athens" (Bardon, "*Don Quichotte,*" I, 383; my trans.).

22. *Augustan Reprint Society Publication,* no. 95 (1963), ii.

23. "Proceedings at the Court of Censorial Enquiry, &c.," *The Covent Garden Journal,* ed. Gerard Edward Jensen (New Haven: Yale University Press, 1915), I, 281.

24. *The Complete Works of Henry Fielding, Esq.,* ed. William Ernest Henley (New York: Frank Cass, 1902), XI, 70. Cf. *The Coffee-House Politician:* "The greatest part of mankind labour under one delirium or other: and Don Quixote differed from the rest, not in madness, but the species of it. The covetous, the prodigal, the superstitious, the libertine, and the coffee-house politician, are all Quixotes in their several ways" (*Works,* IX, 108).

25. *Works,* XI, 69–70. Fielding apologizes for such a dichotomy in his Preface by distinguishing between "the production of this season," more topically satirical, and the parts "written in my more juvenile years" in which he discovered, he says, that it was difficult to make an English Quixote very different from a Quixote in Spain (XI, 9–10).

26. Paulson, *Satire and the Novel,* pp. 91 ff.

27. "Chastity and Interpolation: Two Aspects of *Joseph Andrews,*" *JEGP* 69 (1970), 26.

28. *The Confidence-Man,* ed. Elizabeth S. Foster (New York: Hendricks House, 1954), p. 271. But see pp. 215–16 above for an analysis of the way Melville goes on to subvert his own distinction here.

Chapter Seven

1. "A Parodying Novel: Sterne's *Tristram Shandy,*" trans. George Isaak, in *Laurence Sterne: A Collection of Critical Essays,* ed. John Traugott (Englewood Cliffs, N.J.: Prentice-Hall, 1968), p. 89.

2. *The Rise of the Novel,* pp. 291, 292.

3. See John Traugott, *Tristram Shandy's World: Sterne's Philosophical Rhetoric* (Berkeley: University of California Press, 1954); Helene Moglen, *The Philosophical Irony of Laurence Sterne* (Gainesville: The University Presses of Florida, 1975); and James E. Swearingen, *Reflexivity in Tristram Shandy: An Essay in Phenomenological Criticism* (New Haven: Yale University Press, 1977). Moglen does consider the novelistic resources of *Tristram Shandy,* but largely in terms of their ironical negation.

4. See Ronald Paulson, *Satire and the Novel,* pp. 248–65; and Melvyn New, *Laurence Sterne as Satirist: A Reading of Tristram Shandy* (Gainesville: University of Florida Press, 1969). John Stedmond in *The Comic Art of Laurence Sterne* (Toronto: University of Toronto Press, 1967) gives some attention to the traditions of satire but broadens his perspective to "comedy" as a literary mode.

5. See D. W. Jefferson, "*Tristram Shandy* and the Tradition of Learned Wit," *Essays in Criticism* 1 (1951), 225–48 (on the tradition of scholastic free speculation); William V. Holtz, *Image and Immortality: A Study of Tristram Shandy* (Providence: Brown University Press, 1970) (on the tradition of literary pictorialism); and Richard Lanham, *Tristram Shandy: The Games of Pleasure* (Berkeley: University of California Press, 1973) (on the traditions of classical and Renaissance rhetoric).

6. *Laurence Sterne: From Tristram to Yorick,* trans. and abr. Barbara Bray (London: Oxford University Press, 1965), p. 17.

7. Robert Alter does consider Sterne in the line of Cervantes and Fielding in his *Partial Magic,* but his notion of the "self-conscious novel" remains limited, being conceived largely in opposition to Leavis's "Great Tradition" and paying little attention to specific historical or intertextual relationships.

8. *The Cry: A New Dramatic Fable* (London: R. and J. Dodsley, 1754), III, 120.

9. *Johnsoniana* (London: G. Bell, 1884), p. 91.

10. *The Rambler,* ed. W. J. Bate and Albrecht B. Strauss, *The Yale Edition of the Works of Samuel Johnson* (New Haven: Yale University Press, 1969), III, 11.

11. "An Essay on the New Species of Writing," pp. i, 16, 37.

12. "The disgraces of Gil Blas are, for the most part, such as rather excite mirth than compassion: he himself laughs at them; and his transitions from distress to happiness, or at least ease, are so sudden, that neither the reader has time to pity him, nor himself to be acquainted with affliction. This conduct, in my opinion, not only deviates from probability, but prevents that generous indignation which ought to animate the reader against the sordid and vicious disposition of the world" (*Roderick Random* [London: J. M. Dent, 1927], p. 5).

29. *Satire and the Novel,* p. 121; *To the Palace of Wisdom,* p. 298.

30. *Covent Garden Journal,* p. 281.

31. Preface to *David Simple,* Oxford English Novels, ed. Malcolm Kelsell (London: Oxford University Press, 1969), p. 6.

32. Cf. Alexander Parker, "Fielding and the Structure of *Don Quixote,*" *Bulletin of Hispanic Studies* 33 (1956), 1–16. Parker detects a shift in Fielding's attitude from the time of *Joseph Andrews* to the time of his review of *The Female Quixote,* from an acceptance of Cervantes's episodic plot structure to a more critical judgment against it.

33. Fielding does anticipate such objections at the end of the Preface, however, giving four reasons for his departure from his own rules. One of these is that vices "are never set forth as the Objects of Ridicule, but Detestation" (10).

34. *The Moral Basis of Fielding's Art: A Study of Joseph Andrews* (Middletown, Conn.: Wesleyan University Press, 1959), p. 95. Cf. Price, pp. 288 ff., for a more sophisticated discussion of Fielding's rendition of Christian ethical doctrines.

35. "Notes Toward a 'Class Theory' of Augustan Literature," p. 148.

36. See Battestin's "General Introduction," pp. xix–xxi, for a summary of this issue.

37. *Tom Jones,* p. 474 (XII, i).

38. *Pamela* (London: J. M. Dent, 1914), I, 21.

13. *Laurence Sterne: The Early and Middle Years* (London: Methuen and Co., 1975), p. 199.

14. *The Adventures of Ferdinand Count Fathom,* ed. Damian Grant (London: Oxford University Press, 1971).

15. Quotations are from James Aiken Work's edition (New York: Odyssey Press, 1940); page numbers are given in parentheses.

16. On changes in the theory of the novel in England after *Tristram Shandy,* see William Park, "Changes in the Criticism of the Novel after 1760,"

Philological Quarterly 46 (1967), 34–41. For other aspects of *Tristram Shandy's* reaction to the English novel of the 1750s, see Richard C. Boys, "Tristram Shandy and the Conventional Novel," *Papers of the Michigan Academy of Science, Arts and Letters* 27 (1957), 423–36.

17. See Tuvia Bloch, "Smollett's Quest for Form," *Modern Language Review* 65 (1967), 103–13. Bloch shows that Smollett was also increasingly drawn to Fielding in his attempts at more architectonic structure.

18. This idea is advanced by Boys, "Tristram Shandy," p. 429.

19. The relation between such visual quotations and the Augustan mock form is discussed by Martin Price in *To the Palace of Wisdom*, p. 332.

20. See A. P. Burton, "Cervantes the Man," pp. 10–12. To judge from a pamphlet by William Windham, *Remarks on the Proposals lately published for a New Translation of Don Quixote* (1755), which criticizes Smollett's proposal for his translation, it would seem that Smollett had hurriedly changed his mind about Cervantes's artistic intention, on the basis of the biographical information that Windham brings forward. The charge that Smollett's translation of *Don Quixote* was an outright plagiarism of Jarvis's version remains unsubstantiated; see Alexander Parker's review of Carmine Rocco Linsalata's *Smollett's Hoax: Don Quixote in England*, in *Modern Language Review* 54 (1959), 97–98.

21. Quotation from Cooke's Pocket Edition of *The History and Adventures of the Renowned Don Quixote* (London, 1796), p. x.

22. *Resources of Kind*, p. 81.

23. On other aspects of the *Hamlet* connection, see Lanham, pp. 131–50, a fine discussion which suggests among other things that Yorick was too self-pitying a self-portrait of Sterne as parson to survive in the comic play of the novel, and Kenneth Monkman, "Sterne, Hamlet and Yorick: Some New Material," in *The Winged Skull: Papers from the Laurence Sterne Bicentenary Conference*, ed. Arthur H. Cash and John M. Stedmond (Kent, Ohio: Kent State University Press, 1971), pp. 112–23.

24. See Lipking, *The Ordering of the Arts in Eighteenth-Century England* (Princeton: Princeton University Press, 1970), and P. O. Kristeller, "The Modern System of the Arts," *Journal of the History of Ideas* 12 (1951), 496–527; 13 (1952), 17–46. It is a curious fact of literary history that one of Sterne's comically appropriated sources, Ephraim Chambers's *Cyclopedia* of 1728, was the original inspiration for the monumental and seriously systematic French *Encyclopédie* of Diderot and D'Alembert.

25. *Illustrations of Sterne: With Other Essays and Verses* (1798), facsimile reprint (New York: Garland Publishing Co., 1971), p. 182.

26. *The Poetics of Quotation in the European Novel*, trans. Theodore and Yetta Ziolkowski (Princeton: Princeton University Press, 1968), p. 83.

27. For a similar though more discreet play with the distinction between written epitaph and vocal elegy, see Gray's "Elegy Written in A Country Church-Yard." A more profound exploration of graphic and oral alternatives to modern typography is of course provided by Blake's illuminated printing; see, for example, the introductory poems to *Songs of Innocence* and *Songs of Experience*. As a novelist, Sterne is more concerned with exploring the ambiguities of the printed book than with getting beyond typographical form altogether. Cf. William Holtz, "Typography, *Tristram Shandy*, the Aposiopesis, etc.," in *The Winged Skull*, pp. 247–57.

28. *"Tristram Shandy's* Law of Gravity," *ELH* 28 (1961), 70.

29. See *An Inquiry Concerning Human Understanding,* VII, "Of the Idea of Necessary Connections"; e.g., "The first time a man saw the communication of motion by impulse, as by the shock of two billiard balls, he could not pronounce that the one event was *connected,* but only that it was *conjoined* with the other. After he had observed several instances of this nature, he then pronounced them to be *connected.* What alteration has happened to give rise to this new idea of *connection?* Nothing but that he now *feels* these events to be *connected* in his imagination, and can readily foretell the existence of one from the appearance of the other" (Library of Liberal Arts edition, ed. Charles W. Hendel [Indianapolis: Bobbs-Merrill, 1955], p. 86).

30. Introduction, *Laurence Sterne,* p. 9.

31. See in this regard my article, "A Defense of History: the Language of Transformation in Romantic Narrative," *Bucknell Review,* ed. Harry R. Garvin (Fall 1977), pp. 33–56.

32. See Derrida, "La différance," *Marges de la philosophie* (Paris: Les Editions de Minuit, 1972). In the romantic interval, of course, writing becomes conscious of a metaphysical burden, of which Sterne is relatively innocent and from which Derrida is trying to free himself.

33. See Lanham, pp. 131–34, and Overton James, *The Relation of Tristram Shandy to the Life of Sterne* (The Hague: Mouton, 1966), pp. 79–101.

34. But not, as far as I know, in print. The opinion is reported as a scholarly rumor by Lanham, p. 53, who attributes it to Ralph Rader, and by Paulson, "The Pilgrimage and the Family: Structures in the Novels of Fielding and Smollett," in *Tobias Smollett: Bicentennial Essays Presented to Lewis M. Knapp,* ed. G. S. Rousseau and P.-G. Boucé (New York: Oxford University Press, 1971), p. 76 n., who attributes it to Richard Macksey. No one should accuse American academics of responding to Sterne inappropriately.

35. Especially in chapter 3, "Games, Play, Seriousness."

36. *An Essay Concerning Human Understanding,* ed. Alexander Campbell Fraser (New York: Dover Publications, 1959), II, 9.

37. Helene Moglen makes brief comparisons between Sterne, Hume, and Berkeley. Perry Miller discusses Edwards's use of Locke and the contrasting case of Berkeley in "The Rhetoric of Sensation," *Errand into the Wilderness* (Cambridge, Mass.: Belknap Press, 1956).

38. Thus Saussure's first principle is "The Arbitrary Nature of the Sign" (*Course in General Linguistics,* ed. Charles Bally and Albert Sechehaye, in collaboration with Albert Riedlinger, trans. Wade Baskin [New York: McGraw-Hill: 1966], pp. 67–70). Cf. Thomas Weiskel on Locke in *The Romantic Sublime* (Baltimore: Johns Hopkins University Press, 1976), pp. 15–17; "the Lockean model subverts the autonomy of mind or soul; the mind is not its own place, but the space in which semiotic substitutions occur" (17).

39. See *Essay Concerning Human Understanding,* I, 527–35. I realize that this contradicts the critical commonplace that Locke's association of ideas is the basis of Sterne's narrative art. But as I argue below, the primary associations cross semiotic levels: ideas connect with things, things with words, words with things.

40. *The Basic Writings of Sigmund Freud,* ed. and trans. A. A. Brill (New York: Random House, 1938), pp. 659–60. "Displacement" is also used more

widely by Freud and by later Freudians; see J. LaPlanche and J.-B. Pontalis, *The Language of Psychoanalysis*, trans. Donald Nicholson-Smith (New York: W. W. Norton, 1973), pp. 121–24.

41. *"Tristram Shandy's* Law of Gravity," p. 76.

42. *The Pleasure of the Text*, p. 64.

43. See Barthes' *Elements of Semiology* (published together with *Writing Degree Zero*), trans. Annette Lavers and Colin Smith (Boston: Beacon Press, 1970), pp. 89–94. In connection with Toby's project, cf. Bishop Sprat, *The History of the Royal Society*, ed. Jackson I. Cope and Harold Whitmore Jones (Saint Louis, Mo.: Washington University Studies, 1958), pp. 112–13: "Who can behold, without indignation, how many mists and uncertainties, these specious *Tropes* and *Figures* have brought on our knowledge? How many rewards, which are due to more profitable, and difficult *Arts*, have been still snatch'd away by the easie vanity of *fine speaking?* ... [The Society has] therefore been most rigorous in putting in execution, the only Remedy, that can be found for this *extravagance:* and that has been a constant Resolution, to reject all the amplifications, digressions, and swellings of style: to return back to the primitive purity, and shortness, when men deliver'd so many *things*, almost in an equal number of *words."*

44. A similar point in made by Meyer, p. 80. An alternative account of Tristram's concern with signification, from a phenomenological rather than a semiotic perspective, is given by Swearingen, *Reflexivity in Tristram Shandy*, pp. 140 ff.

45. See particularly "La Signification du Phallus," *Écrits* (Paris: Editions du Seuil, 1966), pp. 685–95. The best introduction to Lacan in English is Anthony Wilden's translation, annotation, and commentary, *The Language of the Self: The Function of Language in Psychoanalysis* (Baltimore: The Johns Hopkins University Press, 1968).

46. On Smart, see Geoffrey Hartman, "Christopher Smart's 'Magnificat': Toward a Theory of Representation," *The Fate of Reading* (Chicago: University of Chicago Press, 1975); on Goethe, see Elizabeth Wilkinson, "Goethe's Conception of Form," in Willoughby and Wilkinson, *Goethe: Poet and Thinker* (New York: Barnes and Noble, 1963).

47. See Robert Alter's chapter on *Jacques le Fataliste* in *Partial Magic*, pp. 57–83, and Bernhard Fabian, "Tristram Shandy and Parson Yorick among Some German Greats," in *The Winged Skull*, pp. 194–205. One of the most creative "sequels" to *Tristram Shandy* is an exemplary text for the modern Latin American novel, Machado de Assis's *Epitaph for a Small Winner* [*Memórias Póstumas de Brás Cubas*] (1880).

48. The authorship of Hebrews was in doubt from the time of the early church. I have not been able to determine Sterne's own opinion, but his characters assume it was written by Paul. The humor of the exegesis depends on the fact that the author of the epistle is entertaining no doubts at all about the efficacy of his conscience at this point.

49. *Concluding Unscientific Postscript*, trans. David Swenson and Walter Lowrie (Princeton: Princeton University Press, 1941), pp. 462–63. Lanham's discussion of the comic mode of *Tristram*, pp. 151–67, parallels my own.

50. *Studies in European Realism*, trans. Edith Bone (London: Hillway Publishing Co., 1950), p. 11.

Chapter Eight

1. *The Progress of Romance* (1785), The Facsimile Text Society (New York, 1930), p. 111.

2. For a discussion of the influence of the seventeenth-century heroic romances or "salon romances" on Richardson, see Henry Knight Miller, "Augustan Prose Fiction and the Romance Tradition," in *Studies in the Eighteenth Century* III, ed. R. F. Brissenden and J. C. Eade (Toronto: University of Toronto Press, 1976), pp. 244–47.

3. See Freedman, "The Possibility of a Theory of the Novel," in *The Disciplines of Criticism*, for a critique of this generic polarity.

4. *The Melodramatic Imagination* (New Haven: Yale University Press, 1976), p. 5.

5. "Magical Narratives: Romance as Genre," p. 158.

6. See Fiedler's *Love and Death in the American Novel*, rev. ed. (New York: Stein and Day, 1966), pp. 62–125. On Richardson and Austen, see F. R. Leavis, *The Great Tradition* (London: Chatto and Windus, 1960), pp. 4–5, and Margaret Ann Doody, *A Natural Passion: A Study of the Novels of Samuel Richardson* (Oxford: Clarendon Press, 1974), pp. 358–59, 372–74.

7. "The Melodramatic Imagination," *Partisan Review* 39 (1972), 211.

8. *Oeuvres Esthétiques*, ed. Paul Vernière (Paris: Éditions Garnier Frères, 1965), pp. 39–40 (my translation).

9. "Preface to Lyrical Ballads (1800)," *The Prose Works of William Wordsworth*, ed. W. J. B. Owen and Jane Worthington Smyser (Oxford: Clarendon Press, 1974), I, 128.

10. "Epos and Novel," *The Dialogic Imagination* (forthcoming).

11. *Waverly*, Everyman's Library (London: J. M. Dent, 1906), p. 82. Scott makes a similarly negative allusion to the Spanish picaresque somewhat later in the novel; see Alexander Welsh, "Contrast of Styles in the Waverley Novels," *Novel* 6 (1973), 218–19.

12. In 1837 the *Metropolitan Magazine* called Mr. Pickwick "the legitimate successor to Don Quixote, . . . the cockney Quixote of the nineteenth century" (*Dickens: The Critical Heritage*, ed. Philip Collins [New York: Barnes and Noble, 1971], p. 31). The observation was echoed by John Forster, Washington Irving, and Fyodor Doestevsky, among others.

13. *The Posthumous Papers of the Pickwick Club*, Oxford Illustrated Dickens (London: Oxford University Press, 1966); all further quotations are from this edition. On Pickwick as a satire of the eighteenth-century social economist, see Fred Kaplan, "Pickwick's 'Magnanimous Revenge': Reason and Responsibility in the *Pickwick Papers*," *Victorian Newsletter* 37 (1970), 18–21.

14. There is a good discussion of this aspect of Jingle in Rupert Roopnaraine's "Reflexive Technique in *The Pickwick Papers*," Ph.D. diss. (Cornell, 1972), limited only by an unwillingness to see Jingle's conversion in the Fleet as a legitimate part of the older picaresque formula. There is also an older tradition of the picaro as dramatic actor, beginning with Agustín de Rojas Villandrando's *El viaje entretenido* (1603) and continuing in Scarron's *Roman comique*. Other picaresque novels include theatrical episodes; e.g., *El Buscón* and *Gil Blas*. The latter was most likely a "source" for Dickens's conception of Jingle.

15. "Language Into Structure: Pickwick Revisited," *Daedalus* 101, no. 1

(1972), 195. This judgment of Sam's importance in the novel is echoed and anticipated by a number of modern critics and reflects the opinion of the Victorian reading public.

16. "Converging Worlds in *Pickwick Papers*," *Nineteenth-Century Fiction* 27 (1972), 10.

17. For an interesting attempt to read *Pickwick Papers* as a *Bildungsroman*, see James Kincaid, "The Education of Mr. Pickwick," *Nineteenth-Century Fiction* 25 (1969), 127–41; for a more convincing argument to the contrary, see Philip Rogers, "Mr. Pickwick's Innocence," *Nineteenth-Century Fiction* 27 (1972), 21–37.

18. "Language into Structure," p. 183.

19. I am quoting from Lienhard Bergel's useful survey, "Cervantes in Germany," in *Cervantes Across the Centuries*. See also Anthony Close, *The Romantic Approach to Don Quixote* (Cambridge: Cambridge University Press, 1978), pp. 29–41.

20. Lines 50–162; in the 1850 version of *The Prelude* this dream is the poet's own, but in the 1805 version it is attributed to "a Friend."

21. "Lectures of 1818," *Complete Works of Samuel Taylor Coleridge*, ed. W. G. T. Shedd (New York: Harper, 1871), IV, 268.

22. *Last Essays of Elia, The Works of Charles Lamb*, ed. William MacDonald (London: J. M. Dent, 1903), II, 161.

23. "On the English Novelists," *Complete Works*, ed. P. P. Howe (London: J. M. Dent, 1931), VI, 107.

24. *Works*, VI, 108, 106.

25. Ibid., 121–22. In his own *Lives of the Novelists* Scott assimilates Lesage to the eighteenth-century English novel, but he does not extend the privilege back to Cervantes. Cf. Borges's "Parable of Cervantes and the *Quixote*," which charts a similar reassertion of the romance principle through the medium of historical distance.

26. See the early *Atheneum* review of 1836 that censures Dickens's lack of originality: "A wit or a humourist should remind you of human nature—human nature in its vivid and lustrous colours—and not hunt you back to a foregone work, or a pleasant author-predecessor. . . . The *Pickwick Papers*, in fact, are made up of two pounds of Smollett, three ounces of Sterne, a handful of Hook, a dash of grammatical Pierce Egan—incidents at pleasure, served with an original *sauce piquante*" (Collins, *Dickens: The Critical Heritage*, p. 32).

27. *The Life and Adventures of Sir Launcelot Greaves*, ed. David Evans (London: Oxford University Press, 1975), pp. 164, 165. Marcus adduces the precedent of the prison episode in *The Vicar of Wakefield* in *Dickens: from Pickwick to Dombey* (New York: Basic Books, 1965), pp. 29–30, but the sociological breadth of Dickens's vision and the relative immunity of the hero himself from the degradation are closer to Smollett than to Goldsmith. On reenactments of episodes from *Joseph Andrews*, see H. M. Daleski, *Dickens and the Art of Analogy* (New York: Schocken Books, 1970), pp. 22–29; on elements from other novels of Smollett, see William W. Huse, Jr., "Pickle and Pickwick," *Washington University Studies* 10 (1922), 143–54; Frans Dirk Wierstra, *Smollett and Dickens* (Den Helder: D. DeBoer, Jr., 1928); and Earle Davis, *The Flint and the Flame: The Artistry of Charles Dickens* (Columbia: University of Missouri Press, 1963), 18–27.

28. *David Copperfield* (London: Oxford University Press, 1948), p. 55. See Forster, *Life of Charles Dickens*, ed. A. J. Hoppé (London: J. M. Dent, 1966), I, 7–8, and Harry Stone, "Dark Corners of the Mind: Dickens' Childhood Reading," *Horn Book Magazine* 39 (1963), 306–21. A good summary of the evidence in provided by Steven H. Gale, "Cervantes' Influence on Dickens, with Comparative Emphasis on *Don Quijote* and *Pickwick Papers*, "*Anales Cervantinos* 12 (1963), 135–36.

29. *David Copperfield*, p. 56.

30.   The tales that charm away the wakeful night
        In Araby, romances; legends penned
        For solace by dim light of monkish lamps;
        Fictions, for ladies of their love, devised
        By youthful squires; adventures endless, spun
        By the dismantled warrior in old age,
        Out of the bowels of those very schemes
        In which his youth did first extravagate;
        These spread like day, and something in the shape
        Of these will live till man shall be no more.
        Dumb yearnings, hidden appetites, are ours,
        And *they must* have their food.

(*The Prelude*, ed. De Selincourt and Darbishire [Oxford: Clarendon Press, 1959], V, 496–507, p. 167.) Lines 500–503 seem to be an allusion to *Don Quixote*, one which incorporates the dynamics of such recollections of early reading within itself.

31. *The Lives of the Novelists*, p. 368.

32. *Miscellaneous Papers, Plays, and Poems*, in *The Works of Charles Dickens*, National Library Edition (New York: Bigelow, Brown and Co., n.d.), XVIII, 339.

33. "Unity and Coherence in *The Pickwick Papers*," *Studies in English Literature* 5 (1965), 671.

34. Roger Abrahams, "Toward an Enactment-Centered Theory of Folklore," in *Frontiers of Folklore*, ed. William R. Bascom, AAAS Selected Symposium 5 (1977), 80–81.

35. Katherine Carolan has shown how much even this ceremony is a self-conscious recreation on Dickens's part. It is modeled, in many of its details, on the Christmas at Bracebridge Hall in Washington Irving's *Sketch Book*, and it is part of a persistent nostalgia for the glories of Christmas past in England since the Puritans had originally banned the holiday during the Commonwealth. See "The Dingley Dell Chrsitmas," *Dickens Studies Newsletter* 4 (1973), 41–48.

36. Mary Douglas, "Deciphering a Meal," *Daedalus* 101, no. 1 (1972), 61–81. Cf. Roland Barthes on the sign systems of contemporary (French) mass culture in *Mythologies*, sel. and trans. Annette Lavers (New York: Hill and Wang, 1972).

37. "Deciphering a Meal," p. 80.

38. Cf. William S. Holdsworth, *Charles Dickens as a Legal Historian* (New Haven: Yale University Press, 1929), p. 117: "In 1827 the procedure of the common law courts was perhaps the most artificial and the most encumbered with fictions that any legal system had ever possessed. Its main rules were medieval. But these rules, having become unsuited to a more complex soci-

ety, had been overlaid with a number of conventional practices and legal fictions." Holdsworth shows how acute Dickens was, in *Pickwick Papers* and later in *Bleak House*, in understanding and exposing these fictive legal mechanisms.

39. *All the Year Round* 18 (July 27, 1867), 119. Some scholars believe that Dickens had a hand in this article, if indeed he did not actually write it himself; see Richard Stang, *The Theory of the Novel in England* (New York: Columbia University Press, 1959), pp. 26–27 n.

40. *The Newcomes, The Oxford Thackeray,* ed. George Saintsbury (London: Oxford University Press, n.d.), XIV, 49.

41. *The Letters of William Makepeace Thackeray,* ed. Gordon N. Ray (Cambridge, Mass: Harvard University Press, 1945–46), III, 304.

42. *Thackeray: The Uses of Adversity* (New York: McGraw-Hill, 1955), p. 428.

43. "Fielding's Works" [*The Times,* Sept. 2, 1840], *Oxford Thackeray,* III, 388. For a perceptive discussion of *Jonathan Wild* in the series of the picaresque novel, see C. J. Rawson, "The Hero as Clown: Jonathan Wild, Felix Krull, and Others," *Studies in the Eighteenth Century* II, ed. R. F. Brissenden (Toronto: University of Toronto Press, 1973).

44. *Letters* II, 462: "Doesn't the apology for Fielding read like an apology for somebody else too? God help us."

45. *Oxford Thackeray,* XIV, 49–50.

46. Ray, *Thackeray,* p. 128, quoting the recollections of William Hepworth Thompson.

47. *Jane Eyre,* ed. Margaret Smith (London: Oxford University Press, 1973), p. 4. In several letters Brontë deplores Thackeray's fondness for Fielding on moral grounds. Cf. Scott's *Lives of the Novelists,* where he echoes Dr. Johnson's defense of Macheath: men "will not become swindlers and thieves, because they sympathize with the fortunes of the witty picaroon Gil Blas, or licentious debauchees, because they read *Tom Jones*" (p. 100).

48. *Oxford Thackeray,* III, 389.

49. *Letters,* II, 416. But in his lecture "Hogarth, Smollett, and Fielding" he supposes that "of the heroes of Fielding's three novels, we should like honest Joseph Andrews the best" (*Oxford Thackeray,* XIII, 647).

50. *Catherine, Oxford Thackeray,* III, 186.

51. *Oxford Thackeray,* XIII, 652.

52. *Thackeray: the Critical Heritage,* ed. Geoffrey Tillotson and Donald Hawes (New York: Barnes and Noble, 1968), p. 54.

53. *Oxford Thackeray,* XIII, 649.

54. "Charles Lamb says finely of Jones that a single hearty laugh from him 'clears the air'—but then it is in a certain state of the atmosphere" (XIII, 649). Thackeray knew that the phrase had been used by Forster when he complained of it earlier in a letter to Robert Bell; see *Letters,* II, 424. But it did come originally from Lamb's essay "On the Genius and Character of Hogarth."

55. "Preface" to *Pendennis, Oxford Thackeray,* XII, xxxvi.

56. "Charity and Humour," *Oxford Thackeray,* X, 622.

57. *Letters,* III, 304.

58. *Oxford Thackeray,* II, 98.

59. See in this regard an analysis of both *The English Humourists* and *Henry Esmond* as deliberate challenges to Macaulay's *History of England from the Accession of James II*—Jane Millgate, "History versus Fiction: Thackeray's Response to Macaulay," *Costerus* 2 (1974), n.s., 43–58.

60. "The Cybernetics of 'Self': A Theory of Alcoholism," *Steps to an Ecology of Mind* (New York: Ballantine Books, 1972), p. 323.

61. *Oxford Thackeray*, VI, 128–29.

62. Ibid., 129.

63. Ibid., III, 389.

64. Cf. the pointedly debunking remarks about Frederick of Prussia, Carlyle's "Hero as King," in *Barry Lyndon* and Gordon Ray's remarks about the "anti-Carlylean" thrust of Thackeray's *English Humourists* lectures (*Thackeray*, p. 144).

65. All references are to the Riverside edition of *Vanity Fair*, ed. Geoffrey Tillotson and Kathleen Tillotson (Boston: Houghton Mifflin, 1963).

66. "'Before the Curtain' and *Vanity Fair*," *Nineteenth-Century Fiction* 26 (1971), 316.

67. See, for example, Geoffrey Tillotson, *Thackeray the Novelist* (Cambridge: Cambridge University Press, 1954), pp. 209–27, who argues that this role was quite evident in the first version of *Barry Lyndon*, and John Sutherland, "The Expanding Narrative of Vanity Fair," *Journal of Narrative Technique* 3 (1973), 149–69, who shows that the authorial addresses were worked into a particular stage of the manuscript, and that they are less the representation than the creation of a new ethos.

68. "The Tomeavesian Way of Knowing the World: Technique and Meaning in *Vanity Fair*," *ELH* 32 (1965), 384–85.

69. Cf. the analysis of G. Armour Craig of this passage, in "On the Style of *Vanity Fair*," in *Thackeray: A Collection of Critical Essays*, ed. Alexander Welsh (Englewood Cliffs, N.J.: Prentice-Hall, 1968), which is structurally perceptive even as it disapproves of Thackeray's moral stance. See also Edgar F. Harden's analysis of the pervasive parallelisms in Thackeray's plotting of the novel, "The Discipline and Significance of Form in *Vanity Fair*," *PMLA* 82 (1967), 530–41.

70. "The Cybernetics of 'Self,'" p. 323.

71. *Deceit, Desire, and the Novel: Self and Other in Literary Structure*, trans. Yvonne Freccero (Baltimore: Johns Hopkins University Press, 1966), pp. 6–7. Thackeray eventually read *Madame Bovary* and told Henry Sutherland Edwards, "The book is bad.... It is a heartless, coldblooded study of the downfall and degradation of a woman" (*Letters*, IV, 82 n.). He seems to have been unaware of Stendhal.

72. See D. J. Dooley, "Thackeray's Use of Vanity Fair," *Studies in English Literature* 11 (1971), 701–13.

73. *Letters*, II, 531.

74. For Thackeray's rather extensive use of *Amelia* as an armature for *Vanity Fair*, see E. D. H. Johnson, "*Vanity Fair* and *Amelia*: Thackeray in the Perspective of the Eighteenth Century," *Modern Philology* 59 (1961), 100–13.

75. *Oxford Thackeray*, X, 622.

76. Ibid.

77. Ibid., 625, 627.

Chapter Nine

1. "Literary Consequences of Puritanism," in *The American Puritan Imagination*, ed. Sacvan Bercovitch (Cambridge: Cambridge University Press, 1974). See also Ziff's "The Artist and Puritanism," in *Hawthorne Centenary Essays*, ed. Roy Harvey Pearce (Columbus: Ohio State University Press, 1964).

2. *The Adventurous Muse: The Poetics of American Fiction, 1789–1900* (New Haven: Yale University Press, 1977), pp. 2–3.

3. Quoted in Henri Petter, *The Early American Novel* (Columbus: Ohio State University Press, 1971), p. 10. For a provocative critique of this "thin soil" theory in recent criticism of American literature, see Nicolaus Mills, *American and English Fiction in the Nineteenth Century* (Bloomington: Indiana University Press, 1973), pp. 3–31. James himself was elaborating on Hawthorne's list of negatives in his preface to *The Marble Faun*.

4. Quoted in Petter, *The Early American Novel*, pp. 14–15. The most sophisticated recent version of this argument can be found in Spengemann's *The Adventurous Muse*, which like this passage only errs in underestimating the resources of the European novel for renewal. One should also mention in this connection Charles Feidelson's *Symbolism and American Literature* (Chicago: University of Chicago Press, 1953), which argues powerfully for a view of nineteenth-century American literature as a forerunner of European modernism.

5. *Nature, The Collected Works of Ralph Waldo Emerson*, vol. I, ed. Alfred R. Ferguson and Robert E. Spiller (Cambridge: Harvard University Press, 1971), p. 7.

6. "Allegory," *The Portable Coleridge*, ed. I. A. Richards (New York: Viking Press, 1950), p. 400.

7. *The Puritan Origins of the American Self* (New Haven: Yale University Press, 1975), passim. Bercovitch contrasts American and English romanticism in this regard, pp. 170–73, in a way that is particularly suggestive. Nevertheless, he underestimates the degree to which the Puritan and the romantic programs converged in American literature of the nineteenth century.

8. In the 1846 version of the review Poe attempts to deny Hawthorne the originality he had credited him with in the version of 1842; his change of opinion leads him to such curious assertions as the following: "there is clearly a point at which even novelty itself would cease to produce the legitimate originality, if we judge this originality, as we should, by the effect designed; this point is that at which *novelty becomes nothing novel*, and here the artist, *to preserve his originality*, will subside into the commonplace" (*The Works of Edgar Allan Poe*, ed. E. C. Stedman and G. E. Woodberry [Chicago: Stone and Kimball, 1896], VII, 21–22). I am indebted to Joseph Moldenhauer for pointing out this parallel; my discussion of Coleridge draws on Leslie Brisman's *Romantic Origins* (Ithaca: Cornell University Press, 1978).

9. *Hawthorne, Melville, and the Novel* (Chicago: University of Chicago Press, 1976), p. 20. Both Brodhead and Mills attempt to move beyond the customary dichotomy between English "novel" and American "romance," a distinction formulated by Richard Chase in *The American Novel and Its Traditions* (Garden City, N.Y.: Doubleday, 1957) and reaffirmed most recently by Joel Porte in *The Romance in America* (Middletown, Conn.: Wesleyan Univer-

sity Press, 1969). I would argue that many American novels are simply adopting the reromanticizing strategy of the European novel after Richardson, perhaps because of the more unmediated or unrepressed romanticism of American literary culture.

10. "Hawthorne and His Mosses," in *Billy Budd and Other Prose Pieces,* ed. Raymond Weaver, *The Works of Herman Melville* (London: Constable, 1924), XIII, 131. I have advanced this reading of Melville's career in another context in an essay on *Billy Budd,* "The Measured Forms of Captain Vere," *Modern Fiction Studies* 23 (1977), 227–35. For a similar assessment of Melville's development after *Moby-Dick,* sympathetic though more simply negative, see Alan Lebowitz, *Progress into Silence: A Study of Melville's Heroes* (Bloomington: Indiana University Press, 1970), pp. 151–215.

11. E. G. Samuel Monk, *The Sublime: A Study of Critical Theories in Eighteenth-Century England* (New York: Modern Language Association, 1935); David B. Morris, *The Religious Sublime: Christian Poetry and Critical Theory in Eighteenth-Century England* (Lexington: University Press of Kentucky, 1972).

12. *The American Scholar, Collected Works,* I, 58. Poe's "Philosophy of Composition" is another American version of this antiorganic theory, subjecting *Paradise Lost,* among other works, to a similar transcendental fragmentation.

13. Pessimistic readings, which include readings of the novel as one type of satire or another, have been prevalent since *The Confidence-Man* began to attract serious critical attention in the early 1950s, but a contrasting series of more sanguine interpretations has emerged as well: e.g., Philip Drew, "Appearance and Reality in Melville's *The Confidence-Man,*" *ELH* 31 (1964), 418–42; Paul Brodtkorb, Jr., "*The Confidence-Man:* The Con-Man as Hero," *Studies in the Novel* 1 (1969), 421–35; Warwick Wadlington, *The Confidence Game in American Literature* (Princeton: Princeton University Press, 1975), pp. 137–70. The judgments of the novel's artistic merit range from Newton Arvin's "unendurably repetitious" (*Herman Melville* [New York: William Sloane, 1950]) to H. Bruce Franklin's "Melville's most nearly perfect work" (*The Wake of the Gods: Melville's Mythology* [Stanford: Stanford University Press, 1963]).

14. All quotations are from Elizabeth Foster's edition, *The Confidence-Man: His Masquerade* (New York: Hendricks House, 1954), and give page numbers from this edition following the quotation.

15. The most exhaustive study of these materials is Franklin's *The Wake of the Gods* and his annotations to the Library of Literature edition of *The Confidence-Man* (Indianapolis: Bobbs-Merrill, 1967); Franklin simply errs in overestimating the authority that these alternative myths and religions are given in the novel. See also Foster's Introduction; John W. Shroeder, "Sources and Symbols for Melville's *Confidence-Man,*" *PMLA* 66 (1951), 363–80 (on parallels with *Pilgrim's Progress* and Hawthorne's "Celestial Railroad"); and Edgar A. Dryden, *Melville's Thematics of Form* (Baltimore: Johns Hopkins University Press, 1968), pp. 187–93 (on the possible role of Burton and Bayle in Melville's skepticism toward the Bible).

16. *Melville: The Critical Heritage,* ed. Watson G. Branch (London: Routledge and Kegan Paul, 1974), p. 370. See especially Johannes Bergmann, "The Original Confidence Man," *American Quarterly* 21 (1969), 560–77; John

Seelye, "Introduction," *The Confidence-Man*, A Facsimile of the First Edition (San Francisco: Chandler Publishing, 1968), and Susan Kuhlmann, *Knave, Fool and Genius: The Confidence Man as He Appears in Nineteenth-Century American Fiction* (Chapel Hill: University of North Carolina Press, 1973), pp. 11–32.

17. See Merton M. Sealts, Jr., *Melville's Reading* (Madison: University of Wisconsin Press, 1966), nos. 9 and 324.

18. *Israel Potter: His Fifty Years of Exile, Works*, XI, 69.

19. In the Boston *Christian Examiner* (1855); quoted by Seelye, "Introduction," p. xxvii.

20. Branch, *Melville: The Critical Heritage*, pp. 373, 374.

21. In Calvinist tradition the books of the Apocrypha are generally rejected and are not usually printed with the Old and New Testaments. But a Bible Melville purchased in 1850 and annotated had the conventional Anglican arrangement referred to here.

22. For such an interpretation, which is nevertheless a useful corrective to other interpretative excesses, see the Ph.D. dissertation of Margaret Reed Bruner, "The Gospel According to Herman Melville: A Reading of *The Confidence-Man: His Masquerade*" (Vanderbilt, 1971).

23. See Ursula Brumm, "Christ and Adam as 'Figures' in American Literature," in *The American Puritan Imagination*, pp. 199–201.

24. *A Week on the Concord and Merrimack Rivers*, in *The Writings of Henry David Thoreau* (Boston: Houghton Mifflin, 1893), I, 89–90. Melville did read Thoreau's *Week* in 1850; for the most recent assessment of Melville's attitude toward the transcendentalists, see Hershel Parker, "Melville's Satire of Emerson and Thoreau: An Evaluation of the Evidence," *American Transcendental Quarterly* 7, pt. 1 (1970), 61–67.

25. As Robert Alter also remarks, *Partial Magic*, p. 128. Edward Rosenberry, *Melville and the Comic Spirit* (Cambridge: Harvard University Press, 1955), pp. 146–48, mentions Fielding but concentrates on less formal resemblances to Sterne.

26. Melville's markings and annotations of *Don Quixote* are recorded in vol. IV of Wilson Walker Cowen's Ph.D. dissertation, "Melville's Annotations" (Harvard, 1965), pp. 209–37. My interpretation is based on Cowen's transcriptions. Melville does allude to Don Quixote as a character in *White Jacket* (in Chapters 13 and 54), but the allusions do not suggest an intimate knowledge of the novel. Harry Levin argues, without adducing any further evidence, for the relevance of *Don Quixote* to *Moby-Dick* in an essay in *Cervantes Across the Centuries*.

27. See Elizabeth Foster's Introduction, pp. xxiii–iv, for an account of the apparent chronology of composition; see also Watson G. Branch, "The Genesis, Composition, and Structure of *The Confidence-Man*," *Nineteenth-Century Fiction* 27 (1973), 424–48. As the well-known story of Melville's "discovery" of Shakespeare in the midst of writing *Moby-Dick* shows, he remained open to literary suggestion in the course of writing his novels and was capable of radically transforming them *in medias res*.

28. Cowen, "Melville's Annotations," IV, 221. Cf. IV, 215, where Melville marks the first mention of Cide Hamete Benengeli, in Chapter 9 of the first part, with a double check.

29. Ibid., 229.

30. Ibid., 218; cf. IV, 220–21, 236–37.

31. Ibid., 232. Cf. the marked passage on p. 217 about knights-errant as "God's ministers upon earth."

32. *Pierre, or the Ambiguities*, ed. Henry A. Murray (New York: Hendricks House, 1949), pp. 165–66.

33. *Mark Twain-Howells Letters*, ed. Henry Nash Smith and William M. Gibson, with Frederick Anderson (Cambridge: Harvard University Press, 1960), I, 91–92.

34. Claudio Guillén, "Toward a Definition of the Picaresque," p. 82. I am invoking Guillén's eight-point characterization of the picaresque novel "in the strict sense" here.

35. *My Literary Passions* (New York: Harper and Bros., 1910), p. 107. Wadlington offers a suggestive analysis of the "courtship" relationship between Twain and Howells; see *The Confidence Game in American Literature*, pp. 220 ff.

36. *Adventures of Huckleberry Finn*, A Facsimile of the First Edition (San Francisco: Chandler Publishing, 1962), p. 32. Twain's library and reading have been exhaustively catalogued by Alan Gribben in *Mark Twain's Library: A Reconstruction* (Boston: G. K. Hall, 1980), which documents Twain's familiarity with *Don Quixote* and *Gil Blas*. If Twain did know any of the Spanish picaresque novels, the record does not survive.

37. *My Literary Passions*, pp. 106–7. The earliest American example of this dialectic that I am aware of is Henry Brackenridge's *Modern Chivalry* (1792–1815). In this novel, Captain John Farrago is an idealized Quixote, imagining a nonexistent democratic society. Teague Oregan, ostensibly his Sancho, is in fact a more actively picaresque delinquent and rogue, whom Farrago must continually pursue and correct.

38. *"Magic" Realism in Cervantes: Don Quixote, as Seen Through Tom Sawyer and The Idiot*, trans. Robert S. Rudder (Berkeley: University of California Press, 1970), p. 23. See pp. 81–95 for an interesting discussion of Tom's "Evasion" plot as an interpretation of Don Quixote's freeing of the galley slaves.

39. *A Connecticut Yankee in King Arthur's Court*, A Facsimile of the First Edition (San Francisco: Chandler Publishing, 1963). All quotations from the novel are from this edition and give page numbers in parentheses following the quote.

40.
> Of all tales 'tis the saddest—and more sad,
> Because it makes us smile: his hero's right,
> And still pursues the right;—to curb the bad,
> His only object, and 'gainst odds to fight,
> His guerdon: 'tis his virtue makes him mad!
> But his adventures form a sorry sight;—
>
> . . . . .
>
> Cervantes smiled Spain's Chivalry away.
> A single laugh demolished the right arm
> Of his own country;—seldom since that day
> Has Spain had heroes.

(*Byron's Don Juan*, A Variorum Edition, ed. Truman Guy Steffan and Willis W. Pratt [Austin: University of Texas Press, 1958], III, 363–64 [Canto XIII, 9, 11].) For a good discussion of this element in Twain and Cervantes, see

Roger B. Salomon, "Mark Twain and Victorian Nostalgia," in *Patterns of Commitment in American Literature*, ed. Marston LaFrance (Toronto: University of Toronto Press, 1967).

41. Ed. Willis Wager (New York: Heritage Press, 1944), p. 273.

42. *Huckleberry Finn*, p. 366; McNamara, "Huck Lights Out for the Territory: Mark Twain's Unpublished Sequel," *University of Windsor (Ontario) Review* 2, no. 1 (1966), 68–74.

43. *Mark Twain's Mysterious Stranger Manuscripts*, ed. William M. Gibson, The Mark Twain Papers (Berkeley: University of California Press, 1969), p. 405.

44. Charles S. Holmes, "*A Connecticut Yankee in King Arthur's Court*: Mark Twain's Fable of Uncertainty," *South Atlantic Quarterly* 61 (1962), 472.

45. See especially Robert H. Wilson, "Malory in the *Connecticut Yankee*," *Texas Studies in English* 27 (1948), 185–206; James D. Williams, "The Use of History in Mark Twain's *A Connecticut Yankee*," *PMLA* 80 (1965), 102–10; and Rodney O. Rogers, "Twain, Taine, and Lecky: The Genesis of a Passage in *A Connecticut Yankee*," *Modern Language Quarterly* 34 (1973), 436–47.

46. *Mark Twain: The Critical Heritage*, ed. Frederick Anderson (New York: Barnes and Noble, 1971), p. 154.

47. See Justin Kaplan, *Mr. Clemens and Mark Twain* (New York: Simon and Schuster, 1966), pp. 280–311, on the relationship between this disastrous economic venture for Twain and the writing of *A Connecticut Yankee*.

48. For a discussion of the "situationalism" in Twain's earlier novel, see George C. Carrington, Jr., *The Dramatic Unity of Huckleberry Finn* (Columbus: Ohio State University Press, 1976), pp. 12–31. My analysis of *A Connecticut Yankee* has been aided by Carrington's book as well as by the excellent chapter on *Huckleberry Finn* in Wadlington's *The Confidence Game in American Literature*.

49. *Dramatic Unity*, p. 13.

50. *Labyrinths*, p. 41.

51. *Romances of Roguery*, I, 2.

Chapter Ten
1. T. J. Reed, *Thomas Mann: The Uses of Tradition* (Oxford: Clarendon Press, 1974), p. 403.

2. See *A Sketch of My Life*, trans. H. T. Lowe-Porter (New York: Alfred A. Knopf, 1960), p. 47. The complicated chronology of the composition of *Felix Krull* has been established by Hans Wysling in his and Paul Scherrer's *Quellenkritische Studien zum Werk Thomas Manns* (Bern and Munich: Francke Verlag, 1967), pp. 234–57.

3. *The Story of a Novel: The Genesis of Doctor Faustus*, trans. Richard and Clara Winston (New York: Alfred A. Knopf, 1961), p. 24.

4. *An Exceptional Friendship: The Correspondence of Thomas Mann and Erich Kahler*, trans. Richard and Clara Winston (Ithaca: Cornell University Press, 1975), p. 153.

5. "Ruckkehr," *Gesammelte Werke* (Frankfurt: S. Fischer Verlag, 1960), XI, 530 (my translation).

6. "Ruckkehr," *Werke*, XI, 530.

7. *An Exceptional Friendship*, p. 140.

8. See *The Story of a Novel*, p. 77. Mann wrote a brief introduction for a Swedish edition of *Simplicissimus* in 1944 (*Gesammelte Werke*, XIII, 443–44).
9. *The Hesse-Mann Letters*, ed. Anni Carlsson and Volker Michels, trans. Ralph Mannheim (New York: Harper and Row, 1975), p. 9.
10. *Modern Language Quarterly* 12 (1951), 183–200.
11. *Briefe, 1948–1955*, ed. Erika Mann (Frankfurt: S. Fischer Verlag, 1965), 223 (my translation). Mann also received at this time an article by Henry Hatfield, "Realism in the German Novel," *Comparative Literature* 3 (1951), 234–52, which discussed the debt of Grimmelshausen to the Spanish picaresque. "Your discussions of *Simplicissimus* and the picaresque novel particularly fascinated me," Mann wrote back, "—for personal reasons, since picaresque jests happen to be occupying me once again" (*Letters of Thomas Mann, 1899–1955*, ed. and trans. Richard and Clara Winston [New York: Alfred A. Knopf, 1971], p. 633).
12. *Mythology and Humanism: The Correspondence of Thomas Mann and Karl Kerényi*, trans. Alexander Gelley (Ithaca: Cornell University Press, 1975), pp. 46–47.
13. *Mythology and Humanism*, p. 210. Mann is remarking on the coincidence of the publication of *Felix Krull* at roughly the same time as Kerényi (and Jung's) essays on the trickster figure in Paul Radin's *Der göttliche Schelm* (1954); see pp. 239–41 above.
14. *An Exceptional Friendship*, p. 139. Commenting on *Doctor Faustus*, Mann wrote, "The novel of the era, to the extent that I have been able to do it, at any rate, has been done. But where may the naïve and unreflective epic, the *Adventurous Simplicissimus* of these times, come from? I look vainly around for even the possibility. For the qualities that would equip a young fellow to survive the mess will scarcely make him fit to immortalize it." As several critics have pointed out, one such *Simplicissimus* of the times was to be Günter Grass's *The Tin Drum*, published in 1959, though in a much less naive and unreflective mode than *Felix Krull*.
15. "Thomas Manns *Felix Krull*: Schelmenroman und Bildungsroman," *Untersuchungen zur Literatur als Geschichte*, ed. Vincent J. Günther, Helmut Koopmann, Peter Pütz, Hans Joachim Schrimpf (Berlin: Erich Schmidt Verlag, 1973), p. 557.
16. *Letters*, pp. 119, 125, 152.
17. The term is Erich Heller's, who discusses *Simplicissimus* briefly in *The Ironic German: A Study of Thomas Mann* (Boston: Little, Brown, 1958), p. 282. One can see a similar strategy of reversion to type in Mann's comments in 1953 about *The Magic Mountain* itself vis-à-vis the earlier *Abentteurroman*. "Goethe's Wilhelm Meister—is he too not a guileless fool?... Here we see Goethe's great novel, too, falling within the Quester category. And after all, what else is the German *Bildungsroman* (educational novel)—a classification to which both *The Magic Mountain* and *Wilhelm Meister* belong—than the sublimation and spiritualization of the novel of adventure?" ("The Making of *The Magic Mountain*," *The Magic Mountain*, trans. H. T. Lowe-Porter [New York: Alfred A. Knopf, 1958], p. 728).
18. On the close verbal parallels between these episodes, see Heller, p. 282, and Anthony W. Riley, "Three Cryptic Quotations in Thomas Mann's *Felix Krull*," *JEGP* 65 (1966), 106 n.

19. Johann Jakob Cristoffel von Grimmelshausen, *Simplicius Simplicissimus*, trans. George Schulz-Behrend (Indianapolis: Bobbs-Merrill, 1965), p. 174.
20. *Doctor Faustus*, trans. H. T. Lowe-Porter (New York: Alfred A. Knopf, 1948), p. 372.
21. *Confessions of Felix Krull, Confidence Man: The Early Years*, trans. Denver Lindley (New York: Alfred A. Knopf, 1955), p. 247. All further quotations are from this edition, with page numbers in parentheses.
22. *The Standard Edition of the Complete Psychological Works of Sigmund Freud*, ed. and trans. James Strachey (London: Hogarth Press, 1959), IX, 153.
23. Paul Radin, *The Trickster: A Study in American Indian Mythology*, with commentaries by Karl Kerényi and C. G. Jung (London: Routledge and Kegan Paul, 1956).
24. Ibid., p. 200.
25. Ibid., p. 207.
26. Ibid., p. 190.
27. Ibid., p. 176.
28. See Frank J. Kearful, "The Role of Hermes in the *Confessions of Felix Krull*," *Modern Fiction Studies* 17 (1971), 91–108, and Donald F. Nelson, *Portrait of the Artist as Hermes: A Study of Myth and Psychology in Thomas Mann's Felix Krull*, University of North Carolina Studies in the Germanic Languages and Literatures no. 70 (Chapel Hill: University of North Carolina Press, 1971). Both these studies emphasize the parallels with Jung's alchemical Hermes as well as with Kerényi's mythological investigations.
29. See Hans Wysling, "Thomas Manns Pläne zur Fortsetzung des 'Krull,'" *Dokumente und Untersuchungen: Beiträge zur Thomas-Mann-Forschung* (Bern and Munich: Francke Verlag, 1974).
30. "Ruckkehr," *Werke*, XI, 531 (my translation).
31. On this aspect of *Felix Krull*, see Robert B. Heilman, "Variations on Picaresque (*Felix Krull*)," *Sewanee Review* 66 (1958), 547–77. Heilman's very useful discussion is limited only by its tendency to regard the picaresque in an archetypal and dialectical manner quite close to Mann's own.
32. See Eva Schiffer, "Changes in an Episode: A Note on *Felix Krull*," *Modern Language Quarterly* 24 (1963), 257–62.
33. See Anthony W. Riley, "Humour Plus Morality: An Aspect of Thomas Mann's *Felix Krull*," *Humanities Association Bulletin* 27 (1976), 257–59, on Paul Kammerer's *Allgemeine Biologie* (1915) and Lincoln Barnett's *The Universe and Dr. Einstein* (1948); on the Chicago Museum of Natural History, see Mann's letter to Herman Hesse of October 14, 1951 (*Letters*, p. 631).
34. *Freud, Goethe, Wagner*, trans. H. T. Lowe-Porter (New York: Alfred A. Knopf, 1937), pp. 39–40. For some of Mann's more canon- and tradition-minded pronouncements on the novel, see "Die Kunst des Romans," *Werke*, X, 348–62.
35. An intelligent and wide-ranging study of this familiar side of modernism is John J. White's *Mythology and the Modern Novel* (Princeton: Princeton University Press, 1971), which argues among other things that the phenomenon is not limited to novels of the early part of the century.
36. *Nausea*, trans. Lloyd Alexander (New York: New Directions, 1964), p. 56.
37. See in this regard the writings of Ihab Hassan, e.g., "Fiction and Fu-

ture: An Extravaganza for Voice and Tape," *Paracriticisms* (Urbana: University of Illinois Press, 1975), which catalogues a number of the more ludic examples of recent experimental fiction. The "Map of Vanishing Fictions" which Hassan provides there, with the "Novel of Silence" on the left and the "Fantastic Novel" on the right, is still well within the modernist territory, and the examples of the unprecedented that Hassan offers sound a note that is distinctly familiar on the level of theory—for example, Ishmael Reed in *Yellow Back Radio Broke-Down:* "What's your beef with me Bo Schmo, what if I write circuses? No one says a novel has to be one thing. It can be anything it wants to be, a vaudeville show, the six o'clock news, the mumblings of wild men saddled by demons" (*Paracriticisms,* p. 109).

38. One of the most recent studies of the phenomenon is also one of the best—see Keith Cohen's *Film and Fiction: The Dynamics of Exchange* (New Haven: Yale University Press, 1979).

39. For Poe and Matthews, as well as for other theoretical statements, see *Short Story Theories,* ed. Charles E. May (Athens: Ohio University Press, 1976); the quotation is from p. 54. The modernity of the short story is contested by some theorists, but I am concerned only with the type that emerged within nineteenth-century novelistic culture. The classic statement of the opposition between novel and short story is Boris Eichenbaum's "O. Henry and the Theory of the Short Story," in *Readings in Russian Poetics,* ed. Ladislav Matejka and Krystyna Pomorska (Cambridge: MIT Press, 1971).

40. *Labyrinths,* pp. 41–42.

41. Ibid., p. 242.

42. Ibid., p. 44. A contrasting transformation of *Don Quixote* is provided by Unamuno, who in *Our Lord Don Quixote* treats Cervantes's text as a Spanish national Scripture. His earlier remarks "On the Reading and Interpretation of *Don Quixote*" provide an interesting parallel with Borges's reader-oriented idealism: "If the Bible came to have an inestimable value it is because of what generations of men put into it by their reading, as their spirits fed there; and it is well known that there is hardly a passage in it that has not been interpreted in hundreds of ways, depending on the interpreter.... Of less importance is whether the authors of the different books of the Bible meant to say what the theologians, mystics, and commentators see there; the important fact is that, thanks to this immense labor of generations through the centuries, the Bible is a perennial fountain of consolation, hope, and heartfelt inspiration. Why should not the same process undergone by Holy Scripture take place with *Don Quixote,* which should be the national Bible of the patriotic religion of Spain?" (trans. Anthony Kerrigan, *Selected Works of Miguel de Unamuno,* III [Princeton: Princeton University Press, 1967], 452).

43. Israel Shenker, "Whither the Short Story (or Is It Wither)?" *New York Times,* 21 November 1970, p. 33. Barth mentions Kafka along with Beckett and Borges as the writers of short fiction who helped change his views. In 1966 Barth spoke of Beckett and Borges as "the writers of the last quarter century most comparable—in their extraordinary vision, consummate gifts and probable lasting stature—of the 'old masters' of 20th Century fiction: Proust, Kafka, Joyce, Mann. The irony (and the great problem for their successors) is that each of them in his way brings narrative literature to a kind of ultimacy, or finishing point..." ("A Gift of Books," *Holiday* 40 [December,

1966], 171. Barth seems to have synthesized the minimal and the maximal forms of fiction in his recent epistolary extravaganza, *Letters* (New York: G. P. Putnam, 1979).

44. "The Literature of Exhaustion," *The Atlantic* 220 (August, 1967), 33.

45. *Lost in the Funhouse: Fiction for Print, Tape, Live Voice* (New York: Bantam Books, 1969), p. 110. The speaker is identified by Barth in his "Seven Additional Author's Notes," p. xi. Of his intermedia experiments Barth later claimed, "I did it almost in reaction to McLuhan. Some of the pieces utilize the oral tradition, and God knows I have the greatest love for the voice. But most of [the stories] get back to the special qualities . . . of print." Barth went on to speak of "the stability of the print medium. You can last in it; print hasn't changed all that much since Gutenberg. Just because we can't think of print as an absolute anymore doesn't mean that it's obsolete" (quoted by Douglas M. David, "The End is a Beginning for Barth's 'Funhouse,'" *National Observer*, 16 September 1968, p. 19).

46. John Enck, "John Barth: An Interview," *Wisconsin Studies in Contemporary Literature* 6 (1965), 7.

47. Barth drew on Lawrence Wroth's biographical speculations on Cooke in his facsimile edition of *The Maryland Muse* in *Proceedings of the American Antiquarian Society*, n.s. 44, pt. 2 (17 October 1934), 267–335. For discussion of Barth's use of this information and the poem, see Philip E. Diser, "The Historical Ebenezer Cooke," *Critique* 10, no. 3 (1968), 48–59, and David Morrell, *John Barth: An Introduction* (University Park: Pennsylvania State University Press, 1976), pp. 31–41.

48. See Joseph Weixlmann, "The Use and Abuse of Smith's *Generall Historie* in John Barth's *The Sot-Weed Factor*," *Studies in American Humor* 2 (1975), 105–15.

49. See Alan Holder, "'What Marvelous Plot . . . Was Afoot?': History in Barth's *The Sot-Weed Factor*," *American Quarterly* 20 (1968), 596–664.

50. Barth elaborates on this reversal in an interview with Joe David Bellamy: "We have such a long history, in the history of fiction, of novels that pretend to be anything but novels. The novel starts that way. *Don Quixote* pretends to be an historical record translated [sic] by the Cid Hamete Benengeli. . . . I thought it might be interesting to write a novel which simply imitates the form of the novel, rather than imitating all these other kinds of documents. In other words, it pretends to be a piece of fiction" ("Having It Both Ways: A Conversation between John Barth and Joe David Bellamy," *New American Review* 15 [April, 1972], 150). By "pretending" to be a novel, *The Sot-Weed Factor* suggests its historicity inversely.

51. *The Sot-Weed Factor* (Garden City, N.Y.: Doubleday, 1960). All further quotations are from this, the first edition. Barth made some minor revisions and condensations in a second edition of 1967.

52. See, with allowances for Barth's deliberately whimsical sense of performance, his statements in Enck and in his own manifesto "Muse, Spare Me," in *The Sense of the Sixties*, ed. Edward Quinn and Paul J. Dolan (New York: The Free Press, 1968), p. 440.

53. "The Mother of Us All: Pocahontas Reconsidered," *Kenyon Review* 24 (1962), 392, cited by Weixlmann. Young was a colleague and friend of Barth's at the University of Pennsylvania, and Morrell reports, pp. 43–44, that Barth consulted Young's work in progress while writing *The Sot-Weed Factor*. On

earlier and later satires of the Pocahontas story, see Leslie Fiedler, *The Return of the Vanishing American* (New York: Stein and Day, 1968), pp. 81-83, 150-68.

54. Gerald Gillespie discusses these pairings and triangles in a useful way in "Rogues, Fools, and Satyrs: Ironic Ghosts in American Fiction," in *Proceedings of the Comparative Literature Symposium* 5 (1972), 100-101. Barth's fondness for triangular relationships is obvious in all his fiction, including, according to Harold Farwell, his M.A. thesis at Johns Hopkins entitled "Shirt of Nessus" ("John Barth's Tenuous Affirmation: 'The Absurd, Unending Possibility of Love,'" *Georgia Review* 28 [1974], 292).

55. "The Literature of Exhaustion," p. 30.

56. Ibid.

57. *The Magic Mountain*, p. 496.

58. "Petition," *Lost in the Funhouse*, p. 68.

Chapter Eleven

1. *A Tale of A Tub*, ed. A. C. Guthkelch and D. Nichol Smith, 2d ed. (Oxford: Clarendon Press, 1950), p. 31.

2. See, for example, Robert L. Patten's discussion of the far-reaching consequences of the introduction of serial publication: "*Pickwick Papers* and the Development of Serial Fiction," *Rice University Studies* 61, no. 1 (1975), 51-74. A more systematic and general survey, especially of modern developments in publishing, can be found in Robert Escarpit, *The Book Revolution* (London and Paris: George G. Harrap and UNESCO, 1966).

3. Translation from "Las versiones homéricas" by Alfred J. MacAdam in "Translation as Metaphor: Three Versions of Borges," *Modern Language Notes* 90 (1975), 749.

4. *Reason in History: A General Introduction to the Philosophy of History,* trans. Robert S. Hartman (Indianapolis: Bobbs-Merrill, 1953), p. 75.

5. "The Rhetoric of History," *Doing History* (Bloomington: Indiana University Press, 1971), p. 47. Hexter's emphasis on practice is useful for scholars who wish to avoid some of the theoretical controversies within and without the discipline at present. A convincing rapprochement between the realist and idealist schools of history on the basis of their common practice is offered by Harriet Gilliam in "The Dialectics of Realism and Idealism in Modern Historiographic Theory," *History and Theory* 15 (1976), 231-56. I am indebted to this article and to Gilliam's work in progress on "The Modern Novel as Fictive History" for some of the ideas in this chapter. See also J. Hillis Miller's "Narrative and History," *ELH* 41 (1974), 455-73, and Warner Berthoff's "Fiction, History, Myth: Notes Toward the Discrimination of Narrative Forms," *Fiction and Events* (New York: E. P. Dutton, 1971).

6. A vigorous debate over this question of laws in historical explanation has focused on Carl G. Hempel's "covering law" theory. A convenient selection of the positions is provided in Patrick Gardiner, ed., *Theories of History* (New York: The Free Press, 1959).

7. "History and Fiction as Modes of Comprehension," *New Literary History* 1 (1970), 541-58.

8. "The Fictions of Factual Representation," in *The Literature of Fact*, ed. Angus Fletcher (New York: Columbia University Press, 1976), p. 28. The classic of this literary analysis of historical writing is Francis Cornford's

Notes to Pages 267–71

Thucydides Mythistoricus (London: Edward Arnold, 1907); see also White's own *Metahistory: The Historical Imagination in Nineteenth Century Europe* (Baltimore: Johns Hopkins University Press, 1973), and Leo Braudy, *Narrative Form in History and Fiction: Hume, Fielding, and Gibbon*.

9. "Foucault Decoded: Notes from Underground," *History and Theory* 12 (1973), 53–54.

10. The distinction between epistemological coherence and correspondence, in literature and history respectively, is open to question; Avrom Fleishman challenges R. G. Collingwood's version of such a contrast in his *The English Historical Novel* (Baltimore: Johns Hopkins University Press, 1971), pp. 4–5. But the philosophical uncertainties of a particular formulation should not be allowed to obscure the general difference in cognitive function, culturally defined.

11. *Moll Flanders*, p. 7.

12. *A Portrait of the Artist as a Young Man* (New York: Viking Press, 1964), pp. 59, 223.

13. *Great Expectations* (London: Oxford University Press, 1953), p. 393. Jaggers is of course borrowing liberally from the Sermon on the Mount here.

14. The best discussions of this semiotic transformation in the novel that I am aware of are in Gilles Deleuze, *Proust and Signs*, trans. Richard Howard (New York: George Braziller, 1972), and Peter Brooks, *The Melodramatic Imagination*. Jonathan Culler's *Flaubert: The Uses of Uncertainty* (Ithaca: Cornell University Press, 1974) emphasizes the other side of the dialectic: the collapse of preexisting textual structures of meaning into banality, their loss of significance as well as reference. The ne plus ultra of both these processes may be observed at the end of Gabriel García Márquez's *One Hundred Years of Solitude*, where Aureliano, the last surviving member of the Buendía family reads the prophetic history of the family, including his own life, written "a hundred years ahead of time" by the gypsy Melquides. As he reaches the end of the parchments written in Sanskrit and ciphers, he realizes that his reading of the final lines of the text will coincide with the destruction of the family and the "city of mirrors (or mirages)" they have founded (trans. Gregory Rabassa [New York: Harper and Row, 1970], pp. 421–22).

15. "*Don Quixote*: Story or History?" *Modern Philology* 63 (1965), 1–11.

16. *Joseph Andrews*, p. 185.

17. *On Heroes, Hero-Worship and the Heroic in History*, ed. P. C. Parr (London: Oxford University Press, 1920), p. 14.

18. *The Sot-Weed Factor*, p. 725.

19. The most specific and yet the most theoretically wide-ranging study to date of the novel's critique of history is Michael Holquist's *Dostoevsky and the Novel* (Princeton: Princeton University Press, 1977), which discusses each of Dostoevsky's major novels against the background of European historicism and the problematic Russian reception thereof.

20. "*Don Quixote*: Story or History?" p. 5.

21. Harriet Gilliam, "The Historical Novel: A Review and a Critique," *Clio* 1 (1972), 58. Fleishman's *The English Historical Novel*, which Gilliam is reviewing here, shows the way Scott's novels participate in the widespread historicism of their time and the way they are paradigmatic for a long series of later novels called historical, but it does not deal with the contrast and contradiction between the historian's and the novelist's use of similar data.

See, however, Fleishman's more recent *Fiction and the Ways of Knowing* (Austin: University of Texas Press, 1978), Chapter 1, which makes some acute distinctions between fictional, historical, and philosophical texts that parallel my own distinctions here.

22. *The Heart of Midlothian* (London: J. M. Dent, 1906), pp. [2], 10.

23. "Notes on the Novel," *The Dehumanization of Art and Other Writings on Art and Culture* (Garden City, N.Y.: Doubleday, 1956), p. 56.

24. Ronald Sukenick, *The Death of the Novel and Other Stories* (New York: Dial Press, 1969).

25. See, for example, Charles R. Larson, *The Novel in the Third World* (Washington, D.C.: Inscape Publishers, 1976), for a study of novels from Africa, the Caribbean, India, and the South Pacific.

26. N. I. Konrad, "Problems of Contemporary Comparative Literature," *Soviet Studies in Literature* 9, no. 1 (1972–73), 4.

27. "Literary History and Literary Modernity," *Blindness and Insight*, p. 151.

28. In addition to the work of Eric Havelock, e.g. *Preface to Plato* (Cambridge: Harvard University Press, 1963), and "The Preliteracy of the Greeks," see Jack Goody and Ian Watt, "The Consequences of Literacy," *Comparative Studies in Society and History* 5 (1962), 304–45.

29. Along with Keith Cohen's *Film and Fiction*, some useful discussions of these contemporary sister arts are George Bluestone, *Novels into Film* (Berkeley: University of California Press, 1966), and Edward Murray, *The Cinematic Imagination: Writers and the Motion Pictures* (New York: Frederick Ungar, 1972).

30. Herman P. Doezma, "An Interview with Carlos Fuentes," *Modern Fiction Studies* 18 (1973), 493.

31. Hackett Memorial Lecture Series (Austin: Institute of Latin American Studies, The University of Texas at Austin, 1976); a Spanish version was published in Mexico in the same year. As Cervantes wrote in Chapter 9 of the First Part upon discovering the rest of the manuscript of *Don Quixote*, "I needed all my caution to conceal the thrill I felt when the title of the book caught my ear."

32. Anthony Heilbut, "The Theatre of Memory," *Nation*, 25 December 1976, pp. 693–95.

33. *Terra Nostra*, trans. Margaret Sayer Peden (New York: Farrar, Straus and Giroux, 1976), p. 771. All further quotations give page numbers in parentheses.

34. Fuentes acknowledges his debt to Cohn and Yates in *Terra Nostra* itself; he cites Castro and other modern historians of Spain in *Don Quixote, or the Critique of Reading*. A number of other sources are established by Juan Goytisolo's review article, "Our Old New World," *Review* (Center for Inter-American Relations) 19 (1976), 5–24.

35. Cf. *Claude Lévi-Strauss: An Introduction*, trans. J. S. Bernstein and Maxine Bernstein (Ithaca: Cornell University Press, 1970), pp. 33–36, and *Terra Nostra*, esp. pp. 433–34. Another ethnographic detail apparently from Lévi-Strauss is the tattooed lips of Celestina and the Lady of the Butterflies; see the photograph of the Caduveo woman on Plate 5 of *Tristes Tropiques* (New York: Criterion Books, 1961).

36. Fuentes mentions his interest in Faulkner and Lawrence, as well as in

Dos Passos and Malcolm Lowry, in an interview in Luis Harss and Barbara Dohmann, *Into the Mainstream: Conversations with Latin-American Writers* (New York: Harper and Row, 1967).

37. *Don Quixote, or the Critique of Reading*, p. 51.

38. The conflation of Cervantes and Kafka may seem unlikely, but a comparison between *Don Quixote* and *The Castle* forms the basis of Marthe Robert's *The Old and the New: From Don Quixote to Kafka*.

Index

Achilles Tatius, 39, 40, 41
Addison, Joseph, 118, 183
Alemán, Mateo: *Guzmán de Alfarache*, allusions to in other novels, 66, 67, 68, 69, 72; castigation in, 38, 58–64, 73, 114, 293 n. 34; compared to other novels, 73, 103, 138, 236; mentioned, 12–13, 56, 57, 65; popularity of, 26, 55, 205; realism of, 21, 34, 35, 50, 71
Allegory, 3, 36, 200
Alter, Robert, 98
Ancients and moderns, quarrel of, 93, 94, 118, 119, 125, 133, 260
Apuleius: *Metamorphoses (The Golden Ass)*, influence on the novel, 42, 55, 290 n. 78; as romance, 39, 40, 41, 94, 120
Ariosto, Ludovico, 30, 36, 118
Aristotle, 14, 26, 105; influence in seventeenth and eighteenth centuries, 107, 111, 119; *Poetics*, 2, 3, 57; *Poetics*, influence in Renaissance, 13, 30, 31, 64, 82, 83, 118, 267; *Poetics*, parodied by novelists, 11, 121, 122, 130, 162
Arnold, Matthew, 7, 8
Auerbach, Erich, 46
Austen, Jane, 4, 165, 191
Avellaneda, Fernandez de, 85–86
Axton, William, 176

Babcock, Barbara, 43, 74
Baker, Ernest, 19
Bakhtin, Mikhail, 283 n. 36; historical poetics of, 17, 18, 20, 21, 22; on the "carnivalesque," 74, 75; on novelization, 167
Balzac, Honoré de, 15, 23, 165, 284 n. 18

Barnum, P. T., 205
Barth, John, 4, 24, 254; *Giles Goat-Boy*, 12, 252; "The Literature of Exhaustion," 258–59; *Lost in the Funhouse*, 253, 261; *The Sot-Weed Factor*, 252–60, 264, 270–71
Barthes, Roland, 14, 15, 16, 156–57, 284 n. 18
Bateson, Gregory, 186, 190
Battestin, Martin, 132
Beaumont, Francis, 38
Beckett, Samuel, 137, 252
Bellow, Saul, 24, 262
Benjamin, Walter, 31, 116
Bercovitch, Sacvan, 200
Bible, the: American Puritan attitudes toward, 200; in *The Confidence-Man*, 203–4, 206, 207, 208–10, 212, 214, 216, 314 n. 21; in *Don Quixote*, 87; in *Joseph Andrews*, 132; Reformation attitudes toward, 27, 28, 33, 43, 44, 48, 90, 273, 290 n. 3; in the Spanish picaresque, 53, 61, 63, 291 n. 20; in *Terra Nostra*, 278; in *Tristram Shandy*, 159–60, 306 n. 48; in *Vanity Fair*, 193, 194
Berkeley, George, 154
Beyle, Henri [pseud. Stendhal], 191, 192, 193, 271
Bildungsroman: German tradition of, 3, 165, 170–71, 235, 241; as novelistic paradigm, 80, 171–72, 202, 246, 249, 266
Blake, Wiliam, 153, 304 n. 27
Boccaccio, Giovanni: *Decameron*, 74, 75–76, 250, 251
Booth, Wayne, 9, 10
Borges, Jorge Luis, 1, 24, 175, 265; "Parable of Cervantes and the Quixote," 4, 219, 308 n. 25;

325

"Partial Magic in the *Quixote*," 42, 78; "Pierre Menard, Author of the *Quixote*," 71, 230, 251–52, 254
Brackenridge, Henry, 255, 315 n. 37
Brecht, Bertolt, 272
Brodhead, Richard, 201
Brontë, Charlotte, 184
Brontë, Emily, 165
Brooks, Cleanth, 2
Brooks, Peter, 164, 165
Brown, Homer O., 112
Browne, Sir Thomas, 143, 146
Bunyan, John, 194, 200
Burkhardt, Sigurd, 149, 155–56
Burney, Charles, 146
Burney, Frances, 165
Burton, Robert, 143, 146, 147
Butler, Samuel, 95
Butor, Michel, 248, 284 n. 18
Byron, George Gordon, Lord, 220

Calvin, John, 62
Canonical literature: absorption of the novel into, 58, 139, 140, 143, 182, 195–96; modernist redefinition of, 245, 247, 249; novel's critique of, 13, 32, 49, 94, 96, 126, 210, 260; and popular genres, 12, 39, 40, 95, 135; romantic redefinition of, 136, 162–67
Carlyle, Thomas, 188, 227, 266
Carrington, George, 227
Carroll, Lewis. *See* Dodgson, Charles Lutwidge
Cary, Joyce, 182
Cash, Arthur, 140
Castilo Solorzano, Alonso de, 64
Castro, Americo, 33, 275, 288 n. 55
Cervantes, Miguel de: biography mentioned in fiction, 142, 153, 277–79; *Don Quixote* and Avellaneda's sequel, 56, 85–86; —— and canonical literature, 4, 7, 13, 28–29, 30, 82–83, 260; —— and Carlos Fuentes, 274, 277–80; —— and earlier literature, 36, 42, 74–76; —— and English Renais-

sance literature, 38, 89–92; —— and Dickens, 168–69, 174–75, 176–77, 182, 195; ——, eighteenth-century English reception of, 118, 120–21, 139–40, 141–42; —— as exemplary novel, 20, 22, 24, 162, 165, 171, 251, 262–65; —— and Fielding, 117, 119, 121, 122, 123–34; ——, First Part of, 77–82; ——, French reception of, 39, 94–95; ——, generic inclusiveness of, 11, 46, 74; —— and historiography, 186, 268, 270; ——, "idle reader" in, 25, 26–27, 33, 77–84, 161; —— and John Barth, 252, 253, 254, 256; —— and Melville, 212–15, 216, 217, 231, 256; ——, nineteenth-century English and European reception of, 167–68, 172–74, 192, 271; ——, origins of the novel in, 24–27, 28–29, 93; ——, realism of, 9, 12, 21, 73; ——, Second Part of, 62–63, 83–89, 286 n. 31; ——, seventeenth-century English reception of, 95; —— and the Spanish picaresque novel, 1, 55–56, 57, 66, 71–74; —— and Sterne, 142–47, 150, 157; —— and Thackeray, 182–83, 184, 194; —— and Twain, 218–21, 222, 230, 231; *Exemplary Stories*, 60, 71, 72, 77, 250; literary intentions of, 76–77, 263, 282 n. 25; *Persiles and Sigismunda*, 13, 42, 77
Challe, Robert, 94
Chandler, Frank Wadleigh, 65, 98, 231
Channing, Wiliam Ellery, 209
Chapelain, Jean, 119
Chariton, 39, 40, 41
Cibber, Colley, 123, 133
Cleland, John, 156
Clemens, Samuel Langhorne [pseud. Mark Twain]; *A Connecticut Yankee in King Arthur's Court*, 168, 219, 220–30, 254; *Huckleberry Finn*, 11, 217,

218–19, 220–21, 227, 228; and
literary tradition, 199, 217–18,
219, 220, 222, 227, 231, 255, 260;
The Mysterious Stranger, 221
Cohn, Norman, 275
Coleridge, Samuel Taylor, 164,
173, 200, 284 n. 16
Coley, W. B., 104
Colie, Rosalie, 49, 56, 143
Comedy: as classical genre, 94,
116, 122, 128, 145; as popular
genre, 97, 98, 99–100, 101, 103,
131, 222–24
Congreve, William, 111
Cooke, Ebenezer (American poet),
253, 254, 259
Cooper, James Fenimore, 201
Criminal biography, 95, 97, 98, 99,
100–103, 114, 299 n. 31
Culler, Jonathan, 282 n. 28,
282 n. 29
Curtius, E. R., 10, 32

Dante Alighieri, 173
Davenant, Sir William, 119
Davis, Walter, 36, 37, 289 n. 64
Defoe, Daniel: criminal literature
of, 100, 101–2; on *Don Quixote,*
124; influence on American literature, 205, 220, 253; and
literary tradition, 23, 39, 95–97,
104, 105, 134, 263; *Moll Flanders,*
135, 183; —— and canonical literature, 96–98, 102, 111, 162;
—— and historiography, 116,
268; —— and popular literature,
98–101, 103; ——, problem of
value in, 105–16; and the picaresque novel, 98–103, 113, 168;
realism of, 4, 11, 20–21; *Robinson
Crusoe,* 105, 176
Derrida, Jacques, 151, 286 n. 29,
305 n. 32
Dickens, Charles, 6, 169, 170, 178,
201, 274; *All the Year Round,* 182;
Great Expectations, 12, 171–72,
269–70; *Hard Times,* 166;
Pickwick Papers, ceremonial observances in, 178–82, 224; ——
and the picaresque, 168–70, 172,

174, 176, 177; ——, Quixotic
nature of, 168–70, 172, 173,
174–76, 177, 181–82; and Thackeray, 182, 185, 186, 191, 194,
195; use of eighteenth-century
novel, 23, 174–76, 199, 230
Diderot, Denis, 8, 159, 165, 166,
304 n. 24
Dodgson, Charles Lutwidge
[pseud. Lewis Carroll], 217, 221
Donne, John, 89
Dostoevsky, Fyodor, 169, 192, 214,
262, 282 n. 25, 307 n. 12, 322
n. 19
Douglas, Mary, 180
Drama: compares with romances,
40, 121; and the novel, 6, 56, 57,
58, 273; and the novel in the
eighteenth century, 125–26, 127,
131–32, 145, 300 n. 45, 307 n. 14;
and the novel in the Renaissance, 25, 38–39, 46, 89–90, 91,
131, 307 n. 14; and the novel in
romanticism, 166, 167, 171, 272;
in Melville's novels, 201, 216–17;
relationship to novel in modernism, 250, 251, 266, 272

Edwards, Jonathan, 154
Eisenstein, Elizabeth, 26, 28
Eisenstein, Sergei, 274
Eliot, George (Mary Ann Cross,
née Evans), 5–7, 191, 201, 204
Eliot, T. S., 232, 297 n. 27
Elliott, J. H., 31, 33, 34
Emerson, Ralph Waldo, 199, 202,
209
Enríque Gómez, Antonio, 65
300 n. 1
Epic: allusions to in novel, 11, 40,
54, 87, 89, 121, 163; contrasted
with novel, 7, 21–22, 25, 119,
122
Epistolary novel, 54, 165
Erasmus, Desiderius, 26, 33,
43–45, 47, 48
Espinel, Vicente, 57, 65
"Essay on the New Species of
Writing," 125, 140, 141
Estevanillo Gonzalez, 65

286 n. 34, 297 n. 25; in prose,
36, 38, 44, 45, 75, 296 n. 10
Ortega y Gasset, José, 7, 20, 265,
272

Parker, Alexander, 30, 31, 64, 68,
98
Parker, Theodore, 209
Paulson, Ronald, 129, 298 n. 14
Paz, Octavio, 277
Perrault, Charles, 125
Perry, Ben Edwin, 41, 289 n. 72
Petronius Arbiter, Gaius, 39, 40,
41, 47, 120, 290 n. 78
Phillips, John, 124
Piozzi, Hester, 139
Plato, 26, 206, 207
Poe, Edgar Allan, 200, 251,
312 n. 8, 313 n. 12
Poetics, 2, 10, 11, 13–16, 207,
281 n. 5; classical, 2, 3, 16, 103,
125, 134; historical, 2–3, 17;
structuralist, 2, 14–16, 281 n. 5,
282 n. 29
Poetry: contrasted with the novel,
6–7, 11, 12, 57, 273, 282 n. 25;
contrasted with the novel in the
Renaissance, 13, 25, 36, 38, 89,
90–91; relationship to the novel
in modernism, 249–50, 251, 266,
272; relationship to the novel in
romanticism, 166, 167, 173, 200,
202, 217, 272
Poggioli, Renato, 3
Pope, Alexander, 11, 117, 123, 124
Popular literature: generic segre-
gation of, 39, 50, 93, 95; role of
in humanist satire, 45, 48; role of
in the novel, 4, 12; romances as,
28, 97, 121; transformed in *Moll
Flanders*, 97, 98–102, 103
Pound, Ezra, 266, 272
Predmore, Richard, 5
Price, Martin, 4, 97, 98, 129,
304 n. 19
Printing of books: awareness of in
Don Quixote, 25, 26–27, 28,
84–85, 89, 92, 279; as continuing
determinant of the novel, 97,
148–49, 250, 259, 264, 273; as enabling condition for the novel,

25–31, 40, 75, 263; heightened
awareness of in Counter-
Reformation Spain, 33–34, 36,
286 n. 27; 272, 280, 320 n. 45
Procter, Bryan Waller, 185
Protocol, novelistic: in *A Connecticut Yankee*, 223–24; in *Con-
fessions of Felix Krull*, 236; in *The
Confidence-Man*, 206, 215; de-
fined, 49–50, 56; in *Don Quixote*,
77, 82, 83, 214; in *El Buscón*, 66,
67; in *Guzmán de Alfarache*, 59,
60, 62; in *Joseph Andrews*, 133; in
Lazarillo de Tormes, 51, 52, 54,
55, 59; in *Moll Flanders*, 107; in
Pickwick Papers, 178; in *The
Sot-Weed Factor*, 254; in *Terra
Nostra*, 275–77; in *Tristram
Shandy*, 148; in *Vanity Fair*, 186
Proust, Marcel, 8, 9, 15, 137, 192,
248, 272, 275
Pynchon, Thomas, 4, 12

Quevedo, Francisco de: *El Buscón*,
compared with other novels,
115, 138, 236, 295 n. 51; and the
Counter Reformation, 13, 69; as
a picaresque novel, 65–66,
291 n. 16; realism of, 21, 34,
50–51; role of the reader in, 25,
66, 67, 68, 294 n. 45; subversion
of literature in, 38, 65–67, 68–70,
71, 72, 81, 270, 294 n. 37

Rabelais, François: *Gargantua and
Pantagruel*, considered as a
novel, 45, 74–75, 94, 290 n. 7;
contrasted with *Don Quixote*,
74–75; contrasted with the picaresque novel, 44–47, 48, 55;
influence of on later novels, 75,
143, 253, 257, 264
Rader, Ralph, 105
Rapin, Nicolas, 124
Ray, Gordon, 183, 188
Readers: dramatization of in *Don
Quixote*, 25, 75, 76–84, 89–92,
214–15; effect on the novel of,
33, 34–35, 56, 96–97, 169, 263,
264, 280; nonnovelistic types of,
27–28, 33; novel's recognition of,